The Modeling Tutorial

17 Essays on How Human Experience Works

by

David Gordon

Graham Dawes

The Modeling Tutorial:
17 Essays on How Human Experience Works

by David Gordon and Graham Dawes

Copyright © 2017

ISBN: 9781520332994

For information, contact:
David Gordon, P.O. Box 42281, Tucson AZ 85733
modelingbook@gmail.com
www.expandyourworld.net

The essays in this book are intended to take you into the foundational details and conceptual subtleties of the processes of modeling. Its companion book, *Expanding Your World: Modeling the Structure of Experience*, is a practical presentation that includes video demonstration, and is designed to give you a working understanding of the process of modeling using the Experiential Array. You can find this eBook at:

www.expandyourworld.net

Le seul véritable voyage, le seul bain de Jouvence, ce ne serait pas d'aller vers de nouveaux paysages, mais d'avoir d'autres yeux, de voir l'univers avec les yeux d'un autre, de cent autres, de voir les cent univers que chacun d'eux voit, que chacun d'eux est...

Marcel Proust
La Prisonnière

The only true voyage, the only bath in the Fountain of Youth, would be not to visit strange worlds but to possess other eyes, to see the universe through the eyes of another, of a hundred others, to see the hundred universes that each of them sees, that each of them is...

Marcel Proust
The Captive

"We can't start perfectly and beautifully...
  Don't be afraid of being a fool; start as a fool."

Chogyam Trungpa Rinpoche

Table of Contents

Elements of the Experiential Array

iii

Elicitation

Working Models

Introduction

Laying Down the Path

A memory snippet from one of the authors:

One of the many magical places you can visit in this world is Yosemite Valley. Yosemite was carved out of solid granite eons past by relentless glaciers. When the climate changed, the glaciers receded, leaving behind a gorge carpeted with trees and enclosed by towering rock walls. From many places along the upper edges of these walls, unseen streams spill their snow melt into the valley, creating coiling, lacey curtains of water endlessly dropping down the faces of the cliffs. My parents often took me to this valley as I was growing up. On one of those visits we were walking along a dirt path that wound its way through the trees, more or less following along the nearby stream. The path was taking us to the foot of one of those waterfalls. For reasons that I don't need to explain beyond saying that I was ten years old, I slipped away from my parents and ran to the stream. Without hesitating, I began hoping from rock to rock to log to rock, making my way upstream, up through the very middle of the stream. I heard my parents calling—yelling—to me to come back *immediately*, but I naturally decided that I had unfortunately already gone too far to hear them, and so kept going. I don't recall slipping or getting my feet wet. If I did, it did not matter. It was exhilarating to move up the center of a stream toward the growing roar of falling water. At last I came around a bend and to a stop on a rock with the cold water whooshing past. In front of me was a cloud of mist, boiling like smoke, and pouring into it and towering over my head was an eternal torrent of falling white water. Then my parents showed up. We had gotten to the same place. But we were not *in* the same place. They were seeing the falls from the bank, leaning against the wooden rails put there to keep them safe. I was seeing the falls from a rock out in the middle of the roiling water.

Some decades ago now, when we first began our explorations into the nature of human experience, the work of Francisco Varela introduced us to a fundamental idea, an idea captured in the phrase, "Laying down the path in walking." We don't know its true origins. Varela himself cites a 1936 poem by Antonio Machado reminding us:

> ...caminante, no hay camino,
> se hace camino al andar.

> ...wanderer, there is no path,
> you lay down a path in walking.

As we understand it, this idea is also integral to Buddhist thought and teachings, pushing its origins even further into the past. Whatever the historic provenance of the concept being captured in words, the *living* of it undoubtedly stretches into the deepest history of human beings, and of all beings, for that matter. We have always been, and continue to be, laying down our paths in walking.

That is what you have been doing all along. Laying down a path in walking is how "you" got "here." That is how all of us have lived into who we are now. Indeed, every person you meet has walked themselves into a world, a world that is a unique enfolding and embodying of perceptions, beliefs, attitudes, ideas, predilections, skills, and behaviors.

We are bodies interacting within an environment, and in that ongoing interaction we create our ongoing, subjective worlds. Of course, there is much, *much* to say about how that all comes into being, how bodies and systems of neurons and environments weave with one another to create experience. However, the details of how experience comes into being is not the focus of these essays. (You can begin to explore this emerging of experience in the works of Maturana, Varela, Merleau-Ponty, Hofstadter, Lakoff, Bohm, and Bateson, to name a few.) Instead, our interest here is on what is going on when human experience *is* happening. How are we to understand, to get our arms around *that*? These essays grew out of our interest in doing just that, in trying to understand how experience works.

Our particular vehicle for this exploration was that of "modeling." Regardless of whether it takes its form in clay, plastic, paper, computer code, or thoughts, a model is a representation—or, perhaps better, an *analogical capturing*—of something else. A model is not the thing it models, but a form that preserves the significant elements and relationships of the thing being modeled. Modeling, then, is the process of identifying, codifying, and expressing in some form (in the clay, computer code, thoughts) those significant elements and their relationships.

Why bother to explore the world of human experience in this way?

Just as it is inherently pleasurable to discover a new variety of rose, with its unique array of thorns, petals, color, and scent...or a jazz riff that transforms a familiar tune into something wild...or an idea that brushes away cobwebs to let in new light, in the same way it is inherently pleasurable to have a window into the unique, and often startling, world of another person. These little discoveries, these revealings of who we are and can be, have often been enough for the authors to walk the modeling road.

But of course there is more. What else can you expect to discover from taking this trip? Here are a few of the possibilities:

Modeling ensures quicker and easier access to abilities.

All of us have personal dreams of being able to do certain things that we cannot do now. These dreams may reflect deficiencies we believe we have. (For example, the manager who is responsible for regular reports but cannot seem to organize himself to get them done; or the person who cannot seem to stick to an exercise regimen.) These dreams may also flow from our being inspired about what is possible to do. (For instance, fluently speak a foreign language, play a commanding game of chess, enjoy solitude, or capture the imagination of struggling students.) Modeling allows us to efficiently and effectively draw from others those abilities we either need or would like to have, and then manifest them in ourselves. When modeling is discussed, this ability to transfer abilities from one person to another is always offered as its primary goal and utility.

But there are additional reasons that, to our minds, are equally compelling and make the pursuit of modeling worthwhile:

Modeling honors—and helps us learn from—the unique contributions that each of us brings to the world.

A second reason to model grows out of the recognition that there is more to the uniqueness of every person on the planet than just his or her thumbprint. Each of us also represents a unique web of life experiences, the threads of which have been braided into a singular personality, an individual with characteristic, amazing and peculiar perceptions, talents and abilities. There are many wonderful violinists, many people are good at telling jokes, many can relax easily, can write a good letter, can power through a complex task, and so on. And yet, no two of those wonderful violinists will approach their music or play in exactly the same way. And when one of these wonderful violinists is gone, her particular approach to music is gone as well. Similarly, no two humorists will tell their tales the same way. And there are many ways of relaxing, of writing a good letter, and of powering through tasks. Modeling, then, can make it possible to not only capture the workings of a certain kind of ability, but some of the unique attributes of a particular individual's way of manifesting that ability as well. The idiosyncratic and fortuitous attributes of that person may end up being a revelation to us all, bringing into our experience of that ability a subtlety and effectiveness previously unknown.

And there is more:

Modeling can play a significant role in the evolution of culture and society.

If indeed it becomes possible to readily model the desirable abilities of others AND make those models usefully available to anyone, then personal and societal notions about what is possible and how to bring about change will necessarily transform in some fundamental ways. For example, few people would be asking, "Can I do this?" Instead they would be asking, "*How* can I do this?" This is a very different question, one that presupposes capability, and shifts attention to the structure of one's experience and behavior. Instead of unnecessarily accepting limitations, the question, "How can I do this?" makes an individual's pursuit of self-fulfillment and expression in his or her professional and personal life much more a matter of choice.

The widespread availability of abilities through modeling would not rob us of our personal identities, reducing a world of individuals to a herd of equally capable performers. On the contrary, because of the infinite variety of personal histories and life experiences, different people will make different choices as to which abilities they want to acquire. Furthermore, the manifestation of the same ability by any two individuals will be expressed through each person's unique personality, rather than in spite of it. In fact, it is our belief that the widespread availability of models for developing the vast array of human abilities would create many more opportunities to tap and bring forth into the world the unique potentials latent inside each of us.

And one last reason to pursue modeling:

Modeling makes accessible what are often considered "life's little pleasures."

The promise of modeling often stirs people to conquer the big things in life, the things that are societally mandated, applauded and valued. At last, we think, we can learn how to make a killing in the stock market, negotiate to win, be an inspiring leader, or write a best seller. In all the hustle and bustle of conquering, however, it is easy to overlook the fact that it is the small things that contribute the most to the fabric and quality of our lives. Making a killing on the stock market is fine. But so is being able to dance and enjoy it, to tell a joke, accept criticism, find joy in gardening, make someone feel welcome in your home, appreciate a work of art, capture your thoughts in a letter, let go of worries while on vacation, delight in helping your children with their school work, adore your lover, and feel adored by your lover. These are the "small" modeling projects that can be tackled on a small scale, on a daily basis...and can make all the difference in the world. *Your* world.

Now... There is a companion eBook to this one: *Expanding Your World: Modeling the Structure of Experience*, and it is primarily intended to be a how-to book. It is designed to give you a sufficient understanding of the concepts, distinctions, and processes of modeling to allow you to actually do it. And, toward that practical and useful end, it includes video of a complete modeling elicitation and acquisition. Writing a book that was geared toward coming quickly to grips with the process of modeling, as that book was, meant that we were frequently sacrificing depth and richness of understanding in order to produce something that was immediately applicable. Okay, we succeeded in doing that.

But there is still that depth and richness to explore. And that is what you will be doing in this book. In these seventeen Essays we will go beyond the information in *Expanding Your World*, and take you "behind the scenes." If you are someone who is interested in understanding how human experience works, as well as gaining a deep understanding of the process of modeling, then you are the person for whom we have written this book.

To model is to hit the road of human experience, a journey into the heart of human experience, how it works, how it can be shared. Put on your walking shoes.

PART I

The Foundations of Modeling

Foundations

Essay 1

What Is Modeling?

Human experience has structure, and modeling is the process of usefully describing those structures of experience that give rise to human abilities. This makes it possible for us to pursue the acquisition of abilities found in other individuals ("exemplars") for the purpose of our personal evolution (or, of course, to make those abilities available to other people). Since a model is a co-creation of the modeler and the exemplar, the most important attitude the modeler brings to this process is one of intense curiosity about human experience.

People ask us, "What do you do?" Our answer, "We do modeling." This is inevitably followed by a long moment of silence while the person stares at us, trying to imagine what we have to do with chic anorexics parading down catwalks to show off this year's latest evening wear and bikinis. We want to be helpful, so we explain, "Modeling is the process of creating useful descriptions of the structure of human abilities." This explanation immediately evaporates the model in the bikini, of course. And, really, this is a shame; before our explanation, at least they had a model in a bikini to imagine.

Still, the definition "Modeling is the process of creating useful descriptions of the structure of human abilities," is modeling in the proverbial nutshell. And like every nut, packed inside that shell is all the information needed to grow the tree of modeling. There is a lot packed in there, as you will see. At least this time we are not engaged in a chance meeting on the street. We have the luxury of more time. So, let's see how we can crack this nut.

Maps and Models

When we want to go somewhere we use a map. Maps identify significant aspects of a particular area, show us how these elements relate to each other, and provide guidance as to where and how to move within that area. Of course, no map is as detailed as the place it describes. A map of the United States that contained all the information that could be mapped would have to be as big as the United States itself (at least). This means that the intended use of a map necessarily defines and limits the kind of information that it portrays. A map of the United States that shows cities and highways allows us to efficiently travel from one place to another. Our vacation map shows us roads, cities, campgrounds and national parks. But it does not help us decide where to start a wheat farm. For that we need a map that shows areas of annual rainfall, seasonal temperatures and length of growing season. A map never contains within it everything that is true of the terrain it covers. What a map does do is capture what is essential for a particular use, presenting only what we need to know to get around effectively.

Models are much like maps. Models are representations that describe essential structures; that is, they capture the elements, patterns and relationships characteristic of something. Obvious examples are the model airplanes, boats and cars one finds in hobby stores. But a plastic model of a Space Shuttle is not a Space Shuttle. It does, however, have the same shaped wings, fuselage and tail, the same arrangement of windows, rocket thrusters and landing gear. And all of this is on a smaller scale. This plastic model captures enough of the essential elements (wings, fuselage, thrusters) and patterns of relationships (wings are set parallel at mid-fuselage, thrusters at the rear end of the fuselage) for us to recognize it as a representation of a Space Shuttle.

Street Map of London

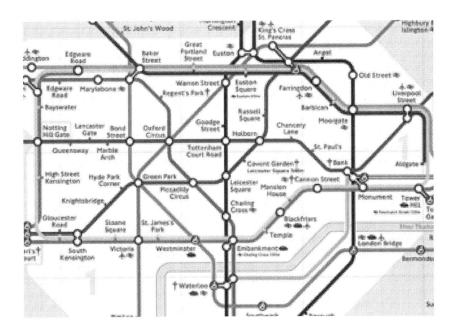

Tube (*subway*) Map of London

The presence of models in our everyday lives, however, goes way beyond that of toy space ships. These models not only capture structures, but also establish structures that influence and guide our experience and behavior. For instance, architects create two-dimensional and three-dimensional models of buildings, which are in turn used by their clients to have enough imagined experience of an actual building to make decisions regarding its aesthetics, functionality and so on. Those same architectural models rendered in more detail (blueprints) serve to guide the builders through every step of constructing the structure. Similarly, a dressmaker uses paper patterns to guide the cutting and piecing together of material into a dress. A recipe is a model of how to create a particular dish. A street map is a model of how your city is organized with respect to its streets, important buildings, parks, and so on, allowing you to move efficiently from place to place.

Not all models are so obvious, however, and so the distinction between a description of something (a model) and the thing itself can become blurred. For instance, Freudians talk about the appetitive id and the superego that keeps that voracious id in check. As soon as we find examples in our experiences matching these distinctions, they quickly become real to us; we forget that they are ways of talking about experience, that they exist only as descriptions. And so we soon find ourselves talking and thinking about our egos as though they actually existed in us in the same way we have hearts, livers and brains. But just as the blueprint is not the building, the id, ego and super ego are not human psychology. They constitute a model of human psychology, as do the Jungian archetypes and collective unconscious, the parent, adult and child of Transactional Analysis, behaviorism's instrumental learning, and the coding of AI computer programs. Each of these models leads to very different understandings of human experience.

In fact, models are operating in every aspect of our daily lives. Other examples of pervasive models are the constitutions that guide our governments and the legal codes that define our civil behavior. Subtler models are the cultural and social conventions that pervade virtually every human interaction. The existence and workings of our social models typically become obvious only when we find ourselves in another country in which models of relationships, government, politics and so on are very different from our own. Even the structuring of these sentences is a function of a particular model of grammar (one of many possible among human languages).

So, blueprints, recipes, road maps, psychologies, legal codes, social conventions and grammars are all models. What all of these models have in common is that they provide structures that guide our experiences and behaviors in the contexts to which those models apply. The street map shows us how to get home, the thriller genre specifies how to put the audience on the edge of their seats, and from the legal presumption of "innocent until proven guilty" flows a river of Miranda rights, bail, juries of one's peers, evidence procedures, and so on.

These models are not the things they describe (a blueprint is not the building, and codes of conduct are not people behaving civilly with one another), but are descriptions of the structures that make those things (buildings, civility, sentences, apple pie) possible. In the same way, a model of a human ability is a description of the essential structures that make it possible to manifest that ability. The structures of human abilities, however, are not built out of bricks, laws, grammars or apples, but out of experience.

Experience and Structure

If instead of modeling we were learning woodcarving, we could simply start chiseling away at wood. Anyone can do that. But we may be able to chisel to more purpose if we first have some understanding of the wood itself; what it is made of and how it grows, how it is layered, creating a grain with a certain direction and density, and so on. Understanding the nature of the wood with which we are working makes it possible to avoid splintering the grain, to select the right chisel and angle of cut. As modelers, our wood is human experience itself.

But what is experience?

To define something is to establish the conceptual borders that, in the process of doing it, create that "thing." But where can we find the borders of "experience?" The immediate difficulty in defining experience is the fact that it is impossible to contemplate something that is beyond the borders of experience. What is there that is outside of experience? Of course we can postulate the existence of something outside of our experience, but the moment we give it any form whatsoever—a name, an image, a place to be—it is no longer outside of our experience. We do not need to have direct contact with Santa Claus, the bogeyman, Satan, or angels for them to be residents of our experiential worlds. And new residents can move in at any time: imagine a creature with phantasmagoric qualities, something you have never seen or imagined before now. Regardless of how amorphous, bizarre and indescribable this imagined creature might be to anyone outside of your head, it is nevertheless now part of *your* experience. And, through the magic of words, gestures and artistry, it could perhaps eventually become a part of other people's experience as well.

This is not to say that there are not things operating outside of your experience. There certainly are. But unless and until they affect your experience you would not know about them—because they are not in your experience. Out of the infinitely rich fog of the world steps a stranger who sits down beside you on a park bench and, so, joins your experiential world (and perhaps becomes a friend for life). Furthermore, these strangers need not be made of flesh and blood. Merely imagining something is sufficient for it to enter your world. For example, learning that whales communicate with "songs" unique to each individual may affect your experiential world from then on in many ways. For instance, you begin to think of them as individuals rather than as members of a "herd." This alteration of your world happens even though you have never had the direct experience of hearing whales sing, or of meeting a whale.

Experience, then, is not merely what you are perceiving through your sensory systems right now. In addition to "sensory experience," we also have "representational experience." That is, we perceive—are aware of—internal representations. For instance, imagine: Walking outside right now... Remembering a recent conversation with a friend... Recalling the smell of fresh cut grass. These are all internal representations of events, rather than direct sensory experiences. Nevertheless, these memories and imaginings are experienced—they come into awareness—and often to a degree that is every bit as compelling as actual sensory-based experiences.

Furthermore, experience is not restricted to conscious awareness. All of us respond to things outside of consciousness, becoming aware of their impact only when that unconscious sensation or perception changes dramatically. For example, perhaps you have had the experience of feeling your body relax when the refrigerator (finally!) stops its incessant thrumming. You were not aware consciously of that thrum and its effect on you at the time, but you were nevertheless experiencing it. Your body was thrumming right along with it. It was a part of your ongoing, unconscious experience, until the dramatic drop in your body tension brought it into conscious awareness. Similarly, all of us have examples of being affected by ideas, thoughts, or memories that were out of conscious awareness, but compelling nonetheless. We perhaps recognized that we were being affected, but had no conscious awareness of what was causing it until some event or revelation brought that unconscious ongoing experience into conscious experience.

As you read these words, you may be aware of hearing them with your internal voice, recalling a conversation with a friend about consciousness, noticing how your hand rests on the table, and hearing the sound of cars passing outside. Experience in the moment, then, is the sum total of everything that you are sensing "outside" and "inside" your body (whether consciously or unconsciously) *plus* everything that you are thinking (again, consciously or unconsciously). Thinking includes the entire panoply of internal processes, such as detecting, remembering, sorting, associating, computing, judging, imagining, and so on. All of these conscious and unconscious sensations and thoughts combine to be your experience at this moment.

Does Experience Have Structure?

Charles Ames created a most incredible room. You look through a hole in the wall at one end of the room as two people enter it from either side. The person on the left is dwarfed by the window and walls and appears to be a midget. The person on the right, however, is clearly a giant, his head barely clearing the ceiling. A miracle occurs when these two people walk past each other to switch places. As they cross the floor you see the giant shrink and the midget expand!

Ames created this very compelling illusion by constructing the room so that it looks square and regular from your point of view, but is in fact very eccentric in its angles. The right corner is near you while the left is actually far away.

There are dozens of other well-known examples of perceptual illusions. You are probably familiar with Necker cubes, M.C. Escher's "impossible" paintings, and the Müller-Lyer lines that appear to be of different lengths, though in fact they are identical. Here is another that may be new to you; look at squares A and B:

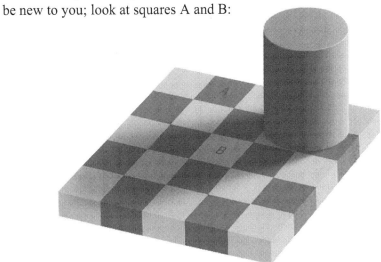

Though square A looks considerably darker than square B, they are actually the same shade, as you can see when they are joined:

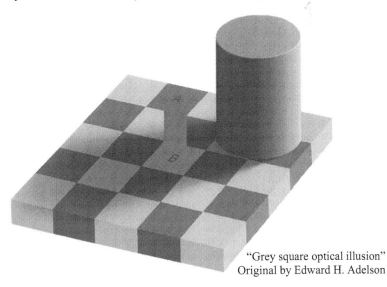

"Grey square optical illusion"
Original by Edward H. Adelson

Another, striking illusion is that of the "Rotating Snakes":

"Rotating Snakes" created by Akiyoshi

What is perhaps most remarkable about these illusions is that knowing they are illusions—indeed, even taking them apart to see how they are constructed—does not stop you from experiencing the illusion. Perception, then, is not strictly a matter of simply recording or taking in that which is being perceived. What we perceive is a product of the interaction between what is "out there" and the perceptual structures we are using to make sense of what is "out there." Sensory system illusions reveal the extent to which underlying perceptual structures generate our perceptions.

The impact of underlying structures extends into every aspect of human experience. Many such examples can be found in Edward T. Hall's books in which he compares the experiences of time and space in different cultures. In *The Dance of Life,* for instance, he describes fascinating experiments by Alton De Long on the influence of scale on the perception of time. De Long created environments that were $1/24^{th}$, $1/12^{th}$, $1/6^{th}$ and full scale, then had his subjects "project" themselves into the test environment and imagine interacting with the human figures he had placed in there. The subjects indicated when they thought thirty minutes had passed, while De Long kept track of the actual time. The interesting result was that subjects who were "in" the $1/6^{th}$ scale room had sixty minutes of subjective experience in ten minutes. Then it got even more interesting. Those projecting themselves into the $1/12^{th}$ scale room had a sixty-minute experience in only five minutes of elapsed time, and those crammed subjectively into the $1/24^{th}$ scale room experienced an hour in two and a half minutes of clock time. Apparently our sense of time is predicated on relative movement through space. If our subjective sense of time is to remain constant, then, being in a smaller space requires speeding up the subjective experience of time in order to cover a "normal amount" of movement and interaction in the limited space available. (Edward T. Hall, *The Dance of Life,* pp. 136-138)

The De Long research, the Ames room and other sensory illusions point to the existence and pervasive influence of underlying sensory structures in perceptual experience. But does the influence of structure extend only as far as sensory perceptions? Can we identify structure operating at the level of human abilities, most of which involve not only sensory perceptions, but behaviors and cognition as well?

During World War II, Viktor Frankl was a prisoner in Nazi concentration camps. His body had been confined, but not his mind. In his book, *Man's Search for Meaning,* Frankl had many profound and moving things to say about his experiences, and about what it means to be a human being in such horrific circumstances. In particular, he tried to understand how it was that some prisoners seemed to give up hope (and usually soon thereafter die), while others maintained hope in the face of constant physical, emotional and psychological battering, and persevered (even when facing death). Frankl recognized four patterns that were characteristic of those who continued to hope in a seemingly hopeless situation.

The first of these common patterns was believing that whatever has been lost could be regained, that "health, family, happiness, professional abilities, fortune, position in society—all these were things that could be achieved again or restored" (Frankl, p.103). The second pattern they shared was that of realizing that the future was unknowable and, so, could in an instant bring about significant changes—including good changes—in their situation. Frankl describes the third pattern:

> But I did not only talk [to my fellow prisoners] of the future and the veil which was drawn over it. I also mentioned the past; with all its joys, and how its light shone even in the present darkness. Again I quoted a poet—to avoid sounding like a preacher myself—who had written, "Was Du erlebst, kann keine Macht der Welt Dir rauben." (What you have experienced, no power on earth can take from you.) Not only our experiences, but all we have done, whatever great thoughts we may have had, and all we have suffered, all this is not lost, though it is past; we have brought it into being. Having been is also a kind of being, and perhaps the surest kind. (Frankl, p.104)

The fourth pattern characteristic of those who continued to hope was that they maintained a compelling future, that is, they were responsible for something or someone in the future and, so, had to live to fulfill that responsibility:

> A man who becomes conscious of the responsibility he bears toward a human being who affectionately waits for him, or to an unfinished work, will never be able to throw away his life. He knows the 'why' for his existence, and will be able to bear almost any 'how.' (Frankl, p.101)

So, what is the "structure" we are pointing to here with these examples? In the context of modeling, structure is the set of interacting elements of experience that make it possible to manifest a particular ability. The four elements that Frankl identified (believe that what has been lost can be regained, recognize that the future is unknowable, recognize that one's past and thoughts are not lost, and have a compelling future) together constitute the structure underlying the ability to hold onto to hope, even when one is in a horrible situation.

This is not an isolated example. In fact we can look at virtually any human ability and find that there is always an underlying structure that generates that ability. You can test this out for yourself right now with a small experiment: Select one of your own abilities—for instance, the ability to dance gracefully, or find solutions to business problems, or enjoy making cold calls, or explain math to children—and identify just one belief you are holding when you are manifesting that ability. (For example, suppose you are good at explaining math to children; perhaps you believe, "Every child is capable of learning.") Now imagine you are in that context, manifesting your ability, only this time you are holding a belief that is opposite from the one you identified. (In our example, you would imagine explaining math to a child while believing that "not every child is capable of learning.") What happens to your ability? You probably found yourself feeling somewhat different, making different assessments in the situation, and saying and doing things differently. In fact, inverting that one belief may have even entirely undermined your ability.

Repeat this little experiment with any ability you wish, changing any element you identify as part of your experience (belief, feeling, pattern of thinking, behavior) while manifesting that ability. You will discover that making even one change does, in some way, affect the manner in which you manifest your ability. Some changes will have a small or subtle impact, and others will have a substantial effect, perhaps utterly changing your responses in that situation. But in all cases, *any change will affect you.*

The simple experiment you just ran with yourself is actually quite profound in its implications. First of all, it demonstrates that:

There are structures underlying human abilities.

That is, underlying each of our abilities there is a set or array of elements of experience that make it possible to manifest that particular ability. Second, your experiment demonstrates that:

Human experience is systemic in nature.

When you ran the experiment you probably noticed that altering that one belief resulted in some change in your behavior as well, or what you were feeling changed, or that you started noticing different things in the situation. If instead you try the experiment again, but this time alter only your behavior, you will discover that this also changes other aspects of your experience (how you are feeling, what you are thinking, even what you are believing). In fact, changing any one element of an ability will have ramifications throughout many or all of the elements of that ability (though, as we shall see in later Essays, to varying degrees and of varying kinds, depending on the system and the nature of the change). The underlying structure operates as a dynamic system, and not a simple checklist of elements. The third point made by your experiment is that:

You can change your experience by changing its underlying structure.

Clearly, abilities have underlying structures, and changing those structures systemically transforms the ability. If instead of merely imagining the belief change you tried in your thought experiment, you integrated that change as a consistent aspect of your experience whenever you actually manifested that ability, you would be feeling, thinking, and behaving differently. That is, you would have changed.

These three observations—that there are structures underlying human abilities, that human experience is systemic in nature, and that you can change your experience by changing its underlying structure—form the conceptual basis for all modeling of human abilities.

Structure and the Acquisition of Abilities

It is one thing to recognize that structure gives rise to the experiences and behaviors that comprise our abilities, and quite another to assert that it is possible to acquire new abilities by taking on the structures that give rise to them. After all, there is certainly more to any ability than just its structure. There are also the myriad details, points of information, subtleties of behavior, and subtleties of understanding that, taken together, are the ability itself in action. The structure, then, is clearly not the ability; the structure is what organizes all of those points and subtleties into the ability. A pile of bricks, window frames, and doors is not a house. Neither is a blueprint a house. A house is what happens when the bricks, windows and doors are organized in relation to one another according to the structure prescribed by the blueprint.

Now a door opens for us. Behind that door is the idea that the cultivation of a particular ability in a person who does not already have it would be immeasurably assisted by acquiring the appropriate underlying structure. This may sound like a radical notion, but it is not. Modeling is, in fact, something all of us already have done and occasionally still do.

As children, all of us were "natural" modelers, devoting ourselves to acquiring the structures we needed to use language, understand the nuances of social interactions, ride a bicycle, do algebra, behave ethically, study, work, entertain, learn, and so on. This modeling was generally implicit. That is, we acquired our models through trial and error, learning to use what worked and was reinforced. (Of course, in this same way we also acquired abilities that may not have served us well as we matured, such as the ability to be violent, or the ability to procrastinate, or the ability to hide our feelings.)

In addition, most of us have had role models, people who impressed or inspired in ways that made us want to emulate them. Your role models may have been a mother, father, grandparent, sibling, teacher, neighbor, or even a character in a movie or book. In these cases the modeling you did was probably both explicit and implicit. Once a person attained the luster of a role model, you probably explicitly (consciously and intentionally) started to emulate that person's appearance, patterns of speech and movement. You tried to say things the way that person said them, do what she did, read what she read, think the way she thought. In the process of matching yourself to the role model's behaviors, you were also implicitly learning (modeling) some of the subtler, presuppositional aspects of that person's world.

A similar, though more formal example of natural modeling occurs in any apprentice relationship, such as when one is the personal student of a

Zen master, journeyman carpenter or a corporate executive. Unlike emulating a role model, an apprenticeship is an explicit modeling relationship in which the master of an ability is trying to pass on that ability to the apprentice. In addition to teaching the student to emulate the outward manifestations of the ability, the teacher often also tries to impart the subtler aspects of the ability, such as how the student needs to think about what he is doing, what he should care about and what he should ignore, and perhaps even help him cultivate feelings appropriate to the ability. But what are the necessary aspects of the ability that somehow need to be imparted if the student is to eventually master it himself? That is, what is the underlying structure that naturally gives rise to that ability?

An excellent and particularly accessible example is given in Dr. Betty Edwards' approach to drawing. As an art teacher she was baffled by the fact that some students readily learned to draw while others seemed never to "get it." In her, *The New Drawing on the Right Side of the Brain,* Edwards writes:

> "Well," I would say carefully, "you look at the still-life and you draw it as you see it." "I was looking at it," the student replied. "I just don't know how to draw that." "Well," I would say, voice rising, "you just look at it..." The response would come, "I am looking at it," and so on. (p. XI)

Demonstration and remonstration produced little success. So Edwards looked deeper. She looked into how those who can draw well are thinking about and seeing their subjects. The result was a model and, from that, techniques that make drawing an acquirable skill for anyone. The efficacy of her approach was brought home to us by Janet Pesvner, a student in one of our modeling seminars. In her work as a speech therapist she uses drawing as a means of helping her students to learn self-monitoring and to discover that they can change their behavior by changing their perceptions. The students begin by taking 10 minutes to make their own drawing of a line drawing she shows them. Following the model described by Edwards, she then spends 5 minutes discussing with them how to look at what they are drawing. This is followed by 5 minutes during which they reassess their first drawing and then 10 minutes more to make a second drawing. A few examples of the results can be seen in Figure 1:

Figure 1.

The Advantages of Models

Modeling and the acquisition of abilities, then, is something we can do deliberately. But why bother? As we discussed above, it is something that all of us already do informally and naturally. So why do we need to create a formal modeling process for the acquisition of abilities?

The first and primary reason is that the informal modeling that all of us engage in is haphazard. Whether we are talking about childhood trial and error, emulating role models or apprenticeship, what we learn depends for the most part upon our picking out of the welter of observed experience those elements of experience and behavior essential to manifesting an ability. Of thirty children in a classroom learning drawing, some will "get it" and others will not. As we have already seen, being able to draw is not a genetic endowment, but an ability made possible by having the necessary underlying conceptual and motor structures. Those children who "get" drawing either walked in the door with those underlying structures or were able to intuit and absorb them from the descriptions and examples given by the teacher. Other children presented with the same descriptions and examples may not divine the necessary conceptual structures and, so, drawing remains a realm of mystery and confusion to them.

All informal modeling experiences are haphazard. What we end up learning is a function of what the parent/model/mentor does, what they consciously know about what they do, how they convey what they do and know, the understandings and abilities the student has to begin with, the student's ability to notice patterns and make sense of their experience, and so on. All of these variables create a myriad of opportunities for essential elements of an ability to either not be conveyed by the parent/model/mentor or, if conveyed, missed or misunderstood by the student.

Imagine instead that the drawing teacher has an explicit understanding of the essential cognitive and conceptual elements that underlie the ability to draw. And further imagine that the first thing the teacher does is to make sure that all of her students have access to those cognitive and conceptual elements. Having the underlying structure does not mean that now the students can draw beautifully; what it does mean is that now they can learn to draw beautifully. All of them.

That is a pretty ambitious word trio: "All of them." How can we say that?

Well, if human abilities have underlying structures, then presumably anyone who has the underlying structure for a particular ability can develop that ability. Notice that it is "can," not will. Having the structure does not in itself confer the ability. Fully manifesting the ability requires that the structure be applied until a rich supporting set of skills, understandings and distinctions is generated. (We will have more to say about this in the Essay on Acquisition.) The structure creates the framework upon which we usefully and effectively hang our experiences.

So, the underlying structure does not guarantee the expression of the ability. But without the underlying structure, we can never manifest the ability.[1] If it is important to you to have access to a particular ability, then, at some point you must acquire its underlying structure. One way to do that is to, in a sense, apprentice yourself to that ability. Emulate what is obvious and, through trial and error, try to discover its inner workings, its underlying structure.

Another approach—the modeling approach—is to first identify what are its essential inner workings, adopt those workings, and then emulate the ability. Now all of your experiences will be guided and tempered by that structure, freeing you to devote your attention and learning to gaining further useful distinctions and a facility with the ability.

Of course, even after acquiring the underlying structure, not all of the algebra students will learn algebra (for reasons we explained above). But, for those who do not learn, it will not be because they cannot, but because of other factors, such as motivation. And the same is true of any other

---

[1] Of course, it is true that all of us have had the experience of operating in a context for which we did not initially have the underlying structures. After a period of fumbling and confusion and mistakes and triumphs, we eventually acquired the necessary abilities. But what was happening as we struggled was that we were acquiring, piece by piece, the essential structural elements of that ability. Sometimes that was from observation of how others handled that context, and sometimes it was through making an analogy between the context and a similar one in which we already had the necessary abilities.

human ability we can think of. If it is possible for one person to learn to do, it is possible for anyone to learn to do. Those possibilities are there, resident in each one of us, and waiting only for a good map and a good reason to put the rubber to the road.

Useful Descriptions

We began this Essay by defining modeling as "the process of creating useful descriptions of the structure of human abilities." Until now, most of our attention has been on the last part of that definition, that is, exploring the relationship between structure, experience and human abilities. A few things also need to be said about "creating useful descriptions."

Models are descriptions. But not all descriptions are equal. A map that helps us get where we want to go is a useful map. And that is just what we want our models to do. A model is "useful" if it helps make it possible for us to reproduce through our own experience and behavior an ability that someone else has. The question is, "Does the model work?" That is the test. The usefulness of a model can be judged in only one place, and that is in experience. It must be tested in human experience.

Initially, the human experience in which the model description is tested is yours, the modeler. As you create this description, it is important to remember that a map is not the thing being mapped, but a representation of that "territory." The mapmaker decides what features to use in making the map (roads, rainfall, elevations... an infinite number of possible features), and how to represent them. You are doing the same thing when you model. As you gather information from your exemplar you note those aspects of his experience that you consider significant (by testing them in your own experience), and set aside (or not even notice) those that you do not consider significant.

Keeping in mind that the model is something you are creating can serve as an inoculation against projecting your own structures into the model of your exemplar. Perhaps the deepest pit one can fall into when modeling is thinking you are ferreting out the truth. This often leads the modeler to look for confirmation in the exemplar for what the *modeler* thinks and believes, rather than discovering the ability from the exemplar's point of view. Knowing that you are creating the model will actually keep you more cognizant of the assumptions you are bringing to the process, as well as more interested in the differences between your experience and that of your exemplar. (We will explore this in depth in Essay 6, on Stepping-In.)

In fact, a model is most properly seen as a co-creation, something that emerges as the result of the unique interaction between you, the modeler, and your exemplar. The exemplar is not a frog pinned to a lab tray, passively giving up his internal secrets to the modeler's incisive questioning. Modeling is not something you do to your exemplar. It is something you do with your exemplar. Modeling is a process of interacting with someone until you have created a useful map of how he does what he does. Over the course of a few minutes, hours, days or weeks, you trade information, understandings and descriptions back and forth with your exemplar as the two of you move toward a description of the exemplar's ability that allows you to manifest it as well. It is a process of adjusting your own thinking and experience to be more in alignment with that of your exemplar, until you discover what structure of experience works to manifest the exemplar's ability.

* * *

Discovering what works is not something that necessarily happens automatically just because you are asking exemplars questions about their experience. We are after a level of understanding that is qualitatively different than what we usually get when we talk with others. In modeling, we are seeking a description of those essential patterns that naturally support the manifestation of a particular human ability.

There are three general prerequisites for doing modeling:

A methodology for eliciting information. The gathering of information is never a passive act, as if you were some kind of vessel being filled with your exemplar's explanations. The gathering of information is, instead, an active interaction in which your questions not only invite responses from the exemplar, but influence those responses as well. Because of this, it is necessary to consider how to approach the gathering of information in such a way that it both respectfully influences the exemplar and supports the modeling process.

A set of distinctions that identify what is significant or relevant. Human experience is infinitely rich, as is our ability to generate descriptions of those experiences. If we are to discover patterns in that vastness (as well as have a common language to talk about the world of patterns we find there) we need a set of distinctions about the nature and qualities of experience.

A methodology for organizing patterns into a model. Ultimately, we will want to transform those patterns we have discovered into some form that makes them accessible, a form that allows ourselves or others to experience the worlds of our exemplars.

It is to these three modeling prerequisites that the rest of these Essays are devoted.

It is a rare privilege to explore another person's experience to the depth and detail you will go when you model your exemplars. And the most important thing you can bring with you on this journey is a fascination with the varieties and qualities of human experience. From that curiosity and wonder everything else will flow.

Foundations

Essay 2

Getting Started

Anything that human beings do can be modeled, and everything we do is worthy of being modeled. It is crucial to model "exemplars," people who in fact have the ability you are interested in. Therefore, you must have a clear and appropriately specified idea of what you want to model before selecting your exemplars. The modeling process itself involves discovering significant patterns of experience and behavior through contrasting examples of the ability in action.

"Jachin-Boaz traded in maps. He bought and sold maps, and some, of certain kinds for special uses, he made or had others make for him. That had been his father's trade, and the walls of the shop that had been his father's were hung with glazed blue oceans, green swamps and grasslands, brown and orange mountains delicately shaded. Maps of towns and plains he sold, and other maps made to order. He would sell a young man a map that showed where a particular girl might be found at different hours of the day. He sold husband maps and wife maps. He sold maps to poets that showed where thoughts of power and clarity had come to other poets. He sold well-digging maps. He sold vision-and-miracle maps to holy men, sickness-and-accident maps to physicians, money-and-jewel maps to thieves, and thief maps to the police."

(*The Lion of Boaz-Jachin and Jachin-Boaz*, by Russell Hoban)

So, what do you want to model?

Notice that we did not ask, "What should you model?" Nor did we ask, "What is worth modeling?" Those questions assume that some abilities are more valuable or important than others. But this is not the case. In fact, nothing in human experience is inherently more or less worth modeling than anything else. A statement like that, of course, puts us way out on an ethical limb. Before you get out your saw, give us a chance to explain.

When the prospect of modeling is raised, most people reach right away for the brightest stars. Our thoughts and aspirations naturally fix upon those incandescent human abilities that most of us consider represent human beings at their best. There is nothing wrong with that conceptually, surely. In practice, however, it is often the case that what are identified as human abilities at their most luminous are actually glowing from the applause of society. Again, there is nothing wrong with that. But there is something stifling about it. In seminar after seminar, when our participants have been given the opportunity to select something to model, their thinking immediately goes to what we as a society seem to value. They want to model being a great business leader, trading stocks, making killer investments, winning at negotiations, being an entrepreneur. Of course, all of these are worth modeling. Brilliant stars, true, but a mighty small universe.

As we mentioned in the previous Essay, the quality of our lives is determined far more by the myriad of "little" human abilities that fill the millions of moments of our days. Making money is fine, but as you journey through your day making it there are disappointments to be dealt with, a joke you would like to tell, the abstract painting in the lobby you don't understand, the criticism of an associate that makes you feel small, a shaft of sunlight through your office window that you would like to stand in but can't justify the time, an employee who needs help understanding something and you just don't know how to get it across, the lunch at which you order foods you know you will pay for later in Alka Seltzer, the boss who is asking you to do something that is against your values, a moment of emptiness when you wonder if there is meaning to your life, the phone call from your teenage daughter with whom you cannot seem to connect, and your nervousness during a presentation to the Board.

But there are people who bounce back from disappointments. There are others who are good at telling jokes. There are those who can be delighted by an abstract painting, or respond to criticism as an opportunity, or take time to step into a shaft of sunlight. Some know how to explain things clearly, while others care for their bodies, or maintain their values in the face of demands to do otherwise, or feel an ongoing sense of meaning in their lives, or connect with their teenagers. You can even find people who consider a Board presentation fun. These are not the kind of abilities that will get any of these people on the cover of a national magazine. In fact, the people who have these abilities probably do not recognize them as anything special or worthy of modeling. And, of course, to them they are NOT special; it is just what they do. But for someone who has always been sucked dry by disappointments or fumbled the telling of a joke, or who is mystified by art or infuriated by criticism, or yearned for the sunlight, felt helpless when trying to help others, anguished over not caring for their bodies, easily let their values slip, felt meaningless, estranged from their teenagers, or petrified by Board presentations...these are priceless abilities. For those of us whose daily lives would be enhanced by these abilities, it is obvious that they are worthy of modeling. And for some of us, a particular ability may be worth anything it would take to have it. The smallest, most seemingly mundane ability you can think of is something of inestimable value to someone who needs it, whose life would be improved by having access to it.

And we will scoot even further out on our limb by including "problems" in the category of human abilities worthy of modeling. Obviously, modeling a problem is useful as a way to gain a deeper understanding that reveals clues for intervention and change. But problems ought not to be thought of only as things that need fixing. "Problems" are just as much human experience and behavior as are the laudable and worthy things we do and, so, are also the natural manifestations of some underlying structures. Or, to say it the other way around, all of us have structures of experience that work perfectly to generate both the experiences we want to have, as well as those we do not want to have.

A useful and more accurate way to think about problems is that they are effective and potentially useful structures that are being inappropriately used. For example, we all agree that procrastination is a problem. But for someone who finds it impossible to be on vacation without worrying about what needs to be done back at the office and at home, the ability to procrastinate may be precisely what he needs. Procrastination is only a problem when there is something that truly does need to be done and you can do something about it; procrastination is a blessing, however, when it is time to let go of doing things for a while. The same is true of, say, the problem of responding to criticism with indignation. Clearly this is a problem for the person who always responds this way, as it may preclude him from ever getting useful feedback. But the ability to respond with indignation may be precisely what is needed by someone who constantly subjects his sense of self to the judgments of others. That is, this "wide-open" person would benefit from being able to consider giving his self-judgments more weight than the judgments being made about him by others.

Notice that we have said that the "person would benefit from having access to the ability." We are not suggesting that he simply trade one ability for the other, discarding the old for the new. In fact, what serves us far more is to have access to a wide range of abilities that we can call upon depending upon the demands of the particular situation we are in. This makes us flexible and robust in our responses and experience. There is much more to say about this topic, but it would take us deep into the realm of therapy. For now, suffice it to say that there is undeniable value in having access to the full range of human experience and abilities.

So, when considering what to model, it is not necessary to limit yourself to the relatively few obvious stars of human abilities, the few that we can point to through the haze of city lights. Stand under darker skies and you will discover millions of experiential stars. They may appear to be small, but that is only because they are further away. Each one, however, is an ability of great value to someone and, so, worthy of modeling.

The delightful and wonderful pool of human abilities is as deep as the universe of human experience, a well from which we can draw endlessly. What will you draw out of those depths?

Specifying the Ability

Where to start? Pursuing a model can be a long journey down some pretty tangled paths. The first (and perhaps most important) step of your journey is to specify what it is that you want to model. If you are not clear where you want to get to, you could end up anywhere, or nowhere. Furthermore, you need to know where you want to go so you can find guides (your exemplars) who already know the way there.

You begin by answering the question, "What do I want to be able to do?" This is an important question in two respects. First, it puts your attention on what you value in the realm of human abilities, and second, it puts your attention on *doing*. Every ability is a means to an end, that is, it has some effect or outcome. Often when we think of what we want for ourselves, we put our attention on that outcome, and not on the "doing" that makes that outcome possible. It is the difference between saying, "I want to get an 'A' in chemistry" (the outcome) and "I want to be able to learn chemistry" (the "doing"); the difference between "I want to be a leader," and "I want to be able to inspire and motivate people at work"; the difference between "I want there to be harmony with my spouse," and "I want to be able to harmonize with my spouse." When you model, you are not acquiring a fish, but learning how to fish.

For many abilities, the answer to the question, "What do I want to be able to do," will be straightforward and you can dive into finding an exemplar. For instance, if you want to be able to hit a solid backhand in tennis, find someone who hits a solid backhand. If you want to tell jokes well, find someone who knows how to deliver a joke. If you want to be able to take a compliment with grace, find someone who already does.

For other abilities you may need to dig a bit deeper than your initial answer to the question, "What do I want to be able to do?" Suppose that you want to model how to write books. Does, "I want to model how to write books" point you well enough in the direction you really want—and need—to go? Well, is writing technical books the same as writing non-fiction books for the mass market? Probably not. Is writing non-fiction the same as writing fiction? Again, probably not. And is writing in any of the various fiction genres—science fiction, mysteries, novels, children's books—manifesting the same ability? No, there are undoubtedly some different abilities involved in writing in each of these forms. Of course, there will also be some similarities. The fact that all of these different kinds of books involve writing means that we will surely find some patterns that are shared by people who write books, regardless of the genre. If what you want to model are the patterns that underlie writing in general, then you would certainly want to draw your exemplars from various genres. If instead what you are really interested in is writing children's books, then it is essential to specify that as the target of your modeling and find an exemplar who writes fiction for children.

This process of greater specification (called "chunking down") can continue, of course. You might not be interested in children's books in general, but specifically books for preschoolers, or science books for grade schoolers, or adolescent fiction. Again, if your interest is at that level of specificity, then it is in your interest to find exemplars of that particular ability. How fine you need to split these hairs depends both upon what you want to end up with in terms of a model, and what you find as you begin modeling. For instance, you may discover that writing fiction for 13-year-olds is not significantly different than writing for 17-year-olds. In that case, people who can serve as possible exemplars include anyone writing Adolescent Fiction. On the other hand, you may find that writing fiction for adolescent girls is different than for boys. In that case, you need to decide if you want to model writing for girls, or for boys, or for adolescents in general.

Sub-Abilities

Even then you may not be done nailing down what you want to model. The process of writing probably involves a number of "sub-abilities." We can think of these as a set of foundation ("smaller") abilities that combine to make possible the global ("larger") ability of writing a book. For instance, it may be that the ability to successfully write adolescent fiction involves the sub-abilities of "Keeping current on the adolescent world," "Formulating a plot," "Creating characters," "Writing text," "Editing," "Interesting a publisher or agent in the work," and so on.

Each of these sub-abilities can be considered (and, indeed, is) an ability in itself, and can be modeled as such. It is probably becoming obvious to you now that it may be possible to chunk down any sub-ability into its own set of "sub-abilities" (or, if you prefer, "sub-sub-abilities"). As the modeler you might choose (or perhaps find it necessary) to approach the modeling of "Writing text," for example, as a set of sub-abilities: "Ordering ideas in a useful way," "Describing clearly," and "Compelling the reader's attention." Each is a modelable ability in its own right which, when combined with its companion foundation abilities, work together to create the global ability.

Sequential or Parallel

All of the sub-abilities work together to make possible the larger ability. This does not mean that the sub-abilities are necessarily operating simultaneously. It may be that the action of one sub-ability is a prerequisite to the action of another sub-ability, and so they are *sequential*. "Formulating a plot" generally precedes and informs the "Writing," which in turn precedes "Editing."

A set of sub-abilities may be sequential, but that does not mean that the objective of each one is necessarily completed before the exemplar moves on to the next sub-ability. For instance, the exemplar may step into "Editing" mode periodically as she is writing. What it does mean is that when the exemplar is unable to fulfill the objective of a particular sub-ability, she will likely drop back into a prerequisite sub-ability. As an example, if she is having difficulty writing the text, she may need to reconsider her plot structure or characters (both the products of prerequisite abilities). If she still cannot resolve the writing problem, she may step even further back in the sequence and consider again what is going on with adolescents, which can then newly inform her characterizations and plotting, which in turn form the basis for her writing.

Alternatively, it may be the case that two or more of the sub-abilities are operating in *parallel*, that is, they come into play at the same time. Our exemplar's sub-abilities for "Writing text" are an example of parallel abilities: "Ordering ideas in a useful way," "Describing clearly" and "Compelling the reader's attention" are all, for the most part, operating at the same time as the exemplar is writing the text. All three sub-abilities represent ongoing evaluations and operations, with no one of them a prerequisite to the operation of the others. All work together in "Writing text," but none are dependent upon each other. Poorly ordered ideas can nevertheless be described clearly and be compelling, for example. Likewise, the ideas may be well ordered but not clearly described, and descriptions can be clear but not compelling.

What Do You Really Need to Know?

Okay, that seems like a lot to get our arms around...

Whether you want to pursue an ability at a relatively global chunk size, or pursue it at the level of its sub-abilities depends upon your particular needs and interests. You can certainly model the ability "Writing adolescent fiction" at that general level. And, in doing so, you will glean a set of patterns that will in some way include or reference many of the sub-abilities of "Writing adolescent fiction" ("Keeping current on the adolescent world," "Formulating a plot," "Creating characters," "Editing" and so on). If instead you model one of those sub-abilities (the ability to "Edit," for instance), you will glean a set of patterns that will also in some way include or reference *its* sub-abilities. (In the case of editing, for instance, these sub-abilities might include "Reading from the reader's perspective," "Accepting criticism" and "Letting go of things you like.")

Discovering that the ability you want to model is made up of some important sub-abilities does not mean that you must choose either to model all of those sub-abilities or to ignore them and model the ability as a "whole." What it does mean is that you must decide what are the abilities (sub-abilities) you specifically want to have "in focus" as you model. In looking at those sub-abilities, you may decide that there is only one (or perhaps a few) that you really want; the others are either (1) not of interest to you or (2) are ones you already have in some measure. For example, in "Writing adolescent fiction," you may be interested only in writing stories to be given to the teenagers in your classes, and so there is also no need to model the ability to "Interest publishers and agents." Or, you may recognize that you already are adept at "Keeping abreast of the adolescent world" and at "Creating characters." And so there is no need for you to model those abilities. Perhaps what you DO need, however, are the abilities to "Formulate a plot," "Write text," and "Edit." Those, then, will be the abilities you will want to have in focus as you gather information from your exemplar.

Finding Where You Are as You Go

Okay, now take a breath.

As you can see, the number of possible sub-abilities for any one ability is potentially enormous (perhaps infinite). And so, as the modeler, it is necessary for you to choose the ability—or abilities—that will be the focus of your modeling. This will help ensure that you pursue what is, in fact, of primary interest to you, and that you select those exemplars who are most likely to give you the kind and quality of information you need. This is the ideal.

In practice, however, it often happens that even the most rigorous pre-elicitation specification of the ability must be re-assessed when you discover the reality of the ability. After all, you are delving into an aspect of the human world that is not an area of competence for you. It is very likely that you do not know all the relevant distinctions in terms of areas of application and of activity significant for successfully manifesting that ability. In the course of gathering information from your first one or two exemplars you will, at the same time, be discovering just what application and activity distinctions are important. And so you may well find yourself readjusting your expectations and needs regarding the focus of your modeling.

You cannot know everything ahead of time, and you do not need to. It is useful to be as specific as you can before selecting exemplars and plunging into elicitation. But as you gather information, be ready to discover that you need to rethink what you want to model, that there are other areas of specific application or sub-abilities you need to focus on. This reassessment may mean that you need to find different exemplars than the ones you had already lined up. But far better to do that and end up with the ability you want than to exhaust yourself modeling abilities that are either not of interest to you or are already in your personal repertoire.

Selecting Exemplars

While it is true that every person is a potential source of fascinating abilities to model, it is most likely the case that you have selected something specific that you want to model. If you are to avoid eliciting confusing and inapplicable patterns, it is essential that you select individuals who are, in fact, exemplars of the ability in which you are interested.

Exemplars can come to your attention through your personal experience of them, recommendations of others, hearsay, or their own declarations. Regardless of how you become aware of this person as an exemplar, you need evidence of their competence. You need to satisfy yourself that she or he does in fact manifest the ability you want to model. The best way to do this is to arrange to witness them in action, as well as see the results of their efforts. This will tell you two important things.

First, witnessing your exemplar "in action" will tell you whether or not he has the ability. He is supposed to be a wonderful teacher; do the students learn? She is great at telling jokes; do people laugh? She creates easily accessible magazine layouts; do people actually find them accessible?

Second, direct experience of the exemplar manifesting his ability will give you a sense of the manner in which he manifests the ability. For example, you may have two exemplars of good teaching, both of whose students are clearly learning. One of those teachers, however, is a calm presence at the front of a placid classroom. At the end of her day, she is both happy and tired. The other teacher ricochets through the classroom, a blur of energy and interaction. At the end of the day, she is both happy and exhausted. Both of these teachers can serve as exemplars of excellent teaching, and will share fundamental patterns that make that ability possible. If, however, you want to model a calm-classroom style of teaching, then the first exemplar is the one you want to model.

In some cases the perceptions of others will be significant in assuring you that your exemplar is someone who indeed has the ability you want to model. For instance, if you are modeling a person who is good at establishing rapport with groups, you would want to talk with people who have been in groups with this person to find out what was, in fact, their experience. Evidence of an exemplar's ability may come in other forms as well. The magazine layout artist who has been recognized with a national publishing industry award for her work probably knows what she is doing when it comes to creating compelling magazine layouts.

How Many?

Models are typically either "idiosyncratic" (made up of patterns particular to an individual exemplar of the ability) or "generic" (made up of patterns particular to all exemplars of the ability).

In modeling we are trying to discover those essential patterns that make it possible to manifest an ability. Finding what is essential requires weeding out the masses of non-relevant things people say, think and do, so that you are left with only those patterns essential to your exemplar's ability. In the case of an *idiosyncratic* model, we do this by comparing several (typically, three) examples of the exemplar manifesting his ability.

We contrast these examples in order to reveal the patterns of experience that are the same in all three of them. For instance, Joe is an excellent elementary school teacher AND you want to be able to teach just as Joe teaches. That is, you want not only to get his kind of results, but also to actually manifest his distinctive manner as he teaches. In that case, you want to include Joe's idiosyncratic patterns in your model, rather than weeding them out by contrasting him with other exemplars who are also excellent elementary school teachers. Joe, then, would be your sole exemplar.

Instead, it may be that you are not interested in modeling what makes it possible for *Joe* to manifest a particular ability, but in modeling what makes it possible for human beings *in general* to manifest a particular ability. In that case you are after a generic model. To create a generic model, you will need more than one exemplar, so that you can compare them, weeding out the masses of idiosyncratic things your exemplars say, think and do. Your goal here is to leave standing only those sturdy patterns characteristic of the ability across all of your exemplars.

For generic modeling you will want at least three exemplars of the ability you want to model. Contrasting two exemplars will certainly provide you with patterns that the two of them share. That is, you will probably find things about the structure of their experiences that are the same (as well as differences—patterns that belong to only one of the exemplars—which you will leave out of the model). But having a third exemplar makes it possible to:

- Confirm the patterns you have found.

- Resolve questions about patterns you are unsure about.

- Alert you to patterns you may have missed in the first two elicitations.

Of course, you can model more than three exemplars, and may need to if you are not recognizing the patterns in the first three. But if you have selected three exemplars who really are exemplars of the ability, you will probably find few surprises during your elicitation of the third individual.

This consistency strongly indicates that you have indeed culled the essential patterns from your first two exemplars. When this is the case (as it often is), going on to model a fourth, fifth and sixth exemplar is likely to be unnecessary.

And, of course, if you are NOT finding essential patterns common to all three of your exemplars, you then need to do one of the following:

- Model additional exemplars.

- Reassess whether or not some or all of your exemplars are truly competent at the ability you are modeling.

- Reassess whether you have appropriately specified the ability you want to model.

We will have much more to say about generic modeling in Essay 16: Generic Models.

Framing for Exemplars

Some people are reticent when asked to be the subject of modeling. Usually this is because either they do not see what they do as being anything special (and, so, not "worthy" of your time and effort), or they are concerned that they do not know enough about how they do what they do to be able to tell you what you want to know. Both of these concerns can be addressed by simply telling the truth of the situation. The first of these truths is that she is able to do something that you admire, consider of great value, and want to understand well enough that you can do it too (or help others do it). The second truth is that she does not need to consciously know how she does what she does. She needs only to be herself, and that it is your job to ask those questions that will help reveal to both of you just how she does what she does.

Almost invariably, once the modeling begins, exemplars become completely engaged in the process. Most of us find it fascinating to see how we are "put together," as it were. You will find that the exemplar will almost immediately become a co-modeler with you, working hard to help you make sense out of her experience. What is more, if your exemplar thinks you are off on a wrong track, she will probably correct you. After all, it is her experience that is being described, and all of us want to be described accurately. Indeed, it is almost always the case that exemplars report truly enjoying the experience of being modeled, finding it "interesting," "gratifying," and even "ennobling."

The General Process of Elicitation

Now you have your exemplar before you and you are ready to begin eliciting information. Where and how do you begin?

In general, the process of elicitation will take two forms: (1) observing the exemplar manifest his ability, and (2) asking questions regarding the nature of his internal processes. All abilities will have both external and internal components, though the ratio between these two will vary greatly depending upon the nature of the ability. If the ability involves significant external behavior, then of course it is essential to observe your exemplar. However, simply observing is rarely sufficient. As we shall see in the Essays to come, even abilities that seem to be purely about manifesting certain external behaviors are, nevertheless, tremendously influenced by internal processes. Ultimately, it is internal processes that are most responsible for generating abilities. And, so, it is the internal processes in which we are most interested.

Of course, internal processes are generally not as evident as external behaviors. Nevertheless, they are accessible. As he describes his experience when manifesting his ability and responds to your precise questions, your exemplar will be revealing his internal processes through the content of those descriptions, through his use of language, and through his external behavior. As he relates his experience, you are initially trying to notice what seems significant in his experience. As you proceed, gathering more descriptions and more examples, you can begin to identify what truly is significant, that is, what are the essential patterns operating in his experience when manifesting the ability. (What distinctions to pay attention to, and how to identify them and their patterns, are the topics of Essays 3 through 14.)

In addition, there is something you can do to foster your exemplar becoming your collaborator in the modeling process. The most effective way to do this is by recording the information you are gathering in such a way that your exemplar can *see* how you are understanding and representing his experience. Flip charts work very well for this purpose, as do chalk boards, white boards, or large pieces of paper. A computer display or even regular sheets of paper can work as well, provided that they are situated in such a way that your exemplar can see what you are writing on them. As you capture bits and pieces of their experience and start to organize them, the exemplar can see how he is being represented.

Typically the question and answer of the current moment quickly fades and is lost as it is supplanted by next question and answer when the conversation moves on. The virtue of having the information on a visible page—where it does *not* fade—allows exemplars to check again and again that you are accurately representing their experience. They may correct you immediately, or they may correct you an hour later. But they *will* correct you if what you have on the page does not quite fit with their experience. This is precisely what you want to happen; you could not ask for a better collaborator than that.

The Core Dump

You could plunge right into the elicitation, having your exemplar access examples and asking him your pointed questions. But those waters may be pretty deep, deeper than they at first appear. For this reason, we suggest that you begin your elicitation with a "core dump." This is a term we have borrowed from the land of computers, and refers to the phenomenon of a computer "dumping" all its stored data at once. Doing a core dump with your exemplar means simply asking him to tell you, in general, how he goes about doing what he does. The core dump is useful in a number of ways:

- **The Core Dump can be a great relief for the exemplar.** Wanting to be helpful, almost certainly he has been fretting prior to the modeling session about what exactly it is that he does, will have thought it through as best he can, and will be primed to tell it all to you. (It is much like when you go to the doctor with a complaint; you rehearse how you will describe what has been going on with you, and you are ready to deliver that speech. You know how very unsettling it can be if you do not get to make that speech to the doctor.) The core dump, then, allows the exemplar to make good on their rehearsed intention to be as helpful as possible.

- **The Core Dump creates an opportunity to get an over-all sense of the ability, giving you a better sense of "where" in the ability you are as you pursue the more explicit elicitation.** In elicitation, it often happens that you ask about one particular element of the exemplar's experience, and he answers by telling you about some other element. This can really get you in an informational twist if you do not recognize that this is happening. The core dump, however, makes it much easier to avoid this confusion. Because it gives you a sense of the lay of the exemplar's experiential land, it is easier to recognize where in his experiential terrain his answers are coming from. You can then either choose to follow that new lead, or to bring him back to the path you are currently interested in. But in either case, you know where you are.

- **The Core Dump gives you a first opportunity to note any aspects of their experience that seem significant to you.** Later, when you get into the more explicit modeling elicitation, these noted "pieces" of experience might prove to be—or at least point to—important patterns in the exemplar's experience when manifesting the ability.

- **The Core Dump provides an opportunity to discover how the exemplar naturally organizes his ability in terms of "steps."**

These steps we call the "flow of the outcomes," and they may represent either strategy steps or sub-abilities.

The Flow of Outcomes

During the core dump you are likely to hear your exemplar mark out the distinct steps they take as they manifest their ability. These are typically indicated by such phrases as "First I...," "then I...," "after that it becomes necessary to..." "I also have to..." "An important step is to..." and "Finally, I..." These kinds of linguistic markers indicate that these phases of their ability are, for this exemplar, distinct from one another. This sequence of phases is called the "flow of outcomes."

For instance, a teacher being modeled for his ability to teach high school algebra may offer (abbreviated here): "I work on my lesson plan the night before, checking that it will fit with where the students are in their studies. Then I consider if I can come up with any new ideas for presenting that material. If so, I work that out ahead of time. When it comes to the class itself, first I review where we have been, then I give them a preview of the day's lesson, then I get into it. Usually, as I present the material, I will stop to check with them on their understanding." This exemplar is marking out as separate steps:

- Checking the fit of the lesson plan.

- Considering new ways of presenting the material.

- Working out new presentations.

- Reviewing for the class.

- Previewing the lesson.

- Presenting the lesson.

- Checking on class comprehension.

As we discussed earlier in this Essay under "Sub-Abilities," any one, some, or all of these steps could be modeled as separate abilities. Or they could be subsumed into more general and inclusive abilities, such as "Preparing algebra lessons" (which will likely include, as parts of the Strategy, "Checking the fit of the lesson plan," "Considering new ways of presenting the material," and so on), and "Presenting algebra lessons" (which will likely include, as parts of the Strategy, "Reviewing for the class," "Previewing the lesson," and so on). Or the ability could be modeled at the most inclusive level, namely, "Teaching high school algebra," in which case probably all of the exemplar's core dump steps will appear as parts of the Strategy.

The chunk size at which you decide to do your modeling depends on what will work for you (or for those for whom you are creating the model). If modeling at the largest chunk size will allow you to manifest the ability—that is, makes it possible for you to do what you want to do—then that is what you need. However, if one of those sub-abilities is necessary for manifesting the larger ability AND you do not have that sub-ability in your own repertoire, then you need to model it. As we pointed out earlier, discovering that the ability you want to model is made up of some important sub-abilities does not mean that you must then choose either to model all of those sub-abilities or to ignore them and instead model the ability as a "whole." What it does mean is that you must decide what are the sub-abilities you specifically want to have "in focus" as you model. In looking at those sub-abilities, you may decide that there is only one (or perhaps a few) that you really want; the others are either (1) not of interest to you or (2) are ones you already have in some measure.

It is also worth noting that you may discover that your exemplar puts most of his attention on one particular sub-ability. For instance, during the core dump, does the algebra teacher go into rich and animated description about the preparation of lessons, while his coverage of the teaching itself is perfunctory? In that case, what may be most worth modeling in this exemplar is his ability to prepare lessons. If instead he cursorily mentions preparation, but works up a sweat talking about the classroom presentation, then classroom presentation may be the richer vein to mine with this exemplar.[2]

---

[2] More can be found about the significance of, and working with, the flow of outcomes in *The Emprint Method,* by Cameron-Bandler, Gordon and Lebeau. In

The Flood of Description

Shortly after you utter the words, "In a moment I will be asking you some very specific questions, but first I would like to have you describe to me in general how you do what you do," the flood of information will begin. At first it may seem to be aswirl with currents you cannot negotiate and worrying depths. But as you understand more and more about the world of your exemplar, you will also find an increasing ability to swim in those same waters. You will start to hear the patterns that resolve a rain of words into a single drop that is simply being replicated a hundred times, but in slightly different forms each time. In other words, this person's patterns will start to make sense to you.

Of course, you will miss a great deal at first. There is no need to be concerned about that. Anything that is, in fact, characteristic of your exemplar—truly a pattern of his experience when manifesting his ability— will always be there. So you will pick it up in the second example he gives you. Or the third, or the eighth. If it was there once and it is a pattern, it will be there again, in some form or another. All that matters is that eventually you get there, that you come to understand and make sense of the patterns.

We suggest that you tape your elicitation sessions. This can be useful in case a pearl tumbles from the lips of your exemplar that you want to catch, either during the elicitation or later, when you are evaluating what you have discovered. You may also use the tape to resolve something that you thought you understood during the elicitation, but now need to review. And finally, and most importantly, it will allow you to relax during the elicitation, knowing that if you miss something, it is not "gone forever."

Exploring Specific Examples

As a result of the core dump, you will have some sense (and probably some particulars, as well) of what is going on in your exemplar's

---

that book, sub-abilities are discussed under the name of "sub-activities," but the concept is exactly the same.

experience and behavior when manifesting the ability. You will also know at what level you want to chunk and approach the ability. Now you can ask your exemplar for actual examples of manifesting his ability, and from those begin gathering the information you need. If possible, create in the moment an actual, ongoing example of your exemplar manifesting his ability. For instance, if we want to model the algebra teacher's ability to "Present a lesson to the class," we can ask him to present a lesson to us. As he goes through the process, we can find out what he is doing in his internal experience. In addition to giving you the opportunity to observe your exemplar, he will have the clarity and immediacy of his ongoing (or at least very fresh) experience from which to answer your questions.

It is often not possible or convenient to create an actual, ongoing example from which to gather information from your exemplar. In that case, ask him to think of a specific recent and actual example of manifesting his ability. (For instance, we would have the algebra teacher find a recent example of presenting a lesson to his class.) You can then take him through the process he went through in that example, using your questions to direct his attention to the particular information you are interested in (just as you do when eliciting from an actual, ongoing experience).

When gathering information from a recalled example, you can help your exemplar have easier and more accurate access to his experience by orienting him into the "present" of that past event. That is, have your exemplar step into being "there" again. And you can help him do this by interacting with him as though he *is* there. That is, make sure that the things you say to him—in particular, the questions you ask—are in the present tense. So, instead of asking, "What were you feeling as you stood in front of the class?" ask, "What *are* you feeling as you stand in front of the class?" You will soon discover that your exemplar is answering in the present tense as well, that he "is there." (Your exemplar lapsing back into past tense is simply an indication to you of the need to orient him once again to being in the present of the example.)

Of course, drawing examples from recalled experiences does have possible pitfalls that must be kept in mind. First, memories can fade, sapping the exemplar's recalled experience of some of its richness. Second, memories can warp, so that the exemplar (unintentionally) interprets or alters his experience, instead of reporting it "as it was." These are important concerns, of course, but this same warping of reported experience can happen even when your exemplar is reporting from an actual, ongoing experience. One of the ways we deal with this is by drawing our information from several examples of manifesting the ability. Comparing them may expose differences that, when examined with your exemplar, reveal that his memory or description of one of them was in some way distorted or mis-described.

In addition, we do not suggest that you simply rely on what your exemplar says is his experience. Instead, one of the best ways to ensure the fidelity of the information you are gathering is by testing it in your own experience. If it does not make sense in your own experience, then it is something to explore further with your exemplar. You need to sort out whether they have reported their experience inaccurately, or that you need more help in understanding it so that it can make sense to you. (We devote Essay 6, Stepping-In, to the skill of using your own experience as an information-gathering sounding board.)

The General Process of Forming the Model

There comes a point when you have gathered enough information to begin forming a model of the ability. That point is not when you have gathered all the information; there is never an "all." Nor is it when you have finished with your exemplar or exemplars. Remember that the purpose of modeling is for you to be able to take on the exemplar's ability. Ideally, then, as you are gathering information you are also testing in your own experience what you are discovering from your exemplar. The point when you begin forming the model, then, is the point *during* elicitation when what you are learning from your exemplar starts working for you, as well. In a very real sense, you are testing and building the model in yourself throughout the process of gathering information.

Compare and Contrast

Now, you do not want to be trying on, testing, and including in the model everything your exemplar describes. Most of what is described will be irrelevant content. Instead, you want to put your attention on the structure of his experience. That is, you want to search for the essential patterns for manifesting the ability, regardless of the content details of a particular situation. To do this, compare and contrast at least three actual (ongoing or recalled) examples of your exemplar manifesting the ability. As you compare the examples, ask yourself: What is the same across all of them? Any aspect of the exemplar's ability that is truly essential—that is underlying structure—will be found in all examples of the exemplar manifesting the ability. The result will be an *Idiosyncratic Model.* If you want to do something the way a particular exemplar does it, you need only compare and contrast examples from that one exemplar.

If instead you want a *Generic Model*, that is, a model that leaves out individual idiosyncrasies and preserves only the structure common to anyone who manifests the ability, you need to compare and contrast at least three exemplars. This, of course, means that you are comparing the idiosyncratic models you already have for your three exemplars. Comparing across these three models will make obvious the idiosyncratic patterns that can be set aside, leaving only those patterns that are operating in the ability regardless of who has it.

Refine

As we mentioned, when you are gathering information you will, at the same time, be identifying how your exemplar's patterns work in your own experience. So, by the time you are done with elicitation, you will probably have much of the model defined. However, now that you are no longer busy with your exemplar(s) and the spaghetti of elicitation, you are free to "be alone" with what you have discovered and its effect on your experience. Now you can turn your full attention to just what, in all that you learned from your exemplar(s), is essential in being able to reproduce his/their ability in yourself or in someone else.

Of course, the way you discover what is essential to manifesting the ability is by taking on the structure and using it yourself. As you do this, look for those elements of the structure that are effective in taking your experience and behavior toward manifesting the ability. The goal is to retain in the model only what is necessary and sufficient to manifest the ability. The simpler the model, the easier it will be for you and others to acquire. (Essay 15, Elegance, goes into the process of refining in detail.)

Test

The first test of your model comes as you rehearse it in imagination. Take on the structures of experience described in the model and imagine being in situations in which you want to manifest the ability. (This is not only a way to test the model itself, but is also the beginning of model acquisition.) Does it generate the ability? Perhaps there are some elements missing, or that need to be understood in a different way, or are not needed. This is an opportunity to experiment with the model in the safety of your imagination.

Then comes the real world, and the real test of the model. The focus of these initial sorties into actual situations is to discover what might still need to be refined in the model (or in how you are using it). Actually using the model in the real world may generate questions to ask that you did not know to ask before, during the initial elicitation. This may mean talking again with your exemplar, so be sure to leave that open as a possibility when you finish your initial modeling session with him.

* * *

In general, that is how it is done.

Like a quick tour of a house to get an idea of where to find the kitchen, the bathroom, the den, now you have an idea of how modeling is laid out. Of course, we are about to return to each of those rooms and take our time to explore them for the details they contain. And, we admit, there will be plenty of them: details regarding how to think about experience and modeling, details regarding what to elicit, details regarding how to gather information, details regarding how to find essential patterns, details regarding how to take on those essential patterns... This is a big house. But take heart. We are not going to explore the dust balls lurking in the corners of these rooms. We will concern ourselves with only those furnishings that make each of those rooms what it is; that is, we will cover only those details that give substance—indeed, life—to the process of modeling presented in these Essays, details that transform notions about "what to do" into doing.

PART II

Capturing Experience

Capturing Experience

Essay 3

Distinctions

The fact that experience always comes as a "package" of simultaneously operating elements makes it necessary to make distinctions in order to "capture" it in description. When we pull into the foreground of our experience something that previously had been in the undifferentiated background, we are making a distinction. Distinctions matter because they determine what we attend to in experience. The distinctions we use to do modeling are intended to take us inside the experience of the exemplar. These distinctions are employed in a graphic called the Experiential Array. The Array operates as an information gathering tool, helping us keep track of patterns as we model. The Array is also a conceptual tool that helps us perceive how significant dynamics within the exemplar's experience operate to generate their ability.

One of the many ways we have of dividing ourselves into groups is by race. It seems obvious that the light-skinned, fair and straight-haired folks in Scandinavia form a distinct group from the dark-skinned, black and curly-haired folks of sub-Saharan Africa, and that the olive-skinned, black and straight-haired of people of southeast Asia are distinct from Scandinavians and sub-Saharans, and on and on. When we see someone, we notice their skin and hair color, hair texture, eye color, body form, and so on, and instantly classify that person according to race. Differences in skin and hair color are real, of course. And they are so manifestly there for all to see, that classifying folks by these features into races seems obvious and even objective. As it turns out, however, using these features as a basis for assigning race is completely arbitrary.

In taking up the question of what constitutes race, physiologist Jared Diamond describes how the peoples of the world would be grouped into races if we used qualities other than physical appearance. For example, some groups of people carry genes (such as the sickle-cell gene) that give them significant resistance to malaria. If resistance to malaria were the quality by which we divided folks into races, then the race of "resistants" would be made up of people from tropical Africa, Southeast Asia, the Arabian Peninsula, New Guinea, Italy and Greece. The "non-resistant" race would include folks such as the Swedes and the Xhosas of South Africa. If instead we identified races by their ability to digest cheese and milk (those that have the enzyme lactase, and those who do not), the race of "milk digesters" would include Swedes and the Fulani of Africa, while the race of "milk avoiders" would include most black Africans, the Japanese and American Indians. Even fingerprints are characteristic of groups. The "loops" race would include most Europeans, black Africans, and east Asians; the "whorls" race Mongolians and Australian aborigines, and the "arches" race Khoisans, some Indonesians, Jews and other central Europeans. (Jared Diamond, "Race Without Color," Psychology Today, November 1994, 83-89.)

If these new racial divisions seem fanciful, it is only because they are not the ones we grew up with. They are just as real as skin color, however, and just as arbitrary. Given a different social evolution of humankind, characteristics like these could have formed the basis for how we distinguish the races today. They would have become virtually transparent to us, just as the classificatory "truth" of skin color and facial features is transparent to us now. Had that twist in attention occurred, perhaps today the race of "digesters" would be casting aspersions on the "avoiders" as people with "no real stomachs," and the "avoiders" scorning the "digesters" as creatures obviously willing to swallow anything. And, of course, perhaps a different course of human developmental history could have left us today without any notion of race at all.

Making Distinctions

But we do have the notion of "race." It is one of the distinctions we make about people. When we look into the endless abundance of our background experience and, within that, identify something as being different, discreet or separate, we are making a distinction. And usually, once it has been pulled from that background welter of experience—made distinctive—it remains distinct to us. The experience had always been there; but now it is singled out and *noticed*. It is much like looking at a photograph of a crowd of people, perhaps a school class photograph, a dance, the bleachers during a sporting event, or a wedding reception. It is just a mass of human faces, and then suddenly you see the face of a friend. It "jumps out" at you, becoming distinct from the rest of the crowd. In fact, it becomes forever distinct; you can never look at that photograph again without noticing that friend. In the same way, somewhere along the developmental line, we looked into the family album of humanity and recognized groupings of visible physical characteristics, and called that "race." We have also found good, bad, liberal, conservative, anarchist, libertarian, right, left, moral, immoral, amoral, trustworthy, successful, kind, generous, stingy, powerful, loving, and on and on.

Of course, we make distinctions about things other than the qualities of people. In fact, we can and do make distinctions about everything in experience. For instance, we notice changes in weather during the year and make the distinctions spring, summer, fall and winter. (Of course, these are distinctions for those of us who live in temperate latitudes. People who live along the equator will make different distinctions about yearly changes in the weather. In the American Southwest, five seasons are recognized. The fifth—"monsoon"—occurs between summer and fall.) Crimson, fire-engine red, scarlet and cranberry are some of the distinctions we make regarding "red." In the world of chairs, there are armchairs, deck chairs, Adirondacks, Eames chairs and rocking chairs. And in the world of art, expressionism, abstract expressionism, neo-expressionism, neo-impressionism, post-impressionism and postmodernism are all distinct styles of painting. You get the idea (or perhaps for you it is closer to being a notion, or a sense, or an impression). Human beings are relentless makers of distinctions, marking out differences in their experiential world whenever and wherever they are noticed.

Do making all these distinctions matter? Is this just playing with words? Julian Jaynes answers this clearly following his charting of the evolution of words, such as the transforming of "psyche," which meant "physical life" (blood and breathing) in the Iliad, but later evolved into "conscious subjective mind-space" in the Odyssey:

> Let no one think these are just word changes. Word changes are concept changes and concept changes are behavioral changes. The entire history of religions and of politics and even of science stands shrill witness to that. Without words like soul, liberty, or truth, the pageant of this human condition would have been filled with different roles, different climaxes.

> (Julian Jaynes, *The Origin of Consciousness in the Breakdown of the Bicameral Mind*, p.292)

Jaynes goes on to argue that this transition of "psyche" created a consciousness "imprisoned in the body," laying the foundation for the "huge haunted career" of dualism throughout subsequent human history in the Western world.

The distinctions we make orient our attention and, so, our experience. That which was in the background—there but without meaning, significance or even presence—now comes into the foreground of experience; indeed, becomes experience. The distinction may be as trivial as the difference between an armchair and an Eames chair (trivial unless you are an interior decorator, of course), or as profound as the difference between good and evil. Regardless, it will affect what and how you perceive your world.

Many of the distinctions that we make are "held" and passed on by culture through language, art, architecture, food, tempos and so on. Despite being subtle and often completely transparent, these cultural distinctions are undoubtedly the most pervasive and affecting. Superb explorations of the subtle, yet profound, distinctions operating in different cultures can be found in any of Edward T. Hall's books. As just one example: regarding "time," all American-European languages make the distinctions of past, present and future, and this creates a world in which time is spent, lost, managed, things disappear into the past, work for the future, and so on:

> The Hopi language does not do this. No past, present, or future exists as verb tenses in their language. Hopi verbs have no tenses, but indicate instead the validity of a statement—the nature of the relationship between the speaker and his knowledge or experience of that about which he is speaking... Summer and hot are the same! Summer is a condition: hot. There is nothing about summer that suggests it involves time—getting later—in the sense that is conveyed by [American-European] languages.

> Edward T. Hall, *The Dance of Life*, p. 35

Clearly, distinctions matter.[3]

Useful Distinctions

Whether they come to us through the cultural waters in which we swim, through encounters in education or on the street, through books, or through personal discoveries, distinctions bring new experiences into awareness. In your travels through life you have probably seen Dante chairs, murrey red, and pointillist paintings, but they did not stand out in your experience as distinct from other funny-looking chairs, reds and paintings. Like the photograph of the crowd containing an unrecognized

---

[3] Also, works by Lakoff and Johnson explore the pervasive effects on experience and behavior of distinctions and of distinctions as metaphors. See their *Philosophy in the Flesh* and *Metaphors We Live By*.)

friend (whose image is falling on your retina, even though you do not "see" it), the world of experience is an infinitely rich crowd; distinctions allow certain of the experiences milling about in that crowd to pop into perception.

A painter friend of ours gave us a lesson in this while crossing a bridge one afternoon in a small town in Denmark. We stopped halfway across to admire the gently rippling, gray-green waters below us. At least that is how the water appeared to us, until she remarked on the lovely pinks. After the requisite, "Pink? What are you talking about?" we began to see the pink as well. In fact, it became obvious. It also made it possible to notice pinkness and other (unexpected) colors whenever we looked at bodies of water from that time on. (And, not insignificantly, could then see the verity in paintings—by Monet, for example—that depicted water swirling with colors, including pink.)

"Water Lilies" by Claude Monet (1917-1919)
THE PINK IS THERE; SEE THESE PAINTINGS IN COLOR AT:
HTTPS://EN.WIKIPEDIA.ORG/WIKI/WATER_LILIES_(MONET_SERIES)

Our experience on that bridge was an unexpected gift of a distinction from a friend. There are times, however, when we are intentionally pursuing a deeper understanding of something. Since the distinctions we use in that pursuit will determine what and how we perceive, it makes sense to consider the appropriateness of the distinctions we are bringing to that exploration. For instance, to describe the structures that create the ocean patterns we call "waves," oceanographers specify such things as "trough height," "speed," "littoral incline," and so on. These are some of the distinctions they use; these are not the only ones that can be made. Distinctions could as well be made about the colors of the water (pink?!), the kind of plankton it contains, its temperature, and the grain size of the sand it stirs up on the beach. However, this alternative set of distinctions is probably not useful in describing how waves form along the shoreline. (Of course, these distinctions may be very significant to an ecologist, a painter, or a geologist.) The oceanographers' distinctions allow them to usefully describe the formative patterns of the phenomenon of waves. Similarly, we want to usefully describe the patterns inherent in experience that come together to form the waves of human abilities. And for that we, too, need distinctions.

There are not good and bad or right and wrong distinctions. Rather, different distinctions will influence you in different directions. The test for any distinction or set of distinctions is, Do they take us in the direction we want to go? In the case of the oceanographer studying wave formation, if she devoted her time and attention to the kinds of plankton populating the surf she would probably not come up with a description of wave formation that would be of much use. The distinctions that she does use, however, are ones that have proven useful in describing the patterns of wave formation.

Human experience is far more complex than waves, or weather, or computer programs by many orders of magnitude. Nevertheless, here we are, setting out to explore experience through modeling, to understand how it works and, ultimately, to change and evolve our own experiences through that exploration. And so we will want to use distinctions that give us experiential access to someone else's ability. That is, we want distinctions that describe an exemplar's ability in a form that we can use to re-pattern our own experiences and behaviors. How can we engage with the mass of "stuff" of human experience in a useful way, in a way that fosters both understanding and access?

This is exactly the question the authors found themselves grappling with late at night at the abbey of Saint Gerard in 1988. Participants in a residential seminar there were finding themselves overwhelmed with, and confused by, the flood of information they were getting from their clients. They needed distinctions that would help point them toward the most revealing and useful aspects of human experience and behavior. Our answer to that need then was—and still is—the Experiential Array.

The Experiential Array

The usefulness of a map is largely determined by whether or not the distinctions used to draw it are appropriate for its intended purpose. In looking at the range of the human "terrain," it is clear that, in broad terms, most of the things we do as human beings involve some combination of Beliefs (patterns of believing), Strategies (patterns of thinking), Emotions (patterns of feeling) and External Behavior (patterns of behaving).

Obviously, these *elements of experience* are significant to varying degrees depending upon the particular ability we are considering. Creating a comedy monologue, for example, relies heavily on Strategies (patterns of thinking) and very little on External Behavior. Delivering the comedy monologue, though, probably relies more on External Behavior and less on Strategies. Regardless of the ability, however, most human abilities involve the simultaneous expression and interaction of all of the elements of human experience. When modeling, then, we want to at least consider all four areas in terms of their contribution to the ability we are modeling. One way to "capture" these elements of experience is in the Experiential Array:

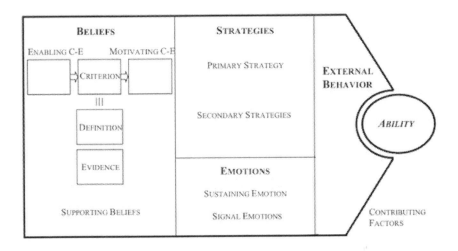

One of the virtues of the Array is that it provides places within which to capture the different elements of experience.[4] As was made evident by the folks in the seminar at Saint Gerard, we need more than a bathing suit when we go swimming in another person's experience. It may well be a flood of information. The Array helps us both stay afloat and maneuver by providing a way to organize the flow of information. Because the Array gives specific places to place specific elements of experience, it helps make obvious what we already know about the exemplar's experience, as well as what elements of their experience we have yet to dip into.

In addition, and perhaps more importantly, having these places for the specific elements of experience makes information redundancy much more evident. The exemplar will often use different words and phrases as she tries to give us a rich and understandable description of her experience. As modelers, we are after the underlying patterns that generate that experience. And, so, we need to be alert to the redundancy in how people express themselves, pulling from those various content descriptions the essential patterns that unite them all. The Array helps us do that by gathering together descriptions about a particular kind of distinction,

---

[4] As you can see, inside most of these elements of experience boxes there are smaller boxes with even more distinctions. We go into great detail about all of these distinctions in later Essays. For now, however, we will refer only to the larger distinctions of Beliefs, Strategy, Emotions, and External Behavior.

allowing them to be compared more easily and, so, more easily reveal the patterns they have in common.

Elastic Boxes

The Array is a conceptual tool. None of us have boxes in our heads, let alone boxes as small as those depicted in the Array graphic. The boxes in the Array are places to put certain kinds of information. The different sizes of the boxes in the Array is a matter of convenience and economy. Their size does not denote relative importance, nor how much information you "ought to" find and put into any one of those boxes. The limitation on information is always its relevance to the ability, and not whether there is room in the box for it. There is endless room in each of the boxes for information.

Furthermore, the Array is more than just a repository for information. That is a function that could be served as well by any number of formats. The Array, however, also captures some of the dynamics of the system. Once you have identified any two (or more) places (like discovering where your friend lives in your neighborhood, or finding Denmark and Sweden on a map) you can see how they relate to one another; how far apart, they are, how to get from one to another, where they are in relation to *other* places, and so on. In the same way, the boxes of the Array show the relationships between the different kinds of information to be found in the "places" of human experience.

The Flow of Effect

All of the elements of experience interact to make possible the expression of an ability. But this simultaneity does not mean that the elements necessarily exert equal influence on each other. Instead, there seems to be a "flow of effect." While your behavior does affect what you are feeling and thinking, the impact is not as great as that of your thoughts and feelings on your behavior. Similarly, your beliefs have a greater impact on what you think, feel and do than any of these elements has on what you believe. All of us can point to examples of trying to change our behavior even though our beliefs had not changed. In those situations, maintaining that change required you to be vigilant regarding your behavior. And it probably did not last through time. This is in contrast to times when you have changed what you believed, instantly and naturally causing changes in your behavior.

Keep in mind that we are talking about what is going on in experience at the time an ability is being manifested or expressed. Clearly, over time, what you think, feel and do can contribute experiences that ultimately do change what you believe. But at the moment we are manifesting ourselves, the "flow of effect" is more from beliefs toward behavior than it is toward the other direction (the relative size of the arrows indicates the "flow of effect"):

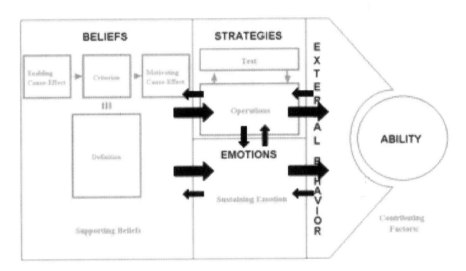

As you can see, there is no arrow going to "ability." In fact, "ability" is not even joined to the rest of the Array. This is because the ability *is* the rest of the Array. That is, when the elements of experience are there and operating, the ability is being manifested. Nevertheless, we have put the labeling of the ability in close relationship to "external behavior" because it is generally through external behavior that an ability affects, and is known to, the world. For example, the ability to effectively lead a group involves all kinds of internal beliefs, states, and processing of information. But all that internal structure must be manifested in behavior for it to have an impact on the group. Of course there are some abilities that do not require being manifested in external behavior. One can be exercising the ability to make up stories without doing anything in particular "on the outside." But it is still the case that the only way that this person's stories can be known by, and have an impact on, the world is if they somehow get expressed in external behavior (through the telling or writing of them).

The primary importance of the notion of "flow of effect" is that it reminds us that simply modeling behavior is usually not in and of itself sufficient to manifest an ability. Behind the natural manifestation of that behavior are supportive ways of thinking and feeling, and behind them all are supportive beliefs. It is the dynamic relationships between all of these elements that give rise to the ability; that dynamic relationship *is* the ability.

Simultaneity of the Array

It is important to bear in mind that the flow of effect suggested by these arrows is not indicative of sequence. That is, the flow of effect is not one in which first beliefs are accessed, and then strategies are engaged, and then behaviors are manifested. Obviously, there are sequential things going on when someone is manifesting an ability. In particular, strategies are often sequential. But it is not the case that the exemplar engages his beliefs before engaging his strategy sequences. They engage at the same time and, of course, the beliefs continue to be engaged and exert their influence on the exemplar as he continues to run through the sequences of his strategy.

For the most part, then, all of the elements of experience are engaged and operating more or less simultaneously. The flow of effect, then, is a simply a comment on the degree of influence each of the elements has within and on the system: in general, beliefs have a greater impact on the system than do strategies and emotions, and strategies and emotions have a greater impact on the system than do external behaviors.

And it is worth repeating, as well, that the flow of effect does not suggest that any one element is of greater importance than another. As the organs of the body learned when they argued about which of them is the most important, the functions of all are needed if the body is to live. Without any one of the elements of experience, there is no ability. Each element contributes a different and essential function as they operate in relationship to one another.

* * *

Except for external behavior, the distinctions that we are proposing to use in our modeling are all about what is going on "inside" the person. How do we get in there to discover what to put in the experiential boxes of the Array? The bridge between you and the internal experience of your exemplar will be built out of questions, and it is to the ins and outs of asking questions that we turn in the next Essay, Asking Questions.

Capturing Experience

Essay 4

Asking Questions

To ask a question is to set the frames for thinking. The compelling nature of questions makes it important to have some understanding of the presuppositions operating in the ones you ask your exemplar. In addition, it is important to know what kind of information you want to get by asking your question. Knowing this allows you to recognize if your exemplar's response is in fact an answer to your question.

"Why is the sky blue?" When one of the authors asked this of his daughter, she reflected on the question for a moment and realized that she did not know. She proceeded to propose a possible explanation. When it was rejected, she set sail on another internal voyage of exploration, and soon returned with yet another explanation. But this too sank upon the rocks of science, and she was forced to seek even further for a workable reason. When at last she had exhausted her ideas, she asked to be told the real reason the sky is blue. But her father refused to tell her. Several years later she

photo by Adael Bullock

confessed to him that she still wanted to know the answer to the question, Why is the sky blue?

The Magic Carpet of Questions

Several *years* later? Questions can do that; they can seize our attention, letting go only when they are answered. And it is not only the big questions that grab us, questions about the whys and wherefores of our pasts, presents and futures. Even mundane questions—How long does it take to drive across the United States? Who starred in the movie "Gilda"? Why is the sky blue?—can demand our attention and compel us to search for answers. But do we *have* to search? It is as though questions are special keys that, when turned, inevitably start the motors of search and discovery.

How Do Questions Get Our Motors Going?

How do questions get our motors going? Now, of course, we just asked you a question. Did you just read across it? Or did you take it in and consider it? What happened in your experience? Where did your thoughts go? How did your body react? As we ask each of these additional questions, are you aware of your thoughts shifting to find an answer? Even if you were not aware of doing that, do you feel that brief moment of stillness, of plunging inside, of wondering?

We are meaning-making beings, creatures who use meaning to mold the raw materials of perception into the bricks of experience with which we build our worlds. Indeed, the two brick-making tools of meaning are those of Making Distinctions (which we discussed in the previous Essay) and Asking Questions. While distinctions provide form, it is questions that provide the impetus *to form*. Being asked a question has an undeniably compelling quality to it. The motive power of questions becomes immediately evident when you are asked a question that you do not want to answer. You will nonetheless answer it "on the inside." Even more telling than this, however, is the difficulty you will have in refusing to answer it on the outside. You feel impelled to answer, and it is an act of conscious self-mastery to remain silent.

It is as if our bodies and our nervous systems are set to respond to questions. And indeed they are. At its most fundamental level, the body is constantly posing and answering the most fundamental of questions: What is this? The semi-permeability of cell membranes, the lock-and-key recognition device of antibodies, the pressure-sensitive nerve endings in skin, the dendritic receptors that respond to specific neuro-transmitters, and so on are all, in effect, asking the question, What is this?, and are waiting for the particular molecule, or pressure, or protein, or neuro-transmitter that is an answer to their question. We are neurologically set up to respond to and orient toward that which is new, unknown, different, unaccounted for, or a change in our feelings, environment, senses, and philosophies.

Let's jump from neurons to the whole person. An interruption—from the "outside" or the "inside"—of our normal flow of meaning making immediately generates questions. Consciously and unconsciously, we ask questions when there is something that we must account for or make sensible; in other words, when we need to give meaning to something. That is the only time questions arise. It is not too much to say, then, that the purpose of a question is to alert us to the fact that meaning needs to be made of something. This is so much the case that when we are asked a question (rather than generating it ourselves) we respond to it as though it had been raised within us. That is, the fact that a question is being asked presupposes that there is a need *in us* for meaning-making. In general, we do not first consider whether or not the question is worth answering. Instead, we respond as though we had generated it ourselves; we seek an answer.

How Do Questions Set Our Filters?

So far we have been talking about how being asked a question incites us to make meaning. But being asked a question is more than an experiential nudge that gets us moving; it is a nudge that gets us moving in a particular direction. The content of a question sets our experiential filters, opening up certain lines of thought, and leaving others ignored, out of consciousness, and unexplored. As an example, try the following, small experiment:

> Slowly rub your hand upon a place on your clothing, asking yourself as you do this, "I wonder just how intensely I can experience this?"

If you try this, you will undoubtedly discover that your experience of touching the cloth becomes richer, perhaps in many ways. (And there is no need to stop with clothing! We encourage you to ask yourself this question in relation to all manner of experiences.) The cloth has not changed; but the quality of your attention to it did change. And this change was incited by the content of the question itself. (As an example, you can repeat the experiment, but this time, as you rub your clothing, ask yourself, "I wonder just how *little* I can experience this?")

In the previous Essay we explored the role of distinctions in organizing our experiential filters along certain lines. The distinctions we make determine to a great extent what we notice—that is, what has significance or meaning. Questions set filters through which we perceive and make sense of a situation by suggesting what is relevant. For instance, asking, "Why is the sky blue?" suggests to us that the relevant distinctions at that moment are "sky," "blue" and "causes of color." If instead we ask the question, "Why is the sky cloudy?" a somewhat different set of distinctions becomes relevant. It is the same sky, but now we are considering it with respect to the distinctions of "sky," "clouds" and "causes of cloudiness." The question, "Is the sky bluer than yesterday?" filters our thoughts through the distinctions of "sky," "blue," "yesterday" and "comparisons of more than." And pointing up at a passing jet and asking, "Where do you think that jet is going?" takes our thoughts into an entirely different realm of considerations. As we watch the jet pass overhead, the blueness of the sky recedes into the background of our experience. We are no longer focused on making meaning regarding blueness; instead, we are now intent upon making meaning regarding possible destinations for that jet. Whether asked consciously or unconsciously, a question sets the experiential filters we use to search for meaning that answers that question.[5]

Questions and Modeling

The effects of asking questions are not trivial. Asking a question is NOT an innocuous, neutral act. It is a way of compelling someone's experience along certain lines. There is no avoiding or canceling the compelling nature of asking a question. What we can do, however, is be mindful of this influence and, so, be mindful of how we ask our questions.

One of the authors witnessed a particularly telling and poignant example of the distinction-setting nature of questions at a lecture about a particular approach to relationship therapy. To demonstrate the approach, the therapist brought to the stage a woman who was having a problem with her husband. She explained that he often worked late at the office and, though he was very good about calling to let her know, she still felt annoyed about it. The session proceeded approximately as follows:

Therapist: Where does he call you from?

Client: His office.

Therapist: How do you know that?

Client: Well, he says he's still at his office.

Therapist: Could he have been calling from somewhere else?

Client: (in obvious growing distress) It's possible, I guess.

The session quickly spiraled into this client "realizing" that her husband's behavior may well mean that he was having an affair. Without judging whether the therapist's questions sprang from his prescience or personal agenda, it is still the case that he led his client down a particular

---

[5] A colleague of ours, Bob Smith (who you will meet again in Essay 16), is fond of reminding his clients, "If you don't like the answers you are getting, change the question."

path of thinking with the nature of his questions. Questions set the distinctions through which we filter our subsequent meaning-making.[6]

When modeling, bear in mind that your exemplar will try to answer the question you actually ask; not the question you intended to ask. So it is important that you ask your question in a way likely to take your exemplar down the experiential path you need her to explore. For example, suppose we are modeling an architect and want to know what her thoughts are as she is designing a home. We could ask, "What are you feeling when you are designing a home?" This question, of course, is asking her to identify her *feelings*, and that is probably what she will then tell us about. But at this moment we want to know what she is *thinking*. So, it is more useful and appropriate to ask, "What are you thinking when you are designing a home?" This seems like an example of a fairly obvious and easily avoided misstep. But is, in fact, a common one in the real world of information gathering. We frequently find that, in the midst of pursuing understanding, people are so intent and focused on getting answers that they neglect the form and subtleties of the questions they are relying on to produce those answers. Slips of intention that are obvious to us as they lie here on the page ("feel" instead of "think") can easily be overlooked in the heat of information gathering.

In fact, going deeper, we find that the exemplar will respond to the subtlest aspects of the questions put to them. Suppose we ask the architect the following two questions:

"What is important as you are designing a home?"
"What is important about designing a home?"

Are these two questions directing our exemplar to the same aspect of her experience, or to different aspects? On their faces, both questions seem to be directing the exemplar down the same experiential road; that is, identifying what is important to her when designing a home. But take a

---

[6] As members of the audience, outside of the interaction, we can wonder why the client didn't merely reject the questions as irrelevant or even insulting? Of course, she could have. But it is not so easy to do that when one is *inside* the experience of being asked the questions.

moment to ask those two questions of yourself. You will discover that they tend to take you down different paths, affecting your thinking in different ways. The first question orients you more to being *in the act of* designing a home, asking you for an ongoing report of what is happening in your thinking and behavior. With her attention directed in that way, our architect might tell us, "I need to be aware of how changes in the spaces affect my feelings so I have an idea of what other people will feel when they are in them." The "about" in the second question, however, puts you in a larger frame, one that is outside of, and judging, the whole enterprise of home design. In response to this question, our architect might answer something like, "Coming up with a design that the client will really love." (Substituting your own content into the two questions will help make these subtle differences immediately evident to you. For example, if you are adept at giving useful feedback you would ask yourself, "What is important as I am giving feedback?" and "What is important about giving feedback?")

How significant is the difference between these two—or any two—questions? That can only be answered in use, with an actual and particular exemplar answering the question. Depending upon the exemplar's responses to them, the two questions in our example could generate similar answers or wildly different answers. What we want to make clear, however, is that words do matter.

Though, No Guarantees

The fact that words matter, that they compel experience, does not mean that they will compel the experience of everyone in the same way, or in a way that is necessarily predictable. (As we pointed out above, the significant difference between two apparently similar questions will only be revealed in the use of those questions with a particular exemplar.) Meaning is not in the words themselves, but is connected to those words by the person using (or responding to) them. No matter how careful we are in wording our questions, it is always the case that the exemplar will respond according to her own world of experience. And that response will not necessarily be an answer to the question we asked; she will answer the question as *she* understands it. Of course, it is essential to ask the question you want to ask, using the wording that conveys your intention, so as to help orient the exemplar toward the precise information you are after. But there are no guarantees that the intention in your well-worded question will get you that information.

In the previous Essay we explored the necessary role of distinctions in describing your exemplar's ability. In general, you are asking questions in relation to those distinctions. That is, you want your exemplar to describe her experience in terms of those distinctions. If, for instance, one of your modeling distinctions is "tempo," you might ask our architect exemplar, "How *quickly* are you moving through the design possibilities you are imagining?" She answers, "Well, I'm imagining moving through each space to find out how it feels." This is a reasonable (and revealing) answer, but it is not an answer to the question we asked. Her response is not about tempo, but (perhaps because she seized upon the phrase "moving through" in the question) about her process for testing her design possibilities.

At this point you might be wondering, If the exemplar will respond to my questions according to their own understanding of them, why bother to be precise about how I ask them? In fact, there are three reasons why this uncontrollability of the exemplar's answers makes it all the more important for you to be precise:

The first we have already talked about above, which is that the wording of your questions will always have an effect on the thinking of your exemplar. And because of shared linguistic, cultural and societal histories, that effect will usually be very close to what you (or anyone) would expect. So your precision will probably help your exemplar retrieve the information you are after.

The second reason is that when you know what kind of information your question is intended to retrieve, it will be immediately clear to you whether or not the exemplar's response truly answers that intention. That is, crafting your question to go after a certain kind of information not only helps set your exemplar's filters, it sets your filters as well. Then, when the response comes back, you are already tuned to recognize the kind of information you are seeking. For instance, when we ask the architect, "How quickly are you moving through the design possibilities you are imagining?" we are setting ourselves to notice descriptions of tempo patterns. Her answer, "Well, I'm imagining moving through each space to find out how it feels," is interesting and is filled with potentially important information that we may well want to capture. But it is also important to not let this unexpected fount of good stuff wash away the fact that it nevertheless did not retrieve the information we were after. (If it is worth asking about in the first place, it is worth getting an answer; *then* you can decide if it is useful information.)

Which leads us to the third reason that being deliberate about your questions is important. And that is, if your precise question does not elicit the information you need, you at least know what your first question was and what it elicited and, so, will better understand how to re-tune your next question to help orient your exemplar's thinking. This "tuning" of the question takes us now to the notion of *framing*.

Framing Questions

It is not the exemplar's job to know what you, the modeler, need to know about the structure of her experience; she just has it (and very likely never explored its structure before). It is, however, your job as the modeler to help your exemplar gain access to those aspects of her experience that may be significant in manifesting her ability. And you do this primarily through asking questions. The magic carpet of your questions is a set of frames for your exemplar to think "through," they are conceptual filters that set direction for thinking. Before rolling out such a carpet, it is worth considering where it is likely to fly.

This means considering where you want your exemplar's thinking to go, and what she may need to know or hear in order to go there easily. How can you know what she needs to hear? Sometimes the answer to that will be found in your own experience; you are a human being, just like your exemplar, and so most of the experiential ground on which you both stand is common ground. Consider what would help you better understand

and respond to the question you want to ask. Those same considerations are likely to help your exemplar as well.

But of course there will also be differences in understanding between you and your exemplar. So in addition to considering what would help you understand and respond to the question, it is also important to consider what *this* exemplar—*this* person—may need. To do that you must call upon your knowledge and experience of your exemplar. Whether it is substantial (because, say, this person is a good friend of yours), or almost nonexistent at the outset, as the elicitation proceeds your understanding of your exemplar will deepen, and so will your ability to form questions that usefully orient her.

Jargon

In particular, be wary of using jargon in your questions. Jargon is tremendously useful among those "in the know," but tremendously confusing when dropped upon those who are not. When operating from our own area of expertise—in this case, modeling—it is easy to slip into using its jargon, forgetting that the exemplars have not been initiated into the arcane world of our modeling distinctions. Since they are not privy to your world, consider how you can make your distinctions in language that anyone can understand. It is the difference between saying, "During elicitation, pace the exemplar's model of the world while calibrating their responses," and, "When asking questions, use language and examples that the other person naturally understands, and at the same time notice changes in her comfort and understanding so that you can adjust how you are asking your questions." The first sentence is (accurately) understood only by those already initiated into the modeling world use of "pacing," "map of the world," "exemplar," "calibrating," and "responses." By contrast, *anyone* can get these same ideas from the second sentence.

The need to make sense to your exemplar does not mean that you can never use jargon. The advantage of jargon is that it condenses concepts into a word or two that might otherwise take paragraphs to describe. Jargon can be a big advantage in terms of making communication more efficient. It means that you and another person can communicate with a shared understanding and do it efficiently. When you are gathering information from an exemplar (perhaps for hours) it can very helpful for both of you to share the language—the jargon—of the distinctions you are using in your modeling. When you want to use jargon, however, introduce it. That is, make sure that you first explain it and, ideally, give examples, so that it also becomes meaningful to your exemplar.[7]

Shifting the Frame of the Question

Obviously, you cannot know up front everything that you need to take into consideration in formulating questions for your exemplar. Your exemplar is not a box of informational marbles that you are emptying, one marble at a time; your exemplar is a person you are getting to know. Modeling is a process of discovery, rather than of confirmation. And, so, as you gather information you are learning more and more about how to understand and interact with this person, your exemplar.

You can therefore count on your questions occasionally going awry. When this happens, many people often respond by asking the exact same question again! Not surprisingly, the result is either the same answer from the exemplar (perhaps expressed in different words), or the same answer plus a growing sense of annoyance on the part of the exemplar. After all, she understands the language and she already answered your question...so why are you asking it again?

Perhaps the best way to think of a question that goes awry is that it worked perfectly to take the exemplar where you did not intend her to go. This misunderstanding is feedback to you that you need to frame your question differently. (It is NOT feedback to change your intention and abandon going after the information you want. Again, if it is worth asking about in the first place, it is worth getting an answer; *then* you can decide if it is useful information.) Accordingly, the next question to ask *yourself*

---

[7] Indeed, every word functions in this way, 'standing for' whole complexes of associations that can only be unraveled with a lot of description (which is what dictionaries do). Jargon, then, is really only topic-specific language that has not yet been made meaningful to you.

is: How do I need to re-frame my question in order to get the information I want? Answering that can be made easier by further self-questions such as, Do I need to make my question simpler, or more concrete? Do I need to give examples? Do I need to backtrack so we are both starting from the same frame of reference? Are there terms (perhaps jargon) I am using that need to be explained? Is *she* operating within a frame that is not useful for getting to the information? What frame for thinking would be helpful? Does she need suggestions for *how* to search for or think about the kind of information I am interested in? Do I need to more specifically bring her attention to a particular aspect of her experience?

These questions are offered only as examples of what to consider, not as a complete set. They are useful, but you will give yourself more freedom and spontaneity in the re-formulation of your questions by recognizing that, in general, your exemplar needs either *Clarification*, or an *Example*, or a *Distinction*, or a *Suggestion*. Let's look at each of these:

Framing by Clarification

As we have already discussed, the use of jargon can create confusion or misunderstanding in the exemplar. And of course, jargon is by no means the sole source of misunderstanding. Any of the ways you have of expressing an idea (your choice of words, sentences, sequencing of ideas, and even voice tonality and facial expressions) may lead your exemplar down paths of association that you did not intend, and perhaps all the way to misunderstanding. When you discover that this has happened, one approach is to clarify, explaining as simply and directly as possible the terms or concepts you are using.

As an example, say that we are interested in the architect's internal sensory system experiences, that is, what she is seeing, hearing and feeling in her head and body. So we ask her, "What are you imagining when you are in the process of coming up with possible designs?" We know what we mean, but she can only respond to the question with what it means *to her*. So she answers, "I'm imagining the interests and desires of my clients, of course." Obviously we need to clarify our use of the term "imagining."

Speaking in terms that she is likely to already be familiar with, we could respond with:

> "I think I misled you by using the word 'imagining.' What I want to know is, when you are in the process of coming up with possible designs, what are you picturing in your head, what are you hearing or saying to yourself, and what body sensations are you aware of?"

This explanation will probably give our exemplar the perceptual and conceptual frames she needs to go directly to the kind of information we are after. If your clarification is still not enough, the exemplar will let you know either by again answering from another area of her experience, or by asking you for additional explanations. In either case, you can oblige, this time coming at your explanation from yet a different angle.

Or you might instead decide that a better way to create a shared understanding is through offering examples of the kind of experience you are after.

Framing by Example

Suppose you ask someone who does not speak English to retrieve a "ball" from the next room. Since that person is not sure what "ball" means, she is liable to come back with anything (or nothing). The way words naturally acquire meaning is by being connected to particular classes of experience. So we show her a small, soft, red sphere and tell her it is a "ball." This example establishes for her what "ball" means: it denotes the class of spherical, small, red, soft things. With that in mind, she returns to the room, but again returns empty-handed because there were no spherical, small, red, soft things in there. Then we show her examples of other spheres that are brown or white, hard or soft, and of various sizes. Through these examples, her understanding of what "ball" means becomes more precise: a ball is any spherical object. Now she can go into the next room and retrieve it.

Often the quickest and surest way to establish a shared understanding with your exemplar is by providing examples of the kind of information you are seeking. After all, the examples you use will be those that are meaningful for you and, if they work for your exemplar as well, both of you will then be using a very similar set of associations. In working with the architect, for example, once it was clear that she misunderstood our use of "representing," we could help her by offering:

> "What I mean by 'representing' is what is going on inside. For instance, when I go to select a present for a friend, I make pictures in my head of times when I have seen him particularly pleased, and notice what it was that pleased him. I'm also asking myself things like, 'Would he like that kind of thing again?' 'What could I find that would be similar?' and things like that. I even have feelings of pleasure when I imagine him opening it up. So, for you, when you are in the process of coming up with possible designs for your clients, what are you representing?"

If this example connects to our exemplar's own experiences, she will have a far more accurate idea of where she needs to turn her attention in order to answer our question. Of course, as with simple clarification, there is no guarantee that this one will be enough. She may still need additional examples.

Framing by Distinction

As we said, your exemplar is not a box of informational marbles. Gathering information is an interaction during which you and your exemplar are learning how to understand and communicate with each other. As the modeler, it is obvious that you are working to understand your exemplar. Your exemplar will, however, be working just as hard to understand you. She will need to make sense of the language you use and the information requests you make. And the more educated your exemplar is about what distinctions to make in experience, the easier it is for her to be your partner in discovery. This does not mean you have to teach her modeling. In the process of gathering information you will be implicitly educating your exemplar about what to attend to, and how to make sense of, her experience.

Even so, there may also be times when you can help your exemplar by being explicit about some of the distinctions you are using in your modeling. This is particularly useful when you find that your exemplar seems to be "locked onto" a certain area of her experience, and neither changing the form of your question nor offering explanations seems to help. When this happens, you need to make an explicit distinction for your exemplar between what they are offering you and what you want them to access in their experience.

For instance, suppose that we now know that as the architect comes up with possible designs for a home, she evaluates each possibility with respect to how well it will "fit the temperament" of her client. Wanting to know what motivates her to make that evaluation, we ask her, "Why is it important that it fit their temperament?" She responds with, "Well, when I imagine I'm in the space, I imagine I'm there as the client. And I feel what it's like to be there. Then, if it fits for me it will usually fit for the client, too." This is interesting and undoubtedly useful information about how she decides the room fits (Essay 9: Strategy). But it is not an answer to the question we asked. Her awareness is "locked onto" what she is doing as she designs, rather than the "reasons" for doing it the way she does, which is what we are interested in exploring at the moment. To clarify the distinction for her, we can explain:

> "We know that you want the space you design to 'fit the temperament' of your client. This is your *Criterion* when designing, your immediate goal. And what you were just describing is how you know when a particular design fits or doesn't fit. You imagine the room and when you can feel in it what you know your client wants to feel, and then you have a possible design. That is how you know it 'fits' during the design process. So that is your *Strategy*. It may also be that if you can satisfy your criterion for fitting the client's temperament, that it will somehow serve or help to satisfy some *other* criterion that is, in a sense, outside of the actual process of designing the home itself. I call this the

Motivating Criterion; it is why it is important to you that the home you design fits your client's temperament. So for you, *why* is it important that you design homes that fit the temperament of your client?"

Now we have drawn boundaries around what our exemplar has been putting her attention on, identifying (naming) them, making them distinct, so that it is easier for her to recognize them. Now she knows what to set aside, and what to attend to in her experience in order to answer our question.

Framing by Suggestion

It is often effective to offer your exemplar suggestions about what her experience might be with respect to the particular distinctions you are asking about. In putting forward your ideas about what is going on in your exemplar's experience, you are doing two potentially helpful things. The first is that it may help your exemplar even better understand the particular nature of the information you want her to be attending to. That is, your suggestion about what her experience is can serve as an example of the kind of information you are after.

The second, more significant effect of making a suggestion is that it gives your exemplar something to compare her own experience with and respond to. By giving your exemplar a description that is *not* her experience she can, by contrast, more easily identify what *is* her experience. For example, our architect exemplar now understands what we mean by "representations," but she is having trouble identifying just what she is representing when she is in the midst of developing design possibilities. We can offer:

> "Let me make a suggestion, but you decide if it is close to what you do or not. Earlier you were talking about 'moving through space,' so perhaps what you are doing is constructing an image of a possible room, then seeing yourself moving inside it and getting a feeling about how easy it is to move through it?"

As we make this suggestion, our exemplar will try to imagine it, and will probably notice right away those aspects of the description that do not fit with her actual experience. So she responds to our suggestion with:

> "It's true, I do make a picture of the space, of the room. But I don't see myself in it. I'm actually in the room, seeing it as if I was in there. And I move through it and really get a sense of whether it feels open, or warm, or efficient, or whatever the client wants the room to be."

Offering suggestions is often an effective way of giving your exemplar an opportunity to identify just what is and is not true in their experience.

Ready to be Wrong

Indeed, offering suggestions can, on occasion, be too effective. So let's wave a small red flag of warning. When modeling, we are as much as possible opening ourselves to who our exemplar is, rather than trying to install *our* ideas of who she is into her. Two dynamics that operate during elicitation make dangerously fertile ground for the planting of suggestions. The first is that, being a normal human being, the exemplar will probably be able to imagine to some extent doing whatever it is we are suggesting, and may then conflate the imagining of the experience with their actual experience. The second factor is that most exemplars want very much to be accommodating and helpful. Together, these two dynamics create a potential for suggestions to prejudice the exemplar's experience. Yet we do want to be able to offer suggestions for the purposes of clarification; it can be very helpful for the exemplar. How can we use this tool without hitting our thumb?

In the above example with the architect, we prefaced our suggestion with, "Let me make a suggestion, but you decide if it is close to what you do or not." This helps to clearly set a frame for the exemplar that what is coming is to be taken only as a suggestion, that there is no expectation on our part that what we are suggesting is necessarily correct. We typically preface our suggestions to the exemplar with some such cautionary words in order, as much as possible, to help them maintain a separation between what is being suggested and their actual experience.

But more important than any cautionary words is what must be behind them. And that is that you are *always ready to be wrong*. By this we mean that any concerns you might have about being right, not wanting to make mistakes, not wanting to look foolish, appearing all-knowing, and so on are all subordinated—if not completely swept aside—by the one thing that really does matter, which is being able to understand the world of this exemplar, this person. Indeed, when you make a suggestion about what your exemplar's experience is, you are offering it with the intention of being wrong, wrong so that your exemplar can more easily get to what is "right" in her experience. (An additional check on inadvertently influencing the exemplar is "calibration," which we talk about in Essay 6: Stepping-In.)

Answering Un-Asked Questions

The exemplar is *always* telling you something about her experience. She may not have answered the question you asked, but she is certainly telling you something. That is, whatever your exemplar offers you will come from her world, and will be a manifestation of how she is operating within the context of the ability she is describing. And so almost every response is relevant. When we asked the architect why it is important that her designs "fit," she answered, "Well, when I imagine I'm in the space, I imagine I'm there as the client. And I feel what it's like to be there. Then, if it fits for me it will usually fit for the client, too." This is not an answer to the question we asked. But it is an answer to one we did not ask, namely, "How do you determine that a space will fit for a client?" (And this is a question we would undoubtedly ask at some point in the elicitation.)

A useful way to think about this is that the exemplar is always offering you her experience. If her response is not an answer to your question, ask yourself, "What has she just told me about the structure of her experience?" Whatever it is, you can be sure it is characteristic of this person operating within the context of her ability. And it may prove to be useful to you in understanding and, ultimately, replicating her ability.

Though always relevant, this un-asked for information may or may not be useful. For instance, our architect exemplar might reveal, "You know, I'm always tapping my teeth with a pencil or whatever while I'm thinking of possible designs." That behavior is certainly relevant in the sense of it being characteristic of how she manifests her ability to design. However, it may not be necessary for us to also tap our teeth in order to design buildings. Sorting out what is essential and non-essential is explored in depth in Essay 16: Elegance and in Essay 17: Generic Models.

* * *

Suppose you have gathered information regarding one example of your exemplar manifesting her ability. You then explore a second example. But this time you get a description couched in different terms (words and phrases). What are you to make of this? Do these differing descriptions actually represent two separate abilities? Of course that is possible. But if you have been careful to draw your exemplar's examples from the same kind of situations, it is probably the case that these two descriptions are different expressions of the same underlying set of patterns. We call this "redundancy," by which we mean that the same pattern or element of experience is being expressed in a variety of ways.

Of course, we use words as a medium for capturing the otherwise hidden experiences of our exemplar. But keep in mind that we are after the structure of those experiences, not necessarily the words used to describe them. Words are fluid and often have fuzzy boundaries in terms of meaning. What is more, there is usually more than one word that can be used to denote an experience. In addition, we can express the same thing in many different ways. Beyond this, it is more the rule than the exception that language provides the freedom to represent something in a variety of ways. (As the previous three sentences illustrate.)

Nevertheless, differences in the words we use to express ourselves do convey subtle differences of experience. The question for us as modelers is, Are those differences significant in terms of the structure of experience of the exemplar? To answer this question, we must not necessarily rely on the exemplar's words, but look instead to the underlying patterns those words are intended to describe. And this is the subject of the next Essay.

Capturing Experience

Essay 5

Patterning

Ultimately, the process of gathering information about an ability is intended to reveal the patterns of beliefs, thoughts, feelings and behaviors that combine to make that ability possible. This is done by comparing across examples to find where and how they are the same. Differences between examples may turn out to actually be the same once linguistic differences in their descriptions are resolved. Actual differences may be worth noting as useful patterns for special circumstances, or they may indicate the need to recheck the appropriateness of how you have defined the ability.

Amidst the hundreds of wonderfully distinctively British comedies in the 50s, 60s and 70s, there was one dynasty of farces that starred much the same cast and all were titled, "Carry On..." ("Carry On Nurse," "Carry On Sergeant," "Carry On Constable," and so on). In "Carry On Teacher" (1959), the school's beloved headmaster is being promoted to another school. The kids, however, are determined to keep him. When an inspector from the Ministry of

Education shows up, the boys do their best to demonstrate what a failure the place really is, hoping to ruin their headmaster's promotion. The prideful and superior inspector decides he will "conduct a little experiment on logic." He asks someone in the class to give him any two-figure number. "27" offers a lad, and the inspector writes on the blackboard, "72." He favors the teacher with self-satisfied smirk, then asks for another number. This time the offer is "81!" The inspector writes "18" on the blackboard. Again, he flashes a condescending glance at the teacher, and then asks for another number. A lad triumphantly shouts out, "33! Go on, then, muck about with that!"

What You Are Looking For

There you are, asking questions of your exemplar, and he obliges with responses. But experience is infinitely deep, subtle and complex. In order to find your way, you apply the filters of your distinctions to bring into the foreground of your awareness (and that of your exemplar, as well) those aspects of experience to which you want to attend. But just what is it that you are looking for as you use your distinctions to sift through the layers of the exemplar's experience?

You are looking for patterns. A pattern is two (or more) things relating to one another in a reliable and predictable way. For instance, when you meet someone and hold out your hand in greeting, they will almost certainly respond by shaking your hand. Similarly, flowers blooming in spring, questions initiating searches for answers, exercise increasing stamina, and the level of street traffic rising dramatically at the end of the work day are all examples of patterns. A pattern about patterns is that violating them predictably causes great consternation and the need to explain how it is possible that the pattern did not hold in this instance. (Recall, for instance, a time when you met someone who ignored your outstretched hand.)

Patterns usually create generalizations about the world. After enough examples of two things relating to one another in a predictable way, we often create a rule or generalization about how those things connect with each other. Hold your hand out to greet a two-year-old child and he will probably just look at it, perhaps wondering what you want to give him (which, in the child's world, is what such a gesture has always meant). But then you take his hand in yours and shake it. After a few more such experiences, the child will probably recognize the pattern and create a new generalization: "When someone extends a hand to you held vertically, extend your own and shake theirs." Of course, the number of experiences one needs to have in order to recognize a pattern and, perhaps, form a generalization depends upon the person, the circumstances, and so on.

Also, it is important to note that recognizing patterns and forming generalizations need not be done consciously. Nor do pattern recognition and generalization need to have been expressed in language in order to impact our experience. Generalizations can be "understood" by the body-mind system, etched into the experiential templates that then get expressed through patterns of thinking and behavior. In fact, the majority of generalizations that organize our experiences and behaviors are not languaged, but nonetheless form the vast architecture of our experience. This does not mean, of course, that these generalizations—even those regarding the minutiae of experience—cannot be languaged. Turning the spotlight of attention upon that which has previously been unconscious may well make it available to description.

Patterns are important precisely because they create the basis for making generalizations. By making generalizations, we do not have to continually rediscover the patterns of relationships operating in our world. Whether explicit or implicit, generalizations reflect what we have learned about how the world works, about the patterns we have perceived, and they can therefore automatically guide our moment-to-moment responses. The generalization, in effect, perpetuates the pattern that originally gave it birth.

This reflective relationship between patterns and generalizations is what makes patterns so useful to us when modeling. Because they are the behavioral expressions of generalizations, patterns can reveal to us those generalizations that form some of the underlying structure of the exemplar's ability. When we say "reveal," we do not necessarily mean in language. A generalization does not need to be described in words in order for it to be operating in our experience. A pattern that we observe in our exemplar, however, can directly reveal the generalization behind it; it does this through how it affects our experience when we use that pattern ourselves. For example, a seminar leader has a pattern of turning his whole body to, and focusing only on, the person who is asking him a question. We do not know why. That is, we do not know the generalization being expressed by that pattern of behavior. Even so, if we then manifest that same pattern of behavior when *we* lead groups it may well have the same effect on our experience and the interaction as it does for our exemplar. (Let's say that the effect is that it not only grabs the questioner's attention, but it also tends to grab everyone's attention.) And of course, through time and experience, we might come to consciously recognize what difference that way of focusing attention makes and, so, recognize the generalization from which we have been operating. (In our example, the *explicitly expressed* generalized pattern might be, "When you fully focus on one person asking a question, you grab everyone's attention.")

Sameness

In the context of modeling, patterns are any aspects of the exemplar's beliefs, thoughts, feelings and behaviors that are consistent to the point of being predictable. These patterns reveal themselves through contrasting and comparing examples of the exemplar manifesting his ability. We are looking for what is the same in all of the examples in terms of beliefs, behaviors and so on. Whatever shows up as a consistent and predictable element in the exemplar's structure of experience is one of his patterns.

How many examples do you need to be confident enough to consider something a pattern? One example is obviously not enough. With just one example you have no way of knowing what is peculiar to the particular situation the example comes from, and what is characteristic of the ability regardless of the peculiarities of the situation. For instance, suppose we have an exemplar of the ability to forgive, and he describes an incident in which he forgave someone who cut him off in traffic. Regarding this example, he tells us, "I recall having done the same myself once" and "I see the humor in the situation." There are no patterns revealed in this; there is only description. So we turn his attention to a second example of forgiveness. In this example he forgave a friend who had betrayed him. But in this instance the exemplar sees no humor in the situation. He does, however, "recall having done the same myself once." Obviously, "finding humor in the situation" is not a pattern for the ability to forgive. "Recalling having done the same myself," may well be a pattern, however. Having the same element of experience appear in both examples is certainly very suggestive of a pattern.

But it could also be a coincidence. This why we suggested in Essay 2 (Getting Started) that, before you start gathering information, you have your exemplar identify three examples of manifesting his ability. The third example is often needed to confirm whether or not what you think is a pattern is, in fact, a pattern. Of course, if the third example does not confirm the patterns apparent in the first two examples, perhaps the previous examples need to be reexamined, and perhaps additional examples may be needed to make clear just what the relevant patterns are. In all cases, however, what we are doing is searching for patterns by looking for sameness across examples.

Difference

When the exemplar consistently uses the same description (or demonstrates the same behavior) across every example, the patterns are obvious. While you certainly will find obvious sameness across examples, you can also expect to find many differences as well.

But are these all truly differences? Not necessarily. We must bear in mind that our observations of the exemplar are subject to our interpretations. Also, the exemplar's descriptions of his experience are subject to both our interpretations and his language choices (which can have quite a range). This means that what at first appear to be differences between examples may, in fact, be merely differences in expression and interpretation. (We will have more to say about this in Essay 8.)

You can be certain that there will be differences in how your exemplar describes each of his examples of manifesting his ability. What you cannot be certain of is that these different descriptions correspond to different *patterns of experience*. The richness of language makes it possible to express the same ideas in endless ways. It is true that different words for the same "thing" will convey subtle differences. But those subtle differences may or may not be significant to the exemplar. For one person, being "delighted" and being "pleased" describe much the same experience, while for someone else being "delighted" and being "pleased" are distinctly different experiences.

Separating actual from apparent differences in this case is often as simple as feeding back to the exemplar the two descriptions and asking, "Are these the same, or are they in fact different?" This gives the exemplar the opportunity to test out in his own experience the two descriptions to discover whether they connect him to the same or different aspects or shadings of his experience. (Indeed, you will probably see your exemplar flipping back and forth between them as he compares the experiences.) Almost always, the exemplar is able to resolve the discrepancy, by confirming either that they are different descriptions for the same experience, or that they are indeed different experiences and explain the discrepancy.

Omission

One kind of obvious difference occurs when an element of experience that is found in one example in not found in another. For instance, our exemplar of the ability to forgive talks about the humor he experienced when forgiving one person, but says nothing about finding humor when forgiving another person. The fact that humor was not mentioned in the second example does not mean it was not there. It may, instead, have simply been omitted when being described. Perhaps the gravity of the second situation overshadowed the humor, but it was there nonetheless, though muted and brief. Or perhaps the exemplar feels a bit embarrassed to admit that he was finding humor in an obviously serious situation. There can be any number of reasons and factors that prevent a particular element from surfacing into awareness (or description) in a particular example.

Omissions can usually be separated from true differences by pointing out to the exemplar the fact that there is such a difference, and then asking if what is true in the one example is also true for the other example. (Remember that you are asking questions to give the exemplar something to respond to, rather than asking questions to convince the exemplar of something you already believe.) If that element is, in fact, a part of that particular example, having your exemplar put his attention on it will usually either make him aware of it, or it will confirm that, no, it was not operating in his experience in that example.

Useful Differences

Because we are searching for the patterns that make up the exemplar's experience, our attention is on plucking out what is the same across examples, and setting aside what is different. Differences, however, should not be completely ignored.

Every opportunity to manifest an ability will generate the need for ad hoc responses. The world is just that rich and complex. Though not patterns that run across all examples of the ability, these "situational" elements of experience may still be worth noting and adopting. This is especially the case when a particular "situation" is one that is likely to reoccur in the real world. For instance, our exemplar of architectural design might relate an example of when she had to go to her client's home and walk around in it before she was able to get anywhere in coming up with a design that "fit the clients' temperament." Normally, this is not necessary, but it turns out that there are some clients who simply do not reveal enough of their temperament in the architect's office, and in those situations, she wanders around their home. Adding this situational pattern to our model of the architect can make it more robust, giving us an effective way to respond in those occasional situations where the usual approach is not sufficient. (In fact, the Experiential Array intentionally makes room for these situational patterns under the heading of "Secondary Operations." See Essay 9: Strategies.)

Real Differences

Resolving discrepancies in description and filling in omissions are not going to account for all differences between examples, of course. Some of those differences will, in fact, be differences. As we said above, some of those real differences will be artifacts of the particular situation and, so, irrelevant to the structure of the ability itself (though they may also be worth capturing as situational patterns).

Another possibility is that the differences between examples are revealing the fact that you do not have the ability appropriately defined. When you define the ability you want to model, you create the net that you and your exemplar cast upon the waters of his experience. The characteristics and dimensions of that net will greatly affect what the two of you dredge up. For instance, suppose you want to model the ability to "maintain rapport with others." Your exemplar obliges with three good examples, and in the first two of these you find many possible patterns. The third example, however, nets you some similarities with the first two, and a bunch of real differences as well. The sudden appearance of these differences alerts us to reconsider the contexts of the examples. We notice that the first two involved maintaining rapport with friends and coworkers as *individuals*, and the third maintaining rapport with a *group*. We now need to consider whether what we are really interested in is "Maintaining rapport...

> ...in general" (in which case we can use all of the examples we already have, and focus on their similarities)

> ...with individuals" (in which case we must set aside the group example and ask for an additional example involving individuals)

> ...with groups" (in which case we must set aside the two individual examples and ask for additional examples involving groups)

Finding real differences between examples, then, is an opportunity to make sure that you are gathering information from examples that are examples of what you want to model. If it turns out that you do not have examples of what you actually want to model, you need to appropriately re-focus both you and the exemplar by more accurately defining the ability, and then have your exemplar identify new examples of *that*.

Between Exemplars

So far we have been considering the process of finding patterns within the set of examples offered by one exemplar. If you are after an idiosyncratic model, then, of course, that is as far as you need to go. If, however, you are after a generic model, you will need to also compare at least three exemplars, distilling from their individual experiences the patterns that they share.

The process of patterning across exemplars is much the same as that of patterning across examples. You are still searching for that which is the same, resolving if possible the differences (through recovering omitted information, or through working out discrepancies in description), retaining idiosyncratic patterns that seem particularly useful, and using differences between exemplars to check on the possible need to refine the definition of the ability.

When patterning across exemplars, however, all of these concerns become more marked, and more complicated to resolve. This is because each exemplar will have his or her own ways of describing the patterns of experience that they nonetheless share. The patterns we discover are not likely to be expressed by the exemplars using exactly the same words and phrases (though this does happen on occasion).

There are a number of important subtleties to this process of distilling out the patterns across exemplars, and we will explore them in more detail in Essay 16: Generic Models, after we have covered the elicitation of the elements of experience using the Experiential Array. The reason for putting off the discussion of cross-exemplar patterning is that, at this point in the modeling process, your focus is best placed upon thoroughly understanding the experiential world of the individual in front of you, your exemplar. Your allegiance is to that person's experience at this point in the modeling process. When you move on to the next exemplar, however, your allegiance will then be to *that* person's experience. Allegiance to the exemplar in front of you helps ensure that, as much as possible, you capture each exemplar's structure of experience, rather than shoe-horning all of them into the same shoe before you even know the true size of their feet. Once you have modeled all of your exemplars for an ability, then it is time to distill the patterns that all of them share.

* * *

Obviously, you are not going to try to match up all of the examples of an ability, word for discrepant word, and ask a thousand times, "And are these the same or different?" That would be tedious (and, of course, generate even more descriptions to evaluate). It is also not necessary. There is another way to identify patterns, and that is by comparing and testing in your own experience what your exemplar is describing. When you discover that two differently described patterns gives you much the same experience, probably they are pointing to the same generalization or structure. If they give you somewhat different experiences, however, then that is a discrepancy to ask your exemplar more about. We call this essential process of testing information in experience "stepping-in," and it is to that to which we turn in the next Essay.

Capturing Experience

Essay 6

Stepping-In

Where experience makes sense is IN experience. Therefore, modeling is best done by "stepping into" the experience of the exemplar. This makes it possible to check your understanding directly through experience, to directly discover possible connections and implications operating in the structure of the experience, and to eventually reproduce the ability itself. The process of stepping into another person's experience involves learning to distinguish what is "me" from what is the "exemplar," and gaining range and flexibility in adjusting the elements of your experience.

Half of the livestock handling facilities for meat processing plants in North America use systems designed by Dr. Temple Grandin, an Assistant Professor of Animal Science at Colorado State University. Because of her ability to understand farm animals in ways that few others do, Dr. Grandin has brought to the industry a unique perspective on the humane handling of animals, namely, the perspective of the animals themselves. Her lectures, her television appearances, and her over 300 publications continue to influence and change how animals are handled in slaughterhouses throughout the world. In addition to her publications about animal processing plants, she has written several books on her own life. What makes her personal life interesting—and her professional life all the more remarkable—is that Temple Grandin is autistic.

Autism is a term that covers a wide range of developmental abnormalities, including repetitive behavior, extreme narrowing of attention, impaired language development, and impaired ability to interact with others. There is also a range of severity of impairment among people with autism, from those individuals who are "low-functioning" to those who are "high-functioning." Temple Grandin is certainly a "high-functioning" autistic, making her way in the world brilliantly. Nevertheless, many experiences most of us take for granted are either not available to her, or come only through struggle. Because her experience is organized differently than most of us, Grandin's accounts of her world and her struggles open many windows on the often hidden experiential dynamics that operate in all of us. One of those experiential dynamics is our ability to empathize, to understand the emotional and experiential significance of other people's verbal and facial expressions and behavior:

> When I have to deal with family relationships, when people are responding to each other with emotion rather than intellect, I need to have long discussions with friends who can serve as translators. I need help in understanding social behavior that is driven by complex feelings rather than logic. I do not read subtle emotional cues. I have had to learn by trial and error what certain gestures and facial expressions mean. (Grandin, *Thinking in Pictures*, p.134-135)

Her experience with animals is different, however. During an interview with Oliver Sachs, she remarked, "'With farm animals I feel their behavior'...'With primates I intellectually understand their interactions'" (Sachs, *An Anthropologist on Mars*, p.281). For reasons we can only guess at, Temple Grandin is able to enter into the subjective world of farm animals with the same ease and naturalness that most of us enter into the worlds of other human beings. And it is clear that she truly is empathizing with these animals; she can predict how they will respond in various interactions, and therefore knows how to create environments for them that respect their experience. Her understanding of farm animals does not seem to be something that is simply given to her. Rather, it is something she discovers. That is, she re-creates in herself the subjective world of these animals and then discovers in her own experience what they themselves must be experiencing in that world:

> When I put myself in a cow's place, I really have to be that cow and not a person in a cow costume. I use my visual thinking skills to simulate what an animal would see and hear in a given situation. I place myself inside its body and imagine what it experiences. It is the ultimate virtual reality system, but I also draw on the empathetic feelings of gentleness and kindness I have developed so that my simulation is more than a robotic computer model. Add to the equation all of my scientific knowledge of cattle behavior patterns and instincts. I have to follow the cattle's rules of behavior. I also have to imagine what experiencing the world through the cow's sensory system is like. (Grandin, p.143)

Temple Grandin is not the first person to try to make sense out of the behavior of farm animals, of course. But as her accounts of what is generally found in the stockyards and slaughterhouses of the world make clear, the behavior of animals is typically viewed from the human perspective of those charged with caring for and handling them. To understand these animals, Grandin instead enters into their world, taking on as her own—as much as she can—their perceptual worlds. She makes sense of their experiences in the only place and in the only way that experience makes sense: in experience.

Making Sense

How do we make sense of someone else's experience? Suppose you meet an Indian on a street in Calcutta and ask him if he would like to join you for lunch. He responds by wagging his head from side to side. How do you make sense out of that response? That is, what does it mean? The meaning of this person's head wagging is not inherent in the gesture itself; it does not contain meaning, like a box of chocolates that actually contains chocolates. To speak of words and gestures as "carrying meaning" is misleading. The meaning is not in the words and gestures themselves. Instead, the meaning emerges as an interaction between those words or gestures and the person who is perceiving them. 'Meaning' is what happens when the observer of that gesture connects it to his own experience. Meaning is made by the connecting of perception to experience.

For instance, we know what a smile means because we have had experiences in which we discovered that smiling people are feeling pleased about something, that there is a connection between the expression of smiling and feeling pleased. When our Indian acquaintance smiles, we immediately connect it with our experiences of this facial expression and recognize that he is pleased. If we had never made that connection, smiling would make no sense; we would perceive it (see it), but it would have little or no meaning for us.[8]

The fact that we are always trying to connect our ongoing perceptions to our personal history of experiences becomes obvious when those connections are *not* immediately available. For those of us who live outside of India, the Indian man wagging his head side to side has no immediate meaning because it does not immediately connect with anything in our previous experience. Nevertheless, the implicit question, What does this mean? sends us on a search through our personal histories of experiences, seeking some kind of connection with what we know. We

---

[8] The accounts of feral children, for instance, reveal that responses we consider innate—such as smiling—may still require timely experiences to be "released" or "imprinted." Without these experiences, these responses may never become meaningful.

may decide that the wagging head means he is unsure (or that he has a crick in his neck, or is trying to empty water out of his ears, or is trying to hypnotize us). We search for meaning and, finding it—regardless of whether or not it is in fact accurate—we feel we understand and can move on. Suppose, however, we have an Indian interpreter beside us who explains that wagging the head from side to side means, "I am very pleased with this suggestion!" This is a moment of new connection for us. We have plenty of experience in our personal history regarding what it is to be pleased by a suggestion, and now we can connect those experiences to this Indian gesture. From that point on, as we walk the streets of Calcutta and observe people wagging their heads from side to side, we know that they are very pleased about something. Now their behavior makes sense to us. Now it has meaning.

The same relationship between perception, personal experience and meaning holds true for language: words trigger representations of those experiences that have somehow been connected to those words. The sequence of characters (or, when spoken, the sounds) "RED" means something to speakers of English only because they have had that sequence—that word—attached to the experience of seeing a particular color. Similarly, "brother," "run," "love," "divide," and "freedom" all have meaning only because we have attached each of these to particular experiences. For those who speak only English, however, the Swahili words, "saa ngapi" mean nothing; they are just sounds, unconnected to anything in our experience. But when a speaker of Swahili says, "Saa ngapi?" as he runs his finger around the face of a clock, we have the opportunity to connect his words with the notion of asking for the time. Experience can be described in words, but that description is only understood by someone experiencing that description. Words become understood only when we are able to connect our experience to them.

The extent of correlation going on moment to moment between perception and stored experience is enormous. (Just consider the amount—and speed—of correlations you are making to understand these sentences as you read them). This is possible because of your brain's ability to simultaneously process input (parallel processing in the parlance of computer models), and to do that processing largely subconsciously.

Except in those moments when we are offered some input for which we have no experiential connections ("saa ngapi?"), this process flashes along automatically.

The point we want to emphasize here is that understanding is built out of experience. Words, symbols, gestures or behaviors—no matter how concrete or abstract they may be—are only understandable through and within the medium of our subjective experience. The correlating of perception to experience operates automatically and unnoticed in our human interactions because we are swimming in the same species waters, and usually in the same cultural and social waters as well. When we do not understand another person, we have two ways of resolving it. One is to make what that person is doing or saying *somehow* fit into our own map of the world. We rationalize the behavior into something that fits with the connections we already have in our experience for such behaviors (such as when we reasoned that the Indian gentleman's head wagging meant he was unsure).

The other way to resolve a lack of understanding is to change our own map of the world to more closely match that of the other person. Doing that requires seeking new experiential connections. This is what happened when the translator revealed to us that the head wagging signified pleasure at the suggestion of lunch. When we do this we are opening ourselves to someone else's experience; we are "stepping into" the experiential world of another person.[9]

"Teach Me to Be You"

As modelers, our intention is to reproduce in our own experience, as accurately as possible, that which is operating in the experience of our

---

[9] Had we been determined to maintain our existing map of the world—that the Indian gentleman was unsure—we could have done so by deciding that the translator was trying to fool us, or that he was not truly well-informed, or that our degrees in psychology made us superior judges of behavior, and so on. You can find further discussion about the function of deletion, distortion and generalization in maintaining our personal maps in Essay 7: The Primacy of Beliefs.

exemplar. If we simply shave off the corners of the exemplar's experience so it can be jammed into the round hole of our own, already existing experience, we will learn nothing from him. Instead we need to make room in us for the exemplar's experience, corners and all. When modeling, the gathering of information needs to be an active and intentional attempt to understand the exemplar from inside *his* experience. This "teach me to be you" orientation toward information gathering we call "stepping-in."

An obvious and important entree into the experience of our exemplar is through his behavior. Matching our behavior to that of our exemplar may give us important elements of his ability. This is particularly so for those abilities that rely primarily on behavior, such as batting a ball, splitting logs, or administering an injection. In addition, matching the external behavior of an exemplar can reveal aspects of his internal experience as well. Elizabeth Marshall Thomas "always wanted to enter into the consciousness of a non-human creature... to know what the world looks like to a dog, for instance, or sounds like, or smells like... to visit a dog's mind, to know what he's thinking and feeling:"

> In the late afternoon sun we sat in the dust, or lay on our chests resting on our elbows, evenly spaced on the hilltop, all looking calmly down among the trees to see what moved there... I've been to many places on earth, to the Arctic, to the African savanna, yet wherever I went, I always traveled in my own bubble of primate energy, primate experience, and so never before or since have I felt as far removed from what seemed familiar as I felt with these dogs, by their den. Primates feel pure, flat immobility as boredom, but dogs feel it as peace. (Elizabeth Marshall Thomas, *The Hidden Life of Dogs*, pg. 120-121)

Here Thomas is stepping into the world of her dogs through their behavior. This example immediately raises a question of whether her experience really does match that of the dogs. We are using her example because it points up that very important question. When we step into the behavior of other human beings it is easy to assume that what we are feeling, they are feeling as well. Nevertheless, as made evident by countless misunderstandings between human beings, being in the same species does not guarantee that our internal experiences match those of anyone else.

In modeling, however, we need accurate access to the internal experiences of our exemplar. As we discussed in Essay 3, all abilities are the result of beliefs, strategies, emotions and behaviors operating together. Although the contribution of each of these elements to a particular ability will vary, for the most part the structures that make them work will be found in internal processes, rather than in the behaviors through which those internal process find their external expression. Although there are many things we can learn about our exemplar's ability from observing his behavior, most of what is significant in terms of the underlying structure is either not at all revealed by behavior or can only be inferred after a great deal of observation. Even then (like Ms. Thomas with her dogs) we will be faced with the question, Do the internal experiences I am having match those of the exemplar? How can we gain surer access to our exemplar's internal world? Fortunately, we have that emissary of experience: language.

One of the beauties of language is that it can reveal much of the inner behavior and experience of the speaker. The way language reveals that inner world is, in a sense, by recreating it in the listener (or reader). And so we can use the descriptive language of our exemplar to step more deeply, thoroughly and accurately into his experience. That is, we can step into his subjective world by allowing his descriptions to access and form experience in us.[10] The purpose of asking questions, then, is not to simply gather information. The purpose of a question is to stimulate the exemplar to describe his experience in such a way that we can step into it ourselves, by accessing our own references for what he is describing.

---

[10] Of course, since no two people can ever have exactly the same experiences, the fit between language and experience will never be perfect. In casual communication this is fine, since the slippage between the words used and the differing experiential references is usually not enough to create significant misunderstanding. Of course, when the slippage is significant, it *does* become a source of miscommunication and, so, of most of the problems arising between individuals, groups and countries.

The Importance of Stepping-In

Why bother to step in? Why open and adjust your experience to that of your exemplar? The reason is that your intention as a modeler is to do more than understand. You do not want to simply hear about the subjective land of your exemplar; you want to walk in it. Taking this journey means altering the structure of your experience to match that of your exemplar.

We do not want to go just anywhere in experience, however. We want the exemplar, guided by our questions, to describe those aspects of his experience that are relevant to our being able to reproduce *his* ability. The most direct way to know whether or not the exemplar is offering us relevant information is by discovering how our own experience is affected by those elements. Does adjusting our experience to match that of the exemplar's take us closer toward manifesting his ability, or not? That is, Is it useful information? This question can be answered only in experience. When it comes to the alchemy of experience, we must test the information we get in the crucible of ourselves. It is there that we discover whether or not we are getting the elements we need from the exemplar. More specifically, stepping-in allows us to:

Test whether or not the question was actually answered

Remember that the fact that a person responds to a question does not mean that they answered the question. Our modeling questions are intended to orient the exemplar to particular aspects of his experience; but that is only *our* intention. The exemplar will answer as it makes sense *to him* to answer. Whatever his answer turns out to be, however, by stepping into the context of the ability in order to test out what he has told us, we can immediately know whether or not it relates to the specific aspect of experience we had asked about (or at least had intended to ask about).

For example, suppose our exemplar has the ability to forgive others, and we ask him, "What are you feeling as you consider the wrong that has been done to you?" He answers, "I recall times when I have made a similar mistake." When we step into the context of trying to forgive someone, and bring into it, "recalling times I have made a similar mistake," we find that it does not take us to a feeling (but instead to a pattern of thinking). Recognizing this—through our direct experience—we know to ask again for the feeling, perhaps adding clarification or examples this time. (And perhaps this time he answers, "Oh...I'm feeling cautious.")

Discover possible elements of experience to explore

Because of the systemic nature of experience, stepping into the exemplar's world will generate systemic changes in our own experiences beyond those particular elements we have learned from the exemplar. We can then ask the exemplar if the changes in structure *we* are experiencing are ones that are true for him as well. For instance, when we try on, "I recall times when I have made a similar mistake," we notice that we are also feeling curious. We can describe this to the exemplar and check if that is also true for him. Regardless of his answer ("Yes, I do; it's kind of a combination of cautious and curious, actually" or "No, not at all"), we get to fine-tune our experience relative to his. That is, we either keep "curious" as part of the ability or, recognize that it is something from our own experience that we brought to the ability, and eliminate it from our model of the exemplar.

Determine where the "holes" are

By using the exemplar's structure of experience in order to step into the context of the ability, we can directly test in our own experience what is working for us and where we still need clarification. After all, the exemplar should not be expected to know what we need to know about his experience, and he may well be unconscious of significant aspects of the structure of his ability until our questions direct his attention to them. On the modeler's side, an intellectual assessment will not necessarily reveal what we still need. Indeed, such an analysis can be very misleading.

From inside the experience, however, we can more readily identify where, for us, there are still "holes" in the structure. For example, when we step into the context of forgiving a certain friend, and feeling "curious and cautious" as we recall "times when I have made similar mistakes," we might recognize that this friend had hurt us intentionally. It was not a "mistake." This then becomes something to ask our exemplar about, that is, "How do you forgive people who hurt you intentionally?"

Understand the systemic significance of information

All of the advantages of stepping-in are, in fact, branches growing on this trunk:

> Stepping-in allows us to access and assess through direct experience how the ability (or some element of the ability) "works."

Knowing how the ability works is the aim of the information-gathering phase of modeling. A model that makes sense on paper but not in experience is of little use. If it "works" on paper but not in experience, we have good reason to suspect that what is on the paper is either insufficient or does not capture the experience as it is lived. The experience of our exemplars will necessarily be converted into, and communicated to us through, the abstractions of language, and through the meaning we make from observing their behavior. Our goal as modelers is to convert those abstractions back into experience—our experience—with as much fidelity to the experience of the exemplar as possible. To step in is to deliberately pursue that goal.

Red Herrings

We want as much as possible to identify what is genuinely operating in the experience of the exemplar. But how can we know that the elements of experience our exemplar is offering us are genuine? Might not exemplars make up or manufacture their answers? Or confuse what they would like their experience to be with what it actually is? Or simply be misguided about the nature of their own experience?

Yes, all of these red herrings can and will occasionally surface. As a fellow human being, the exemplar will want to be helpful and, so, may make up answers to fill voids in his knowledge of his own experience, or perhaps to satisfy some particular desire he detects in us as we ask our questions. Or, like any of us, the exemplar may occasionally be blinded by the light in which he wants to see himself. Furthermore, the exemplar's experience is the water in which he swims, and may not be something he has paid attention to before we showed up with our (probably) unfamiliar distinctions and questions. Consequently, he may make mistakes in characterizing what is going on in his subjective world.

Because of these potential sources of communication slippage and misinformation, some modelers prefer to pattern only that which they can see or hear while the exemplar is actually engaged in manifesting his ability. There is no doubt that doing this provides useful and important information. But simply duplicating external behavior will often not be sufficient to also produce the underlying cognitive structures that give rise to most abilities.

We must rely on language to create an experiential bridge between us and the interior world of the exemplar. We cannot remove the possibility that the exemplar will (unintentionally or intentionally) mislead us in describing his experience. What we can do, however, is test what we are getting through *calibration*, through considering "does it fit, does it work?" and by using "multiple examples, multiple exemplars."

Calibration

The authors once had in their seminar a professional poker player who amazed us with his account of how he played. For him, the most essential aspect of the game was learning to "read" the other players. As the play of the hands proceeded, he would carefully note his opponents' behaviors (known as "tells"), correlating what he saw with the choices of play they made and the cards they were actually holding. In this way he would eventually be able to "read" by these "tells" what his opponents were holding in their hands and what they were thinking.[11]

---

[11] Other professional poker players "read" as well, of course. And so, when playing together, they try to create *mis*-reads by intentionally displaying false behavior. These too can be read as "false tells," creating many levels of complexity and subtlety during play.

Calibration is the process of getting to know what is going on with other people based on what you see and hear them do consistently, that is, their patterns. All of us have a great deal of experience in "reading" other people. We recognize when someone is uncomfortable, confident, unsure, convinced, struggling, content, and so on. All of these states reveal themselves in external behavior: in the tempo and quality of body movements, in characteristic facial expressions, and in distinctive changes of timbre, tempo and intensity in the voice. During a lifetime of interacting with one another we have calibrated ourselves to recognize the "state significance" of these external behaviors, shared by most or all of us as human beings.

Your exemplar is a fellow human being, so to a great extent you are already calibrated to her. That is, you will probably be able to recognize when she is unsure, confident, confused, pleased and so on. Being calibrated to the exemplar's responses makes possible our initial test of the reliability of the information she is offering. For instance, if, as she answers, her brow is furrowed, lips pursed, face asymmetrical, and she ends with an upturning of her voice, we can be pretty sure that she is unsure of what she is describing. This is an indication to not immediately accept the answer, but instead to probe further and help her sort through her experience until she is (and we are) confident about what she is describing.

Calibration based upon being human beings—even when you share the same culture and society—cannot be taken for granted, however. Everyone is an individual, as well as a fellow human being. Therefore, like a professional poker player, it is important to calibrate to *this* individual exemplar. That is, learn how to read when this particular person is confident about a response, wanting to please, confused, and so on. For instance, you may discover that when your exemplar is answering but not looking at you he is actually busy verbalizing possibilities to himself as a way to thoroughly consider them. (Recognizing this, you know to wait, to not yet take what he is saying as an answer to your question.)

Does It Fit? Does It Work?

Remember that the ability is the natural manifestation of the exemplar's structure of experience, and that this structure is a system in which the necessary elements work together. Any element of our exemplar's experience, then, will satisfy two tests if it is indeed a part of the Array for that ability: first, it will fit with the other elements of experience that we already know are a part of the ability, and second, it will contribute in some way to the ability working.

How do we know whether or not a particular element of experience fits and works? First by trying it on in conjunction with what we already know about the exemplar's structure of experience. When we add that element into our own experience, does it bear little relation to anything else or disrupt everything else, or does it fit in? Does it make sense with the rest of the experience? We want to emphasize again that "making sense" is an assessment that is done as much as possible from *inside* the experience. It is not an intellectual assessment from the outside. Something that sounds odd or counterintuitive may, when it is actually experienced, reveal itself to be completely sensible, something that *fits*.

Furthermore—and this is the second test—when we imagine stepping into the context of the ability with that new element of experience added to what we already know, we will discover if it "works." That is, we can notice if the added experiential element seems to contribute to our being able to more fully manifest the ability, or if it does nothing to help, or even hinders the expression of the ability.

If what our exemplar has told us does not fit with the rest of the Array, or if it does not contribute to the working of the ability, then, again, we need to sort out with the exemplar whether or not that element does, in fact, belong in the Array. And if it does belong, how it contributes to the working of the ability. In the course of sorting that out, you will end up either setting that element outside of the Array, or you will come to correctly understand its role in the ability and include it.

Multiple Examples, Multiple Exemplars

A corollary of the idea that experience has structure is that there is a consistent relationship between a particular structure and the ability to which it gives rise. In practice, then, anything that is truly characteristic of the structure of a particular ability will be found in all examples of the exemplar manifesting his ability.

For instance, our forgiving exemplar describes two incidents: in one, someone cut him off in traffic, he then recalled having done the same thing himself, and he saw humor in the situation; in a second example, he was betrayed by a friend, he then recalled having done the same to someone himself, but he did not see any humor in the situation. If we had explored only the first example, we would likely have concluded that "finding humor in the situation" was necessary to forgiveness. But the second example reveals that whether or not he finds humor in being offended depends upon the situation. What is essential to the exemplar's strategy in both examples, however, is the step of recalling how he has made a similar mistake. So another test of the veracity of the information you gather will be found in the consistencies and discrepancies you discover as you compare several examples of the exemplar manifesting his ability. Similarly, comparing across exemplars can help us identify where there may be red herrings in the information we gathered from one of our exemplars.

It may be that differences in how an exemplar handles different situations reveals what should really be considered two separate abilities. In our example, for instance, perhaps the ability to "forgive a trespass by a stranger" is a different ability than that of "forgiving trespasses by loved ones." Similarly, comparing two exemplars who you assume have the same ability may reveal that they are, in fact, better seen as exemplars of two different abilities. Again, it is for this reason that we recommend getting at least three examples from an exemplar (to sort out what is situational from what is truly characteristic of the ability for this particular exemplar), and three exemplars for an ability (to sort out what is idiosyncratic to each exemplar from what is essential to the ability). These topics were also discussed from a slightly different point of view (that of choosing what to model) in Essay 1: Getting Started, and will be treated in more depth in Essays 15 and 16 son Elegance and on Generic Models.

The Fish in the Dream

Many years ago, we were delighted by a comedy routine on the radio. The host encouraged listeners to call in to describe one of their dreams, then the host—playing psychiatrist—would interpret them. The first call went something like this:

Caller: I was sitting on a hill, out in the country.
Host: Was there a fish there?
Caller: No.
Host: Are you sure?
Caller: Yes. There was no fish there.
Host: Well, you were in the countryside. Was there a stream nearby?
Caller: Maybe. Could have been.
Host: And there would have been fish in that stream, wouldn't there?
Caller: I suppose so.
Host: Aha! Just as I suspected! You have unresolved Oedipal fixations!

And so it went. *Always.* If a caller dreamt of being on a city street, the "psychiatrist" would find a nearby market that undoubtedly sold fish; if the caller dreamt of working in an office, the "psychiatrist" helped him discover a coworker who loved to fish; and so on. And in every case the diagnosis was therefore obvious: "unresolved Oedipal fixations."

How can we know that when we are modeling we are not doing the same thing as this radio psychiatrist, that is, "discovering" in our exemplar's descriptions the fish that we expect or want to find there? The three tests that we describe above—*Calibration, Does it fit/does it work?,* and *Multiple examples/multiple exemplars*—will certainly help us avoid throwing our own red herrings into the exemplar's experience. But they do not guarantee it.

In fact, it is guaranteed that we *will* introduce aspects of our own experience into our model of the exemplar. Remember that we understand through our personal experience, not in spite of it. But because the goal in modeling is to alter the structure of our experience as a way of opening doors to new abilities, we want to tip the scales in favor of the exemplar's experience as much as possible. The task, then, is to sort out what is you from what is the exemplar.

Our suggestion is to be alert for anything you discover in your exemplar that also fits for you, or is *just* what you expected, or you know is true or right, or seems immediately familiar. Whenever you have any of these responses, a red flag needs to be raised. These are the kinds of responses that come from finding a match between your own experience and what you are hearing from someone else. When that red flag goes up, the question you need to ask yourself is, "Is this an element of experience we actually share, or am I putting my fish in my exemplar's dream?" You answer this question by probing a bit more carefully into your own experience and the of your exemplar—perhaps asking for another example—in order to sort out what is "me," what is "him," and what is "us."

How to Step In

The ability to step into the structure of someone else's experience is so essential to the ability to model that we will go into some detail about how to do it. In other words, we will be offering you a model for stepping-in. Like most models of complex abilities, merely reading about it—even if you understand it thoroughly—will not transfer the ability to you. It must be put it into practice for you to become familiar and adept with its elements, as well as to integrate it into the rest of who you are and how you operate. An additional consideration here is that, as we are unable to interact with you personally, the model can only be presented as a description of elements and cannot be tailored to you. For all of these reasons, we encourage you to actually try out the model, to engage with and in its elements as they are described here.

To help you do that, the following descriptions include suggestions for how to access the elements of "stepping-in" into your experience. You will notice that the presentation of the patterns and suggestions for accessing them includes framing discussions that are probably already familiar to you from previous Essays. This is because it is usually *not* effective to simply list the needed patterns and then say, "Okay, now *you* do it." Framing for each of them, often including examples, helps the model's patterns come alive in your own experience. What is to follow, then, is also an example of the general process of model acquisition, about which we will have much more to say in Essay 17: Acquisition.

If you find yourself simply reading through these acquisition suggestions now, don't worry. When you are finished with this Essay those suggestions will still be here, and you can return to them to devote as much time as you need for acquisition. Do so; it will be time well spent.

The Central Belief: "Experience Has Structure"

Essential to acquiring the ability to step in is the recognition that **experience has structure**. We have already discussed this idea as a presupposition fundamental to the very notion of modeling (Essay 1, What is Modeling?). As you gather information, what drives your information gathering is your intention to discover *the structure of this person's experience and how it works in manifesting his particular ability*.

The orientation you adopt, then, is one of wanting to learn how to think, feel and behave as the exemplar does. You are not there to confirm what you know or believe, but to help your exemplar reveal to you those patterns that are significant in manifesting his ability. And you want to know them because, as a fellow human being, you recognize that if you adopt those patterns—his structure—it will organize your experience and behavior in much the same way they organize his.

Taking on and being affected by other people's structure is not an exotic notion, but a fact of everyone's personal histories. During your lifetime you have benefited countless times from other people directly or indirectly sharing with you some aspect of their experiential world. It could have been something you read, heard in a movie, were told by a friend, overheard on a bus, or observed. Regardless of where it came from, that tidbit of behavior or different way to think about the world changed how you understood and responded to the world from that point on. A striking example of this, for example, is the general concern raised in the 1970s regarding "workaholics." Articles, books, television programs, support groups and back fence discussions pointed out the pathology of people who seemed to devote most of their time and energy to their jobs. Plenty of people who previously thought of themselves as "hard workers," "dedicated," or "achievers," suddenly realized that they were, in fact, "workaholics." As a consequence, they saw themselves in a somewhat different (harsher) light, and many of them also changed their behavior. They began setting aside the weekend as sacred personal or family time, leaving work at 6 pm no matter what the state of their inbox, taking yoga, frequenting meditation retreats, and so on. Then, in the 1990's, these same people read articles describing the latest research on the deleterious effects of stress. These articles revealed that, for people who *like* to work hard, *not* working is stressful. Once again how they thought about themselves shifted—this time from "workaholic" to "workaphile"—and so did their subsequent patterns of thinking, choices and behavior with respect to work.

Take a moment now to identify several examples of times when the structure of *your* thinking changed (though you may not have recognized it at the time) and, so, caused your experience and behavior to change as well. It is important to find enough real examples to convince yourself that experience does, indeed, have structure, and that changing that structure *necessarily* changes one's experience.

The Necessary State: "Openness / Internal Space"

The relevancy and effectiveness of your exemplar's patterns must be tested in your own experience. This means that you must "open" yourself to the exemplar's experience; that is, that you must be willing to create "space" in your own internal experience for that of the exemplar. It is through being open that you create the greatest opportunity to have personal access to the experience of your exemplar.

Recognizing that experience has structure will, in and of itself, help open you to the experiences of your exemplar. It is worth taking this a few steps further, however, by accessing examples from your personal history of having been open in this way. We are sure you have such examples, though they may have gone unnoticed by you at the times they occurred. To jog your memory, let us suggest a few that you might recognize:

- Getting down on the floor to play with a child (not to entertain the child, but to *be with* the child in her world).

- Standing before an awe-inspiring landscape.

- Being with someone you love and soaking up that person, noticing and appreciating how she moves, the sound of her voice, what she says, the play of expressions on her face, and so on.

- Being whisked into a theme ride at an amusement park, and giving yourself over to the world of puppetry and painted plaster you are passing through.

- Entering the impossible world created by a movie fantasy.

- Meditating.

- Listening to a dear friend who is hurting and needs to be heard, without judgment and without expectation of solving the problem.

- Being in the presence of a respected and admired mentor as she or he is teaching you what they know (like a grandfather showing you how to use tools, or a professor teaching you how to identify a butterfly).

Re-connect with personal experiences such as these to give yourself an immediate and compelling connection to the state of being "open." In addition, if you find a memory that is particularly effective, "hold" onto it; you can use it to access the state of openness when you are modeling. You can use that memory as an accessing "anchor" until the practice of modeling itself automatically generates in you the state of openness.

The Supporting State: "Reverence"

Your exemplar is not a box to be opened, nor is he a machine to take apart, nor is he a "useful source of information." He is a human being who has a lifetime of joys, sorrows, secrets, triumphs and memories. He has skeletons in his closet, monkeys on his back, pearls of wisdom to offer, and soap boxes on which he likes to stand. And like every human being, he has countless abilities. He is a human being, layered and complex, unique and irreplaceable. It is therefore appropriate that we feel *reverence* for this person.

When it comes to modeling in general, and "stepping-in" in particular, it is especially important to cultivate a feeling of reverence for this person who is serving as your exemplar. When we speak of "reverence" we mean: Appreciating and honoring this person's experience as something that is unique, valuable, hard won, and inseparable from the person himself. "Reverence" is a feeling of deep respect for someone (or something) plus the added quality of awe.

Approaching your exemplar with reverence is not simply an appropriate thing to do. Reverence, with its tinge of awe, is tremendously useful for modeling, as well. First, it helps ensure that you treat your exemplar with respect. It is necessary for your exemplar to feel respected if he is going to freely open his experience to you.

Second, it opens *you* to the exemplar's experience. You probably do not feel reverence for any of the hundreds of postcards you find on display at some tourist trap. But the only postcard you ever received from a loved one may very well be something toward which you feel reverence. When we feel reverence for someone, we recognize that there is something tremendously unique and special about them. They bring that which is unique and special about them into our lives. And so it is with your exemplar, who is bringing something that is unique and special about him into your life. Your relationship, then, becomes less one in which you are doing something to or for your exemplar, and much more one in which your exemplar is offering you something: the gift of himself.

Third, in addition to nurturing respect and trust, the effect of this reverence on us as modelers is to encourage our curiosity about *how this person's wonderful ability works*, and thus further *opens us* to this person and his experience.

Think of several people who you know (or know of) toward whom you feel reverence, so that you create for yourself a solid sense of what that feels like. If you are having difficulty finding examples, begin with something or someplace toward which you feel reverence. Once you have that feeling well in hand (body), hold onto it as you search for a time when you felt the same toward a *person*. When you begin to work with your exemplar, recognize that he, this *person*, has something unique and special to offer—just like that special person in your own life—and recapture that feeling of reverence.

The How: Internal and External Behavior

In the context of modeling, stepping-in requires that you be oriented to *structure*, that you *open yourself* to the experience of the exemplar in order to experience and assess that structure directly, and that you approach the interaction with a feeling of *reverence* for your exemplar's experience. Organizing your beliefs and states in this way will naturally generate many of the internal strategies and external behaviors that are necessary for stepping-in. But probably not all of them. Therefore, it is worth being explicit about those internal strategies and external behaviors that make a significant difference in being able to effectively step in:

1. Make sure that you are sitting or standing either on the same level as your exemplar or that you are below your exemplar as you work

with him. Not only does this help the exemplar feel at ease, but you will find it easier to step into his experience, as well.

2. Get a description of the context in which they manifest their ability, that is, the who, what, where and when. This tells you what "world" to step into as you gather, and try on for yourself, the elements of the exemplar's experience. Knowing the context is essential to assessing the meaning and significance of what you are learning. For instance, if your exemplar says, "I see red," you will understand that experience differently if the context is "my wife is criticizing me," or "I'm planning a painting" or "I'm at a family gathering (Hey, there's Uncle Red!)."

3. When you ask questions of the exemplar, become very still and quiet inside, and devote your full attention to the other person. (This may include tunnel vision and a lower, slower and softer voice.) While the exemplar is thinking about *and* answering your question, remain still. Your stillness will support your exemplar in feeling free to explore his own experience, as well as avoid distracting him from it with speculation about what your behavior (facial expressions, glancing around, etc.) means. In addition, by remaining still you can feel more easily and precisely the effect his description of experience has on you as you take it on for yourself.

4. The exemplar's words will almost certainly carry more of the exemplar's structure than any words that you might use in their place. So use *their* words to affect your experience. Let the exemplar's description take over your body and patterns of thought, using the exemplar's words to guide the reorganizing of your experience:

    *   Feel in your body what you see them doing with their body (especially anything unusual, characteristic or exaggerated).

    *   Things they say as they manifest their ability, either aloud or in internal dialogue, say to yourself (internally).

* Things they describe seeing or feeling, see and feel yourself.

* After your exemplar has offered you an element of his experience, feel free to shift your body as necessary to "try on" the experience. This may involve matching a behavior you have observed in the exemplar or in some movement, change in breathing, facial expression and so on that you need to "try on" in order to more fully access the experience.

Their descriptions—their words—serve to access experiences in you. Ultimately, however, it is not the words themselves that are important, but the *dynamics* they create in your experience. Ask questions of yourself that enable you to make *dynamic* sense out of what your exemplar is describing: The primary, ongoing question is, "How does this affect my experience?"

* Also ask yourself: "What element is it? Is it redundant? Is it relevant to this array/ability or to some other array?"

* Looking for "*the* way" the structure works will help you sort what is new from what is redundant, what is relevant from what is irrelevant (though perhaps relevant to some other ability), and what is essential from what is non-essential for manifesting the ability. Look to see if you can form the structure in more than one way and still support the expression of the ability. If you can imagine more than one structure based on what you already know from the exemplar, ask for more detail until you have identified the one way the exemplar does it.

5. Check your understanding of your exemplar's structure by periodically feeding it back to him. You are also always testing your understanding by being alert to matches and mismatches between your experience and what your exemplar subsequently describes as you continue with the elicitation.

If you should find that you are having difficulty in stepping into the experience of your exemplar, first consider the possibility that, "I have not set myself aside enough." Re-set yourself physically by taking a breath and shifting your body posture. Re-access a personal experience of being open (as described above in the section, "Openness/Internal Space"). Then again take on each element of your exemplar's structure. As you do this, be sure to check your experience with your exemplar to make sure that you are now "getting it."

A second possibility is that, "I've come at this from the wrong direction." That is, you have you have not been eliciting the elements you need in order to be able to successfully step into the exemplar's experience. Again, you first need to re-set yourself (empty yourself of the former structure) by taking a breath and shifting body posture. In this case, however, rather than taking on again the elements you have previously elicited, you need to go after eliciting the element(s) that eluded you the first time around, but this time using a *different* line of questioning (Essay 4: Asking Questions).

Naturally, the real acquisition and integration of the patterns underlying stepping-in comes when you put them into practice while engaged in an actual elicitation. If bringing all of the elements to bear at once is too much to get your arms around at first, start with one or two: for instance, simply make sure you are on the same level as your exemplar and that you remain still while he is thinking and answering your questions. Notice what effect just doing that has on your ability to step into the exemplar's description of his experience. Then add another element to your experiential mix. Naturally, you will be clumsy with stepping-in at first. But, like tying your shoes, through practice it will become something you do effortlessly and automatically.

* * *

Throughout this Essay we have been talking about using the words and phrases of description as passports to stepping into your exemplar's experiential world. We do not, however, want to leave you with the impression that the goal here is to stuff ourselves with the right words, courtesy of the exemplar. Our real quarry is the structure of experience that lies behind those words. We are reminded of the proverbial blind men patting down their first elephant. Each of them has their piece of the creature in hand and mistakes that piece for the whole. Good enough. For our purposes, however, we need to take the tale a bit further. What happens when the mahout standing nearby informs them that they are all holding onto different *parts* of the same beast? What creature will they put together in their heads from the disparate descriptions of their blind fellows? We cannot throw together, "A long muscular thing, a ropy thing, a tree-like thing, a thing like a wall, and a thing like a palm leaf" just any old way and end up with something that looks like an elephant (much less be an elephant). The elements of the elephant need to relate to one another in specific ways for there to *be* an elephant.

Similarly, abilities are not made up of a pile of experiential elements, but of experiential elements operating in relationship to one another in particular ways. **Structure is the dynamic relationships—the patterns— operating between elements**. And it is structure that gives rise to cells, blind men, elephants, ideas, and human abilities.

When modeling, we step into the exemplar's world with what we know about the elements of his experience in an effort to discover how those elements alter and create new patterns of relationships—new structures—in *us*. And when we elicit descriptions that re-structure our own experience in a way that allows us to manifest the same ability as our exemplar, we have a model. Identifying and eliciting the most significant of those underlying patterns and structures is the subject of the next six Essays.

PART III

Elements of the Experiential Array

Elements of the Experiential Array

Essay 7

Beliefs I: The Primacy of Beliefs

Beliefs are anything we hold to be self-evident, and it is this quality of self-evidence that makes beliefs so compelling. Furthermore, the pervasive—and generally transparent— influence of beliefs makes them of central importance in giving rise to most human abilities. Beliefs have structure, and that structure will take the form of either equivalence relationships ("this means that") or causal relationships ("this causes that").

In 1989, Russian psychic and mentalist E. Frenkel stepped onto the train tracks in the city of Astrakhan and, lowering his head in concentration, held up his hands to stop an onrushing train. In a note left nearby, Frenkel explained, "First I stopped a bicycle, cars and a streetcar. Now I am going to stop a train." Whatever powers Mr. Frenkel may have had, they were not sufficient to stop the train, which ran over and killed him ("Soviet who relied on psychic power killed," reported The Associated Press, in The Denver Post/International, October 2, 1989). Mr. Frenkel's *belief* in his psychic powers, however, *was* sufficient to allow him to do something he surely recognized as normally extremely dangerous. And this despite the apparent drive for self-preservation that all animals, including human beings, demonstrate. How could he have done such a thing?

We can simply dismiss Mr. Frenkel as another deluded person who foolishly sacrificed himself to his delusion. But if we do that we will miss the wonderful lesson his actions exemplified. That lesson is that behavior springs from beliefs. Nor is his example an isolated one. It is not even uncommon. Throughout history millions of men and women have put themselves in the path of mortal danger, even certain death, in the service of their beliefs: Crusaders, American revolutionaries, Jeanne d'Arc, Sir Edmund Hillary and Tenzig Norgay, Thor Heyerdal, Jesus of Nazareth, Chief Joseph, Yuri Gagarin, Mahatma Gandhi, the "freedom riders" of the 1950s, Che Guevara, and the anonymous Chinese man standing in front of the tanks in Tiananmen Square. Certainly, all of these people had their own reasons for doing what they did. But in every case they *had* reasons. None of them did those things because they happened to be in the neighborhood at the time.

Of course, the neighborhood you happen to be in *does* matter. During times of war, citizens are often swept up against their will (or at least better judgment) into military service. Given a choice, they would stay home. Yet, they go. Is their submission an argument against Mr. Frenkel's object lesson on the primacy of beliefs? No. After all, not everyone submits; there are also citizens who refuse to put on a uniform (risking ostracism, jail or death by their refusal). Both groups are living in the same world, but respond differently to the situation. The biggest determinant of their differing responses are the beliefs they hold. For instance, those who join the army perhaps believe that they have no choice in the matter. Or that the needs of the State are more important than those of the individual. Or that religious faith requires fearless sacrifice. Or that it would be cowardly to refuse. On the other hand, those who refuse to join the army may believe that they do have a choice. Or that the individual is more important than the State. Or that religious faith requires doing harm to no one. Or that it would be cowardly not to refuse. The possible reasons are endless; what is finite is the fact that there will be reasoning based on certain beliefs. And the nature of those beliefs will profoundly affect the behavior that results from that reasoning.

The situations that most reveal the compelling nature of beliefs occur when one of our strongly held beliefs is challenged by apparently disconfirming events. Extensive and clear examples of how compelling beliefs can be was documented by Festinger, Riecken and Schachter in their now classic study of a doomsday group (Festinger, Riecken, and Schachter, *When Prophecy Fails: A Social and Psychological Study of Modern Groups That Predict the Destruction of the World*). Members of this group believed aliens were about to destroy the world, but would pluck the faithful of the group into the safety of outer space just prior to Armageddon. Members quit their jobs, gave away possessions and endured scorn and ridicule. The appointed day arrived and the group assembled to await the flying saucers that would take them to safety. Not only did the saucers not show, but the destruction of the world did not occur either. This created a serious problem for these people who now had to somehow square their beliefs regarding the prophecy with the fact that it did not come true. For a few members, the lack of fireworks was too difficult to reconcile with the beliefs they held and so they left the group. The solution for most of the group members, however, came in the form of a new "communication" from the extraterrestrials: because of the group's demonstration of faith, the aliens had decided to give humankind another chance.

We can debate about whether or not there are aliens, whether or not these people were justified or not in holding their beliefs, and whether or not they are appropriate beliefs to hold. But what is, in any case, evident is that beliefs profoundly influenced these people's choices and behaviors, and that when faced with the necessity of resolving a challenge to these closely held beliefs, most of them responded by finding a way to perceive events so that they did not disconfirm their beliefs. In fact, many found ways to understand the events so that they *supported* their original beliefs. To have denied the beliefs they held so ardently would have been to deny the world as they knew it. Not a small thing for them.

Nor is it a small thing for any of us. The extreme circumstances in the examples we have been considering make obvious the central significance of beliefs in compelling behavior. But of course this same process is also at work in all of us in the most mundane of daily circumstances. Indeed, the organizing influence of beliefs is evident in virtually everything we do. A moment's reflection upon the subtle, swift and often unconscious background to any of our thousands of daily choices and responses makes evident the pervasive impact of beliefs:

- Walking down the street you finish a candy bar and, believing that *it is important to respect your environment,* look for a trashcan. You make your way to one and toss the wrapper. Then you spot someone casually dropping a candy wrapper on the sidewalk! You are suddenly flooded with disgust that someone could be so *disrespectful of the environment.*

- You are trying to get that report done, but not getting very far. Thinking about what is making it so difficult, you remember that *you always seem to have done your best work when you have Afro-Cuban music playing.* So you put some on.

- A friend calls to ask you to help him move next weekend. You had planned to go skiing. Nevertheless, you agree to help him. After all, *that's what are friends for.*

Each of us can multiply these examples a thousand-fold. And in every case the pattern is the same: Your response to the situation is significantly guided by the beliefs you are holding in that situation.

So What Are "Beliefs"?

The notion of "beliefs" covers a lot of experiential ground. People believe in God, atheism, self-interest, charity, self-sacrifice, self-satisfaction, capitalism, communism, control, and freedom. People believe that the world is round, that we never went to the moon, that whales and redwoods must be preserved, that if you drop a glass it is likely to break, and that Elvis is still alive. People have beliefs about themselves, about others, about the world in general, about certain aspects of it in particular, about what is possible, and about what is not possible. The range of beliefs is as wide as human experience itself.

The quality that makes these endless judgments about experience "beliefs" (rather than "observations," "speculations," or "interpretations") is that they are considered by the person who holds them to be self-evident. That is, that person has acquired enough evidence of the truth of the proposition that s/he no longer requires additional evidence to take it as true. (To "know" that something is true is to cross over into believing that there is no evidence that could prove otherwise.)

Of course, what constitutes sufficient evidence for one person regarding a particular belief may be different from that required by another person. Evidence may be personal experiences, testimonials or arguments made by a respected source, an idea that fits with other ideas we already have, or our observations of others. We may require one example or a hundred examples. It may only need to be something small, or it may require an earth shattering experience. But however we get there, the destination is the same: we have sufficient evidence to no longer need evidence of the truth of something. It is self-evident. It is a belief.[12]

What is more, most of our beliefs are implicit, rather than explicit. We often talk about and relate to them as though they are always explicit and at hand, as if each of us has a list of beliefs to which we can refer when asked, "So, what do you believe about this?" While all of us certainly do have some consciously held beliefs, we are not conscious of the vast majority of them. Most of what we come to believe seems so evident, so thoroughly a part of our subjective worlds, that they become transparent. For instance, the belief that there is some kind of hierarchy in nature (whether as the result of a divine plan or evolutionary pressure) is a

---

[12] Obviously, established beliefs continue to be subject to the same process that originally brought them into being. That is, established beliefs can be changed as the result of sufficient evidence of the "truth" of a challenging proposition or experience. We will have more to say about this process in Essay 17: Acquisition.

belief that is operating in most of us, unacknowledged, unexamined, and transparent. And tremendously influential. It is a premise that has, for example, justified slavery, the class system, castes, stratification, organizational structures, and humanity's dominion over the planet. Even taking the position that "human beings are responsible for *preserving* the planet and its natural resources" is based on that same, underlying premise.[13]

The fact that a belief can be implicit in one's experience does not, however, mean that it is beyond the reach of consciousness, that it cannot be articulated. It means only that there has so far been no need to explicitly articulate it. Because it has served to effectively guide our responses and maintain the coherency of our subjective worlds, there has been no occasion requiring that it be made explicit and, perhaps, examined. Similarly, we do not have to monitor or understand the beating of our hearts—indeed, we do not even have to know of its existence—for it to fulfill its systemic role in our bodies. But when we discover that we can no longer bound up the stairs without getting woozy, we suddenly become very aware that our heart is there, and it becomes useful to understand explicitly how it functions.

Beliefs, then, are explicit or implicit propositions that, for the individual, are valid to the point of being self-evident.

The Relevance of Beliefs to Modeling

In Essay 2: Getting Started we introduced the notion of "maps" as a way of describing what a model is. Using that analogy, a model is a map of a particular experience or ability. We also noted that we can make different maps of the same territory, and that a useful map/model is one that portrays the experiential landscape in a way that allows us to navigate through it. That is, the usefulness of a model is largely determined by the distinctions used to create it.

---

[13] For many examples and a deeper discussion of these points, see Stephen Jay Gould's *Full House: The Spread of Excellence from Plato to Darwin*, and Lakoff and Johnson's *Metaphors We Live By* and *Philosophy in the Flesh*, and Lakoff and Turner's *More Than Cool Reason*.

The fundamental and pervasive influence of beliefs upon our thoughts, feelings and actions clearly makes beliefs a distinction worth including in any mapping or modeling of human experiences and abilities. In fact, we find very few examples of human abilities in which beliefs do not play a significant and even necessary role. But how are we to make our way through a territory as vast and endlessly diverse as that of beliefs?

Despite the infinite richness of content and linguistic expression of human beliefs, there are nevertheless discernable structures that give rise to that endless variety. How to identify these structures is the specific topic of the next Essay. But before getting into the how, let us first become familiar with what the underlying structures of beliefs *are*. There are two fundamental patterns: "equivalence relationships" and "causal relationships." These two patterns are the basis of all beliefs, and it is to them that we now turn.

Equivalence Relationships

> `Twas brillig, and the slithy toves
> Did gyre and gimble in the wabe:
> All mimsy were the borogoves,
> And the mome raths outgrabe.

> (Lewis Carroll's *Jabberwocky*)

One of the remarkable things about Lewis Carroll's nonsense poem, Jabberwocky, is that we do not read it as nonsense. Every noun and verb in its opening lines is, well, *not* a noun or verb, or at least not one that is known to anyone other than to Carroll himself. And yet we do not simply dismiss it as gibberish and toss it into the trash. Quite the opposite. Instead we *search* for associations with the words. Read it again and you will discover images dancing in your head, and perhaps feelings doing the same in your body. Your images may be of familiar things or of phantasmagoria, and they may be clear, hazy or fleeting. But whatever they are, they are you are busy trying to make meaning out of Carroll's words.

Human beings are meaning-making creatures. That is, we are continually consciously and unconsciously making meaning out of our perceptions and experiences as they occur. We do not run around all day having experiences, then sit home in the evening trying to figure out what they meant. We make meaning *as part of* the experience itself. As we discussed in previous sections, the process of ongoing meaning-making dramatically influences what we do—choices, judgments, behaviors, feelings—from moment to moment. This process is ongoing and endless. As we move through the world and our daily lives, new distinctions are made for us and by us, constantly expanding our experiential vocabulary of meanings.

For instance, in her memoir, *An American Childhood*, Annie Dillard describes a trip with her mother to a branch of the Carnegie Library in Pittsburgh. It was the early 1950's, and the library was in Homewood, "a Negro section of town." Getting out of the car, they encountered Henry Watson, the beau of the Dillard family's maid, walking with some other men:

> It would embarrass him, I thought, if I said hello to him in front of his friends. I was wrong. He spied me, picked me up—books and all—swung me as he always did, and introduced Mother and me to his friends. Later, as we were climbing the long stone steps to the library's door, Mother said, "That's what I mean by good manners." (p. 80)

Dillard's mother made a connection for her between Henry Watson's behavior and "good manners." She was telling her daughter, "this means that," establishing an *equivalence relationship* between the two. We create equivalence relationships any time we mark out an aspect of experience as being distinct by attaching to it a particular significance. "Marking out" is an essential process in establishing both equivalence and causal relationships. The potential richness of distinctions to be made about experience is infinite. You have only to learn how to really taste wine, see colors, display good manners, or anything else in which your experience is opened to distinctions *not noticed* before, to realize the scope of this potential.

Anything in the infinite range of human experience can pulled into the foreground of experience and become distinct in this way. The process of building up a vast and limitless lexicon of equivalence relationships begins in childhood. Awash with undifferentiated experience to begin with, over time the world was marked out and labeled for each of us. There were objects (mommy, daddy, cow, building, Christmas present, George, spinach), qualities (red, rough, soft, loud, sour, fresh), relationships (too much, enough, closed, above, inside), behaviors (running, thinking, whining, squirming, babbling, smiling), personality characteristics (smart, inconsiderate, lady-like, gentlemanly, happy, polite,), abstractions (mind, democracy, ideals, good, bad, relative), and so on. Your world quickly filled with distinctions.

As human beings, the significance of a distinct experience is often captured for us by a word (or words). Indeed, all words are examples of equivalence relationships. That is, words have meaning and operate as words only when they are made equivalent to (attached to, connected to) some kind of experience. Once that equivalence relationship has been established, hearing, reading or thinking the word "calls up" consciously or unconsciously the experience with which it is connected. And of course, as two sides of an *equivalence* relationship, experiencing something (for example, seeing a red ball) can "call up" in internal dialogue the words that label that experience ("Ah, a red ball!"). This is how words work.[14]

How Equivalence Relationships Relate to Beliefs

> When a man wants to murder a tiger he calls it sport; when
> the tiger wants to murder him he calls it ferocity.
>
> - George Bernard Shaw

---

[14] Marking out experiences does not necessarily require linguistic labeling. One can create meaningful equivalence and causal connections unmediated by language. Animals do it; so do we.

Once an equivalence relationship has been established, it tends to operate in the person's experience as a given, as something that is self-evident. As we talk with our friend, Susan, for example, we notice that her scarf is red and that she is happy today, and we find her a warm person. The redness of Susan's scarf, her happiness, and her warmth are self-evident, obvious to anyone. We do not need to ask ourselves, "What is that color?" (*red*), "What does her constant smiling and frequent laughter mean about her emotional state?" (*happy*), or "What does her frequent touching of our arm and her probing questions say about who she is?" (*warm*). The fact that these equivalence relationships are beliefs (that is, accepted as true) and not truth itself is revealed when someone else joins us who has somewhat different equivalence relationships for these same experiences. For this person, Susan's constant smiling and frequent laughter mean that she is "nervous," and her frequent touching and probing questions mean that she is "intrusive." Furthermore, this person is an artist and does not even see the scarf as red. Instead, he insists, "It is actually *maroon*."

Some beliefs, then, take the form of equivalence relationships through which we identify or evaluate something. For example, when we identify an acquaintance as being "a kind man," that assessment of him is based on an equivalence relationship we have between "kindness" and the behavior this man exhibits. That is, the observation that the acquaintance is a "kind" man is based on a belief we hold about what constitutes "kindness." Whether we are explicit or implicit about it, in judging this man "kind" we are saying this man's actions match our belief that (for example) "Kind people are those who try to help others feel better." The equivalence relationship here is between the label "kind" and the action "helping others feel better." (Take a few moments now to list a few of the qualities you value in yourself and others, and then consider exactly what you mean by each of them. This exercise will quickly repay you with a firmer understanding of equivalence relationships as one form of beliefs.)

Causal Relationships

I'm a great believer in luck and I find the harder I work, the more I have of it.

- Thomas Jefferson

Causal relationships are established when we perceive that "one thing" consistently and predictably leads to "something else." Perhaps you have seen a child sitting in a high chair discovering gravity. She lifts her spoon, lets go, and stares in wonder as it clatters to the tray. Hesitantly, she picks it up again and lets go. After a few more trials, the causal relationship between letting things go and their falling is established. Now she lifts her bowl, dangles it over the side of the high chair *and looks at you* as she lets go of the bowl. Now she *knows* what is going to happen to the bowl, and is free to explore the causal relationship between dropping things and your reaction. With enough examples of the reliability of a cause-effect relationship, it becomes a given, something self-evident, and takes its place in the transparent fabric of our reality.

Similarly, Mr. Frenkel (with whom we began this Essay) noticed that there was a causal relationship between his having the intention to stop moving objects and their subsequently stopping. Perhaps he had been threatened by an oncoming bicyclist and thought fiercely, "Stop!" and the cyclist screeched to a halt. Surprised, it may have occurred to Mr. Frenkel to try it again with another cyclist, and again he succeeded. However it happened, he had enough such successes that he came to believe that there was, indeed, a causal relationship between his intentions and moving objects. Then came the train.

While the association in equivalence relationships is one of "this is that," the association in causal relationships is one of "this *causes* that." As with equivalence relationships, causal relationships are established for us when two or more "things" in our experience are marked out as relating to one another; but in this case that relationship is one of cause and effect. For instance, you might notice that when you exercise regularly it causes you to have more energy, that rubbing your hands together quickly makes them feel warmer, that the smooth voice tones of your lover make you feel content, or that wearing snappy clothes tends to engender more respect from your business associates.

What is more, we can "perceive" causal relationships between *any* of the distinctions we make in our experience: masturbating causes blindness (behavior to physical condition), tallness causes stooping (physical trait to behavior), planning causes success (cognitive activity to outcome), hearing owls hoot at night causes blood to thin, making violent movies causes social violence, social violence causes violent movies to be made, and so on. All that is needed is to perceive that a particular "this" reliably seems to precede a particular "that" for us to form a belief about the cause-effect relationship between the two.

How Causal Relationships Relate to Beliefs

Causal relationships form a substrate of beliefs in just the same way that equivalence relationships do. That is, many beliefs are expressions of some causal relationship a person has accepted as self-evident. And once formed, it will operate either explicitly or implicitly to guide the sense or meaning that person makes and how he responds. If, for example, you have had some formative experiences in which you treated others well and they treated you well, you might establish a causal relationship between the two events. Expressed as a belief it might come out something like, "If you treat people well, they will treat you well." The expression of this belief in patterns of thinking will probably include noticing when you are treating people well and when you are not, noticing when others are treating you and other people well and when they are not, and considering how you can treat someone well. And in behavior, you will try to treat people well.[15]

---

[15] To be clear, having the belief does not guarantee success; only that you are likely to organize your perceptions and behavior with respect to it. Whether or not you actually succeed in treating someone well in a particular situation will be a function of who that person is, your perceptions of who that person is, what you

But, of course, you will treat people well according to what you consider to be "treating people well." That is, specifically how you treat people will be guided by your equivalence relationship for "treating people well." For you, it may mean "giving them whatever they want." If that is the case, then you will endeavor to treat people well by discovering what they want and giving it to them (equivalence relationship) in the belief that by doing that they will give you what you want, that is, "treat me well" (causal relationship). You could, instead, hold the same causal relationship ("If you treat people well, they will treat you well"), but have a different equivalence relationship for "treating people well." For instance, that "treating people well" is "telling them the truth." In this case you would assess what for you is the truth and tell it to them. Considerations of "giving them what they want" would be irrelevant, perhaps never even entering into your thoughts.

The interaction of equivalence and causal relationships creating the underlying structure of a belief (as in the previous example) is more often the rule than the exception. As we will see, all beliefs are expressions of equivalence and causal relationships.

The Natural Expression of Equivalence and Causal Relationships

As you continue to attune yourself to recognizing the distinctions of equivalence and causal relationships, you will discover just how rampant they are in discourse of any kind (internal musing, conversation, media, literature, film, theater). Even so, it is not often that people talk about their equivalences and cause-effects, presenting them in the neat packaging of an explicitly stated belief (as with, "If you treat people well, they will treat you well").[16]

---

know to do, social factors operating at the moment, and so on. We will have more to say about this topic in the Essay on Acquisition.

[16] For a masterful and instructive example of the pervasiveness and power of

Nevertheless, it is still the case that we can often find expressions of our beliefs in the things we say. These beliefs may be expressed either explicitly or implicitly. When a visiting friend says, "Could I turn on some more lights? It's kind of gloomy in here," he is expressing a causal relationship between levels of light and his mood, specifically, that too little light makes him feel "gloomy." (Remember, someone else may experience low levels of light as, say, "comforting," or "romantic," or in fact may experience no causality between levels of light and mood.) Similarly, someone who says, "She's a real pistol, the way she is always doing what she wants and telling folks what she thinks of them," is expressing an equivalence relationship: a "pistol" is someone who "does what she wants to do and tells others what she thinks of them." In both examples, the equivalence and causal relationships are not put in the neat form of a standard belief statement. Even so, the elements of the beliefs *are there and stated.*

It is also often the case that the elements of a belief are not stated, but implied. For example, Tom says, "I like taking care of my tools." His statement implies that for him there is something important about taking care of his tools. What is neither expressed nor implied is what "caring" for tools means, that is, what the equivalence is. Nor does he express any causality in relation to taking care of tools. But that does not mean he does not have equivalence and causal experiences regarding "caring" for tools. If we ask Tom to explain, we may discover "Caring for tools means keeping them clean and putting them where they belong," an equivalence relationship. For Tom, caring is not about showering your tools with affection, or scratching your name into each piece, or "using the hell out of them." When asked, Tom might also reveal a causal relationship, such as, "If you care for your tools, you tend to do better work with them." Again, for Tom, it is not the case that caring for your tools causes you to be admired by others, or find things easily, or keep from getting injured. Instead it is Tom's belief that caring for tools affects the quality of work you do with them.

---

equivalence and causal relationships, see James Clavell's novelette, *The Children's Story.*

Since beliefs represent an essential and pervasive set of distinctions organizing our experience and behavior, why are we usually not explicit about them when expressing ourselves? Why do we say, "Martin is a very considerate person" and let it go at that, without describing what we mean by "considerate?" The answer is that it rarely occurs to us that it is necessary to explain. As long as we share the same language and culture, we assume that what is evident to us is just as evident to anyone else who shares our language and culture. "We" know what it means to be considerate. There is no need to state the obvious.

However, what is obvious to one person may not, in fact, be obvious to another. And so there are frequent misunderstandings between individuals, regardless of how close they are linguistically and culturally. There have been times when you and a friend have been as far apart on the meaning of a particular concept as a New York stock broker talking with an Mbuti pygmy from the Ituri forest about "security."

The degree to which we can and do take these shared equivalence and causal relationships for granted often becomes more obvious when we find ourselves in a different culture. Of the authors, one is American (David), the other British (Graham). In the liner notes from a Keith Jarrett recording ("La Scala"), they read Jarrett's account of being thanked by a man who had attended every performance at the La Scala theater during the previous twenty-five years. "He said it was the strongest, most moving (again putting his hand to his heart and with tears in his eyes) musical experience he ever had..." Graham was aghast at the "shamelessness" of Jarrett writing something so self-congratulatory. David disagreed, pointing out that the last line of the story is, "The heart is where the music is," which entirely changes the frame of reference for the incident. For David, that is. For Graham, that line in no way mitigated the shamelessness, and we had a lovely argument. And we speak the same language! ("*Some* of us speak *English*." - Graham)[17]

---

[17] Obviously, the opportunity for miscommunication is exacerbated when people are trying to communicate using a language that is not native to them. These differences can also be the source of new and wonderful experiences. For a fascinating presentation of equivalence distinctions that are made by people in various cultures, see Howard Rheingold's, *They Have a Word For It.*

Equivalence and Causal Relationships and Modeling

In modeling, we want to create a description of the exemplar's experience that includes those patterns most significant in organizing that person's thinking and behavior when manifesting their particular ability. We know that the exemplar is using distinctions that are effective for organizing their experience in that context. We also know that the exemplar's distinctions are different than those used by people who do not naturally manifest that same ability. To a significant extent, this is the difference between "those who can" and "those who cannot." (An additional factor of considerable significance is "practice," something we will have more to say about in the Essay on Acquisition.)

For the most part, the distinctions that make up the warp and woof of the fabric of our reality are equivalence and causal relationships. The infinite possibilities of perception and meaning present in each moment are sifted through that weaving of equivalences and causes. And, as we discussed under the notion of "flow of effect," the perceptions and meanings that emerge from this sifting significantly orient—indeed, profoundly affect—our thoughts, feelings and behaviors.

In creating our model we certainly want to discover and understand the exemplar's feelings and behaviors. But we also need access to the fabric of beliefs that organizes those other "expressive" elements of the ability. Without access to the exemplar's beliefs, we are in the position of someone asking a wine connoisseur for tutoring, but wanting only to be told which are good wines to order and which are to be avoided. No matter how extensive a list we memorize, we are confined to the list. What is more, we are in fact not being wine connoisseurs, but mimicking the behavior of one by ordering the correct wine. What we really want from our teacher is to know what to taste in wine, what distinctions to make as the wine swirls in our glasses and spills upon our tongues. If we can do that, we do not need his list. We can make our own.

* * *

It is not possible to enumerate every belief operating in the exemplar's experience; each one of us is infinitely rich, the deepest of experiential wells. No matter how big the bucket or how furiously and diligently we dip into that well, it will always come up full. And the well will never be drained. We must remember that our intention is not to drain the well, but to quench our thirst. We need, then, to discover only those beliefs—in the form of equivalence and causal relationships—that are most significant in manifesting the ability. In the next Essay, we will explore how to identify those equivalences and cause-effects that are essential to manifesting a particular ability.

Elements of the Experiential Array

Essay 8

Beliefs II: The Belief Template

The Belief Template is a graphic tool for capturing the significant equivalence and causal relationships that form the foundational beliefs for an exemplar's ability. These relationships take the form of Criteria, Definition, Evidence, and Enabling and Motivating Cause-Effects. These underlying structures act as the primary experiential filters the exemplar brings into play when manifesting the ability. These structures also give rise to the infinite ways in which the exemplar verbalizes his or her beliefs. In addition, there may be Supporting Beliefs worth capturing. These are beliefs that, while not crucial to the ability, nevertheless bolster its expression.

Artie Shaw was one of the finest and most innovative jazz clarinetists... ever. He was a real "King of Swing," the first white band leader to hire a full-time black female singer (Billie Holiday), led the Artie Shaw Orchestra to fame, and composed many enduring hits, including one that has settled into the psyche of anyone who has ever listened to big band music, "Begin the

Beguine." In his nineties, Artie Shaw reflected on how he arranged compositions for his band:

> The main thing was to get rid of non-essentials. Basically when you're hearing a piece of music there's the melody and the rhythm pulse behind it. It could be a piano...it could be a piano, bass guitar and drums, whatever. But there's a pulse and a melody. Now anything you add to that has got to be done very carefully, because you are taking away from the attention of the average lay listener, who is interested in the melody and in the beat, if he's dancing. When you make an arrangement, as I put it, make it as simple as you can. If there's too much in there that doesn't belong, get rid of it. My job as a leader was to take the music that was brought to me... These were accomplished musicians but they would forget that the audience wasn't an accomplished musician. They didn't know what was going on. My job was to try to act as intermediary between their complex notions and ideas about the tune and what the audience wanted. And I tried my best to keep it musically as good and exciting and valid as I could and at the same time cut out the irrelevancies.

> "The Mystery of Artie Shaw: Will the Beguine Ever End?"
> Interviewed by Ted Hallock, KBOO, Portland, Oregon

In this extract, Shaw pronounces, explains, recommends, recalls, justifies and judges. He says many things. But are they different things? The answer to that depends upon whether we are looking at the surface content of each of his explanations, recommendations and judgments, or at the underlying belief structure that gives rise to them. "The main thing was to get rid of non-essentials," "When you make an arrangement, as I put it, make it as simple as you can," and "If there's too much in there that doesn't belong, get rid of it" are obviously not the same sentences. Even so, it is also obvious that they are different linguistic manifestations of the same underlying belief; they are three different ways of saying the same thing regarding the importance of "getting rid of non-essentials."[18]

What may be less obvious is that almost everything Artie Shaw says in this excerpt springs from that same, underlying belief. For instance, "Now anything you add to that has got to be done very carefully, because you are taking away from the attention of the average lay listener, who is interested in the melody and in the beat, if he's dancing." His explanation reveals that he is attending to what is essential to his audiences, and tries to not include ("get rid of") anything that is not essential to them. If we were modeling Artie Shaw, we would not want all the ways he has of expressing that one idea. That is an infinite well, and we will never drain it. If that well is full of water, we only need a few drops to know what we will find no matter how many times we cast our bucket into it. Similarly, rather than trying to empty the well of our exemplar's experience, we want to find those "drops" that reveal what "fills" him as he is manifests his ability.

As another example, consider the following beliefs:

"Hard work provides a good foundation."

"I need to get busy on that project if it is to get anywhere."

"You get out only what you put in."

"Without effort there is no accomplishment."

"He will never amount to anything until he breaks a sweat at something."

"Choosing between brains and diligence, I'll take diligence every time."

---

[18] This underlying belief extended beyond his music. Asked to write an epitaph for himself for Who's Who in America, Shaw wrote, "He did the best he could with the material at hand." Later, however, responding to a question about the epitaph during a lecture, Shaw said, "Yeah, but I've been thinking it over and I've decided it ought to be shorter, to make it more elegant...I've cut it down to two words: 'Go away.'" www.artieshaw.com

Although each of these statements is manifestly different than any of the others, they are all expressions of the same underlying causal relationship between "effort" and "attaining goals": that is, "Effort leads to attaining goals." These six examples are, in fact, just a few of the infinite ways that individuals—or even one individual—might, at various times and in different contexts, express this same causal relationship.

Similarly, when your friend goes on for ten minutes describing how his boss "really understands his people," he will cover a lot of expressive ground, coming at the topic from many angles. He may offer you examples, quotes, observations, assessments, questions, comparisons, childhood memories and explanations. It will be a rich weaving of communication. Even so, all of that complexity and richness will also almost certainly be the verbalized expression of only a *few* equivalence and causal relationships that your friend holds in relation to "really understanding people."

When modeling an exemplar's ability, we want to identify those few underlying patterns that are most significant in generating that person's experience and behavior in that particular context. (Remember, we do not want the list for good wines, but the ability to determine for ourselves what is a good wine.) How are we to tease out from the expressive tapestry of discourse the threads of those underlying patterns of beliefs?

We begin by making distinctions about the structures of beliefs. (As we discussed in Essay 3, a distinction marks out particular element within the infinitely rich background of experience and, in doing so, causes it to snap into the foreground of our experience.) We began this process of making distinctions regarding beliefs in our discussion of equivalence and causal relationships in the previous Essay. With those general distinctions now well in hand, we are ready to explore the more refined and more useful distinctions captured in the "Belief Template":

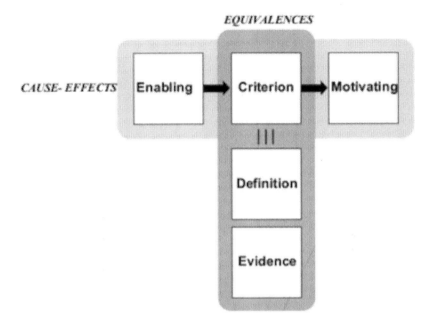

The Belief Template is a graphic model inside the encompassing graphic model of the Experiential Array. As with the Array, the Template is useful in three important ways:

1. It specifies those elements of the exemplar's beliefs that are significant
    and worth capturing for the model.

2. It provides a place to capture them.

These two virtues help us sort through the flood of information by (1) reminding us of those particular aspects of experience (distinctions) we need to focus on, and (2) helping us keep track of what we already have identified and what we have yet to discover. The Belief Template is useful in a third way, as well:

3. It graphically represents the dynamic connections between the elements of the exemplar's beliefs.

The Belief Template lays out in an accessible way the patterns of connection operating in the exemplar's experience. That is, it captures the *structure*. And in so doing, it transforms what would otherwise be an endless list of statements of belief into a set of fundamental relationships that are capable of *generating* that endless list.

Criteria

> In the middle of the fifties, Stravinsky was commissioned by the Venice Festival to write them an original work. His contribution turned out to be fifteen minutes long. The officials of the festival complained to Stravinsky that this was too short. "Well, then," Stravinsky replied calmly, "play it again."
>
> Oscar Levant, *The Unimportance of Being Oscar* (1968)

Imagine for a moment that you are considering buying a home. Outwardly the process involves scanning lists of homes, talking with an agent about what's available, and walking through homes that are on the market. Inwardly the process is one of evaluation: you do not consider every home on the list, you reject some of your agent's suggested properties and are interested in others, and some of the houses you walk through feel right while others do not. When a particular house is not right for you, however, it is not a judgment on the house itself but an expression of how *you* judge that house. That is, it is not *right for you*. Packed inside that phrase, "right for you," are the things you are looking for in a house, what is important to you. If "spaciousness" and "convenience to shopping" are important to you, then you will probably not buy that lovely cottage down the dirt road outside of town. You can see that it is beautiful and quiet and very affordable, but those are not the qualities that are most important to you. Instead, you are attracted to that four-bedroom condominium near the heart of the city's shopping and cultural centers.

In situations involving choices that may have profound impacts on our lives—buying a house, deciding to have a child, getting married, separating from a partner—it is obvious that, in an effort to make those choices, we will evaluate them in terms of those things that are important to us. When buying a home, for instance, one person may be focused on "spaciousness," someone else on "convenience," and others on "low maintenance," or "proximity to good schools" or "affordability." When considering having children, people assess their "emotional readiness," "job security," "time for care-giving," and "expense." These assessments become obvious when we are dealing with something very important to us; these considerations often involve extensive periods of deep thought, sorting through needs, desires, futures, and feelings, talking with others, and perhaps even a certain amount of anxiety.

While it may not be as immediately obvious, this same process of evaluating with respect to what is personally important is also operating in almost everything we do. Even in the mundane and unconscious things we do. For example, suppose we ask you, What is important to you as you read these pages? It may not have occurred to you that something *is* important to you until we asked the question. But if you consider that question for a moment, you will find that there is something you are wanting from your reading. Perhaps you want to "understand" the concepts presented here. Or perhaps as you read your attention is focused on the "usefulness" of the material, or its "clarity," or its "originality." It may instead be that what is important to you as you read is having "fun," finding keys to "personal power," "new possibilities," "freedom," or any of a thousand other human concerns. Each of these different concerns acts as an important standard of evaluation for the people who hold them. That is, a person for whom "understanding" is important will be evaluating how well he "understands" what he is reading. The person placing primary importance on "fun" will be evaluating whether or not he is having fun reading. The person looking for "new possibilities" will be looking for passages that present possibilities she had never considered before. As she reads along she may, of course, also be understanding, having fun, finding keys to personal power, and so on. But the *primary focus* of her attention will be on those passages in her reading that offer "new possibilities." These personally important standards of evaluation are called "Criteria":

The Criterion is the primary standard of evaluation operating within a particular context.

The significance of Criteria is that they have a tremendous impact on what we attend and respond to in our experience. They act as filters on our experience in much the same way as colored lenses filter light. The world may be awash in full spectrum sunlight, but if you are wearing red goggles the only light that is transmitted to you will be shades of red. Similarly, reading these pages while holding the criterion of "usefulness" is like wearing a pair of "usefulness" goggles. As you read "through" those goggles, you will particularly notice any passages that discuss how something might be useful, and think about ways in which the information can be applied. In other words, you will be reading for "usefulness." You will particularly notice any references to how to use or apply the concepts. You are also likely to generate your own ideas about when, where, and how those concepts can be useful. And, ultimately, your experience of satisfaction in reading the book will be largely determined by the extent to which you found it "useful." However, the "usefulness" that you discovered in the book may not occur at all to someone who reads these same pages wearing the criterion goggles of "clarity." She may instead be occupied with noticing how well things are being explained and, when something is not clear, perhaps generate possibilities for how to make it clearer. And again, her reading satisfaction will be significantly determined by her experience of the "clarity" of the writing.

Of course, you could be holding more than one criterion at a time. When you read you could be evaluating both "usefulness" and "clarity." Similarly, when buying a house, "convenience," "affordability," and "spaciousness" may all be important experiential cards played on the table of your decision-making process. In addition to these criteria, there may be a myriad of other things that you take into consideration: the age of the appliances, is there a gas furnace, is the landscaping attractive, and so on. These may be preferences, but they are not important. That is, they are subordinate to "convenience," "affordability" and "spaciousness." (For instance, using these criteria, you probably would *not* reject a convenient, affordable and spacious house just because it has an electric instead of gas furnace.) The fact that those three considerations are important to you means that they will establish the primary experiential filters through which you view the various houses on the market. They constitute your criteria in the context of buying a home.

Context

It is obvious that when you read a book you are operating in a different realm of experience—or "context"—than when you are buying a house, or watching a movie, or working on a report, or explaining something to a child, or painting a picture. The endless variety of place, people, activity, time of day, and so on generates an equally endless variety of contexts.

Whenever we enter into a context, our concerns, thinking, emotions and behavior adjust to the requirements and influences of that particular context. Furthermore, it takes only a slight change in elements to create a different context. For instance, how do your thoughts, feelings and behaviors change when you discover that a report you are working on is not due next week...but tomorrow? The context shifts from "preparing a report due in a week" to "preparing a report due in a day." The shift in your experience may be subtle ("Hmm, well let's see what I can do") or it may be extreme ("This is horrible—I'll never be to do it!"), but your experience *will* change when the context changes. Just what is shifting in you as you shift contexts?

As the context shifts, what is most important or relevant to you in that particular context shifts as well. When the report is due next week, perhaps what is important is "accuracy," "clear writing," "completeness," "classy presentation," and "approval by peers." But if the report suddenly becomes due tomorrow, what is relevant may shift to "accuracy," "clear writing," and (the new concern) "meets minimum requirements" ("completeness," "classy presentation," and "approval by peers" all go out the window). The contextual frame determines what distinctions need to be in the foreground of your experience *now*. These distinctions then act as a set of filters for perception and meaning, significantly affecting how you think, feel and behave in that particular context.[19]

The range of possible contexts is endless because the boundaries that define a context are not necessarily set by the "reality" of a situation. Contexts are defined by the subjective fencing each of us places around our experiences. For one person, preparing a report due in a week is a completely different kettle of fish than preparing one due tomorrow; for someone else those two situations are the same kettle—the same context— and he approaches them both with the same attitude and behavior. Perhaps for him, writing reports for his boss is a totally different context— requiring different thinking—than writing reports for peers, and available time has little to do with what he considers important when preparing reports. Similarly, for one person, planning to build a bird house is a different context than planning to build a dog house, an outhouse or a human house; each context requires its own way of looking at the structure to be built. For someone else, "Listen, a building is a building."

The fact that context is determined by our individual ways of marking out the territory of experience (rather than anything intrinsic to the situation) means that we can shift context while the environment remains the same. Suppose you are conversing at the dinner table, a context that brings to the foreground for you the importance of politeness, openness to ideas, and contributing to the conversation. But as the conversation flows on, you realize that people at the table are trying to avoid talking about something in particular. Now the context becomes one of (perhaps) "interacting with people who are trying to avoid something" (or, perhaps, "figuring out what is being avoided"). And as a result, your criteria shift to concerns about respectfulness, or perhaps privacy, or perhaps telling the truth. The people, wine and conversation go on as before, but what is important to you in that situation has changed.

So far we have been talking about contexts as though they are defined by what is currently going on around us. The realm of experience also includes an infinite landscape of internal contextual spaces as well.

---

[19] See Essay 3, Distinctions, for a review of the impact of distinctions on experience and behavior, as well as a discussion about the Flow of Effect between beliefs and the other elements of experience.

Imagining what your future might be is just as much a context that you can be "in" as is that of shopping for food. Other examples of internally occurring contexts include considering what gift to buy your lover, recalling precious childhood memories, imagining how you will give a friend bad news, visualizing how best to build a bird house, and attending to the subtle sensations in your body. Like externally defined contexts, there are infinite possible internally generated contexts, and they automatically orient our attention, thinking, feeling and behavior along certain lines.

Context and Modeling

In fact, we introduced the notion of context (though not the term itself) in the second Essay, Getting Started, when talking about defining what you want to model. When you specify an ability, you are establishing the context for your exemplar. He will orient his experience to, and answer your questions from, *that* context. This is one reason we suggested that, before you begin your modeling, you consider whether or not you need to first chunk down the ability into "sub-abilities." The example we had used was of modeling the ability to "write fiction." That set the context. "Writing teen fiction," however, would set a different context. And the context changes again when we chunk that down to "writing fiction for 12 to 14 year olds." And of course, within each of these abilities there are the sub-abilities of "creating characters," "plotting," "editing," and so on, each of which establishes a different subjective experiential boundary for your exemplar.

This is why we emphasized the importance of being as precise as possible about what you want to be able to do—that is, specify the ability—before selecting exemplars and beginning to gather information. The context you establish will largely determine the nature of the information you end up gathering. By making sure that you have correctly specified the ability you want, you set a context for your exemplar that helps ensure that he is accessing, and reporting to you, those elements of his experience that give rise to the ability you actually need.

Unlike the land we stand on, then, contexts are fluid frames that separate our world into subjectively different domains. We set the frame and establish the domain for our exemplar (and ourselves) when we specify the ability we want to model in them. If we are to map this territory, we need to plant our flag somewhere as a point of reference. The best place to do that is in the heart of that territory, in the Criterion.

Criteria and Modeling Abilities

Some tracts of land are naturally good for growing grains, while others are naturally good for growing fruit trees. You can go ahead and plant grain where the land is actually best suited to grow trees, but your crop will probably require much more tending, it is unlikely to produce as much, and it may fail altogether. Our exemplars are like wise old farmers; they know what distinctions are most important to cultivate in the context of their particular ability.

The most essential of these distinctions are the exemplar's primary standards of evaluation, that is, his Criteria. The exemplar's criteria act as experiential filters, significantly organizing his perceptions, thoughts, feelings and behaviors along particular lines. It is this meaning-making through the perceptual mesh of the Criteria that forms the basis for how he thinks, feels and behaves in that context.

Furthermore, the fact that the exemplar is consistently effective in that context indicates that the Criteria he is using must be appropriate and useful. Criteria are the beating hearts of most human abilities and, so, are essential to bringing models of those abilities to life.

In one of our modeling seminars, we were treated to a simple and dramatic example of the central nature of criteria to an ability. Derek wanted to learn to take good photographs. From his exemplar he first discovered that an essential sub-ability is, "Recognize a potential picture." When he modeled this sub-ability, he learned that what the photographer is always looking for and responding to—that is, her Criterion—is "contrast," by which she meant any adjacent and marked difference in brightness, color, shape, texture, content, and so on. Derek offered the other members of our seminar just this one Criterion, and suddenly everyone was looking around the room and seeing possible pictures. The shadows cast by the chair upon the floor, the red shirt meeting the blue pants, the curve of the potted plant against the rectangles of the window panes, the smooth hand upon the corduroy, the old man walking by holding the hand of a child, all now jumped out at us as possible subjects for photographs. Though of course Derek had additional elements in the Array for "Recognize a potential picture," none of them made any sense, mattered or even worked without first having in place, *in experience,* the Criterion of "contrast."

Criterion in Focus

Of course, the photographer exemplar probably had many criteria operating in her experience as she was looking about for possible pictures. But there was one Criterion which was primary, that of "contrast." We term this the "Criterion in focus." (In the Array it is simply noted as "Criterion.")

Of course, theoretically, a person could have several Criteria in focus at the same time. What happens in practice, however, is that when we have two or more Criteria in focus at the *same* time, there is often conflict. Exemplars exemplify what *works*; typically, they are not caught up in equivocating, being stuck, conflicted and so on. We usually find that the exemplar in action—manifesting his particular ability—has one Criterion in focus. If there are sub-abilities contributing to the larger ability (which is likely), each of them will have its own Criterion in focus, as well.

If during the gathering of information the exemplar does claim to have several Criteria in focus, we explore each of them with him. Typically, it turns out that each of those criteria is a Criterion in focus for an essential sub-ability. The surprising fact is that when we ask the exemplar what is important to him when he is doing what he does, the answer is almost never a string of criteria, but one Criterion.

Lenny

Lenny had not been feeling well for months, and finally went to the hospital when his symptoms became intolerable. When the nurse heard that he had lost weight, and had been craving water and sugar, she decided to check his blood glucose. "Now a normal reading for a fasting non-diabetic individual is somewhere between 70 and 120," Lenny explained. "And I was 533. The doctor shook my hand and said, 'I'm not your doctor any more. We're going to get you an endocrinologist. See ya.' And he walks away. That was that. The nurse says, 'You're diabetic. You're having a sugar crisis right now.' So they send me upstairs and start pumping me full of insulin, which changed my entire universe about fifteen minutes after the first injection."

Diagnosed as a type II diabetic, Lenny was quickly educated about testing his blood and taking medication, a regimen he would have to follow for the rest of his life. He did not like the idea of taking medication, and when he heard about a diet that had allowed other diabetics to keep their blood sugar stable, he decided to try it. It worked. That was fifteen years ago, and Lenny has been maintaining his blood glucose levels since then through this diet. Impressed by his ability to stick to a demanding diet regimen for so many years, we decided to model him.[20] Throughout the rest of these Essays we will be returning to the Lenny's Array as a way of providing continuity to our examples of the various elements of experience. (Lenny's full Array can be found in the Appendix.)

When we modeled Lenny we found that the Criterion he has in focus as he follows his diet is that of "working":

Criterion
"Working"

---

[20] Lenny follows the Sears "Zone Diet," described in detail in many publications, including Sears and Lawren's, *The Zone: A Dietary Road Map, 1995.*

This is not a surprising Criterion, and is probably akin to the criteria that many people hold when trying to stick to a diet. There is something tremendously significant about Lenny's particular form of the Criterion, however. And that is that it is "work*ing*," and not "works" or "worked." Lenny's "working" presupposes an ongoing evaluation; there is no end point to reach which, once attained, means he is done.

This contrasts with people who evaluate whether or not their diet "works" or has "worked." Their Criteria place them in a very different subjective situation from Lenny. When (for whatever reason) these people hit a snag in their dieting, their evaluation is likely to be that the diet "doesn't work" or "hasn't worked." In both cases, the subjective experience is that there is something wrong with the diet (or with "me"), and that it is all over. (Step into the situation of being on a diet while holding either one of those Criteria, and notice how it affects your feelings, thoughts, and choices. Then shift the Criterion to "working" and notice how your experience shifts.) Obviously, neither of these orientations is supportive of continuing to follow a diet.

The structure of experience presupposed by "working," however, orients us in a fundamentally different way. When Lenny hits a snag, there is no sense that the diet cannot work, just that it is not working *currently*. Also, there is less a sense that something is done, finished or proven; instead there is more the sense of the need for adjustment. Both of these orientations strongly support an endless and ongoing effort, which is just what Lenny needs to maintain his diet regimen.

Definition

Happiness is when what you think, what you say, and
what you do are in harmony.

- Mohandas K. Gandhi

Ask a dozen people which of Mother Nature's animal species is the most successful and most will probably respond, "human beings, of course." Our ability to manipulate our world through language, tools and technology are unparalleled in any other species. We are the obvious choice.

But not for everyone. Some people will nominate the ants. After all, ants are far more numerous than human beings. Or how about crocodiles, which have survived basically unchanged for a billion years. Perhaps the accolade should fall upon the Grey whales, which have learned to coexist with each other without war or cruelty. What we point to as the most successful species, then, depends upon how we define "successful." If it means "able to manipulate the world through the use of language, tools and technology," then human beings are a successful species. But to someone who defines "successful" as "having the greatest numbers," then ants have us humans beat. If "successful" means "enduring throughout the millennia," we humans are just getting started and our ability to last is utterly untested compared to the crocodile. Or, if one considers a "successful" species one that has "transcended the willingness to kill its own kind," human beings are not even in the running. Each of these constitutes a different Definition for the criterion of "successful" when speaking of species:

The Definition is a description of what is meant by the Criterion in focus.

Of course, the subjective nature of definitions means that there are no inherently correct or right ones. As Humpty Dumpty informed Alice, "When I use a word, it means just what I choose it to mean—neither more nor less." That works in Wonderland. But on this side of the mirror, in the wonderland of our daily lives, we rely on consensual or shared definitions. That is, we generally agree on what "success" means—or "trust," "liberalism," "conservatism," "intelligent," "loving," "understand," etc.— and then interact through that shared understanding.

Sharing definitions of words is, of course, the basis of a "common language." What transforms words from meaningless sounds into meaningful experience is that the people using those words are operating out of similar definitions. While definitions within a language-sharing group are usually similar enough that they can communicate with a high degree of understanding, it is still the case that there can be subtle differences between individuals as to what a particular word means. And as misunderstandings reveal, those differences can be significant even within a group that believes itself to be "speaking the same language."

For example, an executive we worked with wanted to assign a staff member to a particular job and, so, told his office manager (using common business jargon), "I need a dedicated resource for this project." Two weeks later, the project still did not seem to be moving forward. The annoyed executive hauled the office manager into his office for an explanation. It then came out that the manager thought that "dedicated" meant "a sincere commitment to the job." What the executive meant by "dedicated" was "someone who devotes all of his time."[21]

There are always possibilities for misunderstandings between individuals because of differences in Definition. This does not mean, however, that it is therefore necessary to be as explicit as possible about everything. In casual conversation the slippage between shared words and unshared definitions is often slight or of little consequence. It is only when understanding is essential (as in the case of the annoyed executive above) that it becomes important to make sure that definitions are shared.

For example, in a paper on software design, Mitchell Kapor cites Vitruvius (a Roman critic of architecture) as asserting that a well-designed building fulfills the criteria of "firmness," "commodity," and "delight," then goes on to say that, "The same may be said of good software." But what does it mean to say that a software program (or a building, for that matter) should be "firm," "commodious" and "delightful?" If we want to apply Kapor's analogy to creating good software, we are faced with

---

[21] Remember that this is the executive's definition of "dedicated" within this particular context. What he means by "dedicated" may be one thing when talking about staffing for specific tasks, and something quite different when the context shifts to addressing "work ethics of employees." In that context, his definition of "dedicated" may be the same as his office manager's (that is, "a sincere commitment to the job").

understanding what "firm," "commodious" and "delightful" software *means*. Are our ideas in accord with Kapor's intentions? Fortunately for us, Kapor goes on to explain:

> Firmness: A program should not have any bugs that inhibit its function. Commodity: A program should be suitable for the purposes for which it was intended. Delight: the experience of using the program should be a pleasurable one. (*Bringing Design to Software*, Terry Winograd ed., p.5.)

By defining each of these for us, Kapor more explicitly connects the criteria with our own experiences. Through that connection we now have a clearer understanding of what he means. If we are software designers, this specification is necessary if we want to incorporate his understanding of good software design into our own work. Similarly, if we are modeling Kapor's approach to software design, we will want to identify and use his perceptual filters, at least some of which are captured in those three criteria and their Definitions.

If our experiential filters were already the same as our exemplar, we would probably already be manifesting the same ability he does. Since that is not the case, we can be pretty sure that he is using at least some Criteria and Definitions that are different from our own. As modelers of the exemplar's ability, we want to use the same perceptual and experiential filters—that is, Criteria and Definitions—that he uses to such great advantage, so that our own experiences and responses will come to better emulate his when we, too, manifest the exemplar's ability.

The examples we have been using, and the way we have been talking about Criteria, may suggest that the equivalence relationship between a criterion and its definition is something that we are typically conscious of. In fact, most of our equivalence (and causal) relationships are unconscious and unlanguaged. The act of noticing them brings them into consciousness and (usually at the same time) into language, as well. Nevertheless, we can be guided by our equivalence relationships without having a conscious understanding of what they are. For example, we have often startled corporate executives bent on success by asking them what they mean by "success." Many discover that, though they are devoting much of themselves to fulfilling the criterion of "success," they nevertheless have little or no conscious understanding about what really constitutes success for them. Consequently, they do not have a way of knowing whether or not they have attained it, a circumstance that contributes significantly to their often feeling driven.

Do We Need Both?

Clearly, Criterion and Definition are two sides of the same experiential coin. A Criterion is a label for a particular set of experiences, which is described in the Definition; a Definition is a description of a particular set of experiences, which is labeled by the Criterion. It is the connecting of these two as "equivalent" that gives them meaning. It is legitimate to ask, however, Why is it necessary to go to the trouble of identifying and specifying a Criterion since:

1. A Criterion is merely a label for a particular set of experiences, *and...*

2. It is that set of experiences that is, in fact, the primary filter operating on the exemplar's experience; that is, it is the Definition that is guiding the exemplar's perceptions and experience, regardless of what it is labeled.

Is it not sufficient to simply have a description of the kind of experience the exemplar is using to orient his perceptions and behavior (Definition) when manifesting his ability?

In fact, it is sufficient to have that description. After all, the experience is what you really want, rather than the label for the experience (Criterion). If you do not have the exemplar's Definition of his Criterion, your only understanding of the experience that Criterion represents will be *your own* definition. And your definition may or may not be one that supports manifesting the ability you are modeling. But you know that the exemplar's Definition *does* support the ability. The Criterion is only a label for the exemplar's essential set of experiential filters when manifesting the ability.

Nevertheless, the Criterion distinction is useful. Its usefulness lies precisely in the fact that it *is* a label for a set of experiences. Since it is one side of an equivalence relationship, to access the label is to access the whole of the relationship, just as taking one side of a coin necessarily brings with it the other side at the same time. (Or, as our colleague, Steve Andreas, aptly describes it, the Criterion is "the handle on the suitcase" of the experience.) Think of the Criterion as a simple way to refer to or access what may well be an extensive and detailed description of the exemplar's essential experiences, instead of having to recapitulate that description every time you need it. Grab the criterial label and you grab the whole of the experience attached to it.

Definition and Modeling Abilities

The ultimate goal of modeling is to alter your own structure of experience to match that of your exemplar when he is manifesting his particular ability. As the "beating heart" of most abilities, the Criterion in focus is critical to this structure. And, as we discussed above, the purpose of defining the Criterion is to help ensure that you are operating out of your exemplar's perceptual filters, rather than your own.

For example, recall the example of the Criterion of "contrast" for noticing that there is a potential picture to be taken. When Derek asked his exemplar what she meant by "contrast," she gave the Definition, "Any adjacent and marked difference in brightness, color, shape, texture, content, and so on." For most of us, if we think about contrast at all when taking pictures, we probably think only in terms of differences in brightness, and perhaps color. Without the exemplar's Definition to open our eyes to her much wider range of the notion of contrast, we could use her Criterion but would still miss seeing most of the pictures she sees (those of contrasting shapes, textures, contents, and so on). Or, we could have somewhat the same notion as the photographer, that is, that contrast can be seen in many different forms, but think of it simply as a "difference" in those forms, rather than as a *"marked* difference." Without the exemplar's qualifying "marked," we are likely to consider possible photographs based on *slight* differences, differences that the exemplar would probably have ignored as not being worthy of a photograph (not offering a *marked* difference). Again, if your intention is to replicate the exemplar's ability, you need to operate out of the *exemplar's* Definition of the Criterion.

As we know, Lenny's Criterion in focus in the context of maintaining his diet is that it is "working." When we asked him what "working" means, he defined it as "My blood is regulated and consistent":

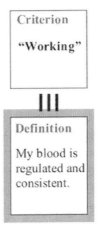

His Definition is very much in line with what is suggested by the Criterion; the Definition describes something that is ongoing, rather than an event or end point. And, again, that matters. Suppose instead that the experience you are evaluating as "working" has the quality of an event or end point, such as "My blood numbers are perfect," "My blood is controlled," or "I'm free of any symptoms." These experiences are much more likely to generate negative evaluations. The normal ebbs and flows of life, behavior, the weather and blood chemistry ensure that your blood numbers will fluctuate, and that there will be moments when you are not feeling just as you would like. Each of these fluctuations and off moments becomes an instance of the diet not working. And after enough instances of "it's not working," it becomes tempting to abandon the effort. The dynamic is the same as that of someone on a weight-loss diet who is evaluating whether or not he is "slim." The answer is *NO* until he is slim. If it will take a year to get there, that is a year's worth of *NO*. That is a lot for anyone to endure, and can quickly become dispiriting.

In contrast, the experience on which Lenny focuses his attention—"my blood is regulated and consistent"—suggests that he is monitoring and adjusting a range within which he wants to keep his blood. Even with the vagaries of life and blood chemistry, this means that most of the time his Criterion will be satisfied. Indeed, his blood varying provides him the opportunity to have the experience he wants (satisfy his Criterion) by giving him occasions to take steps to regulate his blood back to within the acceptable range. Lenny's particular Definition of "working" gives him a lot of ongoing *YESes*, and this naturally reinforces his efforts and supports him in maintaining his diet.

Evidence of Fulfillment

> In the combative 60s, during an interview with rock musician Frank Zappa, talk show host Joe Pyne (who had a wooden leg) smugly said to Zappa, "I see you have long hair. You must be a girl." Zappa coolly replied, "I see you have a wooden leg. You must be a table."

Suppose that you are hammering a nail into a board. Your goal is to hammer that nail until it is flush with the surface of the board, that is, until the head of the nail is at the same level as the surface of the board. The Criterion is "flush," and the Definition is "head at the same level as the surface of the board." Now, how do you know when to stop pounding on that nail head? The answer seems so obvious as to not be worth asking: clearly, you stop when you see that the head of the nail is at the same level as the surface of the board. But suppose you are blind. Now, how do you know when the nail head is flush? The Criterion and its Definition remain the same, but seeing the nail head at the same level as the surface of the board can no longer serve as evidence that the nail is flush. Instead, perhaps you feel with your fingers that the top of the nail head is at the same level as the surface of the board. Or you hear the sound suddenly shift from a metallic clang to a dull thump when the nail is struck. Or you feel a heavy reverberation through your arm and body when the hammer finally hits the nail all the way into the board. (These examples are not inventions. Professional house framers are often already looking at the next nail they will place while they continue to hammer in the current nail. They know by sound and feel when it is flush.)

Similarly, how do you know when the dishes are clean? What is your evidence? Do you look for food or spots? Or perhaps you run your hand over their surfaces, feeling for grease. Or perhaps simply being told they have been washed is sufficient. How do you know when a peach is ripe? By the amount of green relative to the reds and oranges? Or do you squeeze it to feel how much "give" it has? Or smell it? Or maybe it is the sign over the bin that says the fruit is ripe? We understand that some years ago the Canadian telephone company offered a telephone that few people wanted. Customers considered the phone to be "cheaply made." The phone company discovered that this impression was the result of the telephone's light weight. They had assumed that the light weight would be seen as something positive, a benefit of advanced technology. To the customers, however, being both plastic and light was evidence of "cheap goods." The phone company responded by adding lead weights to the telephone, and immediately people began buying it.

If we want our Criterion met (which we do), then we need a basis for knowing when that has happened (or is happening, if it is an ongoing Criterion). That "when" is specified by the Evidence of Fulfillment:

Evidence of Fulfillment is what must be seen, heard, and/or felt to know that a Criterion is being met.[22]

---

[22] For the sake of simplicity, we usually omit "taste" and "smell" when talking about the sensory systems. But of course they are always a part of our ongoing experience and, for certain Criteria, may also be essential Evidence.

Unlike Criteria and Definitions, which tend to be expressed as abstractions, the Evidence is described in terms of sensory experience. That is, associated with each of your Criteria are particular visual, auditory and kinesthetic experiences that—for you—mean your Criterion is satisfied (fulfilled, there, happening, etc.). Of course, all of your sensory systems are operating all the time (even when you sleep). This is more sensory experience than you can attend to in consciousness. So, as you move from context to context, you attend to only certain aspects of your sensory experience, to those aspects you have learned are meaningful with respect to the Criterion you currently have in focus.

In our hammering example, for instance, the novice carpenter hears the same sounds and feels the same reverberations in his arm that an expert carpenter hears and feels, but they do not mean to him that the nail is flush. He has not yet learned to connect those experiences with the Criterion of "flush." Instead, he relies on seeing the surface of the nail head matching the board surface as evidence that the nail is flush. Out of the richness of sensory experiences available to him at that time, he is attending to what he sees. That is how he will know that the nail is "flush." And as the example of the professional carpenter shows, it is just one of many ways to know that.

Our sensory experiences are constantly shifting with the infinite subtle variations of the moment. It would be impossible to specify everything that a person is experiencing at the sensory level in connection with their Criterion. What is possible, however, is to discover what sensory experiences *must* be there for that person to accept that his Criterion is met.

The Range of Evidence

In the examples of Evidence we have considered so far, what "must be there" has been limited to what the person sees, hears and feels with his senses. But we can also represent images, sounds and feelings in imagination. All of us see, hear and feel things on the "inside," as well as the "outside." So, in addition to actually seeing your mother, hearing her speak to you, feeling her hand stroke your head and smelling her scent, you can also imagine seeing her delight, hearing her gasp and feeling the hug she will give you when you tell her some good news. And these internally generated experiences can be as meaningful and compelling as anything we perceive through our senses.

Evidence for a particular Criterion is not determined by what the Criterion is. It is determined by who is using it. What you consider Evidence of "understanding," or "success," or a "good idea" depends upon what life has taught you are reliable indicators of those—or any— Criterion. Some of that teaching comes directly from others, of course, as when a father tells his son, "You will know you are a success when people say they are better off for having known you." Even then, however, the son will refine this Evidence and make it his own through his experiences of trying to live according to that Criterion. For instance, he may come to know that he is a success only when a certain percentage (one, some, most, all?) of people express they are better off for knowing him; or he may discover that there are certain ways people say they are better off that are sincere and matter, and others that are not to be credited; or he may discover that people have ways of expressing it without having to say it directly. However it comes about, through the course of our lives we establish sets of experiences that constitute Evidence of Fulfillment for each of our criteria.

Living on the same planet, sharing the same language, sharing the same culture, and even sharing the same Criterion do not guarantee that you and another person will also share the same Evidence. One of the authors called in a plumber to fix the bathtub, which was taking 20 minutes to empty. The plumber filled the tub with water and opened the drain. The usual gurgling began as the water trickled down the drain, and after a few seconds the plumber announced, "It seems to be working just fine." When the author pointed out that the water level in the tub was hardly dropping, the plumber explained, "Listen, you hear that sound the drain is making? That's what it sounds like when it's draining properly." And he was not kidding. And of course, we are never kidding about our Evidence. It is the basis for knowing and, so, not something to be trifled with, nor is it easily abandoned. If the "threshold" of Evidence is crossed—that is, the sights, sounds and sensations that matter are "there"—then the Criterion is satisfied. And so are we.

Threshold

So far we have been talking about Evidence as though it is always a "satisfied/not satisfied" proposition. And of course, sometimes it is. If you are hammering in a nail, it is either flush or it is not. Similarly, if the way you know that you are having a good workout is "I'm doing more repetitions than I did during my last workout," then you are either doing more repetitions or you are not. But the richness and complexity of human experience does not always (rarely, we would say) make it reducible to such clearly defined Evidence. Often there is a range of experience that will satisfy a Criterion.

In some cases a person will need to have "enough" of a particular experience in order to cross the subjective threshold between "Criterion not satisfied" and "Criterion satisfied." An example is that of testing for a good workout using the Evidence, "I'm sweating." Where is the threshold between "sweating" and "not sweating?" It will vary depending upon the individual. For some of us a thin film of dampness is "sweating," and for others you aren't sweating until your shirt is sopping and water is pooling at your feet.

Threshold may also be reached when one experiences *enough* of the set of experiences that they consider Evidence. For instance, someone asked how she knows her workout is good may say, "When I'm doing more repetitions than I did during my last workout is one way. Also, sometimes I can tell because my muscles are sore the next day. And it could even be that people are telling me I'm looking fit." In this case, having any one of these experiences can be enough to cross the threshold of Criterion satisfaction. And, of course, upon gathering more information from this exemplar we may discover that experiencing any one of these assorted experiences is not enough, but that if two or more are in evidence, her Criterion is satisfied.

Evidence and Modeling Abilities

As modelers, our goal is not to capture every detail of the exemplar's experience; our goal is to capture the structure that generates those details. Criteria are an essential element of that structure. But they are also abstractions that cover a lot of possible ground. That experiential ground becomes a lot firmer when we add the Definition. Still, when modeling, we want to be sure that our interpretation of those experiences—in terms of seeing, hearing and feeling—is the same as the exemplar's. We want what we attend and respond to—the Evidence—to match that of our exemplar.

Evidence serves as much more than an experiential checkered flag, letting the exemplar know that the race to satisfy his Criterion has been won. The moment the exemplar enters the context in which he manifests his ability, his Evidence establishes what specific sensory aspects of his experience he will be attending to in order to satisfy his Criterion. When, for instance, the professional house framer picks up his hammer he is looking at the nail heads relative to the surface of the board, listening to the ring of the nail when it is struck, and feeling the reverberations of each strike. If we want to emulate an expert framer's ability to hammer nails, these are the sensory representations we will need to attend to as well.

Evidence always comes relatively specified. No matter what your exemplar describes as his Evidence, it can always be made more specific. For instance, take the person whose Evidence that he is attractive to others is, "I can see that the other person is enjoying being with me." We can make him be more specific about just what he is seeing at that moment, and perhaps he reveals that the other person is "smiling and laughing." But of course, this can be made more specific as well: "The corners of the person's mouth are pulled back toward his ears, I can see at least some of his teeth, and wrinkles appear in the corner of his eyes."

So, when is enough specification, enough? As we discussed in the Essay on Getting Started, you are at a sufficient level of specificity when you can do what your exemplar does. A model is a way of describing the structure of the exemplar's experience so as to give you access to the same experience. And so, in this case, the Evidence is sufficiently specified when you can access the same kinds of representations as your exemplar. For most of us, "I can see that the other person is enjoying being with me," is probably specific enough for us to use that as our own Evidence. But perhaps you have, in the past, had difficulty recognizing when people are enjoying being with you. In that case you need to go further, specifying that they will be "smiling and laughing," while going as far as, "the corners of the person's mouth are pulled back toward his ears, etc." is more than you need.

This relative specificity is nicely illustrated by Lenny's Evidence of Fulfillment. He knows that his diet is "working" when "I feel energetic, and I'm conscious and have clarity of mind":

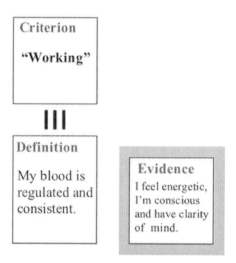

Obviously, "I feel energetic, I'm conscious and have clarity of mind" could all be further specified, detailing their kinesthetic, visual, and auditory nuances. Is this necessary? In the case of "feel energetic" and "clarity of mind," probably not. Most of us know what it is to have those experiences. What he is referring to with "I'm conscious," is not so clear. When we had him specify further, he explained that by "conscious" he means he is aware of, and responsive to, what is going on around him.

Now this description is something we can readily relate to in our own experience and, so, we probably do not need to specify it any further.[23]

In terms of structure, what jumps out at us is that Lenny is using Evidence that is ongoing and internal. This is in marked contrast to the Evidence used by many diabetics, which comes in the form of a read-out from "sticks" (daily self-administered blood tests). If the read-out number is outside a certain range, the diet or drug regimen is askew and needs correction. These folks are using evidence that is periodic and external. Depending upon the daily sticks for feedback about the state of their blood may lead them to be unaware of, ignore or explain away subtle shifts in how they are feeling. This may result in their enduring bigger swings in blood sugar—and a bumpier quality of experience—than Lenny experiences. His ongoing and internal Evidence attunes him to the subtle ebbs and flows of his internal state.

The fact that his Evidence is internally generated is, itself, significant. He is not dependent upon the external world to know how he is. Suppose instead that he knew his diet was working when "people tell me I'm looking great." He could make some dangerously inappropriate judgments about how his diet is working just because some people won't notice that he looks great (or terrible), or notice but not think to mention it, or tell him he looks great (not wanting to alarm him because he, in fact, looks terrible), and so on.

It is also significant in terms of Lenny's ability to maintain his diet that his Evidence is about the quality of his experience, rather than, say, the read-out on a glucometer. The diet is not about controlling diabetes. Of course, that is why he is on the diet, and what is happening through being on it, but that is not where his attention is. Lenny's Evidence for "working" means that for him the diet is about maintaining the quality of his

---

[23] Of course, when it comes time to take on the model for an ability you may discover an element that you thought you understood during elicitation, but for which you actually need more specification. This simply means that you need to gather the additional information from your exemplar. There is no absolute way to know for sure before you do your modeling just exactly what you will need. The process of "stepping in," however, will help you discover these necessary elements during the process of elicitation. These issues are taken up in more detail in the essays on Elegance and Acquisition.

experience. If the diet was (subjectively) about controlling the diabetes, then when it appeared to be controlled there would be a temptation to become lax in following the diet: "The diabetes is under control—I can let go." The quality of Lenny's experience, however, is always shifting and ever-present, and so supports his maintaining the diet by giving him relatively frequent feedback of the need to do—or not do—something.

Enabling Cause-Effect

> "Dreaming won't get you to Damascus, sir, but discipline will."
>
> — Maj. Allenby advises Prince Faisal in
> "Lawrence of Arabia"

While our countless equivalence relationships identify what "things" in our experience *are* ("this is that"), our equally countless causal relationships specify how "things" affect each other: "this causes that." If you think of equivalence relationships as the threads of your experience, then causal relationships are the weaving of those threads. And together they create the fabric of your reality.

Because a Criterion is, by definition, something important to satisfy or fulfill, those situations in life to which it is applied will generate many causal connections. For instance, if it is important to you to be "understood," your life experiences may have taught you that you need to express yourself with a shared vocabulary in order to be understood. Or you may have discovered along the way that one needs to organize ideas hierarchically in order to be understood, or that one must wait until people are in a sufficiently receptive mood in order to understand you, or that you need to believe in what you are saying in order to be understood, and so on. In short, the need to satisfy a Criterion makes it very likely that you have made causal connections between that Criterion and the circumstances or events that you consider will lead to it being satisfied.

In general, we acquire causal beliefs about what must be true, what we must do, or what must happen in order for the Criterion to be satisfied. For example:

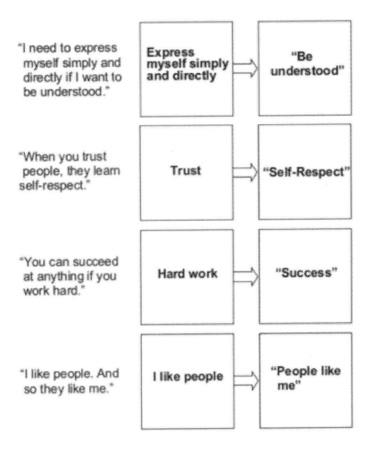

If we consider the Criterion as our destination, then the cause-effects map our route. They are our beliefs about the way to get us to the destination. The way to get people to have "self-respect" is via "trusting" them. The road to "accomplishing anything" is paved with "hard work." And "people will like you" if you take the path of "liking people." The impact of these cause-effects is to instruct or organize our thinking and behavior along certain lines. The person who considers self-respect important *and* believes "When you trust people, they learn self-respect"

will endeavor to trust others; the person who wants to accomplish something *and* believes "You can accomplish anything if you work hard" will endeavor to work hard, and so on.

Of course, a cause-effect does not tell us what *will* happen, but instead what the person *believes* will happen. It is not the case that trusting someone will necessarily foster self-respect in that particular person. There are countless variables operating in any one interaction; some of these variables have their origin in the personal psychologies of those involved and others have their origin in the external circumstances of the moment. What that cause-effect does reveal, however, is what is guiding this person's perceptions, thoughts, and behavior when he is trying to foster self-respect: in this case, "trust the person." A person's cause-effects reveal what he believes enables the satisfaction or fulfillment of his Criterion. We term these causal connections, "Enabling Cause-Effects":

> **Enabling Cause-Effects specify the conditions believed necessary to satisfy the Criterion.**

The range of what can serve as an Enabling Cause-Effect is as broad as experience itself. It can be anything from the grandest abstraction ("Philosophy makes possible self-respect"), to the humblest particular ("Telling someone that they are nicely dressed leads to self-respect"). Despite the enormous difference in specificity between "philosophy" and "tell him he is nicely dressed," in both instances we are being told on what this person is focusing his attention and behavior *in order to* satisfy his Criterion.

Enabling Cause-Effect and Modeling Abilities

Earlier we likened the structure of experience to the weaving of fabric. The threads are our Criteria, and the weaving together of those threads are our Cause-Effects. If we want to reproduce a particular tapestry—as we do when we model an exemplar—it is essential to have the correct threads. But it is also essential to know how to correctly weave those threads together. In modeling, we want to know not only what our exemplar considers important, but also what they believe they need to do to make what is important a reality. We want to know their cause-effects.

If we were reproducing an actual fabric it would be tedious to individually specify each and every intertwining thread as we recreate the whole piece. It is more efficient to identify the patterns of how the threads are woven. Similarly, we do not want to identify every twist and turn in our exemplar's thinking and experience. Rather, we want to discover the patterns that govern how those twists and turns are taken. Granted, what we weave from using these patterns will not be an exact reproduction of the exemplar's experience. To do that we would, in fact, have to duplicate every thread and every intertwining.

There are several good reasons for not taking that exhaustive approach and instead relying on the underlying, formative patterns. The first is that the tremendous complexity of human experience would make specifying every cause-effect an impossible task. The second reason is that it is not necessary to specify everything. Our ultimate goal in modeling the exemplar is to be able to attain the same kinds of outcomes he attains; it is not to say and do exactly the same things the exemplar would say and do. So, we do not need to know everything.

The third reason is that, even if we could reproduce all of the exemplar's cause-effects (and criteria), we would be ill advised to do so. It is not the intention of modeling to churn out duplicate people, as if we were churning out Ken and Barbie dolls. Instead, the intention is to make new experiential structures available so that anyone (who wants to) can express who she or he is *through* those structures. The model brings only a structure; and this structure can only be given life through the unique qualities of the person using the model. Inevitably, the nuances of expression and behavior characteristic of the modeler manifesting an ability will be somewhat different from those of the exemplar. Because of this, each person who reproduces the exemplar's ability is also bringing something *new* into the world.

So, what we want to discover from our exemplar are those cause-effects that are essential, those that are most responsible for organizing the exemplar's experience and behavior when trying to satisfy his Criterion.

For Lenny, this essential Enabling Cause-Effect is, "You have to maintain the focus and discipline if you want the diet to work":

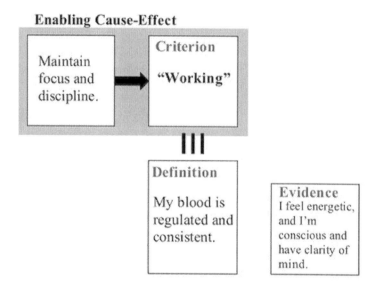

At first glance, the Enabling Cause-Effect seems obvious. We might be tempted to consider this cause-effect trivial because everyone already knows that you have to follow a diet in order to reap its benefits. But does everyone *believe* that? Remember, when we speak of "believing" here, we are talking about those equivalence and causal relationships on which our experience is based, and that drive our behavior. That is, they are *real* or *true* for us. We can know, as *information*, that one has to follow a diet to gain its benefits without that cause-effect being real for us. And because it *is* simply information, it has little or no effect on our behavior.[24]

Clearly, for Lenny, the causal connection between "maintaining focus and discipline" and the diet "working" is not merely an idea or imposed rule; it is real and true for him. It is also clear that many people trying to maintain a diet regimen (or any regimen, for that matter) do not have this same Enabling Cause-Effect operating as a belief. The consequence is both

---

[24] Even believing that it is something you *should* believe is not the same as actually believing it. We will explore this further in the essay on Acquisition.

subtle and significant. Without this belief, the cause (the agent of change) is not considered to be the person, but the diet itself. It is the diet that *causes* the blood sugar to stabilize (or weight to be lost, or increased muscle mass, or better energy). And so, when the person finds that he is not meeting his intended goal (satisfying his Criterion), it is easy and natural to search for another diet, "one that will work." For Lenny, however, discovering that his diet is not "working" means that *he* has not been adequately maintaining focus and discipline, and that he must resume that focus and discipline in order to get the diet working again.[25]

If all that sounds like a lot of work for Lenny, well, it is. To know what keeps him—or anyone—pursuing his Criterion despite the effort required to do that, we turn to the Motivating Cause-Effect.

Motivating Cause-Effect

> The most important motive for work in school and in life is pleasure in work, pleasure in its result, and the knowledge of the value of the result to the community.
>
> — Albert Einstein

An experience to which all of us can personally attest is that of intending to do something... and yet not doing it. Rusting exercise equipment, dusty piano keys, stacks of unread books, overgrown gardens, snow drifts of unpaid bills, fading voices of friends, attractive people allowed to walk

---

[25] Remember that Lenny has personal experience that the diet actually works for him. There are countless diets, but even fierce focus and discipline will be of no benefit if the diet itself cannot be used to reach your goals, whether these are the regulation of blood sugar, losing weight, building muscle, getting healthy, etc. A diet of ice cream isn't going to do Lenny any good, no matter how focused and disciplined he is. A further consideration is that a change of eating, of whatever type, can often have a beneficial effect initially; so short-term benefits cannot be taken to guarantee long-term benefits.

away, swallowed insults, poor negotiations, missed investments, unwritten books... all mutely shake their fingers at us in reproach.

And that's okay. The fact is that none of us has enough time and energy to make everything equally important. Unavoidably, we attend to fulfilling some goals and leave others waiting in the wings. We want to give those behavioral ingénues their chance out on stage, but it is already crowded with the dancers we are familiar with. We suspect that those yet to be tried would be wonderful, and so *should* be given a chance to dance. And when we don't give them that chance, we think we are being reluctant, or fearful, or slothful, that we must be avoiding the unpleasantness of work, of risk, of unfamiliarity. Nevertheless, every day we *do* tackle many things that are difficult, unpleasant, or unfamiliar. We may even take on an onerous task with eagerness and determination, apparently ignoring the effort it demands. How does that happen?

Think of something you did recently despite the fact that it was difficult or unpleasant. Now consider, Why did you do it? You undoubtedly had "a reason," one that was compelling enough to overcome your reluctance to do whatever it was that you did. Recently, one of the authors felt he had to say no to a project that he had previously agreed to do. He knew he would disappoint his colleagues greatly, knew it would be a very unpleasant interaction, and really did not want to do it. But he nevertheless did do it. What motivated him to tell the awful truth? "It was a matter of self-respect. I didn't feel I could respect myself if I didn't do what I thought was right for me." For him, "self-respect" was of fundamental importance. Indeed, making sure that he maintained his self-respect was of *greater* importance than avoiding the unpleasantness of disappointing his colleagues.

Similarly, when you look at your own example of choosing to do something despite its otherwise daunting difficulties, you will probably recognize that the reason that moved you to action expressed something whose importance was bigger or greater than avoiding the unpleasantness of whatever it was that you were facing. That reason that moved you probably expressed or related to some aspect of who you *are* at a fundamental level and, so, was naturally compelling. That compelling reason was the motivating half of what we call the Motivating Cause-Effect:

Motivating Cause-Effects specify "larger" criteria that are fulfilled when the Criterion in Focus is fulfilled.

In a Motivating Cause-Effect, the fulfillment of the Criterion in focus in a particular context contributes or leads to the fulfillment of an even "larger" and often intrinsically important criterion. And so the need or desire to fulfill the larger criterion *motivates* the person to pursue satisfying the Criterion in the present situation. For instance, in the author's example of backing out of a project, his Motivating Cause-Effect was, "It is necessary to be honest with myself and others in order to respect myself." And so he will endeavor to be honest *in order to* respect himself (or, to put it the other way, his desire to respect himself motivates him to be honest):

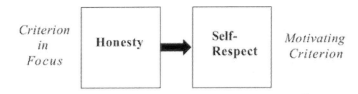

Of course, both sides of the Motivating Cause-Effect are criteria, but they serve different functions. The Criterion in Focus establishes what is essential to evaluate and fulfill when in a *specific* context ("honesty," in the example of the author speaking with his colleagues). The motivating criterion is what is essential to fulfill across *most or all contexts* (which is the reason we often think of it as being a *larger* or *intrinsic* criterion). For the author, "self-respect" is essential not only when he is interacting with his colleagues, but also when exploring the depths of his humanity, vying for parking spaces, and on and on. Intrinsically motivating criteria are often descriptive of personal identity, and are often subjectively experienced as "deeper," "higher," "what it's all about" or "more me" than are context-specific Criteria. (Indeed, motivating criteria may very well be criteria that go to the very core of who you are: self-concept, identity, personality, soul.) To not fulfill—let alone violate—such criteria is extremely unpleasant.

Of course, it is not the case that the motivating criterion is always something from the level of personal identity. For instance, consider a person who, when weeding her garden, believes it important to "do a thorough job, getting all the roots out, so you will have less work in the future" (THOROUGH NOW → LESS WORK IN THE FUTURE). Yes, she does want to avoid work in the future, and so is being thorough in weeding in the present. But this does not mean that "avoiding work in the future" is something that goes to the very heart of who she. (Though, it could!)

Sometimes the Criterion in focus may also be the motivating criterion. That is, the criterion that person wants to satisfy in the present context is also a criterion that is of fundamental importance to who she is. Take as an example a woman for whom "caring" is *intrinsically* important, and she is sitting up with a friend whose father has just died. The focus of her attention is on caring for her friend. She is not caring in order to help her friend evolve, or to grow as a person herself, or bring peace to the world. She needs no additional motivation to care for her friend; caring is in and of itself intrinsically motivating for her.

Though "motivating criteria" sound like what we commonly think of as "values," they are not. Values are criteria that we apply across most or all contexts. Of course, as we have seen above, it may be that an individual's motivating criterion *is* a value (a criterion applied across all contexts). But motivating criteria can also be less lofty, like the gardener who wants "Less work in the future"; an essential criterion when gardening, but not across all contexts. In other words, the weeder in our example can be motivated by the promise of less work in the future *without* "less future work" being one of her values. It does seem to be true, however, that motivating criteria that are also values tend to be more compelling than those that are not.[26]

---

[26] Perhaps the motivating power of values comes from the fact that, because they touch on a great many aspects of our lives, the consequences of fulfilling or not fulfilling them are magnified.

Motivating Cause-Effect and Modeling Abilities

The essential cause-effects are those that are most responsible for organizing the exemplar's thinking and behavior in relation to satisfying his Criterion. The power of these cause-effects—indeed, the power of all beliefs—resides in their ability to organize an enormous set of responses at every level of our experience.

The organizing significance of Motivating Cause-Effects is obvious: they get us to *do*. Unless you have the motivation to actually engage in the ability you are modeling, you are not likely to acquire it, even if you can access its structure in yourself. Being capable is not the same thing as being willing; both are necessary for an ability to manifest itself.

For Lenny, maintaining the focus and discipline required by his diet, as well as paying daily attention to whether or not it is working, is no picnic. Taking the medication would be easier. What compels him to stick to his diet? When we asked him why it is important that his diet be "working," he explained, "So I can have the life I want to have, rather than the one I don't want to have":

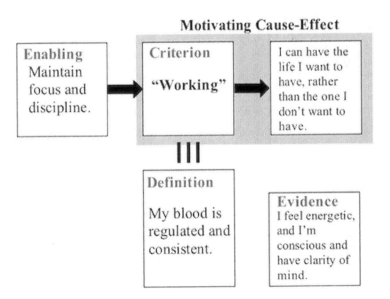

Motivating Cause-Effect

| Enabling
Maintain focus and discipline. | Criterion

"Working" | I can have the life I want to have, rather than the one I don't want to have. |

| Definition

My blood is regulated and consistent. | Evidence
I feel energetic, and I'm conscious and have clarity of mind. |

In most present moments, Lenny is probably just fine. He feels energetic, conscious and clear; he feels good. It is also in the present that a pint of ice cream looks good. For most of us, feeling okay in the present and wanting the ice cream can lead to thoughts such as, "I'm feeling good, so maybe I don't need to be so careful today. And so what if I eat this ice cream now? It's just this once; no real big deal. And I deserve a little pleasure." As long as the significance of eating the ice cream is evaluated in the time frame of the present, it is probably going to get eaten.

But of course, it is in the present that we are also choosing the future. Lenny's Motivating Cause-Effect makes a direct connection between the choices he makes in the present regarding "maintaining the focus and discipline" needed to keep his diet "working" and his future. We all know—as information—that following the diet will be good for us, exercising will be good for us, smoking will be bad for us, and so on. But Lenny believes this; the experience of the causal connection between the working of his diet and his future is real to him. And because of that, when he considers straying from the diet (either because it is a burden in the moment, or because that moment is offering something tempting), the experienced connection between the present and the future helps take him out of the present. The choices of the present are extremely compelling. By adding a real sense of the future, the present compulsion is blunted and Lenny can choose based on a perspective that is driven by the needs of the future, rather than only the desires of the present.

Furthermore, Lenny's Motivating Cause-Effect includes both the future he wants and the future he wants to avoid. This creates the subjective experience of moving toward the future he wants when his diet is working, and moving toward the future he does not want when his diet is not working. As we all know from our own experiences, avoiding unpleasantness is very motivating. For most of us, avoiding an unpleasant future is more immediately compelling than is moving toward a pleasant future.

But then why have both? Why not simply have a cause-effect between the diet working and avoiding the unpleasant future? The reason is that continually having to avoid future unpleasantness can itself become oppressively unpleasant *in the present*. This is what Lenny would be facing many times each day if he represented only the future he wants to avoid. If you try this out in your own experience you will probably find that you quickly get to the point of wanting to avoid (deny) the whole question of what you ought to be doing in the present—"To hell with the whole thing"—and give up on the diet. Having a future to avoid is very motivating, but having only a future to avoid can become demotivating. By holding a cause-effect relationship between his diet working and both possible futures, Lenny has the impetus of both avoiding the unwanted future and of moving in the direction of the wanted future.

Supporting Beliefs

As we first noted in the section on "Criteria," the exemplar will have many other beliefs operating besides the ones that emerge directly from the Criterion in Focus. The beliefs that connect to the Criterion in Focus (Definition, Evidence, Enabling and Motivating Cause-Effects) are essential to manifesting the ability, which is why we capture them in the Belief Template. However, this does not mean that all other beliefs are inconsequential. They are certainly of some consequence to the exemplar. They contribute in many subtle ways to her perceptions, choices, experience and behavior when manifesting her ability. And, while these beliefs may not be essential to the structure that makes that ability possible, some of them may still be helpful to us in taking on and manifesting that ability. We call these, "Supporting Beliefs":

> **Supporting Beliefs are beliefs that, though not part of the Belief Template, support the exemplar's expression of the ability.**

Unlike the Criterion and its Belief Template, we do not go hunting for Supporting Beliefs. As we have said, if you go hunting for beliefs, you will find them. Lots of them. So instead we notice when Supporting Beliefs pop up. Once in a while a particular belief jumps out of the crowd of background equivalences and cause-effects. Because we are not looking for every member of the crowd, when one suddenly stands out, there is good reason to take notice of it and consider how significant it is to the exemplar's ability. One reason these beliefs tend to stand out is that they often come neatly packaged in a clear and assertive statement, much like an epigram ("Look before you leap!" "He who hesitates is lost!").

For example, in one of our modeling seminars, Dee was modeling "Authentic and Respectful Straight-Talking." The Belief Template was:

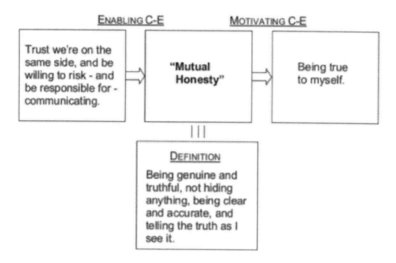

Some of the Supporting Beliefs were (notice how these statements take the form or tone of an epigram):

"Conversation is catalytic in nature."

"Honesty has more value than comfort."

"We are all human and are all doing our best."

"I love people. They deserve to be able to talk about things. It's a gift to them."

None of these are found in the Belief Template for "authentic and respectful straight-talking," and none of them is necessarily needed in order to use that Belief Template. But when you imagine using it while *also* believing any or all of the Supporting Beliefs, you will discover that they significantly affect both the quality of your experience and your ease in manifesting the ability.

In Lenny's case, his Supporting Beliefs included:

> "Insulin is really the enemy. It is more damaging than it
> is good, in excess amounts."

> "I am a diabetic and I'm a diabetic for the rest of my life."

> "The [dieting] system only exists because I remember that it
> does, so I pay attention to it."

> "Now I don't have anyone to rely on except myself."

For Lenny, these Supporting Beliefs are not bells and whistles that have been tacked onto his ability to maintain a diet. They are part and parcel of the whole experiential package involved in regulating his blood sugar. You can operate out of the essential equivalences and cause-effects in Lenny's Belief Template without believing that "insulin is the enemy," or that "I'm a diabetic for life." But the possible usefulness of any of his Supporting Beliefs becomes immediately evident when you step into the context of being a diabetic who wants to stick to a diet, and add those Supporting Beliefs into your experience.

Explicitly knowing your exemplar's Supporting Beliefs can be useful in two ways. The first is that you can make those beliefs something you believe as well (of course, drawing upon your own life experiences to make them real for you; see the Essay on Acquisition). They work for your exemplar, and so they may do the same for you, giving your ability greater depth and making it more robust from the outset.

Second, knowing your exemplar's Supporting Beliefs can be useful when you are having difficulty taking on the Array. Checking whether any of the Supporting Beliefs are difficult for you to embrace (or even just accept) can reveal aspects of the ability and its Array that bump up against aspects of who you are. If so, then at least you will know what you need to accommodate in yourself in order to have full access to the ability. (Again, see Acquisition for some guidance in making that accommodation.)

* * *

Of course, beliefs are not "things," like bricks and mortar are things. In order to have a presence and impact, beliefs must be manifested through some kind of action. This action can be in the form of external behaviors, as when believing "If you treat others with kindness, they will learn kindness" leads you to act with kindness. Beliefs can also be manifested in internal actions, in the form of patterns of processing information, as when believing "to be successful, I have to know what I really want" leads you to think deeply and thoroughly about your desires. Clearly, exemplars of an ability have patterns of internal processes and external behaviors that give effective expression to their beliefs. These patterns are their Strategies, which we explore in the next Essay.

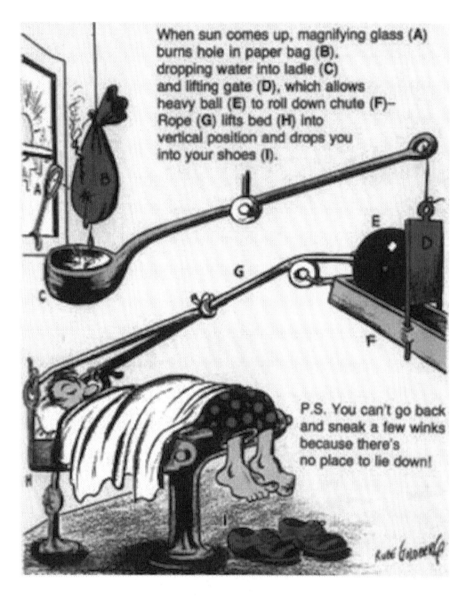

Rube Goldberg TM & © of Rube Goldberg, Inc.
Distributed by United Feature Syndicate, Inc.

Elements of the Experiential Array

Essay 9

Strategies

It is through our Strategies that what we know, believe and intend are put into action. A Strategy is made up of two parts: the "Test"—which is the exemplar evaluating her Criterion—and the "Operations"—which are the internal processes and external behaviors the exemplar engages in to satisfy the Test (Criterion). Because of the inherent complexity of most Strategies, we use narrative description to capture them in a form that is sufficiently rich to be useful.

For 55 years Pulitzer Prize winning cartoonist Rube Goldberg delighted millions of newspaper readers with his cartoons depicting innovative ways to accomplish simple tasks using strategies that were relentlessly logical and, at the same time, fabulously—and hilariously—complex.

It was apparent to Rube Goldberg that when human beings are faced with something to do, they can generally be counted on to find a way to accomplish it in a way that requires far more effort than is really needed. In his cartoons we see reflected not only our penchant for making the simple unnecessarily complex, but also the precariousness of our strategies. They are often so obviously dependent upon the world cooperating—indeed, collaborating—that the desired outcome is not at all assured. In the cartoon above, the man sleeps secure in his faith that the sun will shine through his window, initiating the sequence of events that will get him out of bed. If it is a cloudy morning, however, his elaborate strategy is useless.

Still, we need strategies. We need to get out of bed, engage an audience, sort priorities, make financial decisions, select birthday gifts, plan meals, organize our day's work, find necessary information, deliver bad news to the boss, get the kids to clean their rooms, find out what is really going on with our mates, exercise, correctly spell a word, choose wisely from the menu, and come up with solutions to vexing problems. These are all things we do. For the most part, we do them without resorting to magnifying glasses and balanced bowling balls. Instead, we do a lot of thinking about, and interacting with, the world.

This thinking and interacting is not random, of course. The thinking and interacting we do to get out of bed on time are specific to that specific purpose; it involves different considerations and different behaviors than selecting a birthday gift for a friend or spelling a word correctly. When faced with a desired outcome, we gather information, sort perceptions and float ideas, we pose questions, make statements and push buttons, we twist images, chew words and check our feelings, all in service of attaining that outcome. That is, we employ a strategy. You may not be aware of all of the internal considerations and external actions that make up one of your strategies, but they are there, working to attain whatever your particular goal may be:

Strategies are sets and sequences of internal processes and external behaviors intended to attain particular outcomes.

All of us have numerous strategies for dealing with the countless small and large outcomes, goals and needs that flow through our daily lives. However, as Rube Goldberg's creations remind us, not all strategies are created equal. Some work better than others. People who are good at a particular ability—that is, they consistently attain the outcomes essential to manifesting their ability—are necessarily using effective strategies. How they think and interact works well in that context; that is, they are *exemplars* of that particular ability.

The T.O.T.E.

Like beliefs, strategies have an underlying structure. And, like beliefs, understanding that structure can help us capture an exemplar's strategy in a form that makes it more accessible. Much of the essential structure of strategies was described beautifully by Miller, Galanter and Pribram in their seminal book, *Plans and the Structure of Behavior*. The advent of cybernetics made it evident to Miller and his colleagues that the old stimulus-response model for behavior was inadequate; in particular, it neglected the significance of the feedback loop in governing experience and behavior. A feedback loop is operating whenever a change in the present state of a system precipitates responses throughout the system (that is, makes things happen) to bring it back to the desired state. A familiar example of this is the system loop between a thermostat and a cooler: when the temperature rises beyond a set point, the thermostat turns on the cooler; when the temperature drops back down to the set point, the thermostat turns off the cooler.

Miller et al captured this essential aspect of behavior in a model they called the T.O.T.E. The acronym stands for "Test Operate Test Exit," and was graphically represented as:

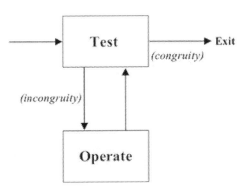

(after Miller, Galanter and Pribram, 1960)

This elegant diagram captures the essential distinctions and relationships fundamental to any strategy. [27] To begin with, the individual is Testing the congruity or incongruity of input. Specifically, what she is testing for is the congruence between her Criterion (desired experience) and the input (actual experience). When the test of the Criterion is satisfied (congruity), she is free to "exit" and move on to the next Criterion that needs to be satisfied. This "next Criterion" could, of course, be a re-testing of the one just satisfied, as when one is engaged in the iterative task of slicing a carrot into pieces of a certain thickness.

If, however, there is incongruence between the input and the Criterion, the person engages in a set of behaviors, called an Operation, in an attempt to satisfy the Criterion. As Miller et al put it, "The test phase can be regarded as any process for determining that the operational phase is appropriate." More simply, an Operation is a set of actions a person engages in order to satisfy a Criterion.

The criteria we test for may be unconscious or conscious, and they range from those concerning the most fundamental, organismic levels of response, such as maintaining blood saline concentration (avoiding pain, standing erect, locating a sound and so on), to the most abstract levels of experience, such as deciding what constitutes the meaning of life (or recognizing facial expressions, understanding words, evolving ideas and so on). Similarly, the range of Operational behaviors spans all functional levels of the organism: the Operation to bring blood saline concentration to normal may involve the behavior of drinking water, while the Operation to feel like a worthwhile person may involve the cognitive process of surveying the history of one's life for meaningful moments.

Nested TOTEs

Obviously it is never the case that we are engaging only one TOTE at a time. Our experiences and behaviors are the sum expression of countless tests and operations going on both simultaneously and sequentially,

---

[27] Miller, Galanter and Pribram define "Plan" as "...any hierarchical process in the organism that can control the order in which the sequence of operations is to be performed." This definition is not significantly different from our definition of Strategies as "...sets and sequences of internal computations and external behaviors intended to attain particular outcomes."

consciously and unconsciously, and at various functional levels. For instance, the slicing of carrots is made possible by the coordination of numerous sub-TOTEs that combine to make up the process of cutting itself. (e.g. "Is the knife where I want to cut?" "Is the knife cutting?" "Is the knife blade all the way through the carrot?") It is probably also the case that the slicing of the carrots is itself a sub-TOTE that contributes to the satisfaction of a larger, more inclusive TOTE. (e.g. "Is this enough carrots to feed the family?") Like Russian dolls, our experience and behavior are made up of TOTEs "nested" inside of TOTEs, which are themselves nested inside of other TOTEs, and so on. A diagram of a very few of the nesting TOTEs for slicing the carrot might look like this:

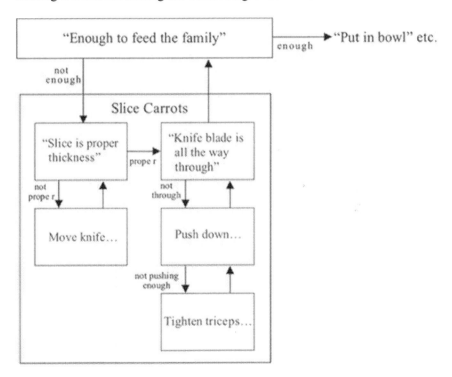

The TOTE also suggests the nested nature of Strategies. Strategies are the sum expression of many layers of TOTEs operating together, from autonomic regulation of body temperature to cutting carrots to preparing a presentation to abstract reasoning. Regardless of the Strategy level we choose to describe, there will undoubtedly be numerous other Strategies nested within it. Those nested strategies, working together as a system, *is* the Strategy we want to elicit from our exemplar. [28]

The TOTOTOTO...

In the examples we have considered so far, an unsatisfied Test triggers the Operations needed to satisfy it, after which the person "exits," moving on to the next TOTE. Often, however, rather than simply attain the goal set by the Criterion, a Strategy works to *maintain* the satisfaction of the Criterion. In this case, the person is not waiting until her Criterion is unsatisfied to engage her Operations. Instead, as soon as she is in the appropriate context, she is engaging those internal processes and external behaviors that support the satisfaction of her Criterion, and she continues using them as long as she is in that context. An example might be a therapist for whom "rapport" is important. From the very beginning of the therapy session she will engage in those behaviors that foster rapport. But she does not abandon those behaviors once she discovers, "Ah, I have achieved rapport!" Instead, the therapist continues to manifest those behaviors that support rapport, and test that she has rapport, throughout the session.

The TOTE and Strategies

The TOTE usefully points out the two fundamental functions of a Strategy—Testing and Operating—and shows how these functions relate to one another: the need to satisfy a Test initiates an Operation until the Test is satisfied.

Or to put it another way, what engages behavior—and keeps it engaged—is the desire or need to satisfy criteria. This is an essential point

---

[28] The notion of "nested Strategies" may seem familiar to you from our discussion of "sub-abilities" in Essay 2, Getting Started. A sub-ability will have its own Array—including the Strategy—nested within the "larger" Array of the ability. Thus, "Slicing a proper thickness" and "cutting all the way through" are both modelable sub-abilities of the ability to "Slice carrots," and "Pushing down" is a sub-ability of "cutting all the way through," and so on.

for understanding Strategies. Strategies are not simply about engaging in a set of internal processes and external behaviors. For three important reasons, those behaviors need to be in service of satisfying a specific (even if unconscious) Criterion:

- Without a Criterion, behavior lacks focus. The Criterion provides ongoing relevancy and an effectiveness check for our behaviors. (When slicing the carrot, knowing the desired thickness allows us to make adjustments in the knife position, rather than whacking away just anywhere on the carrot.)

- A Criterion is a description of what is wanted or desired, and so is naturally motivating. Because it is inherently pleasing to satisfy a Criterion (that is, to attain a goal), it helps ensure that we persist with the behaviors of the Strategy. (Having "enough to feed the family" may well carry us through the tedium of slicing all those carrots.)

- A Criterion lets us know when to stop operating and move on. Without the feedback provided by the Criterion, we may continue to run the behaviors of the Operation long past the point of usefulness. (Told simply to "slice carrots," we could end up knee deep in them when, in fact, only a cup of sliced carrots was "enough to feed the family.")

A Strategy, then, is made up of networks and nests of TOTEs. But how best to capture these often extensive and possibly complex relationships?

Narrative Strategies

The TOTE is useful as a conceptual tool, and is excellent for portraying a Strategy in which the Test and Operation are simple and small enough to be succinctly described. However, the vast majority of abilities that we would want to model involve the operation of whole sets of internal processes and external behaviors. We could reduce all of them to individual, succinct, nested TOTEs. But by the time we had them all described and tied together with input and exit arrows, we would have a plate of experiential spaghetti that no one could digest. In the example of slicing a carrot, for instance, we merely scratched the surface of "the ability to slice enough carrots," and we still generated a TOTE diagram of considerable complexity. What, then, would we end up with if we tried to use such diagrams to capture the Strategic complexity of, say, "the ability to negotiate consensus in groups"?

It can be argued that the TOTE (or some such diagrammatic representation) not only presents the content and the relationships, but also has the virtue of presenting it all at once, as a "picture." But unless such a diagram is relatively simple and made up of immediately known elements, it still must be "read," that is, deciphered sequentially. And that is when it becomes easy to get lost in its complexity. (For example, take a look at the flow chart of any corporation.)

Furthermore, the arrows in the TOTE suggest a sequential flow of events. But is this what really happens in our experience and behavior? Are our Strategies laid out like experiential Rube Goldberg constructions such that, once triggered, there follows a particular step-by-step sequence of events? Perhaps the answer is yes when dealing with very simple, very basic pieces of behavior, such as squinting to protect yourself from a sudden, bright light. But most human abilities—and certainly the vast majority of those we would want to model—are not so pure and simple.

And let's not forget the nested nature of TOTEs. Any of the actions that make up a Strategy will be made up of other constituent actions. And many of those nested TOTEs (or if you prefer, nested strategies, sub-routines, sub-abilities, etc.) may well be operating simultaneously. For example, grasping a cup involves the operation of dozens of simultaneous nested TOTEs governing the movement and coordination of eyes, posture, arms, hands and fingers, all of which combine to "create" the higher level action of "grasping the cup."

Obviously, there is no level of detailed description that can utterly capture any Strategy as it is "lived." (Any description is an abstraction— not a duplication—of an experience.) And even if we could, we would not want to because that sea of specification would quickly swamp our experience. How can we usefully capture the complex nesting of internal and external operations that make up a Strategy? The answer is, through narrative description.

By "narrative" we mean, "telling the story." In the context of describing the Strategy, we are simply capturing the natural language "story" of how the exemplar does what she does. One of the beautiful things about language is that a word or two can conjure up the worlds of experience connected to them. Language has built into it the cues for those "things" and "actions" that are relevant to the communication. For instance, "I keep slicing carrots into thin pieces until there is enough for the family," brings into our experience the relevant actors, actions and objects ("I" "slicing" "carrots" "family"). In addition, language puts them in relationship to one another ("I slice carrots for the family"). Language also provides modifiers that cue us to qualities of those things and of how they relate to one another ("I keep slicing carrots into thin pieces until there is enough for the family"). Each of these words matters in that each one brings with it a host of associations, nested TOTEs, filaments of connection, and nuances of meaning. Just the word, "slice," for instance, calls up a whole network of perceptions, associations and actions connected with the notion of "slicing," a network that is substantially different from those called into our experience by "chopping," "whacking" or even "cutting" carrots. "Slicing" conveys a tremendous amount of strategic information regarding what to do.

And, clearly, the depth and breadth of experience conveyed in a sentence of description will be exponentially greater than that of a single word. Narrative description, then, can be an efficient way to access the complex experiential associations you need in order to make an exemplar's Strategy come alive in your own experience.

The Test

A Strategy is a set of internal processes and external behaviors intended to satisfy a Criterion, and it is this "intention" to have that Criterion met which sets the Strategy into motion. The Criterion (as described by its Definition) establishes a goal; but of course you also need a way to know whether or not—or to what extent—that goal is met. And so you Test for the satisfaction of your Criterion. (This "knowing" is not necessarily conscious, as we discussed in the Essay on The Belief Template.)

Criteria and their Definitions tend to be abstractions. How can we test abstractions? We test them in experience, naturally, where abstractions take forms that we can see, hear and feel. And so a nail is "flush" when you see its head at the same level as the surface of the board (or you feel with your fingers that it is at the same level, or you hear it make a dull thumping sound, or you feel a heavy reverberation through your arm). And a dish is "clean" when you see no spots (or your finger squeaks across its surface, or someone compliments you on its cleanliness). And a peach is "ripe" when it looks mostly red (or it yields to gentle pressure, or is fragrant, or the sign says they are ripe). You probably recall these sights, sounds, textures and smells as examples of Evidence of Fulfillment from the Essay on the Belief Template. And of course, it is the Evidence of the Criterion that you are Testing for in your Strategy:

A Test is what must be seen, heard and/or felt to know that a Criterion is being met.[29]

Imagine, for example, that you want to embark on an exercise program and have turned for advice to a friend who exercises regularly. One of the things she impresses upon you is that "If you want to get

---

[29] As we noted in the previous Essay, because most Evidence for human experiences will be found in the visual, auditory and kinesthetic sensory systems, we will not trouble you with "...and taste and smell" every time we refer to the sensory systems. They are, nevertheless, always there; not cited, perhaps, but not forgotten!

anything out of it, you have to make sure you get a good workout, a workout in which you really exert yourself." So, the workout needs to be "good," which means "you really exert yourself." But how do we know when we are really exerting ourselves and, so know when to either intensify or reduce our efforts? What do we see, hear or feel that signifies that we are sufficiently exerting ourselves? Of course, each of us will have our own answer to that. Just as different people may have different Definitions for the same Criterion, there can be different ways to know when a particular Criterion is satisfied. For example:

"I know I am really exerting myself in my exercise program when...

...my muscles are hurting as I work out."

...my muscles are sore the next day."

...I'm doing more repetitions than I did during my last workout."

...at the end of my workout I've done more repetitions than I did in my previous workout."

...I feel exhausted but relaxed when I finish."

...I'm feeling stronger every day."

...people tell me I'm looking fit."

...I see the rest of my day and see myself having greater energy."

...my breathing is heavy and my muscles are tired."

...I feel exhausted and say to myself that I can't go any further."

...I feel the sweat pouring off me, and people look impressed when they see me working out."

Imagine that you are wanting to exert yourself in an exercise program, and try some of these Tests. It will quickly become obvious that the nature of the Test you use makes a significant difference in determining your experience. Different tests orient you to different possibilities of what to notice and respond to in the world of your experience. For instance, some of the Tests in our example occur during exercise ("my muscles are hurting as I work out," "I'm doing more repetitions than I did during my last workout," "people in the gym look impressed when they see me working out"). Such Tests orient you to ongoing experience, providing feedback that allows you to make adjustments in your workout (increasing or decreasing repetitions, for instance) while you are doing it. If instead your Test is, "My muscles are sore the next day," you will be judging in retrospect how "good" your workout was, and then have to wait to make adjustments until your next workout session.

Since the nature of the Test significantly affects experience, it is worth looking briefly at some of the possible forms Tests come in so that you will be better able to recognize them and their particular contribution to your exemplar's ability:

Sensory / Imaginal

Some Tests are based on sensory experiences, as in "People tell me I'm looking fit" (auditory), or "my muscles are sore the next day" (kinesthetic), or "people look impressed" (visual). In addition, the above examples of knowing that a nail is flush, a dish is clean, or a peach is ripe are all examples of sensory-based Tests.

Tests can also be satisfied by experiences that are largely (or even purely) imaginal. For instance, a person who knows that she has "really exerted" herself when "I see the rest of my day and see myself having greater energy," has a Test based on an imagined visual experience. Or the person who knows she is "finished" with a period in her life when "I hear in my head the gentle clunk of a door closing," has an imagined auditory Test. Likewise, a person who knows that she "understands" when "I can imagine myself using the knowledge," is using a Test that is imagined experience, though we are not sure which sensory systems are involved in her imagining. It is likely that she is seeing something, and she may be hearing and feeling things as well; but in any case it is being experienced through the eyes, ears, and body of imagination.[30]

---

[30] Although we subjectively experience some things as being "outside" ourselves, and others as being "inside" ourselves, *all* experience occurs internally.

Past / Present / Future

Like all experiences, of course, Tests always—and can only—occur in the present. But the Tests may be *about* the past, present or future. Time frames, then, are the subjective "when" of experience; that is, is the person placing her attention on the past, on the present, or on the future? Examples of a present Test include "My muscles are hurting as I work out" and "I can feel the sweat pouring off of me, and people in the gym look impressed when they see me working out." A Test such as "I see the rest of my day and see myself having greater energy," is about the future. An example of a past Test is, "There was a time when I was in poor shape."

Intermittent / Ongoing

In some cases you Test your Criterion intermittently, that is, either once in a while or at a specific time. For example, if you know your workout is good when "I feel exhausted but relaxed when I finish," you are waiting until the end of the workout to know if it was a "good" one. If instead you know by "My muscles are hurting as I work out," your Test is ongoing; you are determining *throughout* the time you are exercising whether or not you are getting a good work out.

Self / Others

Sometimes it is your *own* experience and behavior that is meaningful to you, such as when the Test for a good workout is "I feel exhausted but relaxed when I finish." Judgment of whether or not the Criterion is satisfied, then, comes from the *self*. In other contexts the satisfaction of a Criterion may rest in the judgments of others. For instance, if your "good workout" Test is "People tell me I'm looking fit," the quality of your workout is being decided by what other people think (specifically in this case, How *fit* you *look*.) And, of course, it may be that the judgments of both self and others matter: "I can feel the sweat pouring off of me, and people in the gym look impressed when they see me working out."

Matching / Scaling

In some instances you may be testing for a specific experience, and there is either a *match* for that experience or there is *not a match*. If your "good workout" Test is "My breathing is heavy and my muscles are tired," you will not consider your workout is "good" until and unless you are both breathing heavily and your muscles are tired.

Another possibility is that the experience you are testing for exists on a continuum that ranges from "not there at all" to "completely there." This *scaling* of experience means that the result of your Test will be judged in terms of more/less, faster/slower, better/worse, higher/lower, and so on. For instance, if the person whose Test is "I'm doing *more* repetitions than I did during my last workout," manages to lift the weight just one more time than she did in her previous workout, she is likely to judge it as a "good workout."

Single / Multiple / Assorted Experiences

In some contexts, we are testing for one particular experience (e.g. "My muscles are hurting as I work out"). In other situations we may be after satisfying a set of multiple experiences. For instance, the person whose "good workout" Test is, "I feel exhausted and say to myself that I can't go any further," may feel exhausted, but she will not consider her workout "good" until she is also saying to herself, "I can't go any further." That is, there are multiple experiences being tested for, and all need to be satisfied for the Test to be satisfied.

It may also be the case that the Test involves an assortment of experiences, but that experiencing any *one or some* of them is enough to satisfy the Criterion. For example, "I'm doing more repetitions than I did during my last workout is one way. Also, sometimes I can tell because my muscles are sore the next day. And it could even be that people are telling me I'm looking fit." This person can be satisfied that her workout is "good" when she is "doing more repetitions," *or* when her "muscles are sore the next day," *or* when people "tell me I'm looking fit."

Of course, Tests typically consist of some combination of these six distinctions. For instance:

"My breathing is heavy and my muscles are tired."
[sensory, present, ongoing, self, matching, multiple experiences]

"People tell me I'm looking fit."
[sensory, present, intermittent, other, matching, single experience]

"I see the rest of my day and see myself having greater energy."
[imaginal, future, self, scaling, single experience]

The structure of the Test clearly matters. The experiential dynamics created by the structure underlying, "My breathing is heavy and my muscles are tired," are significantly different from those of, "People tell me I'm looking fit." (Not better, not worse; just different.) The *ongoing self*-assessment of, "My breathing is heavy and my muscles are tired," will naturally lead you to make constant adjustments in your workout, working harder or easing up as needed in order to get that heavy breathing and those tired muscles. In contrast, the *intermittent* and *other* assessment of, "People tell me I'm looking fit," will lead you to seek out periodic feedback from others, which you can then use to judge your past performance and make adjustments for the next time.

Which is the right Test to use when working out? The ongoing self-assessment, "My breathing is heavy and my muscles are tired," sounds like a good idea. After all, it keeps you free from the shifting judgments of others. Furthermore, it has you attending to your body's responses, so you can work hard while not overdoing it to the point of hurting yourself. On the other hand, it may be that this ongoing, self-based Test will leave you vulnerable to not working hard enough—or to even quitting—because your attention is so much on how tired and sore you are feeling. When it comes to working out, perhaps it is better to have the intermittent, other-based Test of, "People tell me I'm looking fit." This Test might allow you to better dissociate from the ongoing discomfort. And it may be that wanting to have other people comment on your "looking fit" promotes greater perseverance than does feeling aching muscles. So, which of these

Tests (or any of the others that we listed above) is the "right" or "best" one?

Answering that question is why we are modeling, of course. Rather than make answering that question an academic exercise in which we decide which one sounds right or ought to be right, we instead look for exemplars; that is, we find people who already successfully work out. Whatever the nature of the Test these people are using is, it is manifestly supportive of, and perhaps essential to, the ability to get a good work out, *the way that the exemplar gets a good work out.*

The Test and Modeling Abilities

Action without direction is, literally, pointless. And an exemplar's actions are, by definition, anything but pointless. Whatever our exemplar is doing, we can be sure that it is in service of some Criterion. The Criterion creates a focal point for her actions and, in particular, the opportunity for feedback. Feedback is essential for evaluating the relevancy and effectiveness of her actions, to know whether to continue, change or stop what she is doing. Indeed, having feedback with respect to a Criterion is so significant that it is often all a person needs in order to eventually attain competency in an ability. There are numerous biofeedback and other learning studies demonstrating that, given accurate feedback regarding the desired response, a person can learn to correctly respond to a subtle pattern, or even control internal metabolic and neurological processes, and do this without any conscious awareness of the behaviors they have developed to attain the goal.

When it comes to specifying the Test, we put a premium on descriptions based on sensory system discriminations. These discriminations include not only what is seen with the eyes, heard with the ears, and felt with the body, but what is seen, heard and felt in imagination as well. This emphasis on describing what the exemplar is seeing, hearing and feeling helps insure that we are getting a description that is closer to the exemplar's Test experience, rather than an interpretation or abstraction (Criterion and Definition) of that experience. Such descriptions help us to access those same Tests in ourselves in a form that is more true to experience as lived by the exemplar.

How specific do we need to be when it comes to capturing the Test? To some extent, this depends upon the ability being modeled. For example, in modeling the ability to play notes on the violin, we are likely to find that the Test for "proper intonation" is precise; there is a particular note you need to create, and being a bit off it is just not good enough. But if our exemplar is testing for, "I'm sweating a lot," do we need to establish how many beads of sweat constitutes "a lot?" Probably not. Remember that it is not our goal to reproduce the exemplar, but to reproduce the ability.

What matters is that we capture a description of the Test that is sufficiently rich to allow us to test our experience in the same way that the exemplar tests hers. And so we elicit a narrative description of the Test. Depending upon the ability and the exemplar, we could end up with anything from a precise micro-experience that must be matched sensation-for-sensation, to a "macro" experience that, although complex, is nevertheless familiar to most people. For instance, suppose our exemplar knows that her employees are "committed" (Criterion) to a project when "I can see they are eager to proceed" (Test). That Test covers relatively extensive and complex discriminations. Still, it is acceptable as a Test because most of us have personal experience of what "eagerness to proceed" looks and sounds like. It only becomes unacceptable if, down the road, we discover that our own perception of "eagerness to proceed" does not sufficiently match what the exemplar actually sees, hears, and feels. Ultimately, it is in using the exemplar's Test ourselves that we discover— directly through trial and error—the level of specification we need to get from the exemplar in order to successfully run her Strategy Test in ourselves.

We already have Lenny's Criterion and Evidence when it comes to maintaining his diet; and so we also already have what he is Testing for in his diet Strategy. (Remember that Beliefs, Strategies, Emotions and External Behavior are different sets of distinctions applied to the same ability. The ability itself is not divided in this way; we do that to help reveal its essential patterns. So it is not at all unusual to find a particular aspect of the exemplar's structure represented in more than one of the elements of experience. The correlation between the Evidence and the Test, however, is the one overlap that we will always find.) Lenny's Test, then, is:

> Test
> **"Working"**: I feel energetic, and I'm conscious and have clarity of mind.

The points we made in the previous Essay regarding the significance of Lenny's Evidence are, of course, true about his Test as well. His Test (*I feel energetic, I'm conscious and have clarity of mind*) puts his attention on his ongoing and internal experience, making him perhaps more able to notice and respond to ongoing shifts in his blood sugar than someone who tested for "regulated blood" using periodic finger 'sticks'. Furthermore, because his Test is internally generated, he is not dependent upon the often capricious responses of the external world. And, finally, because his Test is about the quality of his internal experience, he gets relatively frequent feedback about changes in his state and, so, is frequently faced with the need to do—or not do—something in response to it. This helps keep the importance of his diet present and real for him.

The Operations

Our Operations are what each of us does to satisfy our Criteria. When it comes to "doing," we often fix our attention on our external behaviors; that is, on how we move, what we say, facial expressions, and sequences of observable actions. But of course, we act on the inside as well. Obviously, there are differences between moving furniture in a room and moving furniture in your head. Moving furniture in your head does not, in and of itself, affect anything in the world outside of you. However, much like moving furniture in a room, doing it in your head also involves engaging in actions, although these actions are in the form of "internal processes": computations, representations, spatial manipulations, internal dialogue, internal questions, sensations, memory sorting, shifts in perspective, and so on.

It is essential to recognize the strategic importance of internal processes. In trying to emulate others—whether through some kind of formal modeling, apprenticeship, or mimicry—usually we try to pattern our own behavior after that of the other person. This often doesn't work, however, because the people we are emulating are doing things that go beyond what we can observe in their behavior. They are also "doing" on the inside, engaging in internal processing. Their internal processing is what is informing and guiding their external behavior. (This was also discussed in the third Essay on Distinctions.)

Of course, the relative importance of external behaviors to internal processes depends upon the ability being modeled. Multiplying numbers in one's head, for instance, will certainly involve the operation of a lot of internal processes and few external behaviors. The ability to sink baskets with a basketball requires the operation of many external behaviors and relatively few internal processes.[31]

Furthermore, the mix of external behaviors and internal processes may vary among exemplars. In modeling the ability of architects to come up with ideas for home design, for example, we might discover that one architect imagines combinations and distortions of shapes, volumes and lines until he finds a basic set which fits his client's desires and personality, and that another architect wanders around the actual home site, seeing possible shapes and walking "in" them until she finds those that fit her client's desires and personality. The first architect's Operations are almost entirely internal processes; the Operations of the second architect involve both internal processes and external behaviors. (There are

---

[31] Of course doing *anything* involves millions of internal processes if we chunk down to the level of neurons firing and muscles twitching. Besides not being possible, it would not be desirable to capture experience at that level of specificity, because it is *not* the level of experience. We do not experience the thousands of computations that make it possible to lift a book; we experience lifting the book.

also some obvious similarities between the Operations of these two architects, structures which are probably responsible for *both* of them being good at coming up with design ideas.)

Sequences and Sets

Strategies are usually thought of as a sequence of steps: do this, then do this, then this, then this, and so on. And many strategies are just like that; sequences of operations that take the form of recipes, algorithms, formulas, steps, procedures and techniques for achieving desired outcomes. Cooking recipes, determining the income tax you owe the government, and planting a garden are familiar examples of such strategies. Sugar must be "creamed" into the butter before adding the eggs; the tax percentage is applied to your income after subtracting your deductions; soil is turned over and soil amendments added before seeding. Similarly, internal strategies may be sequential. The strategy of the architect in the above example may run something like: interview the home owners to discover what experiences they want to have in their home, then go to the site at different times of the day and night, then walk around it until you know it from every angle, then begin to imagine shapes and forms that fit with the desires of the clients, then actually walk "inside" those shapes to determine if they are likely to fit with the client, then... and so on. Like beads on a string, each step in such strategies is a prerequisite for effectively taking the step that follows.

But not all strategies can be beaded onto the string of sequence. Many strategies instead involve a "set" of internal processes and external behaviors. In these strategies there is not a first, second and third step to take, but a group of steps that are taken either simultaneously or in an ad hoc fashion. For instance, a strategy for "safe driving" might involve: look several hundred feet ahead and imagine how driving conditions might be changing for you; maintain sufficient stopping distance between you and the car in front; leave a place to go either left or right in case of an emergency; check mirrors every few seconds; shift your body enough to keep it loose and relaxed; and so on. This is not a sequential strategy, but a set of behaviors that are enacted as needed, sometimes sequentially and at other times simultaneously.

As another example of an ad hoc set of internal processes and external behaviors, consider this negotiator's Strategy Operation:

- "Discover things about the personal lives of the people involved."

- "Establish rapport," "Never lie to a participant, but always work to promote trust of me."

- "Search for what is underneath what each side is asking for, that is, what are they hoping to satisfy by a particular demand."

- "Take an entrenched position to its logical conclusion and get agreement that this future is not wanted by the person holding that position."

- "Widen each person's perspective whenever they establish a boundary."

- "If a person becomes angry with the other side, I make him aware of the inescapably human element in the other side."

- "Praise and appreciate any example of willingness to cooperate."

None of these behaviors is necessarily a prerequisite to another, nor are they all necessarily operating continuously. Instead, all of them are available, and some or all of them are enacted depending upon what the negotiator is facing at the moment. Even such an obvious starting point as "establish rapport" might be pre-empted by an unexpected opportunity to "search for what is underneath" a participant's demand or the immediate need to "widen a person's perspective" with respect to a boundary.

Attain and Maintain

Strategies are often thought of as vehicles for getting to a certain destination; once there, you can stop driving. Indeed, the TOTE model suggests this notion with its "Exit" last step; once you have attained the satisfaction of the Test, you are done and can Exit the Test-Operate cycle. Of course, many Strategies are of just this sort. An architect may transform shapes in her mind until she finds a house design that is "Relaxing," then exit that internal process to, perhaps, consider how to actually build that house design. The gardener who likes a "Neat" garden will pull weeds, rake, trim and so on until his garden is, in fact, neat, then pull up a chair for an iced tea. An editor may rewrite a sentence until it "Flows," then move on to the next sentence. In each of these examples, once the person has satisfied her Criterion, there is no need to continue either Testing for it or Operating to satisfy it; it is time to Exit.

But as we pointed out in a previous section, for much of human experience the TOTE model is perhaps more accurately represented by "TOTOTOTO..." It is often the case that the context requires a Criterion be satisfactorily *maintained*. That is, the Operation is continually being enacted and the Criterion is continually being Tested in order to support the ongoing satisfaction of that Criterion. For instance, a negotiator who considers "Trust" necessary to the successful conduct of a negotiation will engage her behaviors to foster trust and *keep* them engaged throughout the negotiation. Just because she has initial success at gaining a person's trust, she does not then abandon her trustworthy behaviors ("Great, they trust me! Now I can treat them anyway I want to!"). Similarly, an athlete may maintain "Focus" throughout her game, a meditator remains "Centered" during a mediation, a lion tamer keeps "Control" while in the cage, an artist continuously looks for "Truth" as she works on her canvas, and so on. Whatever these people do to satisfy their Criterion they keep doing to keep that Criterion satisfied. In these Strategies the Exit comes only when the person is no longer in the context and the Criterion is therefore no longer relevant.

Primary Operation

"Don't you see, Bloom, darling Bloom, glorious Bloom? It's so simple. Step one: you find the worst play in the world, a surefire flop. Step two: I raise a million bucks. (There are a lot of little old ladies in the world.) Step three: you go back to work on the books, only list the backers *one* for the government and *one* for us. You can do it, Bloom. You're a wizard. Step four: we open on Broadway, and, before you can say step five, we close on Broadway. Step six: we take our million bucks and we fly to Rio de Janeiro! Rio, Rio-by-the-sea-o..."

Zero Mostel hatching his foolproof plan
in Mel Brooks' *The Producers*

The fact that a person is an exemplar of an ability—that is, that she consistently attains certain outcomes in a particular context—makes it extremely likely that she is employing the same Operation each time she is in that context. These are the sequences or sets of internal processes and external behaviors that work for the exemplar. We call this the "Primary Operation":

The Primary Operation is the set of internal processes and external behaviors that usually work to satisfy the Criterion.

Of course, all of the general points we made in the previous section regarding Operations are also true for Primary Operations. They may involve internal processes or external behaviors or both; these internal processes and external behaviors may be organized sequentially, or as an ad hoc set of actions; they may be organized to satisfy the Criterion only at certain times, or to maintain the ongoing satisfaction of the Criterion. What makes these Operations "primary" is that they are the internal and external actions with which the exemplar always leads. And the exemplar does this for the very good reason that these particular internal processes and external behaviors usually work to satisfy her Criterion. *Usually*; nothing always works. And so...

Secondary Operations

"How could this happen? I was so *careful*. I picked
the wrong play, the wrong director, the wrong cast...
Where did I go right?!"

Zero facing the disaster of success
in *The Producers*

The world does not always cooperate. It doesn't always offer us the conditions and responses we expect or want. Your Primary Operation may not work—indeed, will not work—all the time. Despite your proven Primary Operation, you run out of carrots before having "enough"; your co-worker seems impervious to your efforts at establishing "rapport"; the house you designed does not feel "comfortable" to your clients; you are too tired to have a "good" workout. Like the sleeper in the Rube Goldberg cartoon, there are times when all of us will face a cloudy day.

The unruly complexity of real life means that an essential aspect of any competency is being able to usefully respond when things are *not* working out in the usual way. The person who has only their Primary Operation on which to rely—no matter how effective it usually is—is standing on thin experiential ice. A little too much sun, an errant crack, a duck landing nearby, anything not normally accounted for, and that person is sunk. In response to the unexpected demands of the real world, most exemplars of an ability have developed "Secondary Operations":

Secondary Operations are the internal processes and external behaviors used to satisfy the Criterion when the Primary Operation is ineffective.

Depending upon the ability and exemplar, there may be anything from none to dozens of Secondary Operations. However, the range of possible Operations can often be usefully divided into three groups according to what extent the Criterion is satisfied:

Criterion is INSUFFICIENTLY SATISFIED:

The complexity of human experience makes it possible to Test for some Criteria along a relative scale, such as "more/less" or "enough/not enough." And so a negotiator has "*some* rapport" with her clients, but not enough to proceed with the negotiation; the fact that the couple is "*pretty* comfortable" with the design of their home is not sufficiently satisfying for the architect; the body-builder is annoyed that her workout is not going "as good as it *should*." In these instances, the exemplar's experience is that her Criterion is insufficiently satisfied, and so a different strategic—Operational—tack is needed. Take as an example the negotiator who recognizes that her Primary Operation of being interested in the background and personal interests of her clients is not working to create sufficient rapport for the negotiation. Instead of either giving up or plowing ahead without the rapport she wants, she switches to a Secondary Operation in which she begins revealing to the clients things about her own background and personal interests. She engages this Secondary Operation because she has found that revealing herself to her clients often creates rapport with them.

Criterion is NOT AT ALL SATISFIED:

It may be the case that the exemplar's Primary Operation is doing *nothing* to satisfy the Criterion. Though the Primary Operation is usually effective, this time (for some reason) the negotiator has no rapport with these particular clients; the couple is not at all comfortable with the house design; or the workout is just no good at all. Rather than abandoning the field in these cases, your exemplar may have another Secondary Operation to put into play. For instance, when the architect realizes that her clients are not at all comfortable with the house she has designed, she shifts to a Secondary Operation in which she has the clients point out homes they *do* feel comfortable in, thoroughly questions them about what they are responding to in those homes, and then imagines walking through those houses to better educate herself about the kinds of environmental experiences her clients want to have.

Criterion CANNOT BE SATISFIED:

There may be times that, as far as the exemplar is concerned, the Criterion cannot be satisfied, or at least cannot be satisfied "now" (for instance, it does not seem possible to get a good workout *today*). This is a bit different circumstance than in the previous two situations. If the exemplar gets to this point, she may have a Secondary Operation that allows her to usefully and appropriately let go of continuing to try to satisfy her Criterion. For example, when the person working out recognizes that she simply cannot have a "good workout" today, she engages a Secondary Operation in which she reviews her workout—how she has prepared for it, approached it physically and mentally—and determines what she needs to do so that *next* time her workout will be "good." The exemplar is letting go of satisfying her Criterion *for now*. This does not necessarily mean that she has to abandon the field now, as well. For instance, the body builder may let go of her primary Criterion of having a "good" workout, but then shifts her current workout Criterion to "increased flexibility."

We have often found these three classes useful in thinking about and, in particular, identifying the various Secondary Operations an exemplar may have available to employ when needed. Though they do not exhaust the possibilities, these classes nevertheless generally cover the range of real life situations for which we are likely to want or need effective strategic choices, namely, those times when our Criterion is "insufficiently satisfied," "not at all satisfied," and "cannot be satisfied."

We are not suggesting that there will always be a Secondary Operation for each of these classes. The exemplar's response to "insufficiently satisfied" may be to simply continue with the Primary Operation until it *is* sufficient. Other exemplars may not consider "not at all satisfied" to be a possibility. These exemplars are always finding *some* evidence of their Criterion being satisfied and, so, at worst they may perceive a situation as "insufficiently satisfied." And some exemplars will have no Secondary Operation to deal with the circumstance of "cannot be satisfied." It is simply not part of their experience and, so, they will persist with their Operations until they have satisfied their Criterion to some acceptable degree.[32]

Operations and Modeling Abilities

An ability is the capacity or competence to act in such a way as to consistently produce a particular outcome. Of course, any action results in some kind of outcome. But we do not want "some kind" of outcome; we want a particular outcome. And so we do not want just "any action," either, but instead those that work; we want the Operations of an exemplar of the ability.

There is an understandable tendency to describe Strategy Operations as a sequence of steps (like those depicted in the Rube Goldberg cartoon). After all, sequences of steps clearly lay out for us what to do and when. For instance, here is the beginning of the Primary Operation for one of the architects:

1. Interview the home owners to discover:
   a. What ideas they have about how they want the house to look.
   b. What experience they want to have when in their home.

---

[32] We have often found that people who are exemplary at maintaining commitments or persevering at tasks do not have a Secondary Operation for "not possible." This *lack* of an Operation is clearly one of the structural pieces underlying their ability to maintain commitments and persevere. We have also found this Secondary Operation missing in individuals who obsess about things, i.e., they have no way to Exit from their Strategy. The contrast between these two examples illustrates that no element of structure is inherently either beneficial or a burden. Every element operates within the nexus of the whole; if it is beneficial, it is because of everything else that is operating around and in relation to it. No single structural element gives rise to an ability; abilities are the result of a constellation of structural elements working together.

2. Go to the site at different times of the day to walk around until you know it from every angle.

3. While at the site, imagine shapes and forms that fit with the property *and* how the clients want the house to look.

4. "Walk inside" those imagined shapes to get a sense of how well they create the experiences the clients want to have.

5. (etc.)

Like this example, Operations can be sequential. But you must also be ready to discover instead that the structure of your exemplar's Operation is organized as a *set* of actions, each of which is enacted according to the changing needs of the situation and the moment. We had an example of this in the Strategy of the negotiator:

- Show interest in the personal lives of the people involved.

- Establish rapport.

- Tell the truth, and if you can't, say nothing and explain why you cannot respond.

- Search for what is underneath the positions each side is taking, that is, what are they hoping to satisfy by each of their demands.

- Widen each person's perspective whenever they establish a boundary.

- Take an entrenched position to its logical—and unpleasant— conclusion, and get agreement that this is a future the person does not really want.

- If a person becomes angry with the people on the other side of the negotiation, make him aware of the inescapably human elements in the other side's position.

- Praise and appreciate any example of willingness to cooperate.

The use of "bullets" is to suggest that none of these Operations is necessarily a prerequisite to any other, nor are any of them necessarily enacted at the same time. They are brought to bear on the situation when needed. For instance, the negotiator doesn't take every stated position "to its logical and unpleasant conclusion." But when one of the negotiating parties digs himself into an entrenched position, the negotiator *will* take that position to its logical and unpleasant conclusion.

And, of course, your exemplar's Operations may be best captured as a mix of both sequences and sets of internal processes and external behaviors. For example, the negotiator's Operations might turn out to be best represented as:

1. Establish rapport.

   - Show interest in the personal lives of the people involved.

   - Tell the truth, and if you can't, say nothing and explain why you cannot respond.

2. Establish a future—no matter how limited to begin with—that both sides can agree on.

   - Praise and appreciate any example of willingness to cooperate.

3. Search for what is underneath the positions each side is taking, that is, what are they hoping to satisfy by each of their demands.

   - Take an entrenched position to its logical—and unpleasant—conclusion, and get agreement that this is a future the person does not really want.

   - Widen each person's perspective whenever they establish a boundary.

- If a person becomes angry with the people on the other side of the negotiation, make him aware of the inescapably human elements in the other side's position.

4.   (etc.)

If you compare your experience of using this "mixed" version of the Operation with your experience of using the previous, non-sequential (all-bullet) version, you will notice that representing the Operation as a sequence imposes sequencing on your own thinking. Now when you think about conducting a negotiation, "establish rapport" becomes a step to complete before moving on to the next step of "establish a shared future," and so on. These become steps that you take, that you make happen. The fact that the behaviors within each of those sequential steps are represented as an ad hoc set imposes a different way of thinking. A *set* of behaviors creates a sense of being on the lookout for, and being ready to respond to, certain situations. For example, during the period of establishing rapport, the negotiator's Operation primes you to notice opportunities to "show interest in the personal lives of the people involved," and, in those instances when you cannot respond by telling the truth, "saying nothing and explaining why you cannot respond."

A mix of sequential and ad hoc Operations is neither better nor worse than a purely sequential or purely ad hoc Operation. They are all just different, and they are all possible. The question (as always) is, How does the *exemplar* organize her experience? If, for our exemplar, negotiation is a sequential set of actions, then that is how to capture her Operation. If instead she relates to negotiating as a set of actions that are employed as they become relevant, then we capture her Operations in a bullet (or similarly non-sequential) form. And of course, if for her there are both sequential and ad hoc actions, then we want to capture them in a form that conveys both.

Lenny's Primary Operation is, of course, to follow guidelines and steps laid out for him by the Zone diet (his Primary Operation, then, would normally be a description of his eating regimen; but since that description already exists in the form of books, it is unnecessary for us to reproduce it in the model itself):

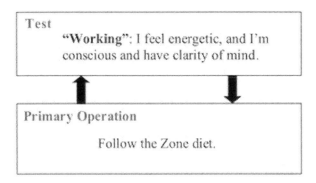

No matter why you are dieting, there is some dieting protocol that has been laid out for you that you need to follow if you want to have the effects of that diet. Most people we know are perfectly capable of following a diet...in the beginning. Where it often becomes a problem is in continuing to stick to it as the days turn into weeks and the weeks into months. The heady and self-reinforcing successes of the initial days are often followed by missteps, by feelings of deprivation, and by frustrations that lead to such thoughts as, "I can't do this," "the diet isn't working," "it doesn't really matter if I don't follow it this once," "I can get serious about this next week," and so on. Regardless of the particular rationalization, the result is the same: the diet is dropped.

Successfully maintaining a diet regimen requires some way of effectively responding to these pitfalls. We want robust models, of course, models that withstand the often uncooperative vagaries of the real world. Much of this resiliency is the result of having effective Secondary Operations, and this is precisely where the particular genius of Lenny's Strategy is to be found.

Like everyone else, there are times when Lenny either makes mistakes in following his diet, or rationalizes choices that violate his diet. If those mistakes or poor choices are significant, his Test has him notice that he is not as energetic, conscious and clear as he wants and needs to be.

(In terms of our classes of Secondary Operations, his Criterion is "not sufficiently satisfied.") Instead of responding to this situation as so many of us do, by tumbling into the well of despondency ("It's no good," "It's no use," etc.), Lenny responds with a Secondary Operation that brings him right back into following his diet:

Test

"**Working**": I feel energetic, and I'm conscious and have clarity of mind.

Primary Operation

Follow the Zone diet.

Secondary Operations

CRITERION NOT SUFFICIENTLY SATISFIE D

1. Remember being back in the hospital and just before, and feel mild panic.

2. Go into the negative future and imagine what that will be like.

3. Go into the positive future and remember that: "If I'm going to get there, I need to follow the diet," and "I am one or two meals/steps away from getting back on track."

4. Feel stronger, back in control.

5. Go back to the beginning of the diet and follow it strictly until I'm back on track.

There are many brilliant aspects to his Secondary Operation. Before pointing them out, it is helpful to first look at what often happens when someone is in that situation of needing to follow a regimen (diet, exercise, quitting smoking, etc.), but it isn't going "well."

Human beings generally try to avoid what is unpleasant. We go away from what is painful. The decision to embark on a diet (or an exercise or health program) is very likely to be triggered by something or some situation that has become so unpleasant in your present experience, that you feel it cannot be ignored and allowed to continue. Okay, so you start the diet. Then another "something" unpleasant happens, this time in relation to the diet: You are being offered cheesecake, which you love and have not had in weeks, and you feel deprived; or you are just feeling unhappy and know that ice cream would be comforting; or you have gone two weeks without losing any weight and feel frustrated, and so on. Now your present experience is (again) unpleasant: "deprived," "unhappy," "frustrated." Naturally, you want to go away from feeling that. And eating the cheesecake or ice cream, or dumping the diet completely, are ways—*in the present*—of getting away from those unpleasant feelings.

Lenny does something different, of course. Let's go through his Secondary Strategy and see how it works to get him back to satisfying his Criterion:

Step 1 -

By beginning with a recollection of the period when he felt physically terrible and ended up in the hospital, he brings into his experiential present the reality of what happens when he does not control his blood sugar. This is very different from what many people do who give up on a regimen. Like Lenny, they have had bad experiences (wheezing on a hike, having to buy larger clothes, fits of coughing), but unlike Lenny, these experiences are either not accessed, or are remembered only as information, as something that happened *in the past*. Lenny remembers *being* in the hospital, he is "there" again, feeling the discomfort and fear of that time.

Step 2 -

Many people who are trying to follow a regimen "know" what the future has in store for them if they do not stick with it (the inability to get around, heart disease, lung cancer, etc.). But again, that future is just information. It isn't real. By recapturing into his present experience the very real pain of the past, Lenny gives himself (in step 2) the basis for a

realistic—in fact, a present and visceral—experience of what his future
will be if he does not control his blood sugar. Taken together, these first
two steps provide a real and compellingly unpleasant (in fact, awful)
experience of his future if his diet continues to not be "Working." This
becomes something he *really* wants to avoid.

Step 3 -

If all he did was to scare himself with that awful future, it could
quickly become something oppressive. Now the unpleasant future creates a
subjective experience of wanting to get away from feeling oppressed by
unpleasantness. In the case of dieting, this need for relief from the
unpleasantness can lead to a wide range of possible responses: indulgent
eating, going to sleep, giving up the diet, and so on.

Like any of us, Lenny will want to get away from unpleasantness, and
could do so by dumping the diet. Instead, he takes the next step of
reminding himself of the future he *does* want. This gives him something to
go *toward*. This not only supports emotional states such as feeling hopeful,
inspired, and determined, but it also re-establishes the goal that "keeping
to the diet" is aimed at. As an analogy for the difference Lenny's strategic
step makes: If you only want to get out of an awful town, then no matter
where else you go, at least you will be out of that town. But of course, you
could wind up in another awful town. By recapturing the future he wants,
Lenny is selecting the town he will go to. The unwanted future provides
the impetus to move; the wanted future provides the worthwhile direction.

Even having the direction of that future may not be enough, however.
It is still the future, something far from the present. Often people feel that
they have gone so far off their diet that the future is suddenly as remote as
it ever was. The task of getting there feels overwhelming, and they give
up. Lenny, however, keeps his future within easy reach by reminding
himself that "I am one or two meals/steps away from getting back on
track." This creates the experience that what he needs to do to be making
the future come true is something relatively small and well within his
grasp.[33]

---

[33] This is an echo of the sequence of cause-effects captured in his Belief
Template: "Maintain focus and discipline → Working → I can have the life I want

Step 4 and 5 -

He supports his renewed experiencing of the string of cause-effects between his present and his future by feeling stronger and then goes back to following his diet. But he does not return to where he "left off." Obviously, he had been slipping in some way or to some degree in following his diet regimen; otherwise it would still be "Working." So he returns to the original focus and discipline of the diet (including the weighing of portions, timing of meals, etc.), which simultaneously reminds him of what he needs to do and ensures that he gets back to feeling energetic, conscious and clear (quickly leading to his Criterion again being satisfied). At the same time, doing this reinforces his belief in the causal connections between these things, as well as providing him with a growing sense of control.

Lenny has no Secondary Operations for "Criterion not at all satisfied" or for "Criterion cannot be satisfied." Which makes sense. He can't afford to be in those situations. To be in a situation in which his diet is "not at all Working" or "cannot Work" is to be in a life-threatening situation. (Or at the very least, having to live on medications, which he really does not want to do.) So his experience is structured to keep him from getting to those critical points. Instead he has (1) a Test that is self-based and ongoing, providing him with always accessible and immediate feedback to which he can respond, and (2) a Secondary Operation that gets him quickly "back on track" before he is in a situation of his diet not "Working."

* * *

Strategies present experience as bits and pieces of behaviors (both internal and external) that come in and out of play as needed to satisfy the Criterion. All of this activity is happening in and through a body, however, and bodies are not bits and pieces. Reaching for a cup is not something that is done just by your arm; your whole body participates in that reaching (by, for instance, subtly shifting your center of balance in order to support

---

to have, rather than the one I don't want to have."

your arm as it extends). Similarly, the perceptual, cognitive and behavioral activities that make up the reach and grasp of an ability are themselves supported in doing this by essential emotional states, and it is to these that we turn in the next Essay.

Elements of the Experiential Array

Essay 10

Emotions

Emotions not only provide feedback regarding "how we are doing" (that is, the "state" of ourselves as a system), but also feed forward, establishing a state that brings into the present certain patterns of thinking and behavior. Emotions that feedforward are necessary to maintain the ongoing expression of an ability, and these are called "Sustaining Emotions." In addition, there are "Signal Emotions," which provide ongoing feedback regarding the extent to which our Criteria are being satisfied. Signal Emotions signal how well a Strategy is working, and provide the impetus to move from one Operation to another.

Where do we live? This is where:

Please, please don't be so depressed—We'll be married soon, and then these lonesome nights will be over forever—and until we are, I am loving, loving every tiny minute of the day and night—Maybe you won't understand this, but sometimes when I miss you most, it's hardest to write—and you always know when I make myself—just the ache of it all—and I *can't* tell you. (Zelda Fitzgerald to F. Scott Fitzgerald in *Love Letters*, by Antonia Fraser)

And here...

Our living conditions were abysmal, yet I had never been happier. We slept on broken bunks or on the ground under the stars. If it rained, we got wet. Our tools consisted of picks, axes and shovels. An older woman among us—she was in her sixties—recalled tales of having done similar work after World War I in 1918. She made us feel blessed for the little we did have. (Elisabeth Kubler-Ross in *The Wheel of Life*)

And here...

When rage or boredom reappeared, each seemed never to have left. Each so filled me with so many years' intolerable accumulation it jammed the space behind my eyes, so I couldn't see. There was no room left even on my surface to live. My rib cage was so taut I couldn't breathe. Every cubic centimeter of atmosphere above my shoulders and head was heaped with last straws. Black hatred clogged my very blood. I couldn't peep, I couldn't wiggle or blink; my blood was too mad to flow. (Annie Dillard in *An American Childhood*)

And here...

In remembering moments such as these, I retain the sad-sweet reflection of being an only child and having a loyal and loving dog, for in the struggles of life, of the dangers, toils, and snares of my childhood hymns, loyalty and love are the best things of all, and the most lasting, and that is what Old Skip taught me that I carry with me now. (Willie Morris in *My Dog Skip*)

As we move through our days and our lives, we are always feeling. Emotions wash over us and through us, bathing every corner of our awareness. Sometimes they stay with us, slowly flowing or ebbing over the course of a day, or even many days. At other times they come as flash floods. They roar in, seemingly out of nowhere...and then moments later are gone, with hardly a wet spot to show they had been there at all.

What *are* emotions?

An Ocean of Emotion

Emotions may be sinewy or diaphanous, they may be enduring or fleeting, pleasant or unpleasant. But in every case, as has been recognized since before Aristotle, emotions are experiences of the body, involving complicated patterns of hormonal, neurochemical and central nervous system responses. However, no description based strictly on the emotionally intoxicating effects of hormones and neurotransmitters, or on the mapping of central nervous system architecture, fully explains the range and qualities of our emotional experience. (For research into the physiological basis of emotion, see Damasio, 2000; Edelman, 1993; LeDoux, 1998; and Pert, 1999)

We often refer to our emotions as "feelings." There is, however, an important distinction to be made here. Not everything we feel is an emotion. Touch a hot stove and you will feel pain and jerk your hand away; neither the sensation of pain nor the behavioral response of jerking your hand away is an emotion. Feeling angry with yourself for touching the hot stove *is* an emotion, however. What distinguishes sensations from emotions? One of the first things we notice about sensations (and behavioral responses, for that matter) is that they are, for the most part, localized in certain parts of the body. The extent of these "part body" feelings can vary. You can feel a pinpoint of heat on the tip of a finger or feel the body-bathing heat of the summer sun. Emotions, however, are "whole body" feelings; people report feeling emotions either "everywhere" or within the trunk of the body (often including the head) and almost always somewhere along the midline. Indeed, when people refer to their emotions you will often see them gesture to, or touch themselves along, the midline of their body. It is also interesting to note that, when relating an unpleasant emotion, people are likely to gesture asymmetrically (their hands' at different levels or moving asynchronously, for instance), and are apt to gesture symmetrically when referring to pleasant emotions.

In any case, emotions are "whole body" in that they are experienced as the state of "me," rather than the state of "my finger." Unlike sensations, which are reports about the state of your body at specific locales, emotions are reports about the state of you as a *whole system*.

Why do we need such whole system reports? As products of evolution, emotions are very efficient ways of organizing the whole organism to respond effectively to those situations that require a full response. For instance, the response of our "animal body" to danger is immediate, extensive and thorough: stillness, orienting toward the danger, crouching, piloerection, accelerated heartbeat, flood of adrenaline, tightening of viscera, keen awareness, etc. This whole body response we call "fear," and is one of the six fundamental emotions—along with happiness, sadness, anger, surprise and disgust—that have been identified as characteristic of most mammals (and perhaps other animals as well). Indeed, some researchers consider this set of "universal" emotions to be the only true emotions.[34]

But fear, happiness, sadness, anger, surprise and disgust do not constitute a complete set when it comes to human beings. When we touch that hot stove, instead of feeling angry about our carelessness, we can just as well feel "chagrined" about being so careless. And feeling chagrined does *not* feel the same as feeling angry. In fact the six universal emotions are better thought of as categories, and within each of these categories we experience whole ranges of emotions.

What is more, we often wander outside those categories, experiencing and naming distinct emotional experiences that do not at all fit into any of those six "universals" (without using a dogmatic shoehorn to do some shoving). Emotions such as "curiosity," "desire," "compassion," and "love" are not simply variations on any of those six fundamental emotions. And yet we can feel curiosity, desire, compassion and love every bit as

---

[34] The classic work on what constitute fundamental emotions is, of course, Charles Darwin's *The Expression of the Emotions in Man and Animals*. For an exploration of the controversies surrounding the identification and classification of emotions, see LeDoux 1998.

strongly as happiness, sadness, fear, anger, surprise and disgust. In addition to happy, we can also have as distinct emotional experiences feeling thrilled, ecstatic, pleased, content, joyful, cheerful, exultant, delighted, gratified, satisfied, excited, tickled, eager, energized and so on. While all of these emotions may be from the same "family," each of them *feels* different. (If you doubt this, access them one at a time and notice how each one affects you.)

To say that emotions are of the body is not to say that is *all* they are. Our bodies are superb responders, constantly recognizing, collating and adjusting to the relentless flow of sensations and perceptions that impinge on us. This affecting flow is not limited to direct sensory experience, however. In human beings, emotions are also responses to *meaning*. Our ideas about the significance of things that exist and happen, both in the world around and within us, is as important a part of the flow of our lived—and emotional—world as are our sensory experiences.

Your body is a fertile ground for emotional experience; whenever the seed of a perception or idea—that is, a distinction—is dropped into your body, emotions will grow.[35] "Mind" and "organism" are always engaged with one another, and in human beings, mind is inextricably linked to language. The penchant for naming that comes with language allows us to pull into the foreground of our experience finer and finer distinctions regarding the patterns of sensations we feel. The layered and ever-changing tides, storms, calms, winds and waves of hormones, sensations, and perceptions are constantly shifting and may or may not be in consciousness. But they are nevertheless always "there." When we bring our attention to them, we make distinctions about those body experiences, noticing and labeling certain sets or patterns as particular emotions. Again, this infinite array of sensations, plus the ability of language to mark them

---

[35] This same point regarding the process of making distinctions and the evolution of experience was made initially in Essay 3, Distinctions, and we have returned to it again and again in every Essay since. It is a fundamental process in human experience – perhaps *the* fundamental process in human experience – and is as significant to the flowering of our emotional experience as it is to the broadening of our perceptions and beliefs.

out, makes it possible for us to distinguish and name an enormous (and perhaps infinite) range of emotional experience.

The range of noticed emotional experience will vary from individual to individual, and this variation is largely due to differences in distinctions being made about experience. For instance, individuals who tend to make few distinctions in their experience might feel either "happy" or "not happy," and not much in between. Other individuals who make unusually subtle distinctions may well experience (for example) "pleased" and "rather pleased" as completely different emotions.

Each of the various emotions we experience not only feels different, each of them has different implications for how we respond as well. For instance, when we feel "satisfied" with a gift someone has given us, our response (what we think, say and do) will probably be significantly different than if we feel "ecstatic" with the gift. That is obvious. It may not be as obvious, however, that feeling "satisfied" and feeling, say, "content" are also likely to lead to different responses. They are very close as emotions go. Nevertheless, if you compare examples of feeling each of them, you will discover that they affect your experience and responses somewhat differently. For example, if you feel "content" when you receive a gift, your thoughts, behavior and words of thanks toward the giver may be a bit warmer than if you feel merely "satisfied."

Your subjective experience of the difference between "satisfied" and "content" may be just the reverse of what we just described above. That is, for you it may be that feeling "satisfied" leads to a warmer response than feeling "content." The quality and texture of your emotional response will be the result of the current situation interacting with your unique personal history of meaning-making in similar circumstances.

Human emotions, then, are inextricably tied to meaning. Whole-body sensations and feelings that coalesce into distinct patterns can become meaningful to us, and we call these distinctive, meaningful patterns "emotions":

Emotions are meaningful physiologically based, whole-system states.

Now we can explore briefly the two significant roles emotions play in determining our experience: expression and influence.

Emotions as Summations of Experience

Imagine that your boss leans in through the door to your office and says, "I really appreciate your work on that report," then ducks back out, and you feel *proud*. That feeling of pride is your body instantly recognizing and weaving together the significance of countless contemporaneous threads: the fact that the boss is stopping by at all, the particular words he says, his sincere smile, the nod of his head, where he puts emphasis as he speaks, your memory of having worked hard on the report, your recent anxiousness about where you stand with the boss, and so on. All of that comes together viscerally as an emotional experience, one that you recognize as feeling "proud." Emotions are the weaving together of the concurrent threads of the moment—sights, sounds, sensations, words, memories and thoughts—into experiential cloaks. A slight change in the mix of the threads of the moment, however, and the emotion may very well come together differently. Had the boss delivered the compliment with a sarcastic tone, your visceral mix might leave you feeling *shame*. Or, if you knew that you had not put as much effort into the report as you should have, perhaps the emotional summing of the moment would be one of *relief*, and so on.

This moment-to-moment summing is the source of our emotional fluidity, the weaving of the texture of our ongoing experience. The fact that emotions are always *there* (you are always "in a state," even if your state is frequently shifting) does not mean we are always consciously aware of them. When you are walking, your brain and body know how you stand in relation to the ground and use that ongoing feedback to make the thousands of adjustments necessary to keep you upright and moving forward, all without intruding on your consciousness. In the same way, our emotions can provide feedback without our being aware of them at the time.

One essential role that emotions play in our experience, then, is that they embody the sum total of the subjective significance of our perceptions and thoughts as they coalesce from moment to moment. This embodying of significance often happens in the wink of an eye, and may be happening outside of our current, conscious awareness. All of us have had the experience of suddenly being awash in an emotion seconds (minutes or, let's face it, even days and weeks) before our conscious minds catch up and reveal to us what our emotions have already understood. Conscious or not, however, our emotions not only embody our subjective present, they influence us, as well.

Emotions as Influencers of Experience

> There is no fire like passion, there is no shark like hatred, there is no snare like folly, there is no torrent like greed.
>
> - Buddha

Emotions do more than express our current states. They also *influence* how we think and behave. Indeed, our emotions occupy a pervasive position of influence that society, culture, behavior, beliefs, "better judgment," and laws can hardy touch. We may alter our behavior in deference to "those in charge," but our emotions rarely also defer. They stubbornly answer to no authority beyond their own, sometimes mysterious, rules. Indeed, it often seems as if our emotions are in charge of our experience and behavior. Consequently, they get the credit both when we are doing well ("Loving you gives me the courage to keep going") and the blame when we are not ("I didn't mean to do that; I was just frustrated").

Even so, our emotions are no more in charge of us than our beliefs, strategies or behaviors are in charge of us. You may have a favorite organ—lungs or heart or liver—but it is not in charge of the body. It is *of* the body, an essential aspect of the system, each element of which contributes to the functioning of the body. Similarly, emotions are an essential aspect of a system; not running the system and yet always influencing it. And so when you feel sad, for instance, that feeling can orient your attention toward what is awful in your world, trigger internal dialogue about how bad things are, decrease your sense of energy, slow your body movements and so on. Then *something significant* happens—a friend says a loving word, a child laughs, you recall a warm memory—and you begin to feel joyful. Now this feeling of joy is influencing what you attend to, say to yourself, sense in your body, and so on. Now the dynamics of the whole system of your experience stabilize around *that* emotion. That is, until the next *sufficiently significant something* happens, stirring a different emotion and compelling the dynamics of the system to reform itself once again.

The Distinctions

In exploring Beliefs we plunged into their underlying structure, and used the Belief Template as a way to help part those deep waters. But we will not be taking that same plunge with Emotions. What we need to capture about Emotions in our model is *unlike* what we need to capture about Beliefs. Explaining this difference requires a brief but important walk over some terrain we already crossed in the two Essays on Beliefs.

Beliefs as expressed in language are "surface expressions" of fundamental, underlying connections or premises. A particular belief can and will be expressed in endless ways. For instance, when an exemplar of negotiation says, "You have to know what makes them tick if you are going to get their heads nodding in unison," our natural logic and experience tells us that this is *one way of describing an underlying principle*. Since our goal is to adopt the exemplar's structure of experience as our own, the question is: Does this particular surface expression of a belief give us sufficient and appropriate access to the underlying structure? In the negotiating example, does attending to what makes people "tick" and looking for head nodding allow us to identify and act from the premises we need to in order to successfully negotiate?

Not wanting to get caught and constrained in a particular surface expression, we try to abstract from it the underlying principle that generated it. The Belief Template is a tool for helping us go quickly and directly to those underlying principles that generate the exemplar's many ways of expressing her belief. There can be many levels of abstraction between these underlying principles and their surface expressions. So we dive through several surface expressions to find the premise beneath, the underlying structure that gives rise to those surface expressions. In so doing, we gain access to the generative structure, the structure that will allow us to generate our own endless surface expressions of that particular belief.

As a "state of the system," an emotion does not have layers of abstraction between its surface expression and the direct experience itself; there is the name of the emotion and the experience to which that name refers. Of course, there may be differences in how a particular emotion is experienced by different individuals. These differences may be in intensity, weight, movement, duration, and so on. Nevertheless, our shared experiences of a particular emotion are usually quite similar. Loneliness, sadness, joy, curiosity, love, contentment, indeed most emotions, are experienced in much the same way by everyone. And so when modeling we have usually found it sufficient to simply identify those Emotions that help give rise to the ability, without delving into their structures.

This is not to say that emotions do not have structure; they do. These structures have already been explored and described by Leslie Cameron-Bandler and Michael Lebeau in their excellent book, *The Emotional Hostage*. In their model the relevant distinctions regarding the structure of Emotions include time frame, involvement, intensity, comparison, tempo, criteria and chunk size. Understanding the structure of an Emotion may be important if we want to understand or change a particular emotion. But we do not need to know its structure to *have* that Emotion. Most human emotions have been experienced at some time or another by all of us. We find that most people have access to the full range of human emotions, and that it is sufficient to know *what* the exemplar's Emotion is to be able to include it in our modeling of her ability.[36]

---

[36] Of course it may be that you are a stranger to a particular emotion, or that you "know" it but find it difficult to access into your experience. In either case, if the model requires an Emotion with which you are unfamiliar, it is necessary to do something that makes it possible for you to have ready access to it. And this

So far we have been talking only about our subjective, internal experience of an emotion. We now need to take a look at the distinction between experiencing an emotion and the outward expression of an emotion.

Emotions as Experienced, Emotions as Observed

We are used to inferring what someone else is feeling by noting his or her behavior. Inferring emotions in this way is essential to the ongoing flow of interactions, judgments, misunderstandings, and rapprochements of our day-to-day relationships. But as we all know (through sometimes painful and embarrassing personal experience), we are not always accurate in our inferences. When it comes to our daily interactions, sometimes misjudging does not matter, and sometimes it matters a great deal. When modeling, however, it *always* matters. We want to be explicit and accurate about what is true *in* the exemplar's experience, and not get lost in our judgment *of* the exemplar's experience.

In this regard, it is important to recognize that a person's behavior may or may not be indicative of what that person is actually feeling in that moment. For instance, a friend is having some difficulty at work and you offer to help him. He shakes his head briskly, waves his hands at you and says, "No, no, it's alright. I can handle it." What are we to make of this in terms of his emotional state? There are many possibilities. For instance, perhaps he feels *embarrassed* discussing his work problems, or he feels *unworthy* of help, or too *overwhelmed* to talk about it at the moment, or *confident* that he can deal with it himself, or *determined* to deal with it himself, or *resigned* to the way things are, and so on. Any of these different emotions might be operating in our friend's experience, while being manifested in his singular behavior of declining our help and waving us off.

When modeling, we need to bear in mind that there may be a difference between the Emotion we attribute to the exemplar based upon *our* observation of her behavior, and *her* self-report of her emotional state

---

"something" may well involve easing yourself into the Emotion through its structure. Again, see Cameron-Bandler and Lebeau for how to do this.

when manifesting that behavior. Since our goal is to walk in the experiential shoes of our exemplar, we want to know what the exemplar is actually feeling, even if it does not accord with how we would judge her emotional state based on her behavior. In making this point (and as we discussed in the Essay on Asking Questions) we are not suggesting that the exemplar's self-report is necessarily or always accurate or true; we are suggesting that we should be ready to discover that there is a difference between the *exemplar's* description of her emotional state and how *we* would judge it based on observing her behavior. If there is a discrepancy between the exemplar's self-report and our judgment of her emotional state, that needs to be sorted out with the exemplar. When doing this, we must not be wedded to our own judgments if we are to arrive at a description that is faithful to the exemplar's experience.

Pleasant Emotions, Unpleasant Emotions

Here is a distinction that everyone recognizes: some emotions feel good, and others feel bad. But to say that an emotion feels bad is not to say that it is bad to feel that emotion, or that one should always try to avoid it. Nor is it the case that, just because an emotion feels good, it is always a good idea to feel that emotion, or that you should seek it out whenever possible. For instance, suppose you are working on a project and it is progressing just as you want it to. You feel contentment, an emotional state that most people find very pleasant. The systemic influence of feeling contentment is likely to keep you continuing doing what you are doing. Suppose you then run into difficulties and your project stalls. You may very well begin to feel frustrated. This is not generally considered a pleasant emotional state; we don't like it and want to get out of it. But consider how feeling frustrated actually affects your thinking and behavior. When feeling frustrated you are *still striving for a solution*. Or to put it another way, feeling frustrated keeps you engaged in trying to resolve the problem, which is a very useful and appropriate response in many situations.[37] If instead you were to continue to feel contentment in

---

[37] You may object, pointing out that for many people feeling frustrated leads them to quit striving, or to even run away from the situation. However, upon close

the face of things going wrong, the systemic effect of that emotion would probably be that you would *not* engage in trying to resolve the problem; it would instead predispose you to accept things as they are. The important point here is that all emotions, regardless of how much we adore or abhor them, have a systemic impact on how we think and behave, and it is that systemic impact that we are interested in when modeling.[38]

We know that whatever our exemplar's emotions are, they support her in manifesting her particular ability. It is natural to assume that someone manifesting wonderful competence at some ability is operating out of a pleasant or positive emotion state. This is not necessarily the case. The office whiz who keeps things beautifully organized could be operating out of an emotional state of worry, the trim neighbor who follows a rigorous daily exercise program could be operating out of fear, and the tireless community activist could be operating out of anger. We may want their abilities, but taking on the emotional experience of these exemplars might not be very enticing. Must we endure those unpleasant emotions in order to enjoy the benefits of these exemplar's abilities?

Possibly. If all exemplars of a particular ability feel the same emotion, this strongly suggests that that emotion is essential to being able to manifest that ability. For instance, if we model several people who are exemplars of keeping an office organized and find that all of them operate with an emotional state of *worry*, it may well be the case that this is an *essential* pattern underlying their ability. Fortunately, however, in most cases we can find *other* exemplars of that same ability who experience a more benign (or even delightful) emotion. So, office organizers who feel playful (rather than worried), regular exercisers who feel challenged (rather than fearful), and community activists who feel daring (rather than angry). Those may be the exemplars we will want to model.

---

inquiry you will find that people who respond in these ways are not feeling frustration; rather, their emotional state has switched to something else, such as feeling overwhelmed or scared or hopeless. (Of course, any of these emotions may also be useful and appropriate, depending upon the situation in which they are being felt.)

[38] Interestingly, when we recognize that an unpleasant emotion is doing something beneficial for us, we can even have pleasant emotions *about* the unpleasant emotion.

Signal Emotions

In a previous section we described emotions as embodying "the sum total of the subjective significance of our perceptions and thoughts as they coalesce from moment to moment." In summing up the coalescing of our perceptions and thoughts, our emotions provide us with ongoing feedback on how well what we are doing (our internal processes and external behaviors) is satisfying the Criteria we are holding from moment to moment. Our emotions are not merely chair-bound idlers, passing comment on passersby; rather, emotions are more like community organizers, actively engaging the citizenry in responding to the needs of the town.

Often the effect of emotional feedback is that it alters how we respond in a particular situation. For instance, when a project is going sour and we feel *frustrated*, we may respond by trying something different to get the project back on track. When we feel *hurt* by a friend's uncaring comments we may express this to them, hoping to re-establish our mutual trust. When we feel *overwhelmed* by a huge task we may break it down into bite-sized pieces so we can eventually succeed; or ask someone to help us with it; or decide that the task isn't worth doing and, so, free ourselves to do something else, and so on. In each of these examples and any others that you can think of, the emotion is in effect saying, "my Criterion is not being satisfied." This then often initiates some kind of response—a change in behavior or thinking—intended to somehow satisfy your Criterion.

When emotions are serving this feedback function, we call them "Signal Emotions" because they signal the fact that something has changed in relation to the satisfaction of your Criterion and, so, alert you to the need to respond differently:

Signal Emotions indicate whether or not—or to what extent— the Criterion is currently being satisfied.

So far, our examples of Signal emotions have been of those (often unpleasant) Emotions that accompany having our Criteria *not* satisfied.

But Emotions signal the satisfaction of Criteria, as well. When the person pursuing the project recognizes that she is "on track" she may feel *happy*; the person who wants "mutual trust" may feel *connected* to her friend when she reveals something personal to him; and the person facing the huge task may feel *confident* as she sees it progressing toward "success." In these instances, their Emotions are signaling that the person's Criteria are being satisfied. The significance of that, then, may be either, "Keep doing what you have been doing," or, "You can stop doing what you have been doing, and move on to another Criterion."

Naturally, the particular Emotion an individual is feeling in a particular situation, as well as the range of Emotions she is likely to experience within that situation, will depend upon that person, the Criterion, the circumstances, and so on. As a generalization, however, the "family" of emotions one experiences is likely to be determined by whether your Criterion is *Exceeded, Sufficiently Satisfied, Insufficiently Satisfied,* or *Violated*. For example, consider the person who wants "Mutual Trust" in relationships. Depending upon what is happening with respect to this Criterion in a particular situation, she might feel any of the following Emotions:

"Mutual Trust" is **EXCEEDED...**

> the emotion may be: ***Loving***

"Mutual Trust" is SUFFICIENTLY SATISFIED...

> the emotion may be: ***Connected***

"Mutual Trust" is INSUFFICIENTLY SATISFIED...

> the emotion may be: ***Wary***

"Mutual Trust" is **VIOLATED...**

> the emotion may be: ***Afraid***

In general, while pleasant Emotions may lead to changes in your expression, they generally do not signal the need to change what you are doing (how you are thinking and behaving). When your Criterion is being satisfied (or even exceeded), as embodied by the pleasant emotion, this is a signal that what you are doing is working. It tells you, "Keep doing it."

However, unpleasant emotions (in the list above, *wary* and *afraid*) do signal the need to change how you are thinking and behaving *so that* you can get back to fulfilling your Criterion.

Signal Emotions and Modeling

As we pointed out in the Essay on Strategies, an important part of excelling at any ability is having Secondary Operations for effectively responding when things go awry, as they occasionally will no matter how effective the exemplar's Primary Operation. As reports of "whether or not—or to what extent—the Criterion is currently being satisfied," Signal Emotions often act as the prompt to engage one of the Secondary Operations.[39] For example, an office manager who is a whiz at maintaining an organized office feels *in control* as long as his Primary Operation for dealing with incoming communiqués continues to work to satisfy his Criterion, "Maintain Order." Feeling *harried*, however, signals that his usual approach is not working and prompts him to shift to a Secondary Operation. (Perhaps reassessing and resetting the categories he uses to sort incoming communiqués.) Signal Emotions are transient in that they will continue to be stimulated until the Criterion is once again being sufficiently satisfied. (The office manager will continue to feel *harried*, alerting him to the need to reset his sorting categories, until he again has "Order" and feels *in control* of his office.)

We can also turn to Lenny for an example of the role of Signal Emotions in a model. When he discovers that he does not "feel energetic, and I'm conscious and have clarity of mind" (that is, the Criterion of "Working" is not being satisfied) he feels the Signal Emotion, *mild panic*. Feeling mild panic spurs him to engage his Secondary Operation, which is intended to return him to the point where his diet is again "Working."

But why the relatively low intensity of *mild panic*? Is that appropriate considering the potentially dire consequences of Lenny's diet not working (i.e. debilitation, amputations, death). Wouldn't an unqualified *panic* (or

---

[39] Someone who is not an exemplar of the ability is likely to respond to these emotional shifts by trying either to damp down or overcome the Signal Emotion, or by abandoning the pursuit of their Criterion.

fear, dread, terror) generate a more reliable compulsion and devotion to getting himself back on his diet regimen? When we step inside his experience, however, and compare the feeling of *panic* to that of *mild panic*, we immediately discover the natural wisdom of Lenny's response. Feeling panic can easily lead to scattered thinking or to grasping at immediate remedies, neither of which supports deliberately and consistently following a diet regimen. Feeling panic can also easily lead to an irrational but nonetheless emotionally compelling desire to avoid the whole, panic-inducing context. This could in turn result in a real crisis as the person tries to soothe himself by ignoring his physical symptoms. In contrast, *mild* panic still generates a sense of the need to respond to what is going on, but without overwhelming Lenny to the point of either frenzy or avoidance.

We want to point out that although Lenny's feeling of mild panic may be an example of "natural wisdom," it was certainly not a matter of choice. He did not sit down one day and decide that mild panic would serve him well as a Signal Emotion. The characteristics of a particular situation will naturally establish the types of emotions that are likely to emerge in that situation. In Lenny's case, the structure of his experience in the context of maintaining his diet regimen sets a certain, relatively narrow range of emotional response: *mild panic*. Indeed, anyone trying to maintain a diet regimen for diabetes who, when they realize that something is awry, responds by feeling *panic*, will almost certainly NOT be operating out of the same structure as Lenny. For instance, a person whose emotional response is *panic* is almost certainly not using ongoing evidence. Without ongoing evidence, the state of this person's blood sugar and her health has more opportunity to dip significantly before being noticed, triggering a crisis that may ultimately become truly worthy of panic. Lenny's attention to ongoing evidence, however, helps avoid this by alerting him to small changes before they have a chance to snowball. To take another example, a diabetic who responds to a change in blood sugar by feeling *mild concern* probably does not have as a compelling belief that there is a connection between the diet working and desirable and undesirable futures. Lenny's solid belief in the cause-effect between the diet working and his having his desired future (and avoiding the one he does not want) creates an experiential environment which naturally leads to more intense Signal Emotions when the diet is *not* working, alerting him to the fact that his future is *definitely* jeopardized.

These examples show that the feedback function of Signal Emotions makes them important in the effective and consistent expression of the abilities we are modeling. Nevertheless, it is rarely necessary to explicitly know and take on the exemplar's Signal Emotions in order to take on the modeled ability. This is because we generally do not need to instruct someone in what emotional response to have when the Criterion is not satisfied or violated (or satisfied or exceeded, for that matter). The Criterion and its web of equivalence and causal relationships, along with the Primary and Secondary Operations, combine to create an experiential environment that naturally predisposes one to access Signal Emotions of a certain family, range, and intensity. The fact that the office manager feels *harried* when the office is not in order is a *natural* response given the structure of his experience in that context. In a real sense, his beliefs and strategies do not easily let him get to other possible emotional responses, such as *overwhelmed*, *hopeless*, or *desperate*. These are emotions that may lead to throwing up one's hands and walking out, a response that, as a whiz at keeping an office organized, our exemplar is not likely to ever get to.

But for some abilities, Signal Emotions cannot be taken for granted. Clearly, when we modeled Lenny and he revealed his Signal Emotion, *mild panic*, it struck us as worth explicit including in the Array for his ability. The significant difference that that emotional state could make in successfully manifesting his ability, plus the fact that it may not be as automatically generated by most people as other, less useful, Signal Emotions, made it something worth specifying in the model. By including it, the person who wants to take on Lenny's ability can make sure to have experiential access to that emotional state, and can explicitly incorporate it into her use of the model. (More about doing this in Essay 17: Acquisition.)

We want to reiterate, however, that in our experience, including the Signal Emotion in Lenny's Array was exceptional, rather than typical. While there may be (and we ought to be on the lookout for) Signal Emotions that are worth stating, most often there is no need to specify them in the model for it to work in someone else. The dynamics of the context of the ability, plus the structure of the exemplar's beliefs and strategies, plus our shared human experiences, typically work together to naturally generate appropriate and effective Signal Emotions as they are needed.

Sustaining Emotions

We all know the difference that our emotional states can make in how our day goes. Wake up on the proverbial wrong side of the bed and your day can easily be filled with endless things going wrong. You huddle beneath a gray sky and chilling rain as you reluctantly make your way to work, where an ominous swamp of papers awaits you. You plunge in and deal with those papers, but you are vexed again and again by their many stupid errors. A co-worker pops in to offer a joke, which you understand, but respond to with only a steely stare. The co-worker backs out of your office. You check the clock and are disappointed to find that there are still hours until you can escape to lunch. And so it goes... Until the next day, when you unaccountably wake up on the "right" side of the bed. It is again gray and rainy, but you enjoy the smell of it and think how good this will be for a spectacular spring flower bloom. At work, the pile of papers on your desk is a gauntlet thrown down that you eagerly pick up. There are as many errors in the papers as yesterday, but today you take pride in finding and correcting them. Your co-worker dares to try another joke and you laugh heartily, and then good-naturedly throw him out so you can get your work done before lunch.

What are we really talking about when we refer to a person's "state"? We are referring to a *background emotion* that is persistent and pervasive, influencing to some degree everything that the person is thinking and doing in the foreground of her experience. As illustrated by the example of going to work in two different emotional states, a particular emotion can persist in the background, generally affecting our responses to everything that we engage in. (At the same time, far more transient emotional responses to what is going on from moment to moment are shifting in the foreground of our experience. These shifting emotional responses are, of course, the Signal Emotions.) In the context of modeling, the function of these persistent and pervasive background emotions is that they keep the exemplar in a state that supports her as she manifests her ability. Such a state is termed the "Sustaining Emotion":

The Sustaining Emotion is a background state that helps keep the person actively engaged in manifesting the ability.

As we noted previously, emotions have underlying structures. When elements of that structure coincide or correspond with the structures operating in the exemplar's beliefs and strategies in a particular context, that emotion can help to sustain those beliefs and strategies. The Sustaining Emotion is a way of "holding" the structural distinctions that are important in a particular context. Another way to put it is that the Sustaining Emotion is holding *in the body* at least some of the essential relationships that are held in the conceptual framework of the beliefs. In this way, the Sustaining Emotion brings the body into alignment with the cognitive elements. The result is not only more congruence in thought and action, but also more ability to continue operating out of those beliefs and strategies. This sustaining of the beliefs and strategies is due to the fact that, as part of the system, the complimentary structures embedded in the Sustaining Emotion are exerting their filtering influence in parallel to, and in support of, those structures operating in the beliefs and strategies. Three examples:

* An acquaintance of ours is devoted to solving crossword puzzles, and feels *challenged* when doing them. Feeling challenged generates a sense that there is something one wants to and *can* overcome, even though it will be difficult. Feeling challenged keeps him engaged in solving the puzzle, even when he finds himself reading the last clue and still has not filled in a single square! Not surprisingly, if he begins a crossword puzzle that is too easy—draining away his feeling of *challenged*—he soon sets it aside.

* Another acquaintance is often in the position of leading teams in her company, and lead them she does. When in that context, her ongoing Sustaining Emotion is that of feeling *responsible*. Because she feels *responsible*, she recognizes that there are things that need to be done, that she is capable of doing them, and that they are hers to do. And so she works diligently with the group, exerting plenty of oversight on their activities (some say too much), never shirks a task in service of the team, and is quick to admit her lapse if she drops one of the balls.[40]

* A colleague of ours is a master at tracking down information. He is clever, bold and relentless in pursuing it, and almost always successful. When on the trail of his quarry, his Sustaining Emotion is *pleasant anticipation*, the effect of which is to hold out the promise that he is inexorably moving toward something that will be very satisfying. Thus, despite going down many blind alleys and facing many locked doors, he persists, fueled by a pleasant anticipation of what will be found around the next corner.

Unlike the Signal Emotion, the Sustaining Emotion is not providing feedback on whether or not the Criterion is being satisfied. Remember that as a person is operating within a particular context, her Criterion will be shifting through a range of conditions of satisfaction ("violated," "insufficient," "satisfied," "exceeded," and so on). These transient emotional responses to the Criterion's ongoing adventures signal the need to make adjustments in strategy to try to satisfy the Test of the Criterion. Whether the Criterion is satisfied or not, however, the Sustaining Emotion is establishing an emotional environment that supports the continuing use of those Strategies and the continuing pursuit of that Criterion.

---

[40] Naturally, her boss and everyone else would agree that, "*Of course* she is responsible for the team – after all, she's a *manager*." But that is a performance expectation of her role. Any person in her role would be responsible for the performance of the team; but that person might not *feel* responsible. Instead they might feel *ambitious*, or *careful*, or *driven*, each of which would dramatically affect **how** this person fulfilled the role responsibility of leading the team.

Talking about the Sustaining Emotion as "setting an environment that supports the ability" may give the impression that it is separate from, and added to, the ability. This is not the case. Like beliefs and strategies, the Sustaining Emotion is an integral element of the ability; without it you do not have the ability. Just as the context of the ability calls up a particular Criterion and Strategy, the context calls up an emotional state as well, one that is congruent with the pursuit of that Criterion and the use of that Strategy. Without a Sustaining Emotion, trying to hold a certain Criterion and execute the needed Strategy will be very much more difficult. This is quite obvious among people involved in sports who, when they take the field, the field takes *them* to sustaining emotional states (such as *determined, confident,* or *focused*), states which help them stay "in the zone" where they can manifest the fullest expression of their abilities.

Sustaining Emotions and Modeling

When you first put on a new sock you are very aware of the sensations of it encasing your foot and constricting your calf. But soon you no longer notice the sock. That is, until the top of the sock slips down to your ankle. Suddenly you are again quite aware of that sock. If you leave it sagging, however, soon you will again not notice it. The phenomenon of accommodation to stimuli is something we all know well: there is no point in putting our attention on something that is unchanging. What grabs our attention is change. This lack of attention is not a decision on our part, but a response built into the nervous systems of all creatures. From the beginning, survival has put a premium on changes in the status quo.

Consequently, the emotions we are most aware of are our Signal Emotions. As they shift frequently and unexpectedly, often from moment to moment, they naturally command our attention. But the fact that Signal Emotions are more obvious does not mean that they are more significant in manifesting a particular ability. In fact, as we discussed earlier, it is usually not necessary to identify Signal Emotions when modeling since they are, to a great extent, prescribed by the interaction between the structure of the ability, the current situation, and shared human experience.

What is **not** prescribed and *is* necessary to identify is the Sustaining Emotion. Unlike Signal Emotions, the Sustaining Emotion does not provide feedback on whether or not the Criterion is being satisfied; rather it is a state that supports the exemplar in continuing to operate out of the beliefs and strategies necessary to the ability. In contrast to the constancy of the Sustaining Emotion, your exemplar will go through a shifting range of Signal Emotions. But the comings and goings of Signal Emotions neither establish nor undermine her ability. The Sustaining Emotion, however, is an integral element of the ability: if the exemplar's Sustaining Emotion should vanish, she will not be able to continue to manifest the ability, or at least not with the same congruence, depth and consistency.

Since the Sustaining Emotion is not a response to the fluctuating satisfaction of the Criterion, it tends to remain constant while the exemplar is manifesting her ability. Like the sock, this constancy of the Sustaining Emotion causes it to quickly recede into the background of awareness and, so, it often goes unnoticed by the exemplar. This means that your exemplar may at first have some difficulty putting her finger on just what her Sustaining Emotion is when she is manifesting her ability. But once she does identify it, invariably it becomes obvious to her that that emotional state must be "there" to do what she does.

As we said, the context of the ability establishes in the exemplar's current experience not only her beliefs and strategies, but the Sustaining Emotion as well. For Lenny, the context of "maintaining my diet to control my diabetes" establishes in his experience the Sustaining Emotion of *powerful/strong*. Why is he using two words to identify what he is feeling? The infinite variety and shades of emotional experience will always outstrip language's ability to generate labels.[41] And so it may be the case that the precise word an exemplar needs to describe what she is feeling simply does not exist, or is not known to her. When this happens, the quality of the exemplar's experience can usually be captured by combining two or more emotion labels. When pursuing his diet, Lenny is not feeling either *powerful* or *strong*, but some combination of the two. In the world

---

[41] For numerous examples of the variety of experience—emotional and otherwise—captured in different languages, see Howard Rheingold's *They Have a Word For It*.

of emotions, they are very close. Nevertheless, if you compare them by taking on one and then the other, you will notice a subtle difference: *powerful* conveys a sense of being able to exert force or your will, while *strong* conveys a sense of being able to withstand great forces. Lenny feels something that is a combination of the two:

Powerful:

> Lenny's diet—like all diets—is demanding. Many people easily or too soon feel inadequate to meet, or are overwhelmed by, these demands and give up ("I can't do it," "It's too hard"). As is clear from his beliefs ("Maintain focus and discipline" and "It won't work by itself; I have to be present"), the onus for the required effort is on him. He must do the work, and it is neither trivial nor easy work. The sense of being capable of exerting his will, of making happen what he wants to happen, comes with feeling *powerful*, and helps sustain Lenny in doing what needs to be done: facing and overcoming the difficulties and demands of the diet.

Just to be clear, it is not the case that Lenny feels powerful *because* he follows the diet. Feeling powerful is part of the experiential package that we call "Lenny's ability to maintain his diet." Feeling powerful was there from the beginning; it did not follow his being successful with the diet.[42] Furthermore, feeling powerful does not fade or evaporate when he runs into difficulty. Indeed, it is what provides the emotional impetus and support to return to following his diet strictly. Undoubtedly, when he gets his diet working again he feels even more powerful, enhancing what is already there.

Strong:

---

[42] Perhaps discovering something that he could do to positively affect his health was the initial source of his feeling powerful, but in any case, the feeling was there at the outset of taking on the diet.

Diets are, by definition, restrictive. They proscribe what you are used to eating and probably *want* to eat. Of course, the diet itself can eventually become what you are used to eating and want to eat. But even if that change does occur, it is normally something that happens over time. In the meantime, there are still all the desires, temptations and social pressures to eat what you were accustomed to before commencing the diet. The sense of being able to **withstand** pressure comes with feeling *strong*, and supports Lenny in holding constant to his diet in the face of the daily temptations the world offers to stray from his "track."

Diets are not only demanding, but are also often *endlessly* demanding. This is obvious in the case of a diet to control diabetes, and may also be the case for people who are on diets to control other health concerns, such as blood pressure, cholesterol and weight. It is not that Lenny has only to muster the power to lift the stone once, and then can dust off his hands and walk away. He must lift it again and again, perhaps for the rest of his life. He must endure. Here again feeling strong sustains him since it is an emotional state that for most people carries with it a sense of power that lasts, that goes through time.

As a Sustaining Emotion, then, feeling *powerful/strong* helps Lenny to feel capable of exerting his will (so he can do what needs to be done), to withstand forces exerted upon him (so he can avoid temptations to stray), and to endure (so he can continue doing what needs to be done and continue avoiding temptations).

* * *

When it comes to describing abilities, people typically focus on an exemplar's external behavior. This is not surprising; behavior is usually what is most obvious and easily described. Even though an ability is much more than just behavior, it *is* through external behavior that what is going on "on the inside" gets expressed and has an impact in the world. We will consider external behavior in the next Essay.

Elements of the Experiential Array

Essay 11

External Behavior

> *External Behavior is significant since it is the interface between you and the world. It is through your external behavior (what you say and do) that you are known to, and have an impact on, the world. External Behavior includes any whole body movements, part body movements, postures, tempos, facial expressions, or verbalizations that contribute significantly to the manifestation of the ability.*

Throughout most of human history, and in most societies, the elders in the community were respected and consulted for their experience. There was good reason for this. There still is:

When the first child of one of the authors was born, the boy did not cry. Instead, he burbled quietly and looked around. This, as it turned out, was a ruse. In fact, he could cry with the best of them. His father held him, walked, rocked, jiggled, cooed, jostled, patted and fed him. These ploys generally had no effect. (This was not entirely true. The author's efforts usually had the effect of intensifying the crying.) And these failures were all the more galling because the author's mother-in-law, Dotty, could comfort the boy within a minute (not *minutes*, but *a* minute). Was this ability to soothe a baby the genetic prerogative of grandmothers? Could it be learned by a man in his twenties?

Dotty rocked the baby in the same creaky rocking chair that the author used. Deciding that it must be the pace of her rocking that made her so effective, he adopted that same pace when rocking his son. The boy only continued to cry. Next the author noticed that grandma also patted the child's bottom in the syncopated rhythm of a beating heart. Confident now, the author added this element to his approach, rocking and pat-patting that bottom just as he had seen it done by Dotty. But his son did not care about his father's confident patting, and continued to cry. His father even experimented with patting variations, all of which either had no effect or had the effect of promoting crying into wailing.

As if he was trying to spot from where a card shark was pulling all those aces, the desperate author began to closely scrutinize grandma's technique, looking for the subtle trick she was playing. What he eventually noticed was that she set her mouth in a very distinctive way as she rocked the baby: her lips were slightly pursed, and the corners turned down a bit. The author practiced this face a few times, then took up his crying son, rocked him and patted his bottom in syncopation. And when the author also pursed his lips and turned down the corners of his mouth... it worked.

The Interface

This will be one of our shortest essays, and this despite the fact that in it we discuss the one aspect of modeling that is of primary interest to people: behavior. It is understandable that the initial inclination for most of us is to focus on behavior. After all, our interest in someone's ability is, ultimately, a desire to reproduce in ourselves that person's behavior. That is what is most obvious about a person and that is where the action is. And those actions make possible the outcomes we hope to attain by making those abilities our own. So, why is this essay short? Because the processes that make all that external behavioral action possible take place on the *inside*.

Previously our focus has been on the structure of internal experience. The mostly internal processes that constitute our beliefs, strategies and emotions capture the lion's share of our attention in our approach to modeling because, as we have pointed out several times, behavior is largely a manifestation of those internal processes. All of us have examples of this, of times when we have tried to behave in ways that were different from how we felt. What happens? The behavior is usually incongruent and difficult to maintain, and requires constant vigilance.

Even if we feel we have pulled it off, it will have taken a lot of effort. Essentially, we were fighting ourselves, or (to be more precise) fighting to squelch the behaviors that would have been a *natural* expression of how we were actually thinking and feeling at the time.

We have also repeatedly tried to hammer home the fact that none of the elements of experience operates independently of the others. Nor is one element of experience responsible for conferring an ability, just as no one musical instrument is responsible for a symphony. An ability is something that emerges from the dynamics of the various elements of experience operating *together*. And of course this orchestra of experience includes External Behavior.

External Behavior can be something as obvious as "running around the room" or as subtle as "leaning slightly forward." It can be simple, like "a raised eyebrow," or complex, like "explaining my perspective to other people." And it can be the use of certain words, as when one typically prefaces an explanation with "I would like to give my opinion," or it can be the tonality with which things are said, as when one says "I would like to give my opinion" in a squeaky and hesitant voice. So, by "External Behavior" we are referring to everything that we do on the outside: anything that can be seen or heard by someone else, and specifically, when it comes to modeling, only those things that are necessary for an ability to work:

External Behaviors are those behaviors, movements, facial expressions, verbalizations and voice tonalities that are significant in manifesting an ability.

It is obvious that we behave, and that our behavior has effects. External Behavior is so evident to us, so much what we notice and talk about, that we do not accord it the level of regard that it actually deserves. And that is this: In terms of the world, our thoughts, cogitations and feelings mean nothing. Our behaviors, however, mean everything. Of course, what each of us thinks and feels means something to us, and that is fine. But it is important to recognize that it is only *through* behavior that we have an impact on the world, or that the world knows us. The only way the world can know the opinions forming, the discoveries unveiling, the ideas sparking, the visions appearing, and the feelings stirring inside the vast world of your experience is through what you *do*, through your facial expressions, and through what you say and how you say it. Behavior is the primary interface between you and the world.

Why Not Use Only External Behavior?

Since it is through External Behavior that we interface with the world, why not simply devote our modeling efforts to identifying essential behaviors and adopting them? There are three important reasons why External Behavior models are usually not enough:

Access —

Of course there are some abilities for which External Behavior seems to be sufficient. Soothing a crying baby is an example of just such an ability. It is important to remember, though, that none of us are ever just our behavior (nor are we ever just our feelings or just our thoughts); we always come as a package. Undoubtedly, when the author set his mouth in just the same way as grandma, that unique facial behavior led to many subtle, though significant, dynamic shifts in how he was thinking and feeling as well. And, in a cascade of effects, these internal shifts probably created other, behavioral shifts that were essential to his successfully soothing his son (for instance, affecting how firmly he patted his son's bottom, or how relaxed he was in the rest of his own body).

Still, for most human abilities, merely mimicking External Behavior does not give us sufficient access to essential internal processes. Being able to forgive someone, debugging computer programs, or appreciating modern art are all examples of abilities for which patterns of belief and thinking are essential. Holding out your hand to someone who has wronged you will not necessarily create the empathy needed to actually forgive that person; but *feeling* that empathy is likely to make it easy and natural to hold out your hand to him. Similarly, scrolling through screens of computer code will not reveal to you what to respond to as you scan those lines; and peering at the paint-spattered canvasses of Jackson Pollock may not reveal to you how to engage with his paintings.

Of course External Behavior are often important or even crucial to successfully manifesting a particular ability; but manifesting *only* those behaviors does not necessarily give us access to the essential internal processes. Internal processes generally guide and inform External Behaviors much more strongly than External Behaviors guide and inform internal processes. (This is the "flow of effect" we talked about in Essay 3.) Because of this, for most abilities, merely manifesting the External Behaviors involved does not give sufficient access to the internal processes that actually make the ability work.

Reliability —

A second reason for not confining our modeling to External Behavior is found in the automaticity with which most true competencies operate. The exemplar of an ability does not consciously put herself through the Behavioral paces of her ability, but instead automatically responds with competent External Behaviors. It is important to keep in mind that experience comes as a package. Behaviors do not operate in spite of thoughts, thoughts in spite of feelings, and feelings in spite of beliefs. The dynamic combining of all of these elements within a context *is* our experience. If an ability is to be reliable—that is, we can be assured of it operating when it is needed—then the person must have the internal structure of experience that supports the necessary External Behavior.

Behavior that is not supported by congruent internal processes will not persist over time. For instance, many of us have had personal experience with trying to hold a teenager to his or her responsibility for taking out the garbage. (In fact, most of us have been on *both* sides of this experience.) Despite explanations, exhortations, promises and reminders, that garbage stays put, even to the point of over-flowing. The concerns that are operating in a parent's experience regarding taking out the garbage are not to be found in the experience of most teenagers. But eventually these nascent adults reach a time in their lives when those concerns *are* found in them, and then they take out the garbage without needing to be told. (And so, years later, can be mystified by their own children's inability to remember such a simple task.) But until then, that behavior is not a meaningful part of their experience, and the way the trash typically gets taken out is through parental vigilance. Indeed, the only way *any* un-integrated behavior can persist is through vigilance, that is, through consciously exerting oneself to manifest the behavior.[43]

Depth —

Exemplary abilities are usually robustly responsive, which is the third reason for modeling the internal processes that give rise to the External Behavior. If you try to manifest an ability solely by clothing yourself in its External Behavior, the unpredictability of the real world will soon unfrock you. Having only the behavior, you become an automaton, and your ability becomes brittle, precarious and easily overwhelmed. Life is not an assembly line, offering you the same two pieces of metal to bolt together again and again. It will instead throw at you all kinds of experiences in endless combinations. Most exemplars of an ability operate within a *range* of External Behavior, rather than hewing to a rigidly specified set. Because of the variability in real life, true competency is revealed when a person can continue to competently manifest an ability even as the demands of the situation change. This flexibility of response comes from those internal processes that guide and inform External Behavior.

Of course, the structure of one's internal processes may themselves be so narrow and regimented that they are just as unresponsive to changing situations as are prescribed External Behaviors. But this is almost never the case with people who are exemplars. One of the reasons they *are* exemplars of a particular ability is precisely because they have a structure of experience that allows them to flexibly respond when manifesting their ability.

---

[43] Of course, vigilance can maintain a behavior long enough that it leads to a reorganization of internal structure, which then supports the manifestation of the behavior without further need of vigilance. We speak more about this in Essay 17: Acquisition.

External Behavior and Modeling

Access, reliability and depth; for these three reasons it is essential to explore the exemplar's internal processes *as well as* her External Behaviors. The flow of effect regarding the elements of experience does not mean that External Behavior can be ignored; only that it is probably not in and of itself sufficient to manifest competence in an ability.

Identifying the External Behavior of an ability is not a problem when we are modeling an ability that operates in a very narrowly defined context, such as that of soothing a baby. But what happens when the ability operates in a relatively wide context that is subject to all kinds of variables? For instance, the ability to forgive is not only a matter of saying, "I forgive you" in a certain tone of voice, accompanied by appropriate gestures. Forgiving a loved one may involve External Behaviors that are somewhat different than those for forgiving a stranger on the street, or a nation, or oneself. Does all this mean that, for most abilities, is it necessary to catalogue ALL of the exemplar's patterns of External Behavior?

Fortunately not. The relationship between External Behaviors and the internal processes that mandate them is actually a great advantage to us in modeling. Very simply, most of the External Behaviors that are significant in an ability will be naturally generated by the ability's internal experiential structures.

Of course, no amount of modeling of an exemplar will encompass all of her experience and, so, will also not account for all of her behavior. But that is okay because we do not want to become the exemplar; we want to acquire enough of her structure of experience to be able to manifest the ability that she has. And so we need to reproduce in our own behavior only those External Behaviors that are essential for the ability.

In addition to what is *essential* for the ability, the exemplar will manifest an endless variety of other behaviors that are either "irrelevant" or "idiosyncratic":

- **"IRRELEVANT" behaviors** are those behaviors that have little or no connection to the ability itself. Suppose we are modeling an architect for her ability to design spaces that fit the people who live in them. We notice that, as she is creating possible spaces in her imagination, she sits, breathes, blinks, sharpens her pencil, answers phone calls, sips tea and so on. It is probably the case that none of these External Behaviors is relevant to the ability to design homes that fit people. They may be important aspects of *other* abilities simultaneously operating in her world. Answering the telephone may be essential to the ability to maintain business connections, for example, and sipping tea may be her way of keeping alert. But these behaviors are not relevant to the simultaneously operating ability of home design. As with any element of experience, one way to determine whether or not a particular piece of behavior is irrelevant is by stepping-in and testing it in *your* experience: does it make a difference in your ability to manifest the ability? Another way to test the relevance of a behavior is to ask your exemplar to *not* do it and find out if she can still manifest her ability.

- **"IDIOSYNCRATIC" behaviors** are those behaviors that are essential to the exemplar when she is manifesting her ability, but are not essential for the *ability itself*. In the example of the architect, for instance, suppose we discover that as she is creating possible spaces she taps her teeth with a pencil. To test out the importance of this behavior, we take the pencil away from her and discover that she suddenly has great difficulty running her internal design strategy. This strongly suggests that tooth-tapping is essential for this exemplar to be able to manifest her ability. Do we then need to tap our teeth as well if we want to be successful using her strategy? Or is this an example of the exemplar's idiosyncratic behavior,

behavior that is not really necessary to reproduce in the model? We can answer this by stepping-in and testing whether or not teeth-tapping makes a difference in *our* ability to manifest the ability. We can also sort idiosyncratic from essential by comparing this exemplar with other exemplars of the same ability. If we find that all of them tap their teeth as well, then probably it is a *naturally* necessary External Behavior for this particular ability. If the other exemplars do not tap their teeth, then this is idiosyncratic behavior, and is not necessary to include in the model.

When modeling we are not interested in capturing External Behavior that is either irrelevant or is idiosyncratic. In addition, we have no need to capture all of those External Behaviors that naturally emerge whenever we operate out of the exemplar's structure of experience. What then does that leave for the model in terms of External Behaviors?

What we want to be sure to include in our model are those External Behaviors which are essential to the ability *and* which one might not automatically do as a consequence of operating out of the exemplar's internal structure. In other words, we are looking for *those behaviors that would not occur to you to do if you had not been told to do them*. For instance, suppose an essential piece of External Behavior for the architect is that she slows and deepens her breathing as she imagines possible spaces. Because this is breathing pattern is something that happens way outside of her consciousness, it may not be discovered during the elicitation of her Strategy. And, more importantly, what we do learn about her Strategy (and beliefs and emotional states) may not lead us to automatically slow and deepen our own breathing when we take on her Array. (Perhaps making the extensive internal visualizations involved in her Strategy actually creates *shallow breathing* in our bodies!) In this case, then, "Slow and deepen your breathing" becomes an element of External Behavior that is both essential to the ability and (because we cannot rely on the rest of the Array to automatically initiate it) necessary to note *explicitly* in the model.

In modeling Lenny's ability to maintain a diet to control his diabetes, we found one External Behavior that emerged as both significant and not necessarily an automatic consequence of taking on the internal structures of his experience: "I talk about it [dieting to control his diabetes] a lot with other people." This External Behavior is not naturally mandated by the structure of experience we had already modeled from Lenny.[44]

And yet, when you take on that piece of External Behavior, you immediately discover its effect on, and importance to, the ability to maintain the diet. To begin with, talking a lot with other people about dieting to control his diabetes reinforces why he is doing it, strengthening his sense of the cause-effects, and keeping in his awareness the effect of his present choices on his future health. In addition, the people he talks with very often praise him for what he is doing, and are obviously impressed and interested. This validates what he is doing and his effort, as well as creating a community of support. And finally, each time he talks about what he is doing and why, it creates a public re-commitment—a personal reaffirmation—to the difficult path he is on. This, then, is a piece of his External Behavior that we want to be sure to include in the model of his ability to maintain a diet.

* * *

One of the simplifying attributes of the Array is that it captures those essential elements of experience that combine to make it possible for the exemplar to manifest her ability. Even so, sometimes we find something that, though operating "outside" of the Array, nevertheless contributes to the ease and competence with which the exemplar manifests her ability. The Array makes a place for these "Contributing Factors," and they are described in the next Essay.

---

[44] Of course, there will also be an underlying structure for "Talk about it a lot with other people," as there is for everything we do. But the ability to do that is not what we are modeling in Lenny, so it appears simply as a piece of his External Behavior. If it turned out that we had difficulty doing *that*, we could also model his ability to talk a lot with others about his diet regimen.

Elements of the Experiential Array

Essay 12

Contributing Factors

Many abilities have prerequisites — or at least reinforcements — in the form of other abilities, skills, information, resources, and so on. These Contributing Factors are aspects of the exemplar's ability that, though not essential to the Array, nevertheless contribute to its effectiveness.

When we specify an ability to model, we establish certain boundaries in the world of the exemplar's experience. This is necessary if we want to avoid getting lost in the layered complexity of human experience. In drawing our boundaries we are endeavoring to fence in those elements of experience that are essential to the exemplar's ability. This does not mean that everything else that gets "fenced out" is irrelevant or not useful. Some of these other abilities, skills, information, tools, or environmental conditions may contribute in significant ways to the ability. We call these "Contributing Factors":

Contributing Factors are other abilities, prerequisites, preparations, conditions or considerations outside of the Array that significantly support the ability.

Contributing Factors make a significant difference in effectively manifesting an ability, *and* they are "outside" of the ability (that is, its Array). They are not a part of the experiential structure of the ability itself. For instance, we may find that someone who has an excellent Strategy for preparing for exams also reports that getting plenty of rest makes that preparation easier, and even more effective. But getting a lot of rest is not an *essential* aspect of how he actually studies the material for the exam. He has found that it can contribute to the outcome of being prepared for the test, but it does not determine the outcome.[45]

Almost anything can constitute a Contributing Factor:

Information:

You can acquire a master craftsman's ability to design furniture, but knowing the strengths and finishing characteristics of various woods would contribute significantly to your design work.

Other abilities:

The ability to create interesting fictional characters might be enhanced by paying close attention to what is distinctive about each of the people you meet in your daily life.

Objects and environments:

Some negotiators who specialize in resolving acrimonious disputes find it helpful to conduct the negotiation in an environment that conveys a sense of their power, and so make sure they have a large desk, Mont Blanc pens, photographs of themselves with prominent people, and so on.

Of course, if a particular Contributing Factor is itself an ability (for instance, "being able to empathize") then it, too, can be modeled and added to your repertoire (if you need it), making you that much more effective in manifesting the primary ability.

In modeling Lenny, two Contributing Factors emerged as significant in maintaining his diet. The first is that he "Understands the mechanics of food and of the body." For Lenny, having this knowledge makes it much easier to understand how what he is doing with his diet relates to what is happening in his body, how it is helping him to control his blood sugar now and, so, is making possible the future he wants (and avoiding the one he does not want). Because of his knowledge of the physiology at work, Lenny is not blindly following the dictates of a diet. Instead, those dictates *make sense to him*. Rules without reason are easily broken or discarded altogether. And rules that are not understood in terms of their cause-effects

---

[45] In the case of this particular and hypothetical exemplar, of course. If, however, our exemplar did have "getting plenty of rest" as *necessary* to how he studies, it would appear in the Array in some form.

are more easily ignored because the consequences are neither obvious nor do they seem inevitable to the person. Because of his knowledge, however, the dietetic rules Lenny must follow have reasons that he understands; to ignore them becomes a matter of choosing to ignore the cause-effects he knows to be *true*, and to invite the predictably grave consequences. In addition, says Lenny, "[Understanding the mechanics of food and the body] allows me to be generative about how I pick foods." His knowledge frees him to go to restaurants or to the homes of friends for a meal because he can figure out from what is available how to eat in a way that is consistent with his diet.

A second Contributing Factor for Lenny is that once in a while, "I celebrate the fact that I'm a Type II diabetic by taking a diet vacation for a day." Although this may at first seem counter intuitive, Lenny's "diet vacation" contributes to his ability to stay on his diet in several ways:

First, it provides a periodic relief from the burden of constantly attending to what he eats.

Second, the effects of going off his diet (having his sense of "energy," "consciousness" and "clarity of mind" begin to become impaired) renew for him the reality of the cause-effects between his eating and his health. (If one has been eating properly and, so, feeling fine, the reason why you are bothering to eat properly can fade; after all, you are feeling fine!)

Third, taking a day off from the diet and then resuming it reinforces the essential notion that, "I am one or two meals/steps away from getting back on track." (Undoubtedly, putting himself "back on track" serves to enhance his feelings of being "powerful" and "strong," as well.)

Fourth, it is a "celebration" in that it could have been worse; had he been a Type I diabetic (or perhaps had some other illness), he would not have been able to even contemplate having such choices. As it is, he can slip up, he has room for error and some freedom to choose, and this is cause for celebration. (The very word itself, "celebration," casts a somewhat different and positive light upon his diabetes, pushing it away from the "tragedy" end of the subjective spectrum and more toward the "blessed" end.)

Despite these contributions, isn't it dangerous to fall off the diet wagon, to invite the very slippage that so many people typically fight or succumb to when following diets? Perhaps, if the person is not operating out of *Lenny's structure of experience*. It must be remembered that it is not just anyone taking this diet vacation; it is Lenny, with his beliefs, strategies and emotions. For example, even though he is taking the day off from his diet, he still has the cause-effect—it is still *real* for him—that "My diet needs to work if I am going to have the future I want and avoid the one I *don't* want." Someone else, who does not have this cause-effect (or for whom it is just words, and not subjectively real), may not have Lenny's experiential resources to resume the diet. For this person, taking the day off becomes something very different, something that is less of a vacation and more of an escape.

* * *

We now have a lot of useful distinctions about the structure of experience. However, knowing what to look for is not the same thing as knowing how to find it. We have already discussed three of the general skills essential to information gathering: the asking of questions, patterning, and stepping-in. With those as our foundation for all elicitation, in the next Essay we can address more specifically how to elicit each of the Array distinctions we have been exploring in this section on the Elements of the Experiential Array.

PART IV

Elicitation

Elicitation

Essay 13

Elicitation: A Platonic Presentation

Elicitation is the process of interacting with the exemplar through questions and observation in order to formulate a useful and faithful description of her experience and behavior. In fact the process of elicitation is anything but neat and straightforward in actual practice; there are no elicitation questions that magically reveal the necessary information. This means that eventually we must be so familiar with the modeling distinctions that we no longer need to depend upon ideal questions to do the work for us. Nevertheless, we will begin our exploration of elicitation by using an ideal approach and ideal questions. We do this because becoming familiar with the elicitation of these distinctions is best done by encountering them first through uncluttered and straightforward examples.

The purpose of elicitation is to identify the underlying and generative elements of human experience. Our job, as modelers, is to ask questions that orient the exemplar's attention and awareness in ways that, though possibly unfamiliar, nevertheless allow them to access the information we need. The situation is much like being faced with a safe containing something valuable. The door has a combination lock. The safe is not trying to keep you out. It has no objection to being opened, and is only waiting for you to turn the tumblers in the right way. However, suppose you don't have the combination. Instead, what you have is an understanding of how tumblers work, a stethoscope for listening, and sensitive fingers to turn the dial for telltale clicks that indicate when a tumbler has fallen. It may take a few tries—you can be misled by errant clicks, or may mishear them—but once you have the pattern of turns and numbers, you can go into that safe any time you wish. Now, of course, that combination will not allow you to open any other safe. But the skills of listening and feeling *will* allow you to discover their combinations as well.

As we discussed in Essay 4, the questions we ask are the first and most direct way we have to gain access to elements of the exemplar's internal experience. Before plunging into our questions, however, we want to remind you that elicitation is not something you do *to* your exemplar, but something you are doing *with* your exemplar. Your exemplar is a person to relate to and understand; a safe to open with a sensitive touch (rather than a stick of dynamite). Together, you and your exemplar create a description of her experience and behavior. That description needs to be, in the first instance, something with which your exemplar resonates. That is, it mirrors her experience sufficiently that her response to it is, "Yes, that's what I do." In addition, the description needs to be usable by you. The purpose of elicitation questions is to help you *and* your exemplar gain access to features of her experience, organizing them in a way that makes those features both recognizable by the exemplar *and* usable by you.

The "Ideal" Sequence

There is no right or wrong sequence for eliciting the elements of the Experiential Array. Nevertheless, there is a sequence we generally try to follow: Criterion, Definition, Evidence, Enabling Cause-Effect, Motivating Cause-Effect, Primary Operation, Secondary Operations, Sustaining Emotion and, finally, External Behavior.

This sequence suggests itself from our experiences in elicitation, which have generally shown this flow to be natural, sensible, and useful:

- The Criterion sets the primary filter or test for the ability being modeled. That is, it sets the essential frame for all of the other elements of the Array.
- The Definition is a refinement of the Criterion, and Evidence a refinement of both of them.
- And obviously it is easier to correctly identify Enabling and Motivating Cause-Effects once you have identified the Criterion that is being enabled and motivated.
- The Primary Operation of the Strategy operates in relation to the Test, which is given by the Criterion and its Evidence.
- The Secondary Operations engage when the Primary Operation is not sufficient to satisfy the Test.
- The Sustaining Emotion is often quite subtle (though, as we have said, it may have a huge impact) and, so, may not have been as much in the exemplar's awareness as the other elements. Eliciting the Beliefs and Strategies first creates a rich and recent re-experiencing of the ability to help the exemplar discern the Sustaining Emotion.
- External Behavior is saved for last precisely because it is where people who have not been trained in modeling generally go first (and, often, the only place they go). Since we want to identify only those behaviors that are unique to the ability *and* are not likely to emerge naturally from the Beliefs, Strategies and Emotions, specifying these other Elements first helps narrow the field within which to look for External Behaviors.

Planting the Flag

The richness of human experience and language being what it is, there is a high potential for ending up neck deep in a plate of information spaghetti. In order to avoid that, we need a way to identify which bits of experience are relevant to the exemplar's ability, and which are not.

What comes to our aid here is the fact that the experiential elements of a particular Array (that is, an ability) will have a special relationship with each other: they all "fit" with each other. Beliefs, Strategies, Emotions and External Behaviors are, in a sense, different languages that are being used to describe the same "thing," the structure of the exemplar's ability. And so there will be both some overlap and some differences in those descriptions. But whatever those differences in description are, the experiences they are describing will nevertheless fit and work with the other elements of the Array. Anything that does not fit and work with the other elements of a particular Array belongs to some other aspect of this person's world (that is, to another Array).

The coherency of the Array helps us avoid getting caught in the spaghetti of information by providing an ongoing check: Does this, or does this not, fit with what else is operating in the Array? Anything that does not fit does not belong in *this* Array. (Though of course it may be worth noting because it belongs in another Array that you are interested in, or may simply be a potentially valuable bit of information that is worth pursuing later.)

Array coherency also frees us from being overly concerned about following the "ideal sequence" of elicitation. Regardless of where we enter the Array or how we carom through it, bouncing from one element to another, we have our ongoing test: *Does this fit with what else is operating in the Array or not?* This question helps keep us focused on what is relevant and what, though perhaps interesting, is nevertheless outside of the Array in focus. In order to help you answer this ongoing relevancy question, we suggest "planting the flag" somewhere in the Array. By this we mean, begin by finding something about the structure of the exemplar's experience that you are confident *does* belong to the ability you are modeling, and from *there* expand your subsequent information gathering.

For reasons we explained above, we try to plant our flag in the Criterion first, and then start exploring from there. For example, we begin our modeling of a copy editor by finding out that his Criterion is "flow." Planting our flag there, we can then find out what he means by flow (Definition), how he knows when the copy is flowing (Evidence), and so on.

But in fact you can plant the flag anywhere in the Array and set off from that point, *as long as* you continue to test your subsequent discoveries against the coherency of the growing Array. For instance, if your sense during a particular elicitation is to begin with External Behavior (because it is easier, or it is what the exemplar wants to talk about, or something about it has come out that captures your interest), then by all means plant your flag there. Using our architect example, you could plant your flag in her External Behavior of walking around the property. With that as your flagged point of reference, you could then move on to the Criterion by asking something like, "As you are walking around the property, what are you evaluating?" You are, in effect, asking your exemplar, "What Criterion relates to that External Behavior?" As long as you make sure that the Array grows into a coherent whole, you can plant your flag anywhere in it, and branch out from there. And of course, if you discover that you have planted your flag in an Array that is not really the one you want to model, you can always pull up your flag and plant it again in the Array you *do* want to model.

Array Elicitation Questions

Just as there is no ideal sequence for elicitation, there are no ideal elicitation questions. This fact has not stopped us from trying to find them. Our many years on this quest have convinced us that if such questions exist at all, they will be found sitting on a shelf beside the Grail. Until we find that shelf, we can offer you questions that generally work quite well to orient the exemplar's experience in a way *likely* to take her to the particular kind of information you want to elicit. In fact, for most of the elements of experience we will offer you two questions. Both versions seek the same information, but use different phrasing. Usually, if one question does not help your exemplar access the needed information, switching to the other question will often be effective.

Now, just because your exemplar responded to your question does *not* mean that your exemplar *answered* your question. It is essential to bear in mind that you need to understand the *kind* of information you want to elicit with your question. Knowing a question to ask is not a substitute for knowing what kind of information you want to get through asking that question. Being familiar with the kind of information (that is, the distinct range and quality of experiences) you are after will allow you to recognize whether or not the information you want is "there" in the exemplar's response to your question.

Nevertheless, we are suggesting that, for a while, you use the standard forms of questions we are offering to you in this section. Words do matter, as we have seen. For instance, a question that we often use to elicit the Criterion is, "What is important when you are...?" Is that much different than asking, say, "What is important about...?" It turns out that it is very different. Compare where the following two questions take your experience:

"What is important when you are reading?"
"What is important about reading?"

Probably they take you to two different aspects of your experience. The "when you are" of the first version tends to put you inside the experience, where you can simply report on what is going on *in* your experience *as* you read (e.g. "I want to be inside the character's experiences"). The "about" in the second version of the question tends to put you outside of the experience, making judgments *on the act of* reading (e.g. "It is way to learn about world").

The wording of each of the elicitation questions we are about to offer you, though not ideal, has been annealed and refined in the crucible of work with countless exemplars. As we already admitted, the result is not a set of perfect questions. There are no perfect questions. But these *are* good ones. We will point out some of their individual merits as we go along to better help you understand why they are the way they are. Once you understand what types and qualities of experiences you are going for in asking *these* questions, you will be free to generate questions of your own that take into account those same concerns. That is, familiarity with the Array distinctions will eventually allow you to let go of the "standard" forms we are starting with here, freeing you to generate your own questions in response to the often changing needs of the elicitation process.

We will begin with Platonic elicitation examples. In other words, all of the examples in this Essay are made up. This is a heuristic for the purposes of illustrative clarity; the messiness of real elicitation will follow soon enough in the next Essay, "Elicitation: Warts and All." Before wading into those deeper waters, however, we can use these "clean" examples to get a clearer impression of what the elicitation questions are aiming for and, therefore, have a clearer idea of what to look for in real-life elicitations.

Beliefs

One would think that there would be no need for instruction on eliciting beliefs. People express them freely and often. Why not simply write them down as they flow out?

The reason is that the exemplar's flood of beliefs is largely made up of repetitions and reformulations of the same structural droplets. Rather than try to get our arms around the exemplar's often enormous and constantly shifting sea of beliefs, we look for the underlying structures that generate that sea. To help us with this, we have the distinction between beliefs based on equivalence relationships and beliefs based on causal relationships. We have also made within these two general distinctions the finer distinctions of Criterion, Definition, Evidence, Enabling and Motivating Cause-Effects. These finer distinctions are portrayed in dynamic relationship with one another in the Belief Template.

Criterion

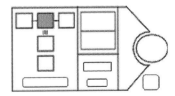

Depending upon the inherent complexity of the ability and the subjective world of your exemplar, there may be only a few criteria operating in her experience, or there may be hundreds. This cornucopia of criteria is initially made more manageable by specifying what particular aspect of her ability you want to model.[46] Modeling is made still easier by recognizing that, although many criteria may be contributing to this particular aspect of the ability, you are primarily interested in identifying the *criterion in focus*, or, more simply, the Criterion.

When eliciting the Criterion, you are asking for that primary and essential standard the exemplar wants to satisfy or fulfill when operating in the context of the ability. It is as if the exemplar is asking herself, "What standard do I most want or need to satisfy right now in this situation?"

ELICITATION QUESTIONS:

"When you are [ability], what is important to you?"
                            or
"When you are [ability], what are you evaluating?"

(In the elicitation questions, we will put [brackets] around the description of the content you need to insert into that question. For example, if the ability is "Running a brainstorming session" and you want to elicit the Criterion, you would ask, "When you are *running a brainstorming session*, what is important to you?" If the ability were "Appreciating abstract art," you would ask, "When you are *appreciating abstract art*, what is important to you?" Naturally, you may need to adjust the question to fit the form of the exemplar's content so that the question makes grammatical sense. We will use **_bold italics_** to mark out the relevant information in the exemplar's answers.)

The three Platonic exemplars we will use for the rest of this Essay on elicitation are "Adam," who has the ability to plan celebrations that people love, "Bridgit," who is able to work patiently with young children, and "Claire," who designs computer interfaces that people enjoy interacting with.

---

[46] We may be modeling several aspects of an ability, of course, but each is modeled separately, or at least is kept separate from the others as we gather information. See Essay 2: The Process of Modeling.

EXAMPLES

> Q: "When you are planning a celebration, what is important to you?"
>
> Adam: "What I really want is that ***everyone is included*** in whatever is going on."

— o —

> Q: "When you are being patient with a child as she is learning something, what are you evaluating?"
>
> Bridgit: "Is there ***movement***. I don't care about the end point, really, only that she is moving in that direction."

— o —

> Q: "When you are designing the user interface for a program, what is important to you?"
>
> Claire: "I want it to be ***elegant***. An interface that has ***elegance*** is just... well, it's just so great when they are."

One of the most common pitfalls that folks fall into when going after the Criterion is that of eliciting one of the many criteria that are relevant to the context of the ability, but not the Criterion that is primary to the ability itself. The introductory phrase, "When you are..." is intended to help address this by focusing your exemplar's attention to when he is *in* the process of manifesting her ability, rather than outside it (where there are, of course, any number of criteria).

Definition

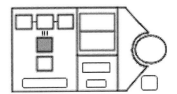

When eliciting the Definition, keep in mind that you are after a description of the *kind* of experience being "named" by the Criterion. Defining the Criterion may include qualities, expectations, boundaries, time frames, behaviors, perceptions...anything in your exemplar's experience that is, for them, what their Criterion *is*. The Definition is much like a dictionary definition, which is an abstraction or description that presents the general nature or essential qualities of something; in the case of modeling this is the Criterion.

ELICITATION QUESTIONS:

"What is [Criterion]?"
            or
"What do you mean by [Criterion]?"

EXAMPLES

      Q: "What do you mean by 'everyone is included'?"
  Adam: "That whatever is going on, each person has a role in it, or is somehow directly involved."

— o —

      Q: "What do you mean by 'movement'?"
Bridgit: "Well, I mean that she can do something she couldn't do before, or understand something she didn't understand before. Even the tiniest of things is enough."

— o —

      Q: "What is 'elegance'?"
  Claire: "A web site where the *things just flow easily from one point to another*, that's elegance."

It is often the case that when exemplars are asked to define a Criterion, they respond with examples of what the Criterion is, rather than the abstracted description of the kinds of experiences that Criterion covers for them. For instance, Adam in the example above could have instead answered with, "If there is a presentation to make—of an award or something—I try to make sure that everyone gets a chance to touch it or hold it, and is present when it is given. Even kitchen staff." This is a very interesting *example* of what Adam does. However, some celebrations don't include awards or kitchen staffs, so the example does not define what 'everyone is included' means.

If instead of a Definition you are getting examples of the Criterion, you can get to the Definition by asking for additional examples. Look for the pattern that ties all of those examples together, and then offer your version of the Definition to your exemplar. She will know right away if it fits her experience or not. "Does not fit" is almost as useful as "does fits," because it will make clearer to your exemplar what her experience is *not*, which will almost always help her bring into focus what it actually *is*.

Alternatively, you can direct your exemplar to "chunk up" from her examples by asking some version of, "What kind of experience are those examples all examples *of*?"

Evidence

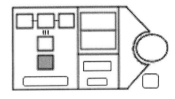

Evidence specifies what the exemplar sees, hears and/or feels that indicates to what extent her Criterion is being satisfied or not. When eliciting Evidence, keep in mind that it is intended to capture the exemplar's sensory experiences.

This does not mean we must slavishly adhere to describing things in minute, sensory detail. We could say, "The corners of her lips are turned up at a 30 degree angle and her mouth is spread wider than normal, thinning her lips—which are also slightly parted—her head is tilted slightly back, there are crinkly lines at the corners of her eyes, which have also been drawn wider" etc. Or we could simply say, "She's smiling." Both are sensory experiences; the first is more specific. The question is, is it unnecessarily specific? Evidence needs to be described at a level of specificity that allows you to see, hear and feel the same things the exemplar does in relation to her Criterion. If the statement, "She's smiling," is enough then there is no need to chunk it down into all its details. However, a statement such as, "She looks at me with a certain expression," is not specific enough to allow you to perceive what the exemplar perceives. There are a lot of facial expressions, so this second statement needs to be chunked down further until it becomes specific enough for you to share the exemplar's perceptions ("What expression? Describe it to me").

ELICITATION QUESTION:

> "What do you see, hear and/or feel that lets you know there is*
> [Criterion]?"
>
>   *(or "you are" "it is" "you have" etc.)

EXAMPLES

> Q: "What do you see, hear and/or feel that lets you know that
> 'everyone is included'?"
>
> Adam: "Well, no one is by themselves, and the groups of people are
> always changing. People feel free to ask for what they want,
> or even complain, and when there are group things, there is
> kind of one sound in the room, not quiet over here, laughing
> there, talking there, and so on."

— o —

> Q: "What do you see, hear and/or feel that lets you know that
> there is 'movement'?"
>
> Bridgit: "You can see it in the child's face, really. She's intent on
> what she's doing, and looks proud. Sometimes smiling."

— o —

> Q: "What do you see, hear and/or feel that lets you know that an
> interface has 'elegance'?"
>
> Claire: "You're not even thinking about how to find something; you
> just go to it. In fact, the best is when you aren't even aware
> that you are jumping from one place to another."

As in asking for the Definition, asking for the Evidence may elicit specific examples, rather than a description of the particular sensory-based experiences that constitute the Evidence. And, as with the Definition, you can abstract that Evidence from the examples, or make the idea of "Evidence" clear enough to your exemplar that she can sort through her examples and pull the description together herself.

Enabling Cause-Effect

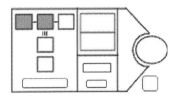

The Enabling Cause-Effect and the Strategy are often related, so it is important to recognize how they are different distinctions. The Strategy lays out what the exemplar *does*, that is, the specifics of her internal and external behaviors. Beliefs, however, are generalizations about how the world works or is organized. As a belief, the Enabling Cause-Effect is the exemplar's *generalization* about what conditions help make it possible for the Criterion to be fulfilled.

As we will see, the Enabling Cause-Effect may include strategically important behaviors. But our attention here is on the belief that our exemplar holds that these particular behaviors are *prerequisites* to satisfying her Criterion. Of course, behaviors that appear in the Enabling Cause-Effect are likely to reappear in the Strategy, as well. But in the context of her Strategy we will be interested in the *doing* of them. As part of an Enabling Cause-Effect, these behaviors serve as goals or intentions, something to be fulfilled, so that the Criterion can be satisfied. In the context of the Strategy, these behaviors are specified things *to do* in service of manifesting the ability.

So, we are looking for the generalization—in this case, in the form of a cause-effect—that is guiding our exemplar when manifesting her ability. But this is what we, as modelers, are looking for; the exemplar is simply going to be reporting her experience of herself as she is accustomed to thinking about it. As human beings, our *doing* is often what is most readily apparent and accessible to us. And so it may happen that your exemplar will start describing elements of her Strategy to you, rather than going to the level of generalization (beliefs) that informs and guides that Strategy. You can sort out for yourself whether or not this is happening by stepping into the context of the ability with your exemplar's answer and ask yourself, "Is this expressing a generalization about how the world works in relation to the fulfilling the Criterion, or is this a description of what the exemplar *is doing* to satisfy the Criterion?"

If you are getting description of Strategy, rather than the causal generalizations, simply point out the difference between the two to your exemplar. This is often all she needs to make the distinction in her own experience and to then focus her attention on the generalizations she operating out of (rather than on the strategic behaviors she uses to bring those generalizations to life).

ELICITATION QUESTIONS:

"What leads to or makes possible [Criterion]?"
               or
"What is necessary for there to be [Criterion]?"

EXAMPLES

Q: "What is necessary for 'everyone to be included'?"

Adam: "You have to **know the group**. Without that, you can't really know what they will naturally enjoy and respond to."

— o —

Q: "What leads to or makes possible 'movement'?"

Bridgit: "***Trust***. If you ***trust the child to know how much she can handle at any one time***, you will be able to help her move. And whenever there is movement, I always praise her."

— o —

Q: "What leads to or makes possible 'elegance'?"

Claire: "If we are talking elegance, it has to be easy and smooth to navigate. And if you're going to get that, you have to ***care more about the experience of the end user than about being clever, getting lost in your own cleverness***."

One way to determine what is Enabling Cause-Effect and what is Strategy is to consider, Does the exemplar's answer tell me what specifically to do? (Strategy) Or is it more of a goal or intention that could be pursued in many different ways? (Enabling Cause-Effect) For instance, Adam says, "You have to know the group." It is easy to imagine that there are numerous ways of coming to know the group: sending out a questionnaire, doing a combined astrological chart, meeting each person privately for a talk, getting a supervisor's assessment of them, gathering information about their cultural and social backgrounds, and so on. Any of these could be Strategy elements. And of course, *all* of the elements of a Strategy are in service of satisfying the Criterion. (It could be that Adam uses all of these tactics as ways of fostering "inclusion.")

The Enabling Cause-Effect, however, describes what *conditions* must exist for the Criterion to be satisfied; not what specific actions bring about those conditions. Adam's belief, "You have to know the group," tells us what he believes must happen so that people are included, but not the actions that will make "knowing the group" come true. That is the province of the Strategy.

Remember that the exemplar's answer to your question may include information that is not an answer to *that* question, but another, perhaps as yet unasked question. Both Bridgit and Claire's answers provide examples of this. Bridgit added, "And whenever there is movement, I always praise her." This is part of her Strategy sneaking into the Enabling Cause-Effect answer. Similarly, Claire began her answer with, "If we are talking elegance, it has to be easy and smooth to navigate," which is part of the description of what "elegance" is, rather than a condition that brings about (causes) "elegance."

Motivating Cause-Effect

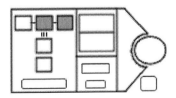

It is often the case that fulfilling the Criterion is motivated by the exemplar's belief that doing so will have a significant impact on something which is of even greater importance to her. Of course, fulfilling the

Criterion is causally linked to attaining the goal of the ability itself. For instance, Adam's ability to ensure that "everyone is included," helps make it possible for him to plan successful celebrations. However, even though it is important to Adam to plan successful celebrations, it is often the case that what is fueling his efforts is something even "higher" (or "deeper," if you prefer) than the Criterion and the immediate goal of the ability. We work competently at our jobs to take care of our families, for instance, or to be a successful person, or to be proud of ourselves. The Motivating Cause-Effect identifies this higher (deeper) goal that is served by the Criterion (and perhaps the ability itself, as well).

ELICITATION QUESTIONS:

   "Why is [Criterion] important?"
              or
   "What does [Criterion] lead to or make possible?"

EXAMPLES

       Q: "Why is it important that 'everyone is included'?"
    Adam: "If they are included they will sort of all feed their
            excitement and joy into each other, and the celebration
            becomes an opportunity to become *a real community*."

                         — o —

       Q: "What does 'movement' lead to or make possible?"
  Bridgit: "*Freedom*, actually. As long as you're moving, you have *the
            possibility of going anywhere*."

                         — o —

       Q: "Why is 'elegance' important?"
   Claire: "A site that allows you to flow through it is one that *you will
            want to stay at, and return to*. You may not even know
            why, but *you will just love that site*."

Motivating Cause-Effects usually address what one perceives as the truly "big" concerns, the truly important concerns in one's life, or in life in general. This is the sense of both Adam's "real community" and Bridgit's "freedom." Motivating Cause-effects need not always be so lofty, however. Claire's "users will want to stay at, and return to, the web site," is an example. Even so, like all Motivating Cause-Effects, it is something of importance to the exemplar *outside of*, or *bigger than*, the context in which the ability is operating. Claire is bringing "elegance" to a web site *before* it is on the screens of the users; Bridgit helps engender movement in children so that they have more "freedom" in their futures; and Adam creates inclusion in a group so that the event can forge a "real community."

A variation that you will find in some exemplars is that their Criterion and Motivator are the same. That is, the criterion in focus in the context of their ability is also something that is inherently important to them, and so is not in service of anything "higher" or "deeper"; it already is that "high," that "deep." For instance, it could be that for Adam "inclusion" is a very highly valued Criterion, inherently important and satisfying. That is, for him "inclusion" is a meaningful end in itself. Indications that your exemplar's Criterion and Motivator are one and the same (that there is no separate Motivating Cause-Effect) are:

- Each time you ask why the Criterion is important, she answers with that same Criterion/Definition (even if phrased differently).
- She can't come up with anything that the Criterion is in service of.
- She says things like, "Well, it just *is*," "What else is there?" "That's what life's about," and so on.
- She looks at you like you are an idiot for even asking.

Supporting Beliefs

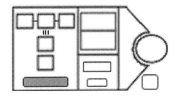

The exemplar will be operating within a web of beliefs, of course. The ones we want to avoid are those that are irrelevant to the ability itself, or are relevant but not needed to be able to manifest the ability. Most of the relevant beliefs will be variations on a few underlying relationships, relationships which we have capture in the Belief Template. By capturing that belief structure, we avoid having to absorb possibly endless versions of the same, underlying equivalence and causal relationships. Still, there may be some beliefs in the experiential "web" of the ability that are very helpful in manifesting it. These Supporting Beliefs are not part of the Belief Template, but they do support the Array.

Supporting Beliefs are not elicited. Instead, they appear fortuitously, and elicitation of them involves noticing you have been "grabbed" by a statement from your exemplar. Usually you are "grabbed" because the belief is expressed in a punchy, evocative or epigrammatic form. If, when you step-in and try on that belief, it also seems to significantly facilitate manifesting the ability, it is worth noting as a Supporting Belief.

EXAMPLES

> Adam: "No one wants to be left out—they just want to be asked in the right way."

> Bridgit: "Think like a child and you will know what to do."

> Claire: "When it comes to the Internet, what annoys you probably annoys everyone else, too."

Strategies

Strategies are sequences or sets of internal and external behaviors intended to fulfill a Criterion. In other words, a Strategy is whatever your exemplar typically *does* to get what she *wants* in a particular situation. Depending upon the ability and the exemplar, a Strategy can involve numerous behaviors, some of which may be complex, and will operate either sequentially, simultaneously, or on an as needed basis, or any combination of those forms. The best way to get our arms around this variety and complexity is through eliciting a narrative of the Strategy.

Primary Operation

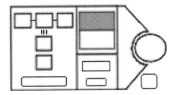 The Primary Operation is a description of what the exemplar typically does to satisfy her Criterion. These doings can cover a lot of behavioral territory. Usually there will be a blend of both internal processes and external behaviors, the ratios of which will depend upon the particular ability.

Probably the most difficult issue to deal with when eliciting the Primary Operation is that of specificity. A strategy step that is "too big" does not give enough direction as to what to do. A strategy step that is "too small" gives superfluous detail, bogging down the model in unnecessary information.

Of course, there is no absolute right amount or level of specificity. The right level of specificity is that level which allows you to manifest the Strategy yourself. So, the ongoing goal in eliciting a Primary (or a Secondary) Operation is to *chunk the description down to your level of competence.* You can do this by asking yourself the question, "From her description of [this step], can I do it too?" The purpose of this question is to prompt you to test whether or not you already have, in your personal experience, the information you need to access the behaviors called for in the exemplar's Strategy. For instance, if a step in the exemplar's Strategy is to "imagine the future I want," and you are already able to do that, there is probably no need to chunk it down any further. If instead you do not know how to "imagine the future I want," then that step in the Strategy *does* need to be chunked down further, until it is described as a set of internal processes and external behaviors at which you *are* (or know how to become) competent.[47]

---

[47] There may also be situations when you already know how to manifest a particular aspect of the exemplar's Strategy, but wonder whether she has something interesting to say on the subject. For instance, she explains that she "strikes up a rapport with her client." As it turns out, you already are able to do that yourself. Still, you are interested in how *she* does it because there might be something useful to learn there. Curiosity is legitimate.

ELICITATION QUESTIONS:

"What are you usually doing to [satisfy Criterion]?"
                   or
"How do you usually go about making sure that [Criterion is satisfied]?"

EXAMPLES [48]

> Q: "When planning a celebration, how do you usually go about making sure that 'everyone will be included'?"
> Adam: "If I don't already know the people who will be coming—I mean their sub-culture, age range, where from, social and work background, their relationships with each other, and so on—I find out. And, of course, I find out what the agenda is for the celebration. Then, for each of the events on the agenda, I imagine I'm one of the people attending—not as me, but as them—and ask myself, 'What do I wish would be happening here now?' And then I imagine someone coming who is likely to not feel comfortable and part of the group, and ask myself, 'What would draw me into this?' I take those two answers and figure out how to make sure both happen."

— o —

> Q: "What are you usually doing to help bring about 'movement' with a child who is learning something?"
> Bridgit: "Several things. I'm always noticing what the child can do already. I consider what would be a small step from there toward where she eventually needs to be in her learning. And we take just that step. If she's pleased with that, it goes smoothly, we can take the next step. I'm always paying close

---

[48] Remember that these are Platonic examples, and do not include the back and forth questioning that would probably be necessary to elicit the full extent of the Primary Operation, or to elicit from some of the strategy steps the details that we might need to competently manifest that particular step.

attention to her attention level and comfort. As long as these are okay, we can keep going. And when she moves forward in any way, I make sure to let her know that, so she can be proud of herself, which, of course, she has every right to be."

— o —

Q: "What do you usually do to ensure that an interface is 'elegant'?"

Claire: "I just blank myself out, set Claire aside for a while. I come to this web site like it's my very first visit, and as someone who is fairly new to the web. And I notice, where do my eyes go? Do I have to search for what I want? Which is a problem. Is there stuff I would never use, or at least not here? Also a problem. I also ask myself, how can this whatever-it-is be misunderstood? If it's a search problem, I move things around until it is right where my 'blank' person can find it easily. If it's something superfluous, I put it either on another page or (if at all possible) in the trashcan. And stuff that can be misunderstood...well, if it's a graphic, I work with the graphics people to clean it up, and if it's text, the writers."

Notice that in some Primary Operations there are sequential steps, such as with Adam's for planning a celebration:

1. Find out "who" is coming, and the event agenda.

2. For each event, imagine I am an attendee and ask myself, "What do I wish would be happening here now?"

3. Imagine I am an uncomfortable attendee and ask myself, "What would draw me into this?"

4. Take those two answers and figure out how to make sure both happen.

Other Primary Operations, such as Bridgit's, include behaviors that are more simultaneous:

+   I'm always noticing what the child can do already.
+   I'm always paying close attention to her level of attention and comfort. As long as these are okay, we can keep going.

And finally, Claire's Primary Operation provides an example of ad hoc strategy steps, steps that are taken only when the situation calls for them:

- If it's a search problem, I move things around until it is right where my "blank" person can find it easily.

- If it's something superfluous, I put it either on another page or (if at all possible) in the trashcan.

- Stuff that can be misunderstood...well, if it's a graphic, I work with the graphics people to clean it up, and if it's text, the writers.

Secondary Operations

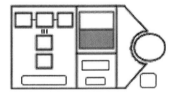

An exemplar of an ability is someone who consistently has good (excellent, desirable, successful...) results in a particular context. This does not mean that it is always easy, or that it is always smooth sailing, or even that good results are always attained. But an exemplar is not thrown by difficulties that are not handled by her Primary Operation. Instead, she has additional useful and effective ways to deal with difficult situations, and these additional ways are the Secondary Operations.

There are three classes of Secondary Operations that we explore directly: the exemplar's response when his Criterion is not sufficiently satisfied, when it is not at all satisfied, and when it cannot be satisfied.

You may not find all three of these types of Secondary Operations represented in your exemplar. An exemplar may simply not have one of these Secondary Operations, or may respond with the same Operation to different situations (for instance, responding with the same behavior both when his Criterion is "not satisfied" and when it "cannot be satisfied").

ELICITATION QUESTIONS:

"What do you do when [Criterion not sufficiently satisfied]?"
"What do you do when [Criterion not at all satisfied]?"
"What do you do when [Criterion cannot be satisfied]?"

EXAMPLES

Q: "What do you do when you are not sure if what you have come up with will allow everyone to be included as much as you would like?"

Adam: "I start again, with the imagining and so on, but this time I first think of some different aspect of who these attendees are; I bring out something that I was not considering before about who they are. Often that will give me some new ideas."

Q: "What do you do when you aren't at all able to come up with a way for everyone to be included?"

Adam: "Well, then obviously I am missing something about these people, so I will gather some more information; actually talk with a couple of them to find out what they like, hate, and so on."

Q: "What do you do when you determine that you will not be able to plan the event so that 'everyone will be included'?"

Adam: "I do the best I can, go for the most people I can. I hate doing that, though."

— o —

Q: "What do you do when the child is having difficulty in moving in relation to her learning?"

Bridgit: "That is a clear signal that *I need to reduce the size of the steps.*"

Q: "What do you do when the child is not moving at all?"

Bridgit: "Well, then probably something is going on in her life that is more important at that time, something is occupying most of her attention. So I will drop the lesson and try to find out what is going on and, if I can, help her deal with it."

Q: "What do you do when you realize that the child is not going to be able to move?"

Bridgit: "THAT does not happen."

— o —

Q: "What do you do when you are having difficulty making a web site elegant?"

Claire: "They're always pretty difficult, I find. I just keep working at moving things around, looking for possible misunderstandings, and so on until it's flowing."

Q: "What do you do when you are not at all able to make a web site elegant?"

Claire: "I try to think of other sites I have worked on or seen that were similar in content, in what they were trying to do. I look at some of those to see how I or someone else organized them. And that usually gives me some clues I can take to the site that's giving me trouble."

Q: "What do you do when you realize that it will not be possible to make a web site elegant?"

Claire: "This does happen once in a while, and it is because there is something very flawed in the fundamental concept of the site. In those cases, *we have to go back to square one and look at what we want the site to do and be, and rebuild it from first principles.* That's the only way."

For Adam, the situations in which his Criterion is either not sufficiently satisfied, not at all satisfied, or cannot be satisfied are three, distinct possibilities, and he has different Secondary Operations for handling each one. But just because we ask for each of these three possibilities does not mean that they exist for the exemplar. Bridgit, for instance, does not have a Secondary Operation for "Criterion cannot be satisfied." For her, that is not a possibility; it is always possible to take even smaller steps and, as she says, "I trust that the little steps will add up to getting somewhere eventually." And Claire does not have a distinct Secondary Operation for "Criterion is not sufficiently satisfied." For her there is only continuing to engage in her Primary Operation, unless she hits the wall of being completely unable to bring elegance to the web site.

Emotions

Typically, exemplars (like most of us) are ready and willing to talk about what they are feeling, and often there are a lot of feelings to talk about. The quantity of emotions that emerge, the ease with which they are identified, and perhaps the intensity of affect that accompanies them, can mislead us into assuming that all of them are significant, and must be captured in the model. With respect to eliciting our exemplar's emotions, then, our attention needs to be on distinguishing the *function* a particular emotion serves in the exemplar's ability, and then determining whether or not that function is essential to the model. The most important function an emotion can serve is to support or sustain the exemplar as she manifests her ability.

Sustaining Emotion

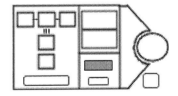 The ongoing, background nature of Sustaining Emotions means that they often go unnoticed by the exemplar. When it comes to elicitation, this also means that they may not be as readily accessible, or as easily languaged as the other elements of experience. And so it may take your exemplar time, as well as searching and experimenting within herself, in order to identify what that (often subtle) background emotional state is for her.

Once again, you can use the process of stepping-in to help your exemplar test whether or not a particular emotion she has identified is likely to be the Sustaining Emotion. Since a Sustaining Emotion is held or maintained in experience regardless of whether the Criterion is being satisfied, not satisfied, violated or exceeded, you and your exemplar can test what happens in your own experiences when you imagine the Criterion being met or not met in various ways. Of course, you will probably feel emotional changes in response to these different situations. The question is, does the emotion you are feeling "stay" in your experience regardless of whether or not the Criterion is being met. If it does, it may well be your exemplar's Sustaining Emotion. If instead it comes and goes depending upon how the present situation is or is not satisfying her Criterion, then it is probably a Signal Emotion. For example, in Essay 10 we talked about the person who feels *challenged* when doing crossword puzzles. He continues to feel challenged even as he is feeling *surprised* by an answer, *frustrated* with a clue, *elated* over figuring out a difficult clue, and so on. "Challenged," then, is his Sustaining Emotion, and the others are Signal Emotions.

ELICITATION QUESTION:

"What is the background feeling that keeps you pursuing [Criterion]?"

EXAMPLES

Q: "What is the background feeling that keeps you pursuing 'everyone is included' in celebrations?"

Adam: "Well, through the entire process it's almost as though it is already happening. I see how great it will be, and I'm feeling this sense of *excitement* about what the celebration can be."

— o —

Q: "What is the background feeling that keeps you pursuing 'movement' with children when they are learning?"

Bridgit: "*Love*. I'm just *loving* that child the whole time."

— o —

> Q: "What is the background feeling that keeps you pursuing
>   'elegance' when designing web sites?"
> Claire: "It's a feeling of 'I'm just going to do it somehow,' you
>   know? It's a challenge, I feel *challenged*."

Using the same word your exemplar uses to help *you* access her emotion does not guarantee that the two of you are having the same emotional experience. However, the exemplar's description often includes explanations and examples that will help you better grasp the specific qualities of her Sustaining Emotion. In some cases, as with Claire and her Sustaining Emotion of *challenged*, the accompanying description can be necessary to properly grasp the correct "form" of the emotion. Her form of "challenged"—"I'm just going to do it somehow"—feels different than other forms of feeling "challenged," such as, "Nothing can stop me," or "What can I come up with that could work?" to take just two possible examples. Similarly, Adam offers us some of the cognitive facets of his experience of *excitement*: "It is already happening" and "I see how great it will be." By adding these to our own experience of *excitement*, we bring our emotional state into closer alignment with Adam's experience.

In addition, the form of the word(s) used to denote an emotion can itself be significant in accurately conveying the exemplar's experience. Bridgit answers, "Love. I'm just loving that child the whole time." If you take a moment to feel *love* and then to feel *loving*, you will notice that they take your experience in somewhat different directions. (For us, *love* has more of a passive sense of "openness or receptivity to"; *loving* has more of an active sense of "extending to.") Of course, having two ways of describing her emotion may not mean that there is any difference between them for *Bridgit*. But if they are different to you, then it is worth asking her, "For you, is there a difference between 'love' and 'loving'?" Doing this will help both of you become more precise about her Sustaining Emotion.

Signal Emotions

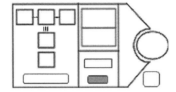 Signal Emotions are transient emotional responses to moment-to-moment changes regarding the satisfaction of criteria, and so there can be a lot of these emotions popping into your exemplar's experience as she manifests her ability. Do we need to include them all in the model? Some? Which ones?

Because these emotional reactions tend to be similar for everyone using the same Criterion, *and* because they typically serve as temporary feedback to your exemplar that she needs to change what she is doing, it is usually not necessary to identify and catalogue Signal Emotions for a model. Of course, there are exceptions; your exemplar may have a particular Signal Emotion that is somehow unusual or (even if usual) so significant to the ability that it is essential to note it. In any case, there is no elicitation question for the Signal Emotion; they readily pop up. The exemplar will certainly offer you many of them in her descriptions. When you step into her experience, if any of those Signal Emotions strike you as possibly significant, check them out with your exemplar and, if essential to the ability, include them in the model.

EXAMPLES

> Adam: "Okay, here I am, imagining I'm the new hire in the company, and while they're presenting the awards and making all of these inside jokes, I feel very ***uncomfortable, isolated.***"

> Bridgit: "I was working with a 7-year-old yesterday, and finally she was able to do subtraction for the first time and I was ***thrilled***!"

> Claire: "Sometimes I realize I am feeling ***deeply concerned***—like you would feel for someone in possible danger—and when I

do I know I am looking at a site that is fundamentally flawed."

We have examples of Signal Emotions from both Adam and from Bridgit, but neither of them is probably worth noting. Most anyone operating out of the Criterion, "people are included" would naturally feel *isolated* as they imagined being in that "new hire" position at the awards ceremony. And as for Bridgit feeling *thrilled*, again, that is something any of us is likely to feel if we have the Criterion of "movement" and have been working with a child who has "finally moved"![49]

In contrast, Claire's Signal Emotion may be worth including in her model. Feeling *deeply concerned* is somewhat unconventional and not what we might expect—or naturally experience ourselves—when using her Criterion of "elegance" and having it violated. What is more, it serves as a signal to her of something very important in terms of her ability, which is that she is dealing with a web site that may well need more drastic measures than she had expected (perhaps taking her to her 3rd Secondary Operation, requiring a complete rebuilding of the website).

External Behavior

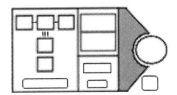

When eliciting External Behaviors, you are not after everything the exemplar does and says. Because much of External Behavior is the natural result of internal processes, it is not necessary to catalogue all of the Behaviors in order to ensure that they will be "there" when you use the exemplar's model; the Beliefs, Strategies and Emotions *naturally* give rise to most of the External Behaviors.

But "most" is not "all." There may be External Behaviors that are important in manifesting the ability, but cannot be counted on to emerge

---

[49] Even if *you* did not feel those same Signal Emotions, you would probably have a response from the same "family" of emotions: instead of *isolated*, perhaps *lonely* or *distant*; instead of *thrilled*, perhaps *delighted* or *deeply pleased*.

naturally and automatically, and were not captured in the Strategy. External Behaviors such as these need to be singled out and made explicit in the model. For instance:

- A woodworker exhales as he glides his chisel forward.
- A teacher spreads her arms wide and inclines her head as she asks her students to settle down.
- A negotiator's voice tonality becomes deep and smooth when speaking of the grievances of the "other side."

These are all examples of distinctive and significant External Behaviors that we might not automatically reproduce in ourselves unless they were explicitly brought to our attention in the Array.

Although we have an elicitation question for External Behavior, the best way of identifying significant External Behaviors comes from observing the exemplar in action, as she is manifesting her ability. You can create an opportunity for your exemplar to demonstrate her ability (hand the woodworker a piece of wood and a chisel). You can go to where your exemplar typically uses her ability and observe (sit in on one of the teacher's classes). You can watch a video of your exemplar in action (have her videotape one of her negotiation sessions). Observing your exemplar in action allows you to directly see the behaviors, hear the words and hear the voice tonalities that she probably takes for granted and, so, may not notice or think to mention during elicitation.

ELICITATION QUESTION:

> "What are you doing on the outside—in your behavior—that is essential to [manifesting Ability]?"

EXAMPLES

> Q: "What are you doing on the outside—in your behavior—that is essential to planning a successful celebration?"

Adam: "Nothing I can think of." (However, when we observe him making a plan, we notice that before he imagines being one of the attendee, he ***takes a deep breath and settles his shoulders***.)

— o —

Q: "What are you doing on the outside—in your behavior—that is essential to being patient with a child who is learning?"

Bridgit: "I never sit above or below the child; always on the same level. And I speak to her directly, like she was another, intelligent adult, even if I am using a simpler vocabulary."

— o —

Q: "What are you doing on the outside—in your behavior—that is essential to designing an easy-to-use web site?"

Claire: "Well, I look at the screen, move the mouse around and try buttons and links. [laughs] When I get disgusted, I growl!"

Bridgit is quite aware of some of her external behavior and can describe it directly. When we step into trying her ability ourselves and include her external behavior of sitting on the same level as the child, speaking to the child like she is an intelligent adult, we find that doing these things significantly affects our effectiveness at manifesting Bridgit's ability. And so we will capture those behavioral elements under External Behavior in the Array.

Claire is also aware of, and can describe, her behaviors when she is designing websites. Even so, we do not note them in External Behavior. "Looking at the screen, moving the mouse around, etc." are behaviors that anyone engaged in designing a website would naturally do. Of course, "Growling with disgust" is not something everyone would automatically do in that context. So, should you include it in the model? If, when you step in, adding that growling behavior does not significantly affect your ability to design effective websites, then it is best not to include it in External Behavior.

Unlike Bridgit and Claire, Adam is not aware that any of his external behavior is essential to his ability. But when we observe him in action, we notice that he does have some distinctive external behaviors, behaviors that turn out to be essential. By stepping-in and taking a breath and settling our shoulders the way he does, we discover that this helps us "clear ourselves out of the way," so that we can more accurately experience the imagined attendee. When we then check this out with Adam, he confirms that, yes, that is what that behavior helps him do. And so we will want to include this behavior as External Behavior in the model.

Contributing Factors

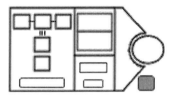 Contributing Factors capture anything that operates outside of the Array itself, but nevertheless can make a significant difference in our effectiveness in manifesting the ability. Of course, "outside the Array" is everything *but* the Array, making for quite a large playing field. There will be many, many "things" in that field that relate to, and bear on, the ability. In Contributing Factors, however, we want to capture only those that seem essential to a truly effective ability. There is not an elicitation question for Contributing Factors. (Such a question would invite being swamped by the sea of possibilities.) Instead (as with Supporting Beliefs and Signal Emotions) we note them when they arise.

EXAMPLES

> Adam: "It's true that I do a lot of reading—magazine articles, books, newspaper articles—about what is going on in society, about the different generations, what they are into, thinking, dealing with, the different industries, and so on. You have to be tuned in."

> Bridgit: "I have a special room set aside for working with the children. And in there, everything is on their scale—not childish—just on their scale."

Claire: *"**I do spend a lot of time just surfing around on the web, to see what's out there.** Mostly it is annoying, but once in a while you find some little piece that's brilliant, that's worth, well, stealing the idea. You have to stay up on what is out there."*

In each of these cases, we could operate out of the exemplar's Array *without* adopting these Contributing Factors: we can manifest Adam's Array for creating celebrations *without* doing a lot of reading; Bridgit's Array for helping children learn *without* having a room on their scale; Claire's Array for designing websites *without* spending a lot of time surfing the web. But it is easy to imagine that our effectiveness might be enhanced if we *do* include those additional elements: By keeping current on what is going on in the various segments of society (as does Adam), our ability to imagine the experiences of celebration attendees will continue to be updated; Having a room like the one Bridgit uses may make the children more comfortable and trusting, and so make working with them easier; Surfing like Claire helps to ensure that the solutions we bring to website design is contemporary, something probably essential in the fast-changing world of the Internet.

* * *

This Essay has familiarized us with the "ideal" elicitation questions. And along with those came ideal responses. This, of course, rarely happens in a real world elicitation. The particular question we use for elicitation matters, of course; if the questions we are suggesting here don't get you directly to the information you are after, they are at least likely to get you into the neighborhood of that information. The best of questions, however, is not a magical incantation; there is no guarantee that it will elicit the information you are after. Ultimately the elicitation questions must be supported by your growing ability to recognize the distinctions themselves, whenever and however the exemplar is describing her experience. In the next Essay we will use a transcript of an actual elicitation to broaden and deepen our grasp of elicitation as it occurs in the real world.

Tomb of the Persian Poet, Hafez
Photo by Pentocelo

Elicitation

Essay 14

Elicitation: Warts and All

The real world process of Elicitation is filled with miscommunications, meanderings, redundancies, and stories. As always, our familiarity with the distinctions and our facility with stepping into experience combine to weave the mesh that sifts through this complexity to find the underlying structure. Your ability to find structure will develop and deepen by using the distinctions to step into, wrestle with, and work through the often labyrinthine layers of the exemplar's description of her ability.

When Gordius, the ancient king of Phrygia, tied his eponymous "Gordian knot," he expected that its impenetrable intricacy would prevent anyone from taking it apart again. That is, anyone but the person who should be the next ruler of Asia. And it did confound everyone who tried to unravel it. What Gordius had not counted on was Alexander the Great and his sword; Alexander simply cut through the knot. The intricate ravel of an exemplar describing his or her experience is often far more bewildering than anything Gordius could have contrived. And we have no sword.

In the previous Essay we presented the Platonic ideals of elicitation sequence and questioning. The "ideal sequence" and the "ideal question" both sound very good, very sensible and neat and encouraging. And so they are...until you sit down with a real exemplar to elicit a real model. In this second Essay on elicitation we complete the trajectory from the Platonic (how elicitation has been designed to work) to real life (what happens when that design hits the dendrites).

This next step takes us closer to our human world, a world in which language entwines with experience, both revealing and concealing its structure. Experience is woven into our language; elicitation doesn't put experience there, it finds experience there. And language is woven into our experience; often our experience comes to us *through* language, or may even be made possible by language; we sometimes reach experiences that are currently beyond language by climbing to them on a ladder of words.

The complexity of this weaving of experience and language means that, regardless of what you intend in your questions, the exemplar will range through her experiential world and answer it in terms that make sense to *her*. What is more, even when she is talking about the specific element that you want her to describe, her description will certainly (indeed, *necessarily*) be entwined with aspects of other elements of her experience.

So, you need to be able to recognize what your exemplar is telling you about her experience, regardless of what you were hoping to hear. This is why we have repeatedly stressed that knowing the question to ask is no substitute for knowing the distinction that the question is intended to draw out. Being familiar with the distinctions allows you to keep your head amidst the swirl of experience your exemplar is likely to offer. This frees you to focus on what you are after at the moment *as well as* to recognize what else you are being offered in your exemplar's answers that could be worth pursuing as well.

Elicitation does not consist solely in exploring through language, of course. There are also all the non-verbal indicators in facial expression, muscle tonus, skin color, body movement, gesture, breathing, voice tone, tempo, volume, etc. Still, even these are often contextualized—that is, given their meaning—by the words that accompany them. So it is through language that we address ourselves to the exemplar's experience, with the elicitation questions as our probes and stepping-in as our laboratory.

Stories

Everyone loves stories, and most exemplars are generous with their stories about manifesting their ability. These exemplary stories captivate us, and well they should. Beyond the inherent charm of stories, they give us a richer sense of this person, of the depth and complexity that is truly their experience, than we can ever have from the underlying structure alone. The exemplar's stories are her structure in action. As the stories unfold and we step into them, our own grasp of her ability is subtly and powerfully enriched.

Exemplars often offer a story as *an illustration of* the answer to your question. That is, as an answer to your question, they offer a story that (they think) exemplifies the distinction you asked them about. In other words, instead of directly describing the precise element of experience you are asking for, they tell you a story about it working in their living world. Naturally, the implication of the story is obvious to your exemplar, and she assumes it will be clear to you as an answer your question. Of course, the significance of the story may jump out at you. If so, it is important to check your understanding with the exemplar, and not just assume you have grasped it. If instead it is not clear to you how the story is an answer to your question, ask the exemplar to help you better understand its significance.

One of the great advantages of stories is that they provide an actual context within which to search for that understanding. Rather than speaking only in abstractions, you and the exemplar can speak of what is happening in the story, with all of its rich content and complexity. Because of that richness, connections and possible paths of exploration become available to you and your exemplar that might not otherwise come to your attention. Suddenly you may chance upon an interesting and important aspect of the exemplar's experience. By following that path you may discover a deeper understanding of a particular element, or the answer to a question you have not yet asked, or the realization that you have planted your flag in the wrong Array and *"over there"* is where you really need to be...and so on.

Or, you may discover a blind alley. And this must be kept in mind. Typically, your exemplar's stories will be easy for them to tell and a delight for you to hear; they will captivate you with their detail and real life situations, and open up many new possible avenues of inquiry. This also makes them easy to get lost in and, so, allow the process of elicitation to slip into a conversation about the exemplar's many experiences. As delightful as that may be, it could easily lead to your being overwhelmed with a mass of information that, when you look at it later, is like opening the door to the bedroom of a teenager. Even as you are learning from and enjoying the ride your exemplar is taking you on with her story, it is important to consider at the same time what that story example reveals about the *structure* of her experience.

The Annotated Transcript

And now, to paraphrase Othello, we will a round unvarnished elicitation deliver (or at least as unvarnished as it gets on the page). Shorn of sound and vision, in a transcript we have only words. This provides us an opportunity to roll around in raw language and gain a sense of the information elicited, the time and freedom to analyze it yourself and, finally, the benefit of our annotations.

As you will see, our elicitation is messy, filled with the "ers," bad grammar and circumlocutions of actual interactions. Unraveling the knots of experience is not easily done, and we do not want to pretend to you that it is. This is the way it really goes. Elicitation is you and your exemplar coming to grips with the structure of an experience and, in wrestling with it, discovering a way to describe that exemplar's experience in a way that allows you to reproduce it in yourself. There is no methodological sword capable of easily and surely slicing through the knots of experience-as-described. If we have anything like Alexander's sword, it is the alloying of our minds, our bodies and our distinctions, wielded in the process of stepping-in.

One thing that will be missing from this elicitation is our behavior as we ask questions (our expressions, gestures, voice tonality) and the exemplar's behavior as she answers them. As we all know, these behavioral qualities can be a huge omission when it comes to understanding what is being communicated. Things that seem to make little or no sense when read on the page, made perfect sense to us at the time because of the exemplar's behavioral cues that accompanied her words. Short of turning these excerpts into novelettes by Proust, we cannot reproduce that richness on the page. However, there are a few places where we will note the exemplar's behavior so that it is easier to follow what is going on at that point in the elicitation.

The transcript can be approached in various ways. It could be read simply as an informational piece. But it can also be approached with a learning frame, as a way to develop sensitivity to the elements of experiential structure (as they appear in living black and white). Our recommendation is that, initially, you ignore the annotations and just read the transcript straight through. This will provide you with a sense of our exemplar and her experiential world as she is manifesting her ability. Then read through the transcript again, and this time note the different experiential elements as they strike you. Finally, on a third reading, whenever you come upon one of the annotation numbers, read our comments. (You will find the completed Array for Ulrike in the Appendix.)

Our Exemplar: Ulrike

At the time of this elicitation, Dr. Ulrike Brandenburg worked in a university hospital in Germany. A medical doctor by background, she specialized in psychotherapy, systemic family therapy, psychosomatic medicine, psychosomatic gynecology, and sexology. Papers, articles, and interviews by or with her have appeared in books, scientific journals, magazines, newspapers, and on

television. She has also presented at many national and international conferences.

After observing Ulrike present at one of her professional conferences, we selected her as an exemplar of the ability, "Engaging an Audience." Although the conference was conducted in German, it was easy to tell that she was engaging the audience. They were clearly responding, at one point banging on the tables with their knuckles (apparently a sign of strong agreement with a point being made), and she received warm applause. A panel discussion between Ulrike and her fellow presenters followed. After the session, her progress off the stage and out of the hall was slowed by a crowd of people who were either expressing their appreciation for the talk or had a question for her. Then a radio presenter pounced, and whisked her away for an interview. Additional evidence of her excellence at engaging audiences included attendee's responses to her presentations, her having won conference prizes for best presentation, and her receiving an award from medical students at her university hospital for best lecturer.

We begin with the "Core Dump," asking Ulrike to describe, in general, how she goes about "engaging the audience." (The transcript has been lightly edited for comprehension, though with the aim of retaining the flavor of her German English.):

"Engaging the Audience": Transcript

Ulrike: Well, I think the main idea is building up a relationship with the audience.[1] And I think this is what most people don't, how you say, put effort in enough. One thing is to give a presentation and tell people ideas; the other, which is the only

In the very first sentence she gives a criterion that will turn out to be the **Criterion: "Building up a relationship with the audience."** (N.B. The Criterion does not always come so easily!) Remember that, while we are being given rich way to wake their interest for these ideas, is first to look after the relationship.[2] So, in a way, I would say it's a matter of risk.[3] You have to risk that you lose your way.

Question: Lose your way?[4]

Ulrike: Well, for me there's always the feeling that, like last time in Dresden I have an anxiety that says, Ooh, if you look after them it might happen that you lose, that I lose my concept, you know. That I get out of the time frame. That I can't say all what I want to say, and that's true. Often I couldn't say all what I wanted to say. I had to put out things. But nevertheless I would say this looking and caring after what can they digest, what can they take, was always worth me having to be flexible.[5]

Question: So, even if they didn't get so much time or, er, information . . .

Ulrike: Yes, last time in Dresden I was able only to give half of the presentation. I threw out that much because I felt they are full. I think I got this high appreciation for my presentation because I noticed that. And I would say, most presentations you can take half of the time, and

material, at this point we don't yet know how it will fit together.

[2] The end of this sentence is a cause-effect. As is often the case, it is expressed "backwards," with the effect being stated before the cause. Nonetheless, she is stating that the relationship with the audience "leads to" their interest in the ideas being presented. We will expect to find this reflected in her Motivating C-E.

[3] "It's a matter of" suggests a cause-effect in relation to "risk". The "it's" does not tell us precisely what it is that risk causes.

[4] Even during the Core Dump you can feel free to ask questions for purposes of clarification. The word "risk" signaled that something significant was being spoken of. (Risk only exists when much is at stake.) The risk is that she will lose her way in the presentation but, at this point, it is not at all clear what that means. So we ask. (Later, Ulrike will give additional details in terms of what the risk involves, and this will become an aspect of the Enabling Cause-Effect.)

[5] She gives three instances of what "losing your way" means: losing her concept (overall plan of what she wants to present), losing track of the time, and, as a consequence, not being able to say all the things she wants to say. So, while she feels building a relationship with the

you still have time enough to say what you think is really important. You can do that more in a telegram style. I think most people don't really, aren't conscious about, yeah, that good presentations live from good relationships with the audience, and this means risk.[6] This means you have to be very flexible, you have to, you lose control, and you get this feeling of losing control.[7] I would say it's like in therapy, it's a matter of, also of love, one could say. Because in a way,[8] um, it only works if you don't take yourself too serious because otherwise . . . For example, this is what I often observe, people who think they absolutely have to tell incredibly interesting things and these are, whatever, THE new informations that they tell people. They are not able to shorten their presentations, they think. Whereas people who think, Oh god, if I do tell it to you or if I don't it doesn't make such a change, they are less narcissistic or less, what is that word, people who go there and want a . . .

Question: Egoistic?

Ulrike: Yeah, egoistic, some kind of, "Me, I want to be the best." You

audience is important, it isn't a free lunch. If you want to build a relationship with the audience, you may have to put aside some of your own aims for the presentation.

[6] This sentence suggests two Supporting Beliefs in the form of cause-effects: "good presentations live from good relationships with the audience," and "having good relationships with the audience means risk." (In the end, these will not appear as a Supporting Belief in the Array because they will already be captured in the Belief Template.)

[7] This sentence carries other elements that will become associated with the Enabling Cause-Effect, having to do with flexibility and losing control, which are aspects of the "risk" she just mentioned. Note that, for Ulrike, "giving up control" is not merely descriptive, but is a *feeling* of losing control, which of course makes it much more challenging.

[8] The "because" suggests that we are about to hear more about love being causally connected to something, but instead she changes direction.

[9] There is a causal relationship

need to have more this: Okay, I want to enjoy it, but I can only enjoy it if *we* enjoy it. A matter of "we," you know.[9]

Question: So, in terms of engaging the audience, what is it that's important to you? What are you, you know, evaluating in that context?[10]

Ulrike: Well, it's a bit, sounds a bit silly, but giving them the feeling you appreciate them.[11] Or some kind of, [clears throat] as I said, or some kind of love towards them.[12] And I think that means bringing up the atmosphere of a "we" and not the atmosphere of, I am the one who can tell you something incredible.[13] So I think this non-hierarchical relationship with the audience is an important thing.[14] I think, um, this, I show myself as a person, what is part of building up a relationship, is important.[15] Not only I appear by my data, by my research, by my success, in a way, but also, yeah, having some personal bits in it. Also I think that, how you say, that increases their interest.[16] Most people are primarily interested in what kind of person is it who speaks, more than what does she or her or he say. At least, it goes

between Ulrike's enjoyment and the audience's enjoyment, which provides a further motivation for her to look after the experience of the audience. (That "we" will soon resurface as part of the Definition.) [At this point the Core Dump ends and we begin the formal elicitation questions. Notice the wealth of information that we have already been given. In the Core Dump you are usually swimming a little bit, feeling your way around the structure, rather than pinning things down. Often it is only after the fact that we can look back at the Core Dump and recognize what elements of the Array we were being given right from the start.]

[10] Formal elicitation questions for the **Criterion.**

[11] This is a different response from what was expected, given what Ulrike had said in the first sentence of the Core Dump. (This difference is resolved by the next question.) In addition, the phrase "giving them the feeling you appreciate them" has more the sense of an Operation (i.e., something you *do*).

[12] It is clear that love is related to appreciation of the audience, and is likely to encourage the expression of that appreciation.

[13] "That means" signals that a Definition is coming; the first part of this sentence is the **Definition:**

together.[17]

Question: Okay, so, let me take you back a bit. You said the important thing is appreciating them. So is this part of this building up a relationship? Is it building up a relationship that is the focus of your attention? That means things like appreciating the audience, developing this atmosphere of "we," that it's a non-hierarchic relationship, and these things like that, and that it has some of this quality of love to it?[18]

Ulrike: Yeah, I think it's a caring thing.[19] I think the speaker is, in a way . . . it's not only the speaker, it's the teacher—I want to tell you something interesting or something new—and I think the teacher has not only to tell interesting things, he has to know is the audience ready. I think this is a very important thing. How is the audience when you start, for example? How is the atmosphere? How is the state of exhaustion? How is the time? How is the pressure that is on us all? And to say things towards these, er, er, items, you know.[20] For example, if you start and you know, Oh, I should give a presentation of twelve minutes and there are only eight

"Developing the atmosphere of a "we." (The change in wording avoids the ambiguity in the phrase, "bringing up.") In the second half of the sentence, the atmosphere of a "we" is further explained by contrasting it with a self-important way of approaching a presentation.

[14] The point about having a "non-hierarchical relationship with the audience" is reflected in a number of ways in the transcript. We did not make this explicit in the Array because the Primary Operation naturally creates a non-hierarchical relationship.

[15] The statement "I show myself as a person" is represented in the Primary Operation as "Include a personal sequence, a sequence with 'I'" (which is how she expresses it later in the transcript). Note that Ulrike describes this as "part of building up a relationship." This might lead one to think it should be represented as an aspect of the Definition. However, it does not have the quality of describing a class or kind of experience, but carries more of the active quality of an Operation. Also: The re-appearance of the phrase "building up a relationship" (heard in the first sentence of the Core Dump) gives additional grounds for thinking that it may well be the Criterion.

[16] This becomes the **Motivating**

minutes, er, most people put themselves under pressure to talk faster or they think, "I crash through, I take four minutes more." I would say it's a much more relaxing thing first to say, "Oh, we have only eight minutes; so either I talk faster, or you stay longer here, or I shorten the presentation." You could do a suggestion that fits to what you see about the atmosphere. Or you could say, for example, with my presentation in Dresden, I started and said that I shorten a lot. And during the presentation people were shouting, "Don't shorten, we stay longer" and so. It was funny. And I thought, now of course I shorten because I felt, if they are so interested they even want to stay longer I probably wouldn't be able to say enough to satisfy them. So I leave it short, you know. And afterwards people had this, "Oh, if you had talked longer we would have got so much" and there wasn't so much I would have had to say more. [laughter]

Question: How do you know when you are building a relationship with the audience?[21]

Ulrike: By how you feel. If you really feel comfortable and relaxed

Effect: "Increases their interest in, and receptivity to, what I have to say."

[17] A **Supporting Belief: "Most people are primarily interested in what kind of person is it who speaks, more than what does she or her or he say."**

[18] Intending to clarify the Criterion, we list the various things she has said are involved in building up a relationship. It makes for a rather long question, but the aim is to help Ulrike differentiate between the (presumed) Criterion and those things that have to do with defining or satisfying it.

[19] Ulrike confirms the supposition regarding the Criterion. The fact that she rushes straight on suggests that the differentiation proposed in the question was rather obvious to her. She seems to pick up on where the question ended, with the point about the relationship with the audience having some of the quality of love. In this instance she expresses it as "caring." (Later, she expresses this same quality as "looking after the listeners.")

[20] For Ulrike, having interesting things to say is not enough. Here she speaks of the necessity to take account of the audience, and gives us a number of the questions she will ask herself (regarding what is happening with the audience) to

you can be quite sure about it's okay.[22] And if you really feel under pressure then this might be also a pressure the audience has, you know. Like in therapy, you have to take that serious. In a way, you have to work on two levels: to talk and on the other level to... um… have a clear perception of the contact. And being able, by what you feel, to take what you feel as being diagnostics about how the audience feels.[23]

Question: Is there anything else that lets you know you are building a relationship with the audience?[24]

Ulrike: I notice it is usually much more silent during my presentation. So, in a way, what happens is, well, the audience is more connected in listening, you know . . . [25]

Question: What, connected together?

Ulrike: Yeah, maybe what comes up is more a group atmosphere. You know, when people don't move that much or talk to each other or so, that is when they are all connected.[26] [pause]

Question: And, so, in terms of this building up a relationship, why is

help her do that. And this process goes beyond taking the "pulse" of the audience. It is also important to let the audience *know* that she is taking account of their experience. These are all things she *does* in service of her relationship with them, and so may well be elements of her Strategy.

[21] The formal **Evidence** question. (It was unnecessary to formally ask for the Definition since she had already given it to us when we were clarifying the Criterion.)

[22] Her Evidence is her internal state of feeling "comfortable and relaxed." Given the nature of the ability, we would be surprised if there was no "external" evidence regarding the audience, as well. But she soon gets to it (see Notes 25 & 26).

[23] Although she is referencing her feelings as Evidence, these feelings are in relation to the internal states of the audience. That is, it is her experience that how she is feeling is a mirror of the feelings of the audience: if she feels "comfortable and relaxed," it is *because* the audience is feeling that way as well.

[24] We are specifically *not* directing Ulrike's attention to external evidence, preferring that she find it herself if it is indeed there. (If she persisted in giving only "internal" evidence, or indicated there was no

that important?[27]

Ulrike: Well, you want them to interest, to be interested in you in a way, in what you did. So you don't get their interest otherwise. I think this is a simple wisdom.[28] Um. [pause] Of course, if they sit there it's clear they have an intellectual interest; otherwise they wouldn't be there to listen to you. But I think you very much increase their intellectual capacity, or their concentration, or that they think with you, and so on, if you get also the emotional basis. And the emotional basis I think you get by this relationship thing.[29] You can see that the atmosphere is completely different with speakers who engage their audience emotionally, they have a special silence.[30] It's completely, you hear everything fall down.

Question: You hear everything fall down? Oh, the noise level goes down?

Ulrike: Yeah, it really goes Zzzssschew and highly concentrated. And after those presentations people usually need a little break before they can enter into the discussion. There is this

further evidence, then we would have asked about external evidence directly. And if for her there were none, then that would be that.)

[25] First example of **external evidence ("much more silent during my presentation")**.

[26] Continuation of the **external evidence ("people don't move that much or talk to each other")**. The mention of "group atmosphere" echoes "the atmosphere of a 'we' " (in the Definition). It also suggests a non-hierarchical relationship with the audience.

[27] Formal **Motivating Cause-Effect** question.

[28] A very clear statement that the interest of the audience is dependent on the relationship you have with them. The phrase "this is a simple wisdom" suggests Ulrike considers the Motivating Cause-Effect completely obvious. (Recall that this is one of those type of responses that often indicates that you have hit upon Motivating Cause-Effect.)

[29] Here there is a clear differentiation between an intellectual interest and an "emotional basis." She holds a chain of cause-effects that run: Relationship → Emotional involvement → Increased intellectual capacity/concentration.

[30] The mention of a "special silence"

stop, you know, and then the chairman says, "Okay, the paper is open for discussion." Nothing comes. I had had that often, already. And then, it's helpful to make a little joke, like, "Obviously, I talked you to death," doof, doof, doof. Or, "You're in trance now so I'm happy I won't get any questions." And then they wake up again. And, and, sometimes, sometimes they don't.

reinforces her earlier point (note 25) that this is **Evidence** of having the kind of relationship she wants.

Question: [Laughter] Sometimes they're *gone*.

Ulrike: Mmm.

Question: So what happens then?

Ulrike: Yeah, the first years when I gave presentations it was often me who didn't get any question in the discussion. And the chairpeople often said things like, "Yeah, it was so round and doodledoo, touching" or whatever. I think it was a bit too perfect, you know, because I had worked it so incredibly out, that people really felt like after a little, I wouldn't say "show," or so, but they were a bit like in trance. Meanwhile, I put much less energy into those presentations and it has the advantage, actually, that the data, or the results, or so, that gets more importance. I think they're more casual now.

Question: Casual in the sense of the relationship with the audience or what? I didn't understand that bit.

Ulrike: I think people now would say, "Ah, she's a really lively speaker and interesting results" and in these former years maybe they would have said, "She creates such a special atmosphere." It had to do with a bit of, yeah, trance or, so touching. And I think I decrease that a bit. Because it, as a, yeah, you could say "performance," took a bit away the liveliness of the audience.[31]

Question: So they weren't so involved back and forth with it, in this developing a "we"?

Ulrike: I'm not completely sure. Maybe it was also my research is a bit different and, mm . . . I think I, by this being so perfect, I also created the anxiety of people to ask. And by being more casual and speaking free and so, I think I decrease that. I think it's easier to get into a debate.[32]

Question: And you want that?

[31] The term "casual" and the idea that she puts much less energy into her presentations was puzzling in view of what she has been telling us, and this motivated the question. As she explains, "casual" has nothing to do with caring less about either her presentations or about her relationship with the audience.

[32] She feels "being more casual" (of which "speaking free" appears to be a part) invites the audience to join her in debate. Ulrike believes that, in the past, she had so worked over and refined her early presentations that

Ulrike: Yes, yes. Also I, I mean, I didn't speak free in former times. I don't now completely, but freer than I did. And there are always lots of parts that are completely free. Whereas in the first years when I was showing the [overhead projector transparencies] I had the words and sentences completely by heart. They were perfect, you know. That's good. That was very important because that's how I started. For me it was only helpful I'd say. I would advise people to start doing presentations like that. But it takes a bit away the liveliness from the audience. You get definitely more interesting debates by . . . [pause]

Question: Okay. So, you've said about a number of things that you *do* to build up a relationship with the audience, yeah. But if you had to sum up in, like, a sentence, what would you say it is that allows, that makes possible, building this relationship with the audience? What is it you have to do, you know, that *anybody* has to do to make this happen?[33]

Ulrike: I think all the things I said already, didn't I?[34]

they had a finished quality, one that did not invite questions nor offer any loose ends to which questions could be applied.

[33] Formal elicitation question for the **Enabling Cause-Effect.** At this point, Ulrike has already given many elements of the Primary Operation. Our question is intended to orient her to the belief level by first restating what she has already said about what she *does* (and so, for the moment, sets those behaviors aside), and by putting the question

Question: Well, you said the specifics. You said lots of specific things. But I'm saying, if you had to say, if you had to capture all those specifics in, like, a sentence, you know . . .

Ulrike: Well, allow yourself that you can't control it. I would say this is like, er, . . . like, er, um . . . [35]

Question: Well, let me say what seemed to be within the different things you said. One thing that seemed to me to be, you know, over all the things you said, so I want to check with you, is that what's important to make that possible is knowing where the audience is and expressing that.[36]

Ulrike: Uh, hmm.

Question: Does that cover those things?

Ulrike: No. This is one point, I would say. [pause]

Question: So this thing about allowing yourself that you can't control it, this is a bigger point?[37]

Ulrike: Mmm. [pause] It's

in terms of "*anybody*." (The "anybody" encourages her to think in terms of generalizations.)

[34] Okay, despite our framing of the question, the question goes phut! On reflection, the last part of the question was a mistake; the "to do" leads her back to Operations, to what she *does*. Which, as she says, she has already told us about.

[35] What Ulrike says here seems to be part of the Enabling Cause-Effect. So at least we are in the right ballpark. She is obviously uncertain, but she is not necessarily uncertain about her experience; she may simply be uncertain about whether she had answered the question properly.

[36] Our taking the step of suggesting an answer is intended to give her something to react to. (If your exemplar is finding it difficult to come up with an answer, simply providing one can give her something to react to. Typically, the exemplar will get an immediate sense of how your suggestion does not quite—or not at all—fit for her and, so, may help point her toward what *does* fit. Remember, it is essential to make your suggestion in a way that conveys that you have no investment in being right.)

[37] Still trying to get the Enabling Cause-Effect straight. Searching for what is the overarching belief.

something about, er, I think you have to have on your mind that, well, at least I have, that to be successful is not the biggest aim. And also, um, the allowance of anything may go wrong. It won't be the end. Something like that also. At least, for me that's important. To know, um, even if I start, whatever, losing my voice, I get a, whatever, psychotic reaction or, you know; it doesn't feel like it but it's okay. If that happens, it wouldn't be the end. I think this is, for me it's the only way to throw myself into the process. If you go into the process you don't know, it may also happen that everything goes horrible. I never know.[38]

Question: So, really, would it be right then to say that what makes it possible, this building up a relationship with the audience is that you, in a sense, dare everything.[39]

Ulrike: Yeah. I would say so. I feel it completely. Going with the process may, is giving up control. That is a, a risky thing. [pause] Risking intimacy, you also could say.[40]

Question: Which do you prefer?

[38] Ulrike's initial "Mmm" was not a complete and robust agreement, nor was it a disagreement. Clearly there is more to be said. Then she again refers to the role of "risk" in the process ("anything may go wrong"). Facing that risk is the only way to be able to "throw myself into the process" (a cause-effect relationship).

[39] This question presents another possible Enabling Cause-Effect by drawing together the many things she said earlier relating to risk and losing control.

[40] She certainly recognizes what the phrase "dare everything" refers to. However, she puts forward another formulation: "Risking intimacy."

[41] It is clear that we are closing in on the Enabling Cause-Effect. The suspects are in the line-up, and it is for the exemplar to identify which one best fits her experience.

[42] **Enabling Cause-Effect:**

[Offers choices—"give up control," "dare everything," "risking intimacy"][41]

Ulrike: This one [pointing to "Risking Intimacy"].[42] "Giving up control" is a bit too radical. You don't give completely up control. You give up control about wanting to be wonderful; but you don't give up control of the whole situation.

Question: Right. Okay. That's clear now.

Ulrike: I think people who are great they, they know they can't completely plan it. Because if they . . . There are those who try to manipulate the audience and many people can, but never it comes off that lively, like with the non-manipulated, and never comes off suddenly great things.[43]

Question: Right. Now, in terms of what you do to build a relationship with the audience, you have mentioned things like the need to appreciate the audience, to have some feeling of love toward them, to develop an atmosphere of "we," and about taking care of the audience. Are there other things you do to build that relationship?[44]

"Risking intimacy." The choice of the term "intimacy," to capture the variety of ways in which risk has been indicated, is intriguing. In terms of what she has said—and will say as the elicitation continues—it is clear that she puts herself on the line. For her, building a relationship with the audience involves joining with them in this atmosphere of a "we," being open to them and what is going on with them. In her experience, this is a personal and intimate relationship. It is not surprising that her comments about risk and the feeling of losing control denote the need for her to be open to a significant degree of vulnerability.

[43] Ulrike underscores her Enabling Cause-Effect by contrasting what she does with what those who attempt to manipulate the audience do. Even when such presenters are successful, they don't get the effects she gets ("lively…suddenly great things").

[44] Formally eliciting the Primary Operation. Since Ulrike has already given many elements of her Primary Operation, this is acknowledged in

the question.

Ulrike: You have to work on two levels. One is what you want to say to them. The other one is, in a way, a group dynamic thing. Getting an idea of what is the atmosphere in the audience. Is the audience exhausted? Is the audience silent? Is there a lot of, whatever, disturbance?[45] And you have to, it's a bit like in therapy, you have to . . . notice these things. Have to mention them, maybe, even. Not in big presentation halls but in groups I sometimes say, "Are you with me? Is everything okay?" And sometimes, if there is a disturbance, I do that also in presentations. I wouldn't say, "Are you with me?" I sometimes interrupt my presentations with sentences…like in Dresden, there were at least four hundred people, asking, "Everything okay?" "Am I too fast?" "I shorten . . ."[46] So, giving them . . . often people don't say anything. But by giving them a break they can relax for a second. And my impression is, my experience is then you get back more concentration afterwards. So having little breaks where you focus on the contact and then go back to what you want to say is also good. Breaks, yeah.[47]

[45] We are given further examples of the kind of questions Ulrike asks herself in relation to the "atmosphere in the audience" (see note 20 for the previous examples).

[46] Whether, to what extent, and how she comments on the atmosphere in the audience depends both on the context and on what she perceives their state to be at the time.

[47] When Ulrike speaks of a "break" here, she does not mean anything like a "tea break," or even a "stretch break." It is a break in the focus of the audience's attention: their minds

Question: So, you would actually say, "Am I too fast?" Or this kind of thing?

Ulrike: Yeah. Looking to them is incredibly important. There are people giving great presentations but they read them and they don't look to the people.[48] Or some free sentences are important, free sentences that are not perfect, you know, where you stumble, humble and doodledye. They make it more . . . [Laughing] . . . Really. "I am only human," you know.[49] Or, sometimes, these things that happen to me. I don't plan them but I have good experiences with them. Like when I suddenly bang into the microphone. Or, in Dresden, I fell against the podium [laughter] when I was just starting. Nothing happened but it was moving. And the whole audience gasped, you know. I said, Whoops! And then the audience was in the first laughter. Before I had said anything. And that was helpful. You can't really plan these things but it's important to think about how can I make people laugh, even when you have a serious thing, um …[50]

Question: So you think about that

are shifted from the topic of her presentation, but only momentarily. She finds that even a momentary "break" allows them to return to the theme with greater concentration.

[48] This becomes an element in the **Primary Operation**. It is also an **External Behavior**. For those who run trainings and workshops, it may seem too obvious to be worth noting. However, in a context where people are typically reading their conference papers, often with no more than the occasional flicked glance at the audience, this can make a distinctive difference in how an audience experiences the presentation. Even trainers and workshop leaders do not always really look at the audience; they may spend much of their time looking over the audience's heads or scanning them in such a way that their eyes never rest on anyone.

[49] "Free sentences" are those which are not read, but spoken freely. They may have been thought through before but, by being spoken free, they will not be as perfectly formed as her written texts. Indeed, she may bumble her way through them. She emphasizes the fact that they make her seem more human (which encourages the non-hierarchical relationship and the atmosphere of a "we").

[50] She is attuned—and always

before?

Ulrike: Yeah, in earlier times, I always had things in my presentations, so I had really planned these laughters. I had jokes worked out, into my presentation. And that was very helpful. Meanwhile, my presentations are not so jokey, I would say. They are serious. But I know I can engage the audience in a way to make a joke or whatever. I more rely on this happens anyway. But laughing is incredibly important. Really.[51] And relaxation. Most presenters don't really take care of that. When there are short presentations [by different presenters], twenty minutes or so, one after the other, people need something to go out of the theme, for then being able to go back into another theme. And people respond, or appreciate it if you notice that. Even if only, maybe, by the question, "Okay, this was a quite a serious theme, I hope you are ready for the next" or der dum. And you could fill this time by telling them who you are, or whatever. All these things are looking after the listeners. This is what I mean by . . . it is like in a therapeutic relationship.[52] And in a way I would say this is, yeah, this relationship is more important

ready—to capitalize on any accidental source of humor. Her own ready laughter means that audiences feel encouraged to laugh *with* her, rather than being inhibited by the worry that they might be thought to be laughing *at* her.

[51] From observing her make a presentation, we know that "jokes" are rarely of the "telling a joke" variety, but more amusing ways of phrasing things, witty asides, etc. She no longer feels she needs to plan these, and instead takes advantage of any opportunities that present themselves. (Considering the importance she gives to laughter, we can surmise that if she had not become confident of being able to find such opportunities, she would have continued to plan humor in advance.)

[52] Again, the cause-effect between Relationship → Increased intellectual capacity/concentration.

[53] **Supporting Belief: "Relationship is more important than what you say."** This is an extreme expression (as Supporting Beliefs tend to be) of her belief that

even, er, er, than what you say.[53] [pause] Hmm.

Question: You say that, in the past, you wrote jokes into your presentation. Did you prepare only jokes or also some other ways to contact the audience?[54]

Ulrike: Also some contact. In my presentations usually were a personal sequence, a sequence with "I," you know.[55] [Gives an example of a story she often used to use in her presentations.] Nowadays, I would rely on that these things happen. So I'm less anxious in terms of that I have to have them under control. But it was good that, even at the beginning, I knew this is important. And this is also a relationship thing, because it's about me risking I present not only what I have to say, I also present me as a person.[56] And once I had the— it was very interesting, I had the experience it didn't work at all.[57]

Question: Yeah?

Ulrike: It was horrible, really.

Question: So what happened then?

Ulrike: Oh, it was last year,

her relationship with the audience is the prerequisite for their having the interest and receptiveness she wants.

[54] Given how much Ulrike emphasized the contact, the relationship, with the audience, it seemed important to check whether she had also been considering contact in her early presentations.

[55] She gives an example of what "contact" means for her. We have heard something similar before, at note 16 in the transcript, where she says, "Not only I appear by my data, by my research, by my success, in a way, but also, yeah, having some personal bits in it. Also I think that, how you say, that increases their interest." She is still including "personal bits." When it came time to select a useful operational description for the **Primary Operation**, we chose the phrase, "a personal sequence, a sequence with 'I'."

[56] A **Supporting Belief** that is another expression of the causal connection between risk (presenting herself as a person) and building a relationship with the audience.

[57] Note that even before we hear about the experience that "didn't work at all," she has indicated that she has a useful ability to benefit from an unpleasant experience ("it

February or so. It was my really
beloved presentation about this one
woman, and it was on the
conference for gynecologists.
Somatic, you know, surgery
gynecologists. I hadn't thought
about, you know, who are these
people? They have no idea about
psychodynamic and doodledye.
Completely different approach. Also
there are no psychosomatic people.
And I wasn't, I was absolutely
exhausted. It was just after my best
friend's death. I went there. I had
my manuscript. The speaker before
me, she was interrupted again and
again but she didn't stop, so she
talked into my time. I had to stop
absolutely on time because
afterwards was a huge international
conference starting in this hall. I
knew that, but I felt, Ugh, I can't
change. I felt too exhausted. I could
have known but . . . And then I
crashed through with my concept.
And I would say I lost the people.
They didn't at all get what I wanted
to say. It was horrible. And I
finished after the case study,
although I could have said much
more, as I felt this is enough. And it
was not a complete mess, but we
were not in contact. It was bad, I
would say. And they probably
thought, What a strange

was very *interesting*").

presentation. What did she actually want to say? Well, some people came and asked for, said you have interesting data but, anyway, it was good for me, this experience, because I could definitely say, this was a mistake.[58]

Question: That's a good example of when you don't do these things. I just want to check, before we move on, are there any other things you think it is important to do in order to build up this relationship with the audience?[59]

Ulrike: Well, liveliness is a big thing. Those speakers who are lively are better speakers, so daring some movement, standing instead of sitting, or moving, you know. I, for example, like to be able to move. I like to change my position. I like walking along a bit.[60] I think the audience gets the impression of a process, not of a…for example, a good thing is letting the audience participate in the process of your thinking. Of course, you have your data to present, but some ideas you still can, um, um, how you say, especially when giving lectures, this is not that much about giving presentations you have completely prepared, but giving lectures I

[58] Because, in this presentation, she did not have the relationship with the audience ("we were not in contact") she felt "it was bad." We can surmise that she thought the experience was beneficial in that it forcefully impressed on her that looking after the relationship is the most important thing.

[59] "Are there any other things" helps Ulrike set aside all that has been discussed and search for any additional elements of her Primary Operation that jump out at her as important.

[60] We noted this as **External Behavior** in the Array. However, Ulrike is not saying that all there is to liveliness is moving around. There can be many other ways in which liveliness is manifested. From our observation of her, it is clear that Ulrike would be considered a lively speaker due to her dynamic manner as expressed through her gestures, voice tonality changes, etc.

would say, students especially are much more interested when they see, Ah, this person is still, we participate in the process of her thinking. Well, also for presentations. I often say, "Coming closer to this presentation I felt . . ." So, meta-comments on how it feels to do this presentation, or so.[61] [pause] This "not being perfect" I think is an important thing because other people can involve themselves. Perfect is a thing that is completely ready [completely finished]. You feel a bit like, Oof, I'm out. And what you have to bring up is the feeling, You can be in if you want.[62] Yeah, that is also an important thing, that you signalize interest in, What do you think?[63] So that you bring up…this again goes with this democratic thing, my research is nothing worth if I don't have your feedbacks. So, again this "we."[64]

Question: Okay, so I'd like to move on now to, well, you gave a lot of examples of things you do to bring up this relationship. Now what do you do if you don't feel that relationship is happening? So, you've done these things but you don't feel that relationship has been built. What do you do then?[65]

[61] Ulrike offers meta-comments on her own experience as one way of "letting the audience participate in the process of your thinking" (something we decided to include in her **Primary Operation**).

[62] **Supporting Belief** that makes the point that something "perfect" does not allow the audience a way into it ("Oof, I [the audience] am out"). Once again, we have an example of the importance to Ulrike of "the atmosphere of a 'we.'"

[63] Ulrike is not saying here that she explicitly asks this question during a presentation, but that she does convey to the audience that she is interested in what they think. (In the discussion following her presentation, there will be an opportunity for the audience to respond to her implicit question.)

[64] Again she makes a clear link between her Primary Operation and its ability to foster "the atmosphere of a 'we.'"

[65] At this point we have the main

Ulrike: Mmm. That depends. It depends on how I feel. Maybe I feel, well, this is the wrong audience for me, you know, they expected somebody completely different, then I would say that. But, maybe if…I don't know, it could be that I feel I am at my end, so I come through only. This also would be okay. Because I would say, being very much in contact with the audience is the optimum solution. And, of course, there can be sub-optimum solutions. One is also, Okay, I do my duty. Also this is, I would say, a matter of flexibility. To see it doesn't work. So I don't put too much energy in it.

Question: So what if, er, …

Ulrike: Or this, I think this is a very important point, because sometimes you immediately can see, Oh, this will be very difficult. Especially when they are disappointed because they expect something else. You can try a bit but then I think it's convenient to think, This is what I can get out, not more. Not to put yourself under pressure.[66] And in a way, "the more effort I put in the better it will be"—that's not true. "The harder I work," this sentence

elements of the Primary Operation. Now we move on to the Secondary Operations. (Note that we do not ask about when her Criterion— "Building up a 'Relationship' with the audience"—is *not sufficiently satisfied*. This is because there won't be a Secondary Operation for that situation. We will explore the reason for this in the Commentary following the transcript.)

[66] There are two Operations, depending on the reason the **Criterion is *not at all satisfied*:**

- If Ulrike feels she is not building a relationship with the audience because she (or her topic, as we find out in her answer to our next question: "Especially when they are disappointed because they expect something else") is just not what they expected, she will comment on this to the group. (This is one of the behaviors of her Primary Operation as well. In this things-not-going-well situation, it becomes *the* way to respond.)

- It may also happen that she is having difficulty building a relationship with the audience because she is exhausted ("at my end"). In this case, she goes for the "sub-optimum solution" of doing her "duty" ("I come through only; I do my duty").

[67] Ulrike does *not* believe that

doesn't work in terms of contact. No. Try to be present. [67]

Question: What about when you don't feel you can build a relationship with a particular audience?

Ulrike: Well, I wouldn't say I don't get contact, because I think that you can get contact with every audience, but maybe it's more this, Bah, I don't want. Or I have to betray myself, or things like that. I'm not interested.[68]

Question: Um. When you are going for this engagement with the audience…right, there obviously are emotions that come up in terms of, if it's going really well, you can be Whoohoo! and if it's not going well it could be Aaargh! But what's the background feeling that is there all the time you are working for that engagement? How would you describe that background feeling?[69]

Ulrike: Uuuum. Well, I would say, there's all the time a . . . nerve, nervousness. I have it changing all the time. I'm never completely relaxed. Although I would like that, you know. Um. So, a slight fear, and also a feeling of excitement.

putting more effort in will lead to a better presentation. For her, good presentations come from having contact with the audience and she indicates a cause-effect between "being present" and having "contact" with the audience (Being present → Contact).

[68] **Criterion *cannot be satisfied.*** "I think you can get contact with every audience," is an extremely powerful **Supporting Belief**. And it means that Ulrike does not have a Secondary Operation to cover instances when her Criterion cannot be satisfied. Instead, for her there is the possibility that she will not *want to* get contact: "Maybe…I have to betray myself or things like that. I'm not interested." (We did not pursue it, but we suspect that in those instances, she would simply "do her duty.")

[69] Formal elicitation of the **Sustaining Emotion.** Precisely because the Sustaining Emotion is in the background of experience, it is usually necessary to make a distinction for the exemplar between Signal Emotions and the *Sustaining* Emotion you are asking for. (Although not a conscious decision at the time, in retrospect we realized that our use of expressive sounds

Yeah, I also, a feeling of Whaaa! That's also there.[70]

Question: Whaaa!

Ulrike: Yeah.

Question: How do we write this? [laughter] So, what's that about?

Ulrike: That's about this feeling, "*Oh*, this is a big challenge! I have the possibility to design great situations." So, I take that possibility.[71]

(when asking the question was matching Ulrike's own predilection for using an extensive range of such sounds.)

[70] From the way Ulrike describes it, it might seem that the nervousness/slight fear, is a Signal Emotion. However, it also seems to be an aspect of her experience of "excitement." (Many people have commented on the similarity in physiological sensations between excitement and nervousness.)

[71] We chose to phrase the **Sustaining Emotion** as **"Excitement, with a slight fear."** This is the reverse of how it emerged in her description. Despite the fact that Ulrike mentions the slight fear first, she speaks in a very spirited way of the excitement. Another compelling determinant of our choice was that, when stepping into each emotion separately, we felt that "a slight fear" by itself *cannot* sustain the Array, but that "excitement" *can*.

Additional Transcript Commentary

This section will cover a few points that were not fully covered in the right-hand column annotations, along with an analysis of how the elements in the Array work together as a whole to manifest Ulrike's ability to engage lecture audiences.

Ulrike's Beliefs

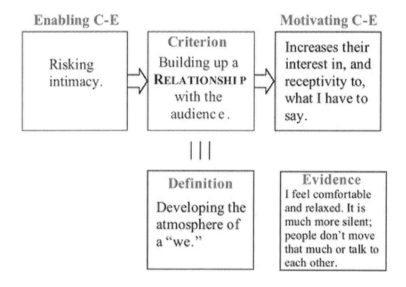

Ulrike's Criterion, "building up a **Relationship** with the audience," may immediately strike you as sensible, even obvious, and so you may not sufficiently credit its significance. Our experiences with seminar conference presenters (both as presenters ourselves and as members of the audience) make it clear that "relationship" is not necessarily the primary filter of choice. As a sampling, "being in control" is important for some, for others it is "thoroughness," and still others "credibility." If you take a moment to step into the context of making a presentation while holding each of these Criteria, you will quickly discover that they engender patterns of thinking and behavior that are very different from Ulrike's. "Being in control" and "credibility" convey a sense of "me versus them" (or at least, "me—them"); and if "thoroughness" is about completely covering the *information*, the audience "them" may be ignored altogether.

Ulrike's Criterion—as underscored by the "we" in her Definition—strongly conveys an "us." The behavior patterns that this attention leads to (self-disclosure, humor at her own expense, acknowledging the audience's states and needs, expressiveness, etc.) are naturally inclusive. As evidenced by Ulrike's ability, patterns that naturally emerge from holding the Criterion "relationship" are certainly excellent for engaging an audience.

Furthermore, notice that Ulrike's Criterion is about "*building up* a relationship." There is an enormous difference between evaluating, "Do we have a relationship?" and "Are we building a relationship?" For her, relationship is something to be fostered, and there is no end to that while she is there; it is always in process and on the way. Hers is not one of those Criteria that, once attained, the person can stop working on satisfying it. Instead, her Criterion keeps her *engaged* with the audience. And they respond to that.

Ulrike's Criterion (as do all Criteria) compels a search for the Enabling Cause-Effect by automatically suggesting the question: How *does* one build up a relationship with the audience? For Ulrike the answer is that it is "risking intimacy" that makes building a relationship possible. Again, we want to point out that this is not the only possible cause to the effect of "relationship" in the world of human experience. For instance, "giving people just what they want," or "complete honesty," or "having agreed on boundaries" are among the (infinite) possible enabling causes for building a relationship. A moment's experience with each of these suggestions will reveal how very different each one would be in terms of its impact when making a presentation. Indeed, even an Enabling Cause-Effect that is close to Ulrike's will still not be the same in terms of its impact. For instance, someone who had "humor" causally connected to building relationships would probably manifest some of the same behaviors as Ulrike (such as making jokes out of mishaps), but might not include anything personal in that humor; the audience may be entertained, and still not have a sense of "we" with the presenter.

Like her Criterion, Ulrike's Motivating Cause-Effect may seem obvious: "Increases their interest in, and receptivity to, what I have to say." Who wouldn't want that? Every presenter might want that, but not every presenter is *holding that in his or her experience* as what is driving him or her. Consider instead as motivations, "my professional advancement," or "a better world," or "understanding." Each of these would engender different qualities of attention and experience in a presenter. Ulrike's Motivating Cause-Effect—like her Criterion, Definition, Evidence, and Enabling Cause-Effect—has the effect of keeping her in the room and in the ongoing present of the presentation, it keeps the audience in her present awareness, and it keeps her being responsive to them.

Ulrike's Strategy

In looking at Ulrike's strategies—*how* she goes about fulfilling her Criterion—it is important to keep in mind the structural patterns already built into that Criterion. Of particular significance is the presupposition of "we" reflected in her Definition, Evidence, and Supporting Beliefs. She knows that she is building a relationship with the audience by whether or not she is feeling comfortable and relaxed, *and that how she feels is reflective of how the audience feels*. It is this connection between her feelings and those of the group that prevents her Criterion from being just about her and ignoring the state of the audience. Instead, it is as if she is one of them and attending to how "we" are feeling. Yes, this is "mind-reading," or in Ulrike's case perhaps, "state-reading." And you may point out (correctly) that she could be wrong about what she is reading. Regardless of how accurate she is, however, the fact that she is using Evidence based on that assumption of "we" naturally orients her to attend to, and care about, what the state of others is. And that orientation will, in and of itself, have ramifications throughout her experience, leading her towards patterns of behavior that seek to build relationship. Judging by the responses of her audiences, these patterns *work* when it comes to engaging them in her presentations.

Primary Operation

* Be present.

* Monitor your own feelings, using them as indicators of what may be happening in the group. Look after the group by letting them know you are aware of questions such as:

    How is the atmosphere?
    How is the state of exhaustion?
    How much are they able to digest?
    How is the pressure on us all [e.g., time]?

* Say some free sentences [not read].

* Include a personal sequence, a sequence with "I."

* Give them breaks to relax for a second by shifting their focus of attention.

* Express appreciation of them.

* Make people laugh.

* Look at them.

* Dare some movement.

* Let the audience participate in the process of your thinking by meta-commenting on your thinking.

Secondary Operations

Not at all satisfied —
There can be two reasons for this:
* If it is because the audience is expecting somebody/something different, comment on this to them.
* If it is because you are exhausted, you are only required to "come through, to do your duty." Don't put yourself under pressure.

When Ulrike is making a presentation, the intention of building up a relationship with the audience is a continuous, ongoing one. It is not something that is achieved once; she is not attempting to build up that relationship at the outset, and then move on to some next stage of her presentation. Instead, she is building up the relationship from the first moment she steps onto the stage, and continues building up that relationship until the moment she leaves the stage.

And so it is not surprising that her Primary Operation is a set, rather than a sequence, of internal processes and external behaviors. Any and all of her processes and behaviors are there to be tapped as circumstances warrant. We also want to point out that most of those processes and behaviors, as we have captured them in her Strategy, are relatively large-chunked. Each one embraces within a few words a whole slew of additional internal processes and external behaviors. For example, consider, "Express appreciation of them." How, exactly, does one do that? We may know how she does it from observing her, or from stories she's told us about her presentations. And so there is no need to make it explicit in the Array. The obvious exception to this may occur when we are creating the Array for others (people who did not participate in the elicitation) to use. Even in those instances, however, it may not be necessary to use more than, "Express appreciation of them." This is possible when those few words are enough to connect us to our own life experiences and resources regarding "expressing appreciation," and that this is enough to give us or others access to the internal processes and external behaviors we need. When this is so, great; as we will discuss in the next Essay on "Elegance," less is often more.

Of course it may happen that we think that "Express appreciation of them" will be sufficient for us (or others) when it comes to putting Ulrike's ability into practice, and it turns out that we were wrong, that we need more explicit information from our exemplar. In that case it may be necessary to return to her for more specification. Depending upon the particular strategy element, it may even be useful to treat that part of her Primary Operation as an ability itself, and model it separately. (An obvious candidate for doing this is Ulrike's strategic behavior, "Make people laugh." That is an ability for which probably most of would need some guidance in order to do it well. And so it may well be worth treating as a separate, "sub-ability," with its own elicitation and Array.)

One consequence of the fact that, for Ulrike, building up a relationship with the audience is a continuously pursued Criterion is that she has no Secondary Operation for situations in which she feels her Criterion is *not sufficiently satisfied*. As we said, she has no expectation that she just runs a few behaviors, she establishes the relationship, and then it's a done deal. For her, an *ongoing* relationship with the audience is essential to getting across what she wants to say, so it must be maintained; there is no end point.

Ulrike's External Behavior

In addition to the external behaviors that Ulrike mentioned during the elicitation ("looking to them" and "daring some movement"), direct observation revealed three additional things that were characteristic of her when presenting.

First, just before beginning to speak, she will sigh deeply. This is something she was aware of, but only because it has been pointed out to her by a number of colleagues; it is not something she does intentionally. For Ulrike, it marks her transition into presentation mode. For all of us, a change in breathing frequently accompanies a change in internal state; and a change in breathing can also *bring about* a change in internal state. When we tried sighing deeply like Ulrike, we found that it tended to bring us into the present, which was very supportive of the rest of the Array. So this is included in the model.

Second, she has a ready laugh, and one that is very infectious. The pertinence of this is that anything amusing in the situation, in her theme, or that inadvertently happens to her in the course of a presentation, is liable to cause hilarity in her, and her infectious laughter amplifies the response of the audience. Clearly, this makes it easier to "Make them laugh," which is part of her Primary Operation. For the model, it seems important to include "have a ready laugh" in External Behavior. But we can't specify that it is "infectious." Unless you are already blessed with an infectious laugh, it does no good to tell you to "laugh infectiously." (To include it we would have to model it as a separate ability.)

The third behavior we include in the model is that her gestures throughout are definite and emphatic. They tend in that direction even during normal conversation, and when she is presenting, this tendency is amplified. Of course, a person's gestures are connected to their internal world. Our inability to speak German hampered our interpretation of her gestures, but it appeared that Ulrike was using her gestures to mark out points she wanted to particularly emphasize.

Ulrike's Contributing Factors

We singled out only one Contributing Factor, but it is an important one to Ulrike: "Be well prepared." Ulrike speaks of writing out every detail of her early presentations, and of their being worked through until they were "perfect." Not only had she written in jokes (as we have heard), but when pointing to her results on overhead projection transparencies (making it difficult for her to read at the same time), she says, "I had the words and sentences completely by heart." When speaking of the difference between lectures and presentations she describes the latter as "presentations you have completely prepared." Although she spoke of using "some free sentences," it is also clear that, because she was presenting clinical research material, it was still necessary to read much of her presentation from well-prepared notes. This was much appreciated, though one might imagine it was in the same way that we appreciate a good reading from a well-written book. As we saw, Ulrike decided to make her presentations less "perfect" in order to encourage more interaction in the subsequent discussions. But this does not mean that she ceased to be well prepared.

In the elicitation, Ulrike tells us of her increasing awareness of the importance of having contact with the audience, and of the factors that enhance contact. But that contact is happening in the context of giving *a prepared presentation*. Because our focus here is on the Array for "Engaging the audience," it is easy to forget that this is only one aspect of her ability to give good presentations at professional conferences. If we wanted to know about the whole ability, we would need to explore the other Arrays that comprise it (one of which would be her ability to prepare).

Final Thoughts on the Elicitation

Core Dumps are always rich in the patterns that we will be sorting into the Array later in the elicitation. It is not always clear just what those patterns are at the time the Core Dump is tumbling out. In Ulrike's case, however, many of the significant elements of her experience stood out immediately. Of course, despite the neon signs flashing around her patterns, we did not know for sure at that point just how they would fit into her Array, or how best to capture them in description.

Ulrike was clear in her thinking and in her expression. She seemed to already have thought a good deal about her presentations. This would certainly accord with the fact that her approach developed over time. An additional factor may have been her psychotherapeutic training. The process of reporting on a case in supervision develops an ability to reflect on the therapeutic interaction as well as on how one's own behavior influences this. With this background, she may be better prepared to link changes in her own behavior as a presenter to the responses she receives from the audience.

Not that the ability to reflect on one's own experience is at all necessary for the elicitation process to work. Nor does the likelihood of Ulrike having reflected on her experiences of giving presentations mean that she was previously aware of everything she said in the elicitation. And no exemplar will have their knowledge of their own experience already structured in a form that fits into the framework of the Array. Regardless of who the exemplar is or her background, it the modeler's responsibility to do the modeling; the exemplar's is to be herself.

The most troublesome element to elicit was the Enabling Cause-Effect. After Ulrike had told us what she *does* (Strategy) to build up a relationship with the audience, we wanted to her belief and retrieve her Enabling Cause-Effect. In Note 34, we pointed out that the wording of our question probably led her astray. When identifying the Enabling Cause-Effect, the tricky thing is to separate out the belief (generalization about the process) from the operations (the process itself). It is tricky because, of course, the person *believes* every element of the Primary Operation plays a part in leading to or making possible the satisfaction of the Criterion. If they did not, at some level, believe the operations worked toward that end, they would not do them.

But they are not beliefs at the level we are after in the Belief Template. For instance, she would not be likely to say, "The relationship with the audience comes from looking at them"; or "from daring some movement"; or "from being present." On their own, those elements are too small to bring about the kind of relationship she wants. They contribute to it, but no one of them *causes* it by itself. To be considered an Enabling Cause-Effect we must have something that Ulrike believes will by itself bring about that relationship. For her, it is, "Risking intimacy," which is made operational by (manifested by) such things as "looking at them," "daring some movement," "being present," and so on.

Theoretically, the description of the Primary Operation could go on forever. The Primary Operation is what a person is *doing* to satisfy her Criterion, and they will be doing all manner of things. It can be difficult to know when to stop. How do you know when you have them all? This is easier to know when the Primary Operation is completely sequential. In that case, the answer is that we know we have the Primary Operation when we have every step of the sequence. However, as we have seen, many Primary Operations include—or even entirely consist of—sets of operations which can be drawn on at will, applied together, or used any which way. This is the case with Ulrike's ability. Where sets of operations are involved, how do we know we have the set?

Well, we don't. As we have said elsewhere, the purpose of gathering information for the Array is not to be exhaustive; it is to capture the essence of the structure. Therefore, our goal is to feel that we have identified the important elements of the Primary Operation.

Although there is no absolute answer to what is enough, we do have our experiential arbiter: the process of stepping-in. We step into the exemplar's context, take on the Array structure, and assess whether the elements we have of the Primary Operation seem to be sufficient to satisfy the Criterion. If they do, then we have enough. Once that point was reached with Ulrike, questioning on the Primary Operation ceased; our attention then turned to the Secondary Operations. We assume that, had questioning continued, Ulrike would have been able to come up with further things she does when presenting. However, through the process of stepping-in, we were in a position to determine that we had what we needed for the ability to function (at least for us).

(You will find the completed Array for Ulrike in the Appendix.)

* * *

In this Essay you took some of the first steps that lead from the ideal into the actual. There are many more such steps to be taken. In fact, there is no end to them; the tremendous richness of human experience is enough to ensure that every elicitation you do will be an opportunity to discover new subtleties of how expression reveals structure, and of how to use the subtleties of your questions to gain access to that structure.

Once we have the information, the Array, then what? We certainly did not go to all that trouble just to have information. Rather, we want that information to serve as the doorway into the dwelling of our exemplar's ability. The next few Essays will explore how to refine the model so that it becomes more accessible, and how to gain access itself.

PART V

Working Models

Working Models

Essay 15

Elegance

Elicitation produces an Array that is lush with information and patterns. Not all of those patterns are necessary for the model to work, however. In fact, a model that is too dense runs the risk of being overwhelming or creating unnecessary barriers to acquisition. Now we can turn our attention from the process of gathering information from the exemplar to that of cultivating "elegance" in the model itself; that is, now we can trim the model to those patterns that are necessary and sufficient for it to work.

To watch Fred Astaire dance is to watch the essence of dance. He dazzles us with movement, revealing what is possible *in* moving. And it is not that he dazzles us with impossible leaps, fluttering footwork too fast to follow, or neon sign gestures. Indeed, the reason we can see and feel in Astaire what dance *is*, is because his movements are *not* obscured by excess. Every movement is all that is needed to express that moment...and to flow

into the next movement. It is elegance in action, drawing us completely into another world.

We don't want our models to stumble under the weighty ornament of unnecessary details; we want them to dance like Astaire, carrying us into and through the ability with movements of subjective experience that are just what is needed—no more, no less. We want our models to *work*. But for that to happen, the model has to become a part of our experience. That is, the model has to become *accessible*.

An "elegant" model is one that captures those elements of experience that are *necessary and sufficient* to manifest the ability it describes. Elegance is a relative and subjective notion, of course. A model that requires us to adopt only one pattern to manifest a certain ability is not necessarily more elegant than the model of a different ability that requires two dozen patterns to be manifested. In each case it takes what it takes; the idea of elegance—whether we are speaking of a dance or a model—is that it not include *more* than it takes.

Models are not intended to serve as exhaustively detailed descriptions of the exemplar's experience. There is no inherent virtue in creating a model that is festooned with dazzling distinctions and abundant behaviors. The virtue of a model is found in its effectiveness at making an ability accessible to ourselves or to others. "Elegance" is one of the qualities that help make a model accessible. In general, models become more accessible as they become more elegant.[50]

The fact is that a relatively small set of structures generates the rich (and endless) content of the exemplar's experience. This set of generative structures is revealed in the patterns that we find threading through the rich mass of the exemplar's content. If we want to make a wing with which to fly, we do not catalogue everything that can be specified about every wing. Instead, we compare enough wings until we discover the patterns of structure that are essential to make "wings that work." Those patterns reveal what is *necessary* for a wing to work and, so, tell us what shape our wings must take if we are going to fly as well.[51]

---

[50] Elegance is particularly important if you want to make your model available to a general audience, people who will have neither your technical background nor your direct experience of the exemplar.

[51] Of course, this does not mean we would – or even could – exhaust the possibilities of patterns that can be discovered regarding wings. We may want to

But isn't elegance something we have already sorted out by stepping into and patterning our exemplar's experience during the elicitation? Not necessarily. To begin with, some of the patterns we found during elicitation will have been important in supporting our exemplar's personal manner or style. Take for instance the two "good teachers" we discussed in Essay 2: Getting Started. Though both were good teachers, the manner of one is a "calm presence," while that of the other is a "blur of energy." Some of the patterns you would elicit from each of these exemplars of good teaching would be directly related to manifesting each of their different styles. These person-specific patterns are necessary to your model only if you want to manifest the ability *just like that exemplar*; they are not necessary if you want to manifest *just the ability*.

In addition, some of the exemplar's experiential elements may be tied to the particular situations that she deals with, and these situations may be significantly different from those you will be in. For example, suppose your exemplar of the ability to forgive is also a member of the clergy. You may well find that her Array includes important beliefs about god, one's soul, and so on. These may be essential aspects of forgiveness for her in the world that she lives in. But it may not be necessary for you to adopt those same religious beliefs in order to use her patterns of thinking when forgiving people in the world that *you* live in.

Allegiance to the Model

A primary goal of information gathering is to capture the exemplar's structure of experience as much as possible in its natural state. We have exhorted you to respect and hold almost sacred your exemplar's description of her experience, to keep it in her words, rather than transform it into your interpretation of her experience. So it may seem strange that now we are urging you to cull those same, carefully preserved descriptions.

---

return to examining wings for their secrets regarding "folding," or efficiency of muscle attachment, airflow through feathers, coloration, and so on.

Throughout elicitation, our allegiance has been to the world of the exemplar. We were trying to answer the question, "What *must* be operating in the structure of the exemplar's experience for her to be manifesting this ability?" Answering this question naturally produces a rich description of patterns characteristic *of the exemplar*. Now that you are setting forth the model for your own use, however, you are stepping into a somewhat different realm. Now that we are ready to refine and explicate the model, that allegiance to the exemplar is over. *Now our allegiance shifts to the model itself.*

In setting forth the model for your own use, you are still going after the structure of the ability, of course. But now you are trying to answer a substantially different question:

"What elements of that structure do *I* need to take on in order to manifest this ability?"

The assumption behind this question is that it may not be necessary to take on all of those rich details and nuances of perception, thought and behavior that elicitation has stuffed into the boxes of the Array, like a week's worth of clothing crammed into an overnight bag.

Why We Do Not Need to Include Everything

But are not all those details and nuances important for true competence in the ability? Yes, of course, they are. Don't we therefore need to include all of them in the model? No, we do not need to include them all. And here is why:

A Change in Structure Changes the System

The first reason that we do not need to include everything is that the effect of any change in the structure of a system will be to reorganize, in some way, that system. Because *you* are a system, even the simplest change in behavior, strategy, emotion or belief will create a cascade of effects throughout your experience. Or another way to express this is to say that even a small change (or addition) to a structure necessarily creates a new set of relationships. You can probably find examples of this in your own experience during the last hour, a moment when you shifted some feeling (or perspective, or behavior), and that change immediately shifted much of the rest of your experience. Obviously, the specific shift that takes place, as well as its extent and depth, depends upon how the "particular structure change" mixes with the "you of the moment." But in every case there *will be* systemic effects.

But not just any systemic effects. As a way of protecting the flocks and herds belonging to farmers and ranchers, wolves were all but eradicated in the United States. The result was that deer and elk populations increased beyond the ability of the forest and prairies to support them. So they starved. In some places today, massive hunts are organized to thin the deer population. And in some places, they are beginning to reintroduce wolves. The wolf was not some appendage stuck onto the body of the land, but an integral part of a predator-prey-forage system. Removing the wolf not only necessarily changes the structure of the system, but also *predictably* changes it. We now know (in general) the systemic effect of removing a predator, and we also know (in general) what the effect will be on a prey-forage system if a predator is *introduced.*

Similarly, when you introduce a new belief (or emotion or behavior) into the structure of your experience, it will initiate changes throughout your system that are "naturally" connected to that new element. Of course, that one new element of experience may not itself be enough to initiate all of the systemic changes needed to manifest the ability you have modeled. But it will certainly move "the system" (you) more in that direction. The point of elegance is to introduce only those elements of experience needed to bring to life the rest of the needed system, that is, the structure that *is* the ability.

Systems Are Self-Enriching

The second reason that we do not need to include everything from the Array is that the new (to you) structure both creates a new set of filters and generates new experiences. Over time, these new filters and experiences reveal to you more and more of those "details and nuances of perception, thought and behavior" that make your grasp of the ability stronger and deeper. Recall the authors' experience on the bridge with our painter friend who showed us that there are many colors in water. We not only saw the colors she was pointing out, but started intentionally *looking* for colors in the water. In fact, in doing that, we noticed other colors and shades of colors that she had not pointed out. Because we continued to look for those water colors, we also found that the palette of colors in a lake is different from that in a stream, which is different from that in an ocean on a cloudy day, a sunny day, in shore, far out, and so on.

Similarly, if you take on Ulrike's cause-effect, "You need to risk intimacy in order to build a relationship with the audience," you will start *noticing* when you are risking intimacy, when you are not, and when you are not sure. Also, this cause-effect will attune you to experiences and feedback that refine and extend your discriminations and understandings regarding risking intimacy. For instance, suppose that at the conclusion of a presentation several people come up to say how "close" they felt to you when you admitted that there were aspects of your presentation topic that you were avoiding because they weren't interesting to you. Though you had not intended it, the feedback of those participants helped you see that you had actually been revealing something about *your personal preferences* to the audience, and that that is another way of risking intimacy.

To recap, the two reasons we do not need to include everything in the model are:

- As the patterns in a model settle into your experience, they will naturally (indeed, inevitably) generate many of the nuances and details of structure that are not made explicit in the model. That is how structure works.

- The structure offered by the model will act as a filter on your experience, allowing you to notice and respond to things that previously were transparent or opaque to you. The structure starts a snowball of distinctions that pick up more and more new distinctions as it rolls down the hill of your experiences as you manifest the ability in the real world.

Okay, even if it is not necessary to include everything, isn't it still a good idea to make the model as rich and detailed as possible?

Why We Do Not *Want* to Include Everything

Elegance is not simply an aesthetic consideration (though elegant models do have an undeniable aesthetic that "kitchen sink" models do not have). Elegance is primarily a practical consideration. Aside from the daunting fact that including "everything" in the model will make the gathering of information a monumental task, a too-detailed model can get in the way of you or another person actually being able to take it on.

A ten ton model for a ten pound ability may overwhelm the person who wants to take on that ability. Mountains of criteria and cause-effects and strategies and emotions and behaviors can be intimidating enough to scare even a motivated person away from trying to take it all on. Or, if he gamely starts scaling that mountain, he may soon be exhausted by its steep demands and give up. The bigger the model (in terms of number of details or complexity), the more daunting it inevitably becomes. Including only what is necessary and sufficient helps ensure that the model is no more demanding than it needs to be.

"Space" for the Person

Rearranging a few pieces of furniture in your house to make it comfortable is one thing. But if making your house comfortable means taking out walls, raising the ceilings, replacing the windows, repainting... that is quite a different enterprise, and not so easily done. Models are not crammed into people; models are *accommodated* by people. The more room there is in the model for the person to find himself, the more readily will he be able to adopt it.

To put the point a bit differently, a model that offers only that which is necessary and sufficient leaves more "space" for the person taking on the ability to merge himself with it. An analogy taken from the world of cartooning may help us understand this more clearly. In explaining the iconographic power of cartoon imagery, Scott McCloud offers the following example:

Understanding Comics, ©1993 Scott McCloud

Of the five images, the photographic image on the left is obviously the most complete and realistic representation. But is it the one we can most easily identify with? That photographic image is so clearly and fully who *that* person is that there is little room in it for us to find ourselves. As the images progressively lose the details of a particular (male) person, they reveal more and more of what is essential to "personhood," and it becomes easier for us to identify with the image. There is, in a sense, more "space" for us to find ourselves in each succeeding the image. And of course, this can go too far, as well. The last image has lost so much detail that it has no character or quality other than "face." Yes, now *everyone* can identify with it, but there is very little information in it, and so it does not take us very far.

A useful model, then, is one that hovers somewhere in the middle ground of identity. Its patterns need to be those that are within your range of possible experience while still pushing you to the unexplored edges of that range. Expanding the range of experience and behavior that you have available to you is what change *is*.

Taking on a new model necessarily requires some reorganization of the person's subjective world, a pushing of oneself to previously unexplored areas of experience and behavior. And that may well take effort. Suppose, for instance, that an essential element in a model for working with children is being able to "feel patient." Simply knowing that does not put "patience" in you. The experience of feeling patient needs to be either already somewhere in your personal history of experiences, waiting to be put to use in this model, *or* you need to acquire the ability to feel "patient"—that is, bring it into your range of possible experiences/behaviors—in order to manifest this particular model. If feeling patient is already within your experiential repertoire, it will be relatively easy to bring it into your experience when manifesting this model for working with children. If feeling patient is not easily accessed by you, or is not at all in your current experiential repertoire, you will have to do the work to bring it "in." This will take effort; how much effort it takes to bring in a new experiential or behavioral element will depend upon who you are and what you are wanting to bring in.

Now, let's suppose that "patience" is *not* essential to this model for working with children, but that we nevertheless include it in the Array. If you do not already have easy access to feeling "patient," you may be stopped from taking on the model. This could happen because you find "feeling patient" too troublesome to learn, or too difficult, or it conflicts with your sense of self, and so on. Obstacles such as these could discourage you from acquiring an element specified in the model, and that could discourage you from pursuing the ability, in this case, the ability to work with children. But remember, in this version of the model, being able to "feel patient" is being included even though it is *not necessary* for manifesting the ability. Now you are walking away from a model that you *could have taken on* if you had not been put off by that unnecessary element.

Of course, having a particular ability may be important enough to you that you do not walk away, regardless of the obstacles. You press onward to acquire it, even though it includes personally troublesome elements, and personal work will need to be done for you to access and integrate them. Obviously, if work is needed to have access to an ability, then we roll up our sleeves and do it. But we do not want to create *unnecessary* work. The more distinctions we include in the model, the more chances we have of bumping up against something that could hinder—and possibly overwhelm—us in acquiring the ability. Elegance does not eliminate hindrances to acquisition. Elegance helps make sure that there are no more hindrances to acquisition than there need to be.

So, paring the model down to what is essential helps ensure (1) that there are fewer points of potential conflict between the demands of the model and the resources of the person, and (2) that the demands of the model do not overwhelm the person. Keep in mind that:

The model is not intended to supply everything, but to make everything possible.

Discovering What Is Necessary and Sufficient

Everything should be as simple as it is,
but not simpler.

– Albert Einstein

Ultimately, where a model needs to work is in our own experience, so that is where we test it for what is necessary and sufficient. Of course, this is something you have been doing all along as you gathered information from your exemplar. As she described her experience, you stepped into the context of using the ability *with* her criteria, *with* her cause-effects, ...*t* pieces of her strategy, and so on as a way of discovering what in her description is significant to manifesting the ability.

But during elicitation this testing was not done only inside of your own experience. It was done in concert with your exemplar. You worked together to come up with a shared description of her experiential world.

Now that your allegiance has shifted from the exemplar to the model itself, the work of testing the patterns you elicited becomes solely interior work. The importance *to the exemplar* of a particular element of her experience is no longer the test. Now the test of whether or not an element is essential is in how it affects *your* experience and behavior.

This is not to say that you cannot or ought not to be comparing what you discover about an element of experience with how that element affects the experience of someone else. If you are working with a co-modeler, for instance, you will certainly want to compare experiences as each of you steps into the Array. The difference is, again, that the two of you are no longer after a description that your exemplar would necessarily agree with, but a description that works for you as modelers now trying to manifest the exemplar's ability.

How shall we go about pursuing elegance in our model? To identify what is *essential* for the ability:

* Bring to mind an appropriate context for manifesting the ability you have modeled, and then "step into" it with as much of the Array as you are able to "hold" in your experience.

* Put your attention on the different experiential elements, each in turn, and ask yourself, "In what ways does this influence my experience and behavior in this context?" Identify how each experiential element affects the ability.

* If you find an element that seems to have little or no effect on your manifesting the ability, discover what happens when you eliminate that element from your experience. Do you still get the full expression of the ability?

If you can still manifest the ability without explicitly accessing one of the patterns in your exemplar's Array, then that pattern is not *necessary*; eliminating it from your model will probably make your model more elegant.

Patterns can prove themselves to be non-essential in two ways, and it is important to recognize the distinction between the two: The pattern may be non-essential because it is "irrelevant," or it may be non-essential because it is "implicit" in other elements.

Irrelevant Patterns

Suppose you are modeling an architect who is an exemplar for being able to design spaces that fit the people who live in them. You notice that when she uses her imagination to create possible spaces she has a pattern of tapping her teeth with a pencil. To test out the importance of this behavior, you take the pencil away from her and discover that she suddenly has great difficulty running her internal design strategy. So now you know that tooth-tapping is necessary for this architect when she is designing spaces. And, of course, you include it in her Array. Do you then need to tap your teeth as well if you want to be able to be successful at using her strategy?

You can answer this by stepping-in (as we described above) and finding out whether or not tooth-tapping makes a difference in *your* ability to use her strategy for architectural design. If it turns out that it just doesn't work without tapping your teeth, then that is a necessary element of the Array, and it stays. If tapping your teeth does not make any difference, then it is an irrelevant pattern, and can be eliminated from the model.

Another way to answer the question of relevancy is by comparing this exemplar with other exemplars of the same ability. If we find that all of them tap their teeth as well, then probably it is a *naturally essential* External Behavior for this particular ability. If the other exemplars do not tap their teeth, then this is idiosyncratic behavior that is probably not *essential* to the model. (We will have much more to say about this in Essay 16 on Generic Models.)

Implicit Patterns

As pointed out earlier, any change in the structure of a system will send echoes of change throughout that system. Consequently, as you introduce one element of the Array into your own experiential system you may find that this, in and of itself, initiates changes in certain beliefs, strategies, states, and behavior that are specified elsewhere in the Array. In that case, you may not need to explicitly include these other elements of the model. Or to put it another way, if stepping into the reduced model—one without certain elements—nevertheless automatically brings those same elements into play, then they are *implicit*. You do not need to burden the model with these implicit elements and, so, will have a more elegant model by eliminating them.

Elegance for Others

As we mentioned above, if the pattern is implicit for you, you can certainly eliminate it from the model...if the model is for you. If instead you are creating the model for others to use, don't be too hasty about leaving out an implicit pattern. What you need for the model to work for you may not be quite the same as what others would need. Your enriched experiences of the exemplar's world through stepping-in during elicitation will have taught you more than you may consciously recognize. Connections you have already made between the exemplar's structure and your own experiences will have made some of the structures implicit for you.

If you intend to make the model available to others, however, keep in mind that what serves as an elegant model for you may be stripped a bit too bare for someone else. They do not have access to your extensive experience of the exemplar: her stories, her descriptions, and her nuances of behavior. And so some of what is unnecessary for you may need to be made explicit for them; for them, the model may need that *additional* information to be elegant.

When making a model accessible to others, then, you need to consider what is necessary and sufficient from *their* experiential point of view.

One way to approach this is to evaluate the Array through the experiential eyes of someone completely unfamiliar with it and your exemplar. In this case you are still stepping into the context of manifesting the ability with the Array, and then running the experiment of eliminating the patterns one at a time (as we described above), but now you are stepping-in as someone who is coming cold and fresh to the ability and its Array.

Of course another, and probably better choice, is to actually take some naive individuals through using the Array, and finding out from them where they have need of less or of more information/patterns in order to manifest the ability you have modeled.

Choosing INelegance

As an essay on "elegance," we have naturally been ignoring the one circumstance in which you might *want* your model to remain filled with your exemplar's irrelevant patterns. This is when you want an idiosyncratic model. By "idiosyncratic model" we mean a model that conveys both the ability and the personal style of the exemplar. In this case getting the model to the point of necessary and sufficient elegance is less of a concern; instead, you have decided that you *want* to incorporate the nuances of thought and style of this particular exemplar. Much of those stylistic nuances will be conveyed in the mass of idiosyncratic details they offer you about their world. Including them in your model will assist you in adopting the exemplar's personal cognitive and behavioral style.

The Proof in the Pudding

Of course, the winnowing for "necessary and sufficient" that we have been talking about will have taken place primarily in the garden of our imagination; the experience we have (through the structure given by the

Array) is real, but the context in which it is operating is imagined. The next test comes when we step through the protective gate of that garden.

Your model needs to work "in the field," where life is often much more demanding and messier than we tend to imagine when stepping-in. It is precisely because of that demanding messiness that it is useful to *first* test out and refine the model in imagined experience. Many of the obvious missing or insufficient elements will make themselves known and can be dealt with then. Instead of dealing with (and recovering from!) a lot of unnecessary missteps and confusion in the field, you are freer to actually *use* and begin to integrate the model.

Still, imagination will furnish only those difficulties we know to imagine. When you put the model to work in the actual context in which you need it, you may discover that something you had previously eliminated from it is, in fact, necessary. Or the reverse; something that seemed essential to the model is not actually needed.

Consider the first few times you use the model as opportunities to test it in the crucible of the real world, discovering what works, what does not, and what you may still need from the Array (or possibly even from your exemplar) to be able to manifest the ability.

* * *

In this Essay we pursued elegance by testing the Array in our own experience, trying to determine which patterns are necessary and sufficient to manifest the ability. Another way to identify these essential patterns is by comparing exemplars of the same ability. These comparisons are intended to produce models that capture only those elements of experience and behavior that are essential to the ability itself, weeding out those elements that have more to do with each exemplar's personality and style, that is, the idiosyncratic patterns. The result is a "generic" model, and this type of model is the subject of the next Essay.

Working Models

Essay 16

Generic Models

A generic model is created by looking for, and making generalizations about, patterns of structure shared by several exemplars of the same ability. The process of creating a generic model is one of stepping into and comparing each of the exemplars' Arrays for similarities in both content and structure, as well as resolving important discrepancies. A potential weakness of a generic model is that the process of generalizing may "wash out" details that are particularly useful or compelling for some individuals. The strength of generic models lies in their ability to winnow out idiosyncratic elements belonging to particular exemplars, leaving a model that better reflects the essential patterns of the ability and is, therefore, accessible to more people.

A generic model is one that captures those structures of experience shared by everyone who is an exemplar of a particular ability. Since there is a *particular* structure that gives rise to a *particular* ability, then each exemplar of it will have that same structure humming away inside the nexus of idiosyncratic patterns that she *also* brings to the ability. Both are operating together. The distinction we are making here is the same one you face when tasting wines. For example, although cabernets are produced by hundreds of different vintners, their wines share particular qualities (underlying structure) that make them all recognizably cabernets. On top of that underlying cabernet structure will be aromas, tastes, and colors that are distinctive of the individual vintners. At a wine tasting, the underlying

structure is known ("these are cabernets"), and our attention is on identifying their individual qualities. The situation we face in creating generic models goes in the opposite direction; for us the challenge is to set aside that which is idiosyncratic so as to identify the universal structure of the ability we are modeling.

In the previous Essay we introduced the notion of bringing "elegance" to our models as a way of making them more accessible. Applying the criterion of elegance to the exemplar's Array helps us separate out what is essential for the exemplar's ability from what is non-essential. This trimming of the model ensures that it is no more complex and demanding than it needs to be, thereby making it more easily acquired by you and others.

There is another level of "trimming" possible. Until now, our attention has been on capturing what is essential for *this* exemplar to manifest her ability. We could also step beyond that and ask the question, What is essential for *anyone* to manifest this particular ability? This is the question we are trying to answer when creating a "generic model."

We do this by comparing exemplars of the same ability, which allows us to sort out personal patterns from those patterns that are characteristic of *all* of the exemplars. Of course, we are not going to model all exemplars of a particular ability. There is no need to. After finding the same patterns in ten exemplars of the same ability, we can be reasonably sure that we will find those same patterns in exemplar number 11, in number 12, and in exemplar number 112. That is why all of them *are* exemplars of that ability. In fact, you will probably find that as few as three exemplars will clearly foreground the patterns they share, those patterns essential to the ability itself.

A model is *always* a generalized presentation, and a generic model hovers at the extreme end of that generalization continuum. As soon as we begin to extract similarities between two or more exemplars, we begin to sacrifice the specifics of the individual exemplars for the generalities of the ability (with the intention of creating a model that is more universally accessible and more easily acquired). Making these generalizations is a messy business. It is almost certain that your various exemplars are not going to reveal their shared patterns by using exactly the same language. The complexity of individuals and the range of human expression ensures that each of them will have their own way of describing what are, in fact, very similar experiences.

As the modeler, it is left to you to come up with those generalizations that best capture the essential experiential structures of the ability you are modeling. Just which generalizations are "best" will be determined by how well they work in you and in others to manifest the ability. Unavoidably, your generalizations will be "fudges" of the specific facts of each exemplar's actual experiences. But keep in mind that it is not the purpose of a generic model to capture all of the elements of experience of your exemplars; its purpose is to capture only those elements that are necessary for *anyone* to manifest the ability.

Now, how do you do that?

Generic Modeling Protocol

The emphasis during elicitation was on allegiance to the exemplar. The goal then was to describe your exemplar's patterns in a way that resonated with her experience, a description she could look at and say, "Yeah, that's me." It was only after reaching that point in your modeling that you then turned your allegiance to the model itself.

If you are going for a generic model, you will have done elicitations with several exemplars. Having done that, you are likely to find yourself facing Arrays that do not obviously fit with each other. In general, your task now is to test and compare each of these different descriptions in your own experience (as always, stepping-in), and compare where they take your thinking and behavior. Which elements, though described differently, affect your experience in similar ways? If different descriptions affect you similarly then, in practical terms, they are expressing the same underlying structure. Of course, some of those differing descriptions may in fact take your experience in somewhat different directions. When that is the case, are those differences *significant*? That is, do the differences significantly affect how you manifest the ability? If the differences do not significantly affect manifesting the ability, then they are not essential to the underlying structure.

We do not have a step-by-step procedure that grinds out a nicely packaged generic model. It is a much messier pursuit than that. It requires moving in and out of the several Arrays that you are trying to resolve, sorting them *through* your experience on various levels. In addition, most of this stepping-in and out and assessing and judging and generalizing and testing is happening simultaneously. So, first we want to give you an idea of the overall (messy) process, and then we will unpack some of its details.

As we said above, in its broadest outlines, the process of creating a generic Array involves comparing two or more exemplars in order to discover patterns of structure or content that they share. It may seem that the logical way to approach this is to begin by laying out on the table all of the Arrays from each of your exemplars, and to then start searching for commonalties. However, there is a much more efficient—and natural— way to make these comparisons:

Generic Modeling Protocol

1. Begin by identifying which of the exemplar Arrays works best for you in terms of being able to take it on. This, then, becomes your "referent Array." You will probably know immediately which Array is your

referent. Typically, you will have discovered during elicitation that one of your exemplars stood out as someone whose way of describing her experience was particularly accessible for you.

2. Using this referent Array as your basis for comparison, contrast it with the Arrays of your other exemplars. Because you are starting with something that *works* in your experience, the effect of trying on differing element descriptions in the other Arrays will be much more obvious to you.

* Some of the elements in these other Arrays will move your experience in ways that are similar to your experience when using the referent Array. When that happens, you have found an *essential element of structure* for that ability, something that belongs in the generic Array.

Since it is likely that the different exemplars had somewhat different ways of describing that aspect of their experience, you then need to decide how to best capture it in language for the *generic* Array.

* Some elements will take your experience in directions that are quite different from where the referent Array takes you. This probably means one of three things:

  • You simply missed capturing a correct or true description of that element of structure during your elicitation with this exemplar. If this seems possible, you can go back to your notes or recordings (or, if necessary, to the exemplar herself) to further explore and, perhaps, revise your description.

  • You have identified an aspect of the ability for which different exemplars have different structures and, so, is a pattern *not* essential to the generic ability. If that is the case, the differing patterns are idiosyncratic and, so, not part of the generic model.

  • One or some of your exemplars are actually exemplars of a *different* ability. That is, what they are good at doing is not precisely what you were wanting to model. If so, you can use this information to clarify your specification of the ability and, if necessary, find another exemplar who does manifest the ability you want to model.[52]

Naturally, this is not how it will actually go. Here is what is more likely: As you step in and out of the Arrays, comparing their effects on your experience, how they are the same and different, numerous, difficult and subtle questions will arise: "Are the discrepancies I am experiencing *real* discrepancies, or am I just misunderstanding them? Is this element *really* true for all of the other exemplars? Is this element really *not* true for the other exemplars? This exemplar differs in a number of ways, so should I just ignore her Array completely? What do I do with this interesting idiosyncratic element? Can I include it anyway? And whose language do I use for the Array? Only that of the referent exemplar?" And so on.

Time to fudge.

The Art of Fudging

There are no formulas or easy answers to these or any of the questions that will be raised when trying to reconcile the Arrays of several exemplars. But what we *can* do is talk about what to consider, and how to go about, answering those questions. For the most part, you will be facing three possible situations. Your exemplars are using:

- Same or similar language to express the same structure.
- Different language to express the same structure.
- Different language to express different structures.

---

[52] It is also possible that this maverick exemplar will instead reveal to you that your idea of the ability you want to model was too narrow, or even misdirected. Finding this out could lead you to widen or correct your definition of the ability, so that it now includes the "maverick" as a legitimate exemplar, and may spur you to find exemplars of this "broader" ability.

Same Language, Same Structure

The hoped for possibility is that there is a close match across the exemplar Arrays in their descriptions of a particular pattern. That is, they use virtually the same words and phrases. For instance, suppose we are modeling grade school teachers who have the ability to "hold the attention of a child" and, in response to the question, "What is important to you when working with a child?" the answers from our three exemplars are:

"I look for what is special in that child."
"The search is for that which is special in any child."
"What's special about this child, that's what I'm after."

This is a little bit of modeling heaven. When this happens, how to capture that element of the Array is obvious and easy: you simply use the language that your exemplars all agree is the way to capture that aspect of their experience (in this case, the Criterion, "what is special").

What To Do

Beyond selecting the particular wording that works best for you, no fudging is needed. Savor these moments. They will be few and far between.

Different Language, Same Structure

What more frequently occurs, however, is that at least one (and often all) of your exemplars will use different words to express patterns that they nevertheless all share. They have the same patterns but, thanks to the richness of language, describe them in different ways. For example, suppose our three teacher exemplars respond to the question, "What is important to you when working with a child?" as follows:

"It's how this child is special. That's what I'm after."
"I look for the lightning in each child."

"The child's particular interest is what matters to me."

The words "special," "lightning," and "particular interest" are different. But are these three responses expressing different structures (different Criteria)? In order to sort out the answer to this question, we test each of the exemplar's descriptions by taking on each of their Arrays in order to discover if their different phrasings affect how we manifest the target ability. To be clear, we are not assessing which one we like, but instead how each of them orients our *thinking and behavior*.

Let us say that, in this instance, our experiences of taking on the different descriptions makes it evident that in fact all three teachers are expressing the same underlying structure: all are looking for what each child is naturally excited by or about (which then becomes the doorway through which the teacher introduces new learnings to the child, etc.). This is what we would expect: if we have chosen exemplars who are all good at doing just what we want to model, then almost certainly they are operating out of the same underlying structures of experience. Because of the richness of language, we are not surprised to find that their individual differences naturally produce different expressions of those structures. But it is only the words describing them that are different; the essential structure giving rise to those varying descriptions is, nevertheless, the same (or very close) for all of our exemplars.

What To Do

When comparing the Arrays of your several exemplars you will find differences between how they describe their experiences. The question is whether a particular exemplar is using different words to express essentially the same structure, or is a "maverick," that is, someone who is truly different than your other exemplars.

Your ongoing experience during elicitation will often reveal whether or not your exemplars are using different language to describe what are, in fact, the same structures. Remember that as you are gathering information you are also trying on their patterns in yourself in order to sort out the experiential significance of what they are describing. This gives you a basis for comparison as you then move from one exemplar to the next. So it is likely that during the process of elicitation with your second and third exemplars you will already be recognizing where there are similarities between them in terms of structure, similarities that are there despite the idiosyncratic language they are using to describe those structures.

Notes, transcripts, and tape or video recordings can also be very useful in helping to resolve these apparent discrepancies. These records will often provide the context, the stories, and detailed explanations (all of which were probably reduced to a few words and phrases in the Array) that you need to make sense of what is going on. We often find when we look back at these records that a "maverick" exemplar *did* express herself in the same or similar way as the other exemplars, but that we had not picked up on that particular languaging or examples at the time.

Once you determine that, yes, these are different ways of talking about the same thing, there is the question of what language to use in the generic model? The goal is not to simply find terms that are general enough to encompass all of the exemplars. The goal is to use language that evokes the necessary experiences and structures. Of the three exemplars above, "particular interest" is the most generally descriptive of their shared Criteria. But it is also bland (at least to the authors' ears and bodies). Much more evocative is "lightning," which engages our experience more immediately, strongly, and (through metaphorical associations) more deeply.[53]

And so it is *in* experience that these judgments of similarity and dissimilarity need to be made. Initially, it will be made in *your* experience. That is, as you try on the range of languaging you have from your exemplars" Arrays, you will discover how they work in your own experience in terms of accessing the ability. In doing this you will also be discovering which descriptions work best to evoke the necessary

---

[53] It is also important to keep in mind that the fact that an apparently maverick exemplar has her own way of expressing her experience does not necessarily mean she would object to describing it in another way. If you have ready access to the exemplar, another way to test whether or not her maverick description truly denotes a different experience is to have her "try on" the description in your referent Array. Does she find that it also works in her experience (or at least well enough)?

underlying structures. Obviously, if the model is only for you, that is as far as you need to go. If instead the model is intended for others to use, you will also need to test your languaging choices on people unfamiliar with the model.

Different Language, Different Structure

The third possibility is that the differences in the exemplars' language reflect true differences in structure as well. In other words, one of your exemplars is, in fact, a maverick and is operating out of a structure that is somewhat different from that of your other exemplars. Going back to our teacher exemplars, we find that while two of them are *Looking for what each child is naturally excited by or about* (labeled as the "lightning," and the "particular interest"), our third exemplar is actually attending to something quite different. For her, the "special" she is after is: *What is difficult for this child*. It is clear that this third exemplar (like the two other exemplars) is able to hold the attention of the children she works with. It is *also* clear that she is operating out of quite a different Criterion/Definition than the other two when she is doing it.

How does this difference in exemplar structures affect our generic model?

What To Do

You selected your exemplars because you considered all of them excellent at manifesting the particular ability you want to model. If, however, you discover that one of them is operating out of a truly different structure of experience, the first thing to do is to recognize that this difference will probably teach you something about your model. Do not simply discard the maverick's Array, or even the part of it that does not fit with your other exemplars. The differences are quite possibly an opportunity to learn more about the ability.

At the very least, her dissimilarity will help you refine the definition of the ability you are modeling. That is, contrasting it with the Arrays of the other exemplars may help you become clearer about what you are actually creating a model *of.* For instance, with the teacher exemplars, the intention was to model the ability to "hold the attention of a child." However, when we look more clearly at what the dissimilar teacher ("what is difficult for this child") does, we realize that she teaches the physical education program, and that she is excellent at holding the attention of children when they are striving to learn a sport. Outside of that particular context, she is not nearly as adept. This difference brings into focus that we are actually creating a model for "holding the attention of a child *in the classroom.*" Now we have a more accurate understanding of where the boundaries are of our model, and if we want to interview additional exemplars, we know more precisely how to identify them.

In addition to perhaps helping you redefine the ability, a maverick exemplar may also shed light on some of the subtle workings of the model itself. Discriminating the many tastes to be found in a particular wine is done by comparing it to wines that are close in taste. This allows the subtleties in each of them to become more apparent precisely because they are otherwise quite similar. Your maverick exemplar is like a comparison wine: significantly different in one or some ways, and yet quite close to the ability you are wanting to model. (Indeed, close enough that you did not recognize at first that hers *is* a different ability.) Because of this closeness, contrasting her structure with that of your other exemplars can lead to a deeper understanding of what they are doing and how that works to manifest the ability. The question to answer is, "How do I make sense of the fact that this exemplar has an element(s) of structure that is different from the other exemplars?"

For example, we can compare the maverick exemplar's *"what is difficult for this child?"* with our other exemplars' *"what is each child naturally excited by or about?"* When we try these two orientations on, one thing that jumps out at us is that the divergent exemplar is more oriented toward the child attaining an outcome, while the other exemplars are more oriented toward the child's ongoing experience.[54] Through this

---

[54] This is not to say that the divergent exemplar does not consider the child's ongoing experience, or that the other exemplars do not hold outcomes for the child. Rather, that there are differences between them regarding the focus of their attention. And, as we discussed in Essays 3, 7 and 8, the focus of one's attention

contrast, something in the model that was previously implicit and opaque is now explicit and clear. And, if having this explicit understanding sheds some useful light on the Array, making it more accessible and effective, you can add it to the model (in our example, we might include in the model explicit instructions about placing one's attention on the child's ongoing experience).

Cherry Picking

In addition to the three situations above, you will also discover tidbits of idiosyncratic structure or content in each of your exemplars that seem to enhance the ability, to help it work better. These idiosyncratic "cherries" can come from any of the exemplars, including one whom you have discovered is really not an exemplar of *exactly* the ability you are modeling. As we noted above, the structure of a maverick's ability will still be close to that of your other exemplars, otherwise she would probably never have appeared to be an exemplar to begin with. And so her Array may well include some elements of behavior, or belief, or strategy that could be useful additions to your model.

For instance, in creating the generic model for "holding the attention of a child in the classroom," suppose we discover the following strategy piece from the physical education teacher: because her focus is on outcomes, and in sports these are often pretty clearly either met or missed, she has developed an effective Secondary Strategy for re-engaging a child who is disappointed in his performance. Since every teacher will face discouraged children, this Secondary Strategy for re-engaging a child who has "failed" at attaining a goal may be a useful addition to the model of our classroom teacher exemplars. Idiosyncratic elements like these, elements that can make a *significant* contribution to the effectiveness of the ability, may well be worth adding to the generic Array.

---

will have profound and pervasive effects on one's perceptions, thought processes, emotions and behavior.

An Example of a Generic Array

Lacking hard and fast rules for creating a generic Array, we will offer you instead an actual example of deriving one. The one we have chosen is for the ability to "Step Into Experience." As has been evident on almost every page of this book, we consider stepping-in of pivotal importance in modeling. We hope that the following discussion regarding a generic Array for stepping-in will not only serve as a useful example of the process of creating such models, but that it will give you a deeper and more functional experience of stepping-in itself. Anything you can do to cultivate this ability in your own modeling work will be worth doing.

This generic Array was originally developed for our modeling programs at the request of the participants. In fact, it was the participants of one of our seminars who did the initial Array elicitations, and who chose us, the authors, as exemplars of the ability to step in. Later, casting about for a third exemplar to include in the distillation of a generic Array, we recognized that a friend, Bob Smith, was a superb exemplar of the ability. In his work as an executive coach, Bob is known for his almost preternatural ability to generate multiple strategies, tactics and choices for his clients that allow them to get past the personal or organizational barriers they face. This process begins with his ability to accurately step into his client's experience. Subsequently, the authors created a generic Array from these three elicitations.

We cannot, of course, take you down the exact road we took to get to the generic Array. There was no road. The process was more akin to running wild in the forest of the exemplar Arrays, smacking into trees and falling into holes until we came to know the terrain well. Obviously, one advantage we had in this experiential rumpus was that two of the three exemplars were us, the authors. That meant that as we sorted through the Arrays—identifying true differences, resolving apparent differences, and deciding on language—we had ongoing access to each other.

Even so, it was not simple.

"Stepping-In"

We begin by identifying our referent Array, the one that initially strikes us as most comprehensive and accessible: this is Graham's. This first step is also the last that we can explicitly mark out for you. As we noted previously, there is no step-by-step sequence or technique that will take you through how we came to our "stepping-in" generic Array. Instead, we will present each element of experience in turn and describe some of the experiencing, thinking, and "fudging" we went through to make the choices we made.

Criterion and Definition

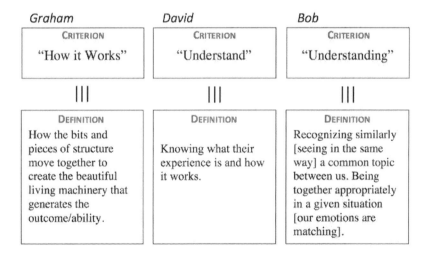

Graham	David	Bob
CRITERION	CRITERION	CRITERION
"How it Works"	"Understand"	"Understanding"
DEFINITION	DEFINITION	DEFINITION
How the bits and pieces of structure move together to create the beautiful living machinery that generates the outcome/ability.	Knowing what their experience is and how it works.	Recognizing similarly [seeing in the same way] a common topic between us. Being together appropriately in a given situation [our emotions are matching].

When we look just at the Criteria, we immediately see that they are from the same "family." Two of them are expressed almost exactly the same: "Understand" and "Understanding," and the third, "How It Works," takes our experience to very much the same subjective place as "Understand."

But, "expressed *almost* exactly the same" is not the same thing as, "expressed *exactly* the same." And "*very much* the same subjective place" is not, "the *same* subjective place." Are all three Criteria in fact just different language for essentially the same experience, or do they actually denote different experiences? (Keep in mind that we are seeking the experiences behind the words.) To sort out the Criteria across exemplars, we need to turn to—and step into—their Definitions.

WE HAVE A MAVERICK - When we do this, it becomes clear that Graham's Criterion is actually much closer to David's than it is to Bob's. Trying on each of the Criteria/Definitions, and comparing where they take our experience, two particularly significant differences become apparent:

> * With Graham and David's "How It Works" and "Understand"
> (as they define them), it is evident that there is an end point to
> the stepping into the experience of the exemplar. They are doing
> it *to get to* "how the bits and pieces of structure move," or
> "knowing...how it works." And once they get it, they are done.

Bob's Criterion, however, does not have an end point. "Understanding" is ongoing; he is continually checking and wanting to maintain a match between how he and the client see things, and between the emotions they are having.

> * More significantly, Bob's Criterion makes stepping-in for him as
> much about maintaining the relationship as it is about gathering
> information. He made clear in the elicitation that his focus is on
> the client feeling understood as much as it is about Bob
> understanding the client.

For David and Graham, the exemplar feeling understood is a by-product of the process of elicitation. It is not an intention to be fulfilled *by* elicitation. Their Criteria are not about their relationship with the exemplar, but about the structure of her experience.

How do we make sense of the fact that Bob does not have the same Criterion as Graham and David? Contrasting theirs with Bob's reveals that the *purpose* for which one is using stepping-in matters. Bob is gathering information with the intention of getting his clients to do something. Bob not only needs to understand his clients so that he knows what to advise, he needs to have a relationship with them that makes it possible to influence them. In the context of modeling, however, Graham and David have no intention of getting the exemplar to change (quite the opposite), and no expectation of having a relationship that continues beyond the elicitation. (Bob's relationships with his clients sometimes span years.)

The difference between a purely information gathering context (modeling) and an intervention context (coaching) seems—now!—significantly different to us. And this difference accounts for the discrepancy between Graham and David's Criteria and Bob's. Graham and David are exemplars of the *specific* ability that we want to model: *Stepping-in when modeling.*

We are not going to discard Bob's Array, however. Despite the coaching aspects of his ability, it is still the case that he steps into his client's experience to gather information. Perhaps the other elements of his Array will either confirm or throw a contrasting light on patterns we find in Graham and David's Arrays, or it may offer some Array cherries worth picking.

RESOLVING THE CRITERION - It seemed best to resolve the Definition first, since that is the experience that is being labeled. David certainly agrees with Graham's more specified Definition, but for David, "Understanding" may also be at a relatively large chunk size (which Graham agreed with as well). And so we decided that the Definition needs to keep open the range of chunk size. In addition, we recognized that the word "knowing" may suggest to some people some sort of pre-knowledge, which is definitely not the case for David. We found that the word "discovery" perfectly captures the relationship that both David and Graham experience with the exemplar. And finally, we felt it important to convey that we are not looking for a static structure, but a dynamic one, as Graham captures in his Definition ("bits and pieces of structure move together"). Taking these together—range of chunk size, discovery, and movement—the Definition for the Criterion becomes, "Discovering what the structure is and how it operates in this person."

As for the Criterion label, David's "Understand" is an obvious choice, both because it is echoed by Bob and because Graham agrees that it would cover his experience as well. However, because the Criterial label may be used as the mnemonic for the whole complex of ideas and perceptions that make up the Criterion (Definition and Evidence), we want to make sure that it leads the person appropriately. For many folks, "Understand" has strong associations with compassion or sympathy with another person's situation. This makes "Understanding" a very appropriate label for Bob's Definition, and one we might use if the ability to step in was within the context of therapy. But in the context of modeling, the focus of our stepping-in needs to be on structure. For this context, then, "How It Works" serves much better as the Criterion (and is even echoed exactly in David's Definition!). The generic Criterion and Definition, then, is:

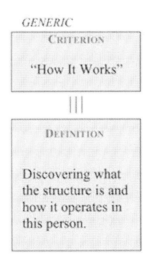

Enabling Cause-Effect

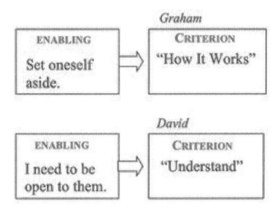

In terms of what makes getting to "How It Works," Graham and David are on either side of the same coin. Scratch the surface of either one's Enabling Cause-Effect, and you find the other. The result in Graham of "set oneself aside," is that it opens him to the exemplar; David opens himself to the exemplar by setting himself "aside."

However, neither of their Enabling Causes works very well in terms of language. "Be open to them" may take many people to a therapeutic stance, or to the cliché notions of "being open" (i.e. willing to consider or listen to something, which is not the same as "setting oneself aside"). And "set oneself aside" seemed too specific in how to open oneself. (A person may bridle at setting himself "aside," but easily accept setting himself "behind," or "being on hold," or "becoming a blank slate," and many other possibilities, any of which would still preserve the essence of the Enabling Cause-Effect.)

Also, it was clear for both Graham and David that being open was an intentional and active state. It is something they are *doing*. This is more obvious in Graham's case: "*Set* oneself aside." But, again, this was the other side of David's "being open," as well. We decided that we could convey this better through "open*ing*." So, the Enabling Cause-Effect is, "Opening to the person's experience is necessary to discover how it works":

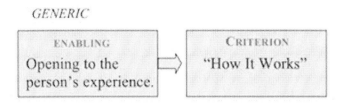

Motivating Cause-Effect

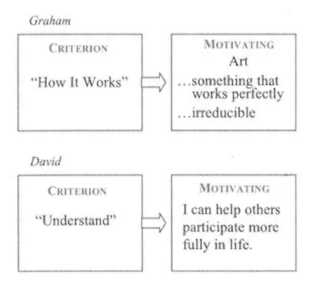

As is usual, the Motivating Effects for David and Graham are expressions of what is vitally significant to them in life, and not just when they are modeling. And, obviously, they are very different from each other. Their Motivators are idiosyncratic, and so there is not a generic Motivating Cause-Effect.

What *may well* be worth including in the generic model, though, is that it is necessary to have a cause-effect between discovering how structure works and *something that is of personal and vital significance.* That is, someone acquiring this generic model for stepping-in will need to identify something significant for him that discovering structure can help make possible (This is in stark contrast to Bob's Motivating Cause-Effect, which relates specifically to the context of coaching: "They will feel safe enough to be themselves, be open and trust me."):

GENERIC

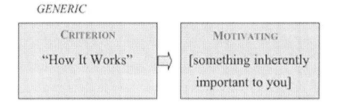

Supporting Belief

David's Supporting Belief, "The price you pay if you open to them and understand them is that you are going to care about them," is not useful for the generic model. It makes sense in relation to his Motivating Cause-Effect ("help others"), but it is not likely to be relevant to anyone who is not holding that Motivating Cause-Effect.

We are not aiming to help the exemplar change or grow during elicitation. Quite the opposite. We want them to be as they are, and find a way to access that in ourselves. The belief that makes such an enterprise even thinkable is that, "Experience has structure." Clearly, Graham's Supporting Belief is essential to the viability of the generic model for stepping-in.

Test

Graham

Test
"How It Works": My amorphous image comes clear, and in my body my amorphous feelings "click" or "kick" in; the experience suddenly has boundaries, and there is more space around it.

David

Test
"Understand" : I suddenly find that I'm generating in my own experience the same kind of things – behaviors, choices, feelings, etc. – as the exemplar, and I start recognizing cause-effects that come from being "that way."

Both Graham and David experience the exemplar's structure coalescing into form and working in themselves as they elicit the information. The pieces of experience that have been accumulating and swirling around suddenly come together in a way that *works*. How they hold that form in experience is different. David holds it in himself as the exemplar's interacting nexus of behaviors, choices, emotions and so on. For Graham, that form is held as "bits and pieces of structure" that coalesce into a "beautiful living machine," something held at more of a distance (where it can be *observed*).

Both Graham and David are explicit that this coalescing is *sudden*. The abruptness of this shift in their experience is a significant convincer that they "know how it works/understand." (It is interesting to note that both Graham and David can have this experience of "knowing how it works/understanding" before being able to *describe* how it is working.)

Graham's "clicking" and shift in focus, and David's perceiving additional cause-effects, are idiosyncratic, so these are not part of the generic Array. As with Graham and David, each person will have his or her own idiosyncratic experience accompanying that sudden coalescing of information; for instance, feeling centered, or tension is released, or there is a "silence," or I see myself doing it, and so on.

It struck us as odd that neither Graham nor David appear to include external feedback from their exemplar as at least part of the Test. And this is despite the fact that in their behavior both of them *frequently* ask for feedback from the exemplar to check their understanding, and make shifts according to the exemplar's responses. How do we make sense of this? For contrast, we turned to Bob's Test for "Understanding":

> "We are moving together no matter which direction it [the exploration] is going. The client agrees with my paraphrase of their requests and descriptions of cause-effects operating in their situation."

The fact that he is clearly using external feedback and that he is operating in a client context made it suddenly clear why Graham and David do not use external feedback. Bob is going to need to take his client somewhere. Graham and David are not intending to take the exemplar anywhere with the patterns that they discover; the exemplar's patterns are going to take *them* somewhere. So the test of understanding is in whether or not they can do what the exemplar does in their own experience.

Interestingly, when things have clicked-in/coalesced for Graham and David regarding some pattern or set of patterns, *feedback from the exemplar that they do* not *have it* is not likely to cause them to doubt that they "understand/know how it works." Instead, they are likely to assume that the exemplar's disagreement must be due to their (Graham and David's) inability to accurately communicate their understanding of the structure, rather than their having misunderstood the structure they had elicited. (As Graham put it, "Feedback from the person that, 'Yes, that's my experience,' is encouraging, but not more significant than my locking in.") Exemplar feedback and confirmation is not a Test, but an Operation in their Strategy for elicitation. That is, it is one of the ways they tune and retune their experience until it suddenly coalesces into something that "works."

AN IMPORTANT POINT: What we have just described may seem to contradict—even violate—our previous emphasis on using the exemplar's description of her experience, rather than our interpretation of it. But it does not. Remember that the goal during elicitation is to create with your exemplar a shared description that she resonates with, that is, that she can look at and say, "Yes, that's me when I'm doing this ability." The goal during the forming of the *model*, however, is to create a description of those same structures that enables you and others to access them, making it possible for you to manifest the exemplar's ability. Hence our adage: When eliciting, your allegiance is to the exemplar's experience; when forming the model, your allegiance is to the model itself. Despite our separate presentations of the processes of elicitation and of forming the model (not to mention our nifty adage), the fact is that you will to some extent be formulating the model even as you are doing the elicitations. That is, as you are gathering information you will, at the same time, be experimenting within your own experience to discover how to make the exemplar's structures "work"; this is what stepping-in *does,* and this is the beginnings of the model itself. Through (primarily) her language the exemplar leads us into the array of cognitive and behavioral structures she operates out of when manifesting her ability. The model we create from this elicitation is a way—again through language—of conveying those same structures to you or to someone else. The goal is not to reproduce the exemplar's language, but to reproduce the exemplar's structure. Often this can best be done by using her own language. If, however, using different language will work better in gaining access to the needed structure, then that is what is best *for the model.*

What needs to be captured in the generic Test, then, is (1) that the structure is being tested in the modeler, (2) that it is working in the modeler, and (3) that this "working" comes about in a sudden coalescing of experiences:

GENERIC

Test
"How It Works": I can do it; in the exemplar's context, I suddenly experience myself feeling and acting like the exemplar.

Primary Operations

Graham

PRIMARY OPERATION

1. I do a bodily shift to begin with, a shift out of "me." I make a space for the person's experience, I'm open and receptive, quiet and still inside. The feeling is of being very central, straight on, straight up and down. I am completely intent on the person, my voice is lower, slower, and softer.

   I am very concerned for the person's experience in terms of:
   • Wanting to know what it is in the context of the ability.
   • That they are fine with the interaction.
   • That it is easy for them to access what I want to know.

2. I ask questions (with a lot of framing). I experience a space in me that extends to this other person, and this space is waiting for the person's experience (it encourages the information to come into it).

3. As the bits and pieces come into the shared space, I experience them.

4. I check for confirmation of how I am experiencing them through matches between my experience and what they subsequently say or through my asking direct questions.

David

PRIMARY OPERATION

1. I need to have a description of the context they operate in.

2. I get very still and quiet inside.
   I create tunnel vision for myself, so the person is the only thing that's important.

3. I ask questions:
   • I'm looking for *the* way that person does it. I'm looking to see if it can be done in more than one way; if so, I ask for more detail.
   • I let what they say take over my body.
   • I feel in my body what I see them doing with their body (esp. anything unusual, characteristic or exaggerated).
   • Things they say I say myself (internally).
   • Things they say they see or feel I make inside myself.

There are some obvious similarities between Graham and David's Primary Operations, even if those similar strategic elements are expressed in somewhat different ways or in different places. Specifically, both prepare themselves for "opening to the person's experience" (Enabling Cause-Effect) by becoming "quiet and still inside," both specify and evoke for themselves the context of the ability (this is the context into which they will step and test the bits of information they are going to gather), both ask questions, and both take on in their own experience "the bits and pieces" of structure as they emerge during the elicitation.

Almost all of the non-matching details of the two Primary Operations were, when checked with Graham and David, confirmed to be true for each of them as well. For instance, though he did not come out with it during elicitation, Graham uses David's approach of "looking for *THE* way that person does it." And like Graham, David always uses "lots of framing" when asking his questions.

The Primary Operation for the generic Array was fleshed out by combining those operations that were true for *both* Graham and David.

In addition, a "cherry" worth picking was plucked from Bob's Primary Operation:

> "As soon as your experience stops making sense, stop the client and say, 'Okay, something's not right. I'm missing something.' Ask further questions until your experience makes sense again."

This turned out to be very true for both Graham and David as well, though neither thought to mention it during elicitation. And so this "cherry" from Bob was included in step 4 in the Primary Operation.[55] So, the generic Primary Operation for stepping-in becomes:

---

[55] It is interesting to compare David and Graham's Primary Operation with Bob's because it shares many similarities and, at the same time, is clearly oriented to the intervention context of executive coaching, rather than to a purely information gathering context like modeling.

GENERIC

PRIMARY OPERATION

1. Get a description of the context they are usually operating in.
2. Become very still and quiet inside, and devote your full attention to the other person. (This may include tunnel vision and a lower, slower and softer voice.)
3. Ask your questions (using plenty of framing):
   - Look for *the* way that person does it. Look to see if it can be done in more than one way; if so, ask for more detail.
   - Let what they say take over your body.
   - Feel in your body what you see them doing with their body (esp. anything unusual, characteristic or exaggerated).
   - Things they say, say to yourself (internally).
   - Things they say they see or feel, access inside yourself.
4. Check for confirmation of how you are experiencing them through matches between your experience and what they subsequently say or through your asking direct questions.
   - As soon as your experience stops making sense, stop the client and say, "Okay, something's not right. I'm missing something." Ask further questions until your experience makes sense again.

Secondary Operations

Graham and David show a lot of similarity in all of their Secondary Operations. Yet these still need to be worked through; they cannot simply be clumped together.

Graham

SECONDARY OPERATIONS

Not Sufficient – I have probably run out of the first level of questions, so I play with it (the experience) a bit to move things around. Anything that is indistinct, I ask the person questions about from a different angle.

Not At All – I assume I'm in the way in some way, and haven't set myself aside enough. I need more concentration and more space. To check where I have missed "it," I start feeding back what they've said and check through their response (checking for disconfirmation or a different quality) whether I've got it or not.

Can't – I'm explicit about not getting it. Depending upon the context pressures, I will go with what I've got (particularly something that I suspect is something the person has not noticed before).

David

SECONDARY OPERATIONS

Not Sufficient – I hold on to everything I've got about the person. Is it a case of:
- Missing - I ask for what's missing.
- Not enough - I ask for more information.
- Misunderstanding - I ask for the same information but in a different way.

Not At All –
1. I drop all the blocks of information I have. (I'm missing it; I've come at this from the wrong direction.).
2. I change my body; get up, move around (shake off whatever I was taking on before).
3. I start over with a fresh body; taking a different tack.

Can't –
1. I'm upfront: "I don't understand."
2. I describe what I *did* get that was interesting.

NOT SUFFICIENT - Both of them hold on to what they have elicited and experiment with their experience to try to discover what they still need to find out from the exemplar. Often this means going after the same information, but in "a different way" or from "a different angle."

NOT AT ALL - This is interesting because of the different presuppositions that are operating. For both of them, the first step is to re-set their bodies to take on the exemplar's structure anew. But because Graham assumes that he has "not set myself aside enough," he again "loads on" the exemplar's structure, checking it carefully. David assumes that he was open enough to the exemplar's experience, but has been coming "at this from the wrong direction" (in terms of questions). So he resumes the elicitation almost from the beginning, but this time taking a "different tack." Both of these Operations seemed worth including, as both address possible impediments to getting anywhere in the elicitation (namely, "not open," or "open but misunderstanding the information").

CAN'T - Both of them acknowledge to the exemplar that they are unable to understand. And, interestingly, both of their responses to being unable to discover "how it works" have a therapy feel. Acknowledging the efforts of the exemplar is intended to leave the exemplar feeling good about the elicitation experience.

The Secondary Operations for the generic Array are:

GENERIC

> **SECONDARY OPERATIONS**
>
> **Not Sufficient –**
>   Experiment with the experience by moving things
>   around a bit. If anything is missing, indistinct or
>   potentially misunderstood, ask the person questions
>   about it from a different angle.
>
> **Not At All –**
> • "I haven't set myself aside enough." Re-set
>   yourself (empty yourself of the former structure)
>   by shifting body posture. Check each element of
>   structure with the person as you "load it on." (You
>   are checking for congruence, disconfirmation, or
>   different quality.)
> • "I've come at this from the wrong direction." Re-
>   set yourself (empty yourself of the former
>   structure) by shifting body posture. Take a
>   different tack.
>
> **Can't –**
>   Admit you are unable to entirely get the structure.
>   Acknowledge, and express appreciation for what
>   you did get from the exemplar.

Sustaining Emotion

Two of the three exemplars identified the same Sustaining Emotion: "love" (in the sense of appreciating and honoring who a person is). The fact that Bob applies his ability to step in to a somewhat different context (coaching, rather than modeling), makes a compelling case for "love" as the Sustaining Emotion for the ability to step in *regardless of the context*. The spiritual aspect of Graham's Sustaining Emotion puts him more in relation to the elicited experience itself than to the exemplar as an individual: experience connects us and is in all of us, and is perfect (see Graham's Belief Template). Still, Graham confirmed that his feeling of "holy/awe" encompasses feeling "love." And so that is the Sustaining Emotion for the generic Array:

GENERIC

> **SUSTAINING EMOTION**
>
> LOVE
>
> (Appreciating and honoring who this person is.)

External Behavior

As with the Strategy, there is a great deal of consistency between David and Graham when it comes to External Behavior. Aside from some idiosyncratic behavior, such as David making sure to be at the same eye level as the exemplar when stepping-in and Graham lowering, slowing and softening his voice, they manifest almost the same behaviors. Bob also shares their behavior of becoming still and attending completely to his clients while they are answering his questions. So this is undoubtedly a significant External Behavior when stepping-in in most contexts. External Behaviors for the generic Array are, then:

GENERIC

> **EXTERNAL BEHAVIOR**
>
> - Put yourself on the same level as the exemplar, or below (it makes it easier to step in).
> - Give the person your direct attention while asking a question and awaiting an answer.
> - Remain still while the exemplar is processing your question and answering.
> - Shift your body to try things on.

The complete generic array for "STEPPING-IN" can be found in the Appendix.

* * *

Of course, no matter how elegant it is, the model is not the ability itself. The model is a description of essential structure. Through stepping-in during the elicitation and refining of the model you probably gained access to at least some of that structure. But some elements may still be unfamiliar. And of course, someone who did not participate in the elicitation will be unfamiliar with most or all of those elements. What is more, the essential elements of the ability not only need to become familiar, they also need to start operating together in your experience, as a system, as well. For an ability to become manifest, the beliefs, strategies, emotions, and behaviors captured in the words of the model must come to life in your experience. And this is the subject of the next Essay.

Working Models

Essay 17

Acquisition

Taking on a model is a process of first gaining personal access to the required structure, followed by integrating that structure with who you are. This is done through "reference experiences," which are examples from your personal history of the structural patterns specified in the model. Once you have experiential access to the structure, you develop competence in manifesting the ability by rehearsing it, first in imagination, and then in the real world.

All of us have examples in our personal histories attesting to the fact that "knowing what to do" and "being able to do it" are two different things. The description of how a wing provides lift is not itself a wing; a model is not the ability that it is a model of. Until now, your modeling work has been devoted to discovering what to do, to describing how your exemplar "flies." Now you know.

Now what?

If a wing is to become something that carries us upward, we must give

some tangible form to the description of how a wing works. Similarly, we must embody the structure described in the Array if we want to manifest the ability it models. That is, the structure you have elicited and refined into a model needs to become a part of you; there must be a transition from information on a page to experience in your body.

Because of stepping-in, some of this transition has probably already occurred during the processes of elicitation and of refining the model. You were not merely testing the structures your exemplar described to you, but often learning them as well. Still, it is probably the case that although you have "tasted" all of the elements of the model, they are not yet digested, that is, not yet operating systematically, smoothly, and automatically in your experience and behavior. The model still needs to be *acquired.*

Already Someone There

Acquisition is a process of both familiarizing yourself with the model and integrating its structure into your own experience. Notice that we did not say "adding" its structure, but *"integrating."* You are not an empty vessel to be filled with the structure of the model. Nor are you clay just waiting to be gripped and molded by it. You are, in a sense, already full of *you*; you already have form. When you or anyone is taking on a new ability—acquiring a model—it is essential to remember that *there is already someone there.*

By definition, taking on an ability means change. In general, change is not a matter of simply supplanting the old "someone already there" with the new patterns. Each of us "someones" is a system. And this guarantees that any shift in our thinking and behavior will have an impact that goes beyond those particular shifts. How much you as a system are impacted by a particular change depends upon who you are and the model you are acquiring, of course. But in every case there will be some impact on the system; that is, on you.

Acquisition, then, is more than merely a matter of supplanting the old with the new. Often it is also a matter of reconciling the new with those existing patterns of believing, thinking, feeling, and behaving that are impacted by the new model. In other words, we do not change in spite of who we are, but instead must fit that change in with the totality of ourselves, or at least with those aspects that are affected by the change.

And there is always "room" for that change. In using the metaphor "someone is already there," we are not suggesting that there is only so much room in each of us for experience. Experience is infinitely elastic and endlessly capable of incorporating new elements. A balloon is already completely full; nevertheless it can still take on more air. It can and will grow as air is added, and will still be just as completely full as it was to begin with. (Like all analogies, this one has its limitations. Balloons pop when they get too much air in them; people don't. They just keep getting bigger.)

The fact that we have that capacity to grow, however, does not mean that we just take on board every new idea or behavior that comes along. As we all know from so many personal experiences, fitting in new ways of thinking and behaving is not always so easy. This is true even when it is a change that we *want*. Why is that?

Maintaining Coherency

Toss a bunch of amino acids, tissues, minerals and water into a bag and shake it all you want. When you empty your bag out onto the table, it is not likely to produce Fluffy the cat, nor anything else alive. Life is not ingredients, but ingredients in particular relationships with one another. A cell gets to remain a cell (or a gardenia a gardenia, or Fluffy, uh, Fluffy) as long as those particular relationships are preserved. If ribosomes stop producing energy in the cell, for instance, the ecology of the cell will unravel and soon there will be no cell, but just a puddle of ingredients.

And so the cell has built into its systems ways of maintaining those interactions and functions—relationships—that keep it "a cell." For instance, the membrane that forms the boundary between the cell and the external environment lets in (generally) only those things that support the cell, and keeps out that which might disrupt it. The cell *maintains its coherency* as a system by selectively filtering *in* that which supports it and filtering *out* that which does not. If living systems have a "prime directive," surely it is to maintain the integrity of the system. It is true of a cell, it is true of Fluffy, and it is true of us.

Similarly, you as a personality are not a bag of ingredients, but a living system that—like you as an organism—has a particular *coherency*. In the context of "self," coherency is the functional integration of the various elements of one's subjective experience. The particular way in which your experience is functionally integrated *is* "you." And, in the same way that our cells maintain their coherency by filtering their environment, so too do we filter our experiential worlds to maintain the coherency of one's "self."

What serves as the cell membrane for the self are the processes of deletion, distortion and generalization. (For a thorough explanation of these universal cognitive processes, processes that shape and maintain one's world, see *The Structure of Magic, Volume I.*) These cognitive processes filter our experiences to preserve our coherency as individuals. For instance:

- An old-school accountant who believes that *true* accounting work is done with pencil and calculator—"that is how it is *done!*"—is terribly disturbed when computers are introduced. He maintains his worldview and sense of self by simply refusing to use computers, branding them "perversions" of his profession. (Or perhaps he avoids this challenge to self by moving to a rural town where pencil and calculator accounting is still fine.)

- Another accountant sees himself as someone who fulfills the role of accountant, that is, someone who engages in the *particular activities* required in doing accounting. He is not at all bothered by the introduction of the computer. To him it is just another tool for engaging in the same kinds of activities he has always done. (Later, however, he struggles terribly when he gets promoted to manager, a role he has never seen himself being in.)

- Unlike the previous example, another accountant is thrilled by being promoted to manager because he sees himself as someone who is competent in the business world. Being promoted is the expected recognition of his inherent competence. (Later, when he is fired, he is crushed; his competence has been questioned! But then he regains his coherency when he realizes that the firm *obviously* doesn't recognize when someone is *truly* competent.)

- Another accountant, who sees herself as being a competent person *in general*, takes being fired completely in stride. As a competent *person,* she knows that she is able to turn her hand to all manner of careers, and so she sees being fired as just another opportunity to try something new.

Similarly, in Essay 7, on Beliefs, we cited the study of the doomsday group that, when the space ships did not show up and destroy the world, decided that the group's sincerity had convinced the aliens to give Humanity another chance. You can pick up any newspaper, newsfeed, or magazine and find endless examples of our drive to, and facility with, maintaining the coherency of our individual worlds. For instance, when hurricane Joaquin devastated the Bahamas in 2015, evangelical Tony Perkins claimed that it was "a sign of God's wrath." When, however, a 2016 hurricane flooded Louisiana—including his own home—he claimed that it was "a great opportunity for the Church to minister." Protecting coherency is something we all do.

Clearly, the particular coherency you are operating out of matters; it determines how you respond at a moment in time in a particular situation. How does one's individual coherency, one's view of the world and the self in that world, come into being?

Reference Experiences

Your coherency emerges from your experiences as you live your life, of course. You make sense of what happens around and within you, learn from your experiences and, from those learnings, assemble for yourself a subjective world. We do not mean to imply here that this is something you do consciously or intentionally. Making sense of experience is something that our bodies and minds naturally do as a way of establishing a coherent system that allows us to respond appropriately to the world. As we make connections and refine connections, a map for living emerges. This is a personal map, of course, an integration of your experiences into your own coherency, into what is for you "the world." Those life experiences that compel us to make new connections and, so, change that personal map, we call "reference experiences."

For example, during a seminar it happened that we inadvertently addressed a participant by the wrong name. She not only immediately corrected us, but became furious as well. We asked her to "ride" what she was feeling back through time. A moment later she was in tears and describing an incident from her childhood: One day while playing with her identical twin sister, her grandmother arrived and joined in on the play, as she had done many times before. But this time grandma said something that betrayed the fact that she actually did not know which twin was which. This was a shock to the little girl who had, until that moment, assumed she had a separate identity from her sister. From that time on, she became very assertive about who she was and incensed when people misrepresented her in any way. This reference experience formed the basis for a pervasive, even existential, feature of her map of the world.

Reference experiences are not only fundamental to the formation of our conceptual maps, but to the formation of our physical maps, as well. Temple Grandin (who we met in Essay 6: Stepping-In) longed to be hugged, but could not tolerate being touched. Noticing how cattle relaxed when they were held for their vaccinations in "squeeze chutes," she decided to build a "squeeze machine" for herself:

> To have feelings of gentleness, one must experience gentle bodily comfort. As my nervous system learned to tolerate the soothing pressure from my squeeze machine, I discovered that the comforting feeling made me a kinder and gentler person. It was difficult for me to understand the idea of kindness until I had been soothed myself. It wasn't

until after I had used the modified squeeze machine that I
learned how to pet our cat gently. (Grandin, 1995 p.82)

Reference experiences are any experiences that forge new
connections in our maps of the world, and these connections range from
the simplest of instrumental behaviors to the loftiest abstractions that form
one's philosophy, from not touching a hot stove to touching the mysteries
of life. A few minutes of reflection upon formative experiences in your
own life or the lives of people you know will quickly supply you with
dozens of examples.[56]

In addition to direct life experiences, you will also have many
examples of change that were instigated simply by words. For instance,
perhaps you were stymied by a problem and a friend pointed out, "Hey,
that's not a problem. That's an *opportunity*!" And suddenly, and for the
first time, you really saw how problems *are* opportunities. This new
perspective embedded itself in your worldview and from then on changed
how you dealt with problems. It was not, however, your friend's words that
brought about the change. Words *evoke* experience; that is what they are
for. The only way you can know what a word means is that it is connected
to your personal history of experiences.[57] And so, the friend who pointed
out that your problem was an "opportunity" was, with his words,
triggering in you whatever personal experiences you have connected with
"opportunity." It was those experiential connections from your personal
history (suddenly dropped into the midst of whatever else was going on in
your experience at that moment) that you accessed and used to make your
new connections; that is, to change.

---

[56] More detail on reference experiences can be found in a paper by Gordon,
"Reference Experiences: Guardians of Coherence and Instigators of Change," in
Zeig and Gilligan, *Brief Therapy: Myths, Methods, and Metaphors.*

[57] These connections quickly become unconscious as, indeed, they must if we are
to avoid overwhelming our consciousness with a kaleidoscope of images, sounds,
and feelings as we make ongoing sense of what is being said.

Change

Once those new connections are there, they tend to preserve themselves by orienting us to pay attention to additional experiences that fit with them, and by deleting or explaining away those that do not. In general, these processes are not a matter of choice. We are set up to maintain coherency, and these processes are how it is done. As the accountant examples showed (and all of us have multitudes of our own examples), we tend to maintain our current coherency even when it is unpleasant or not useful to do so.

But of course, it is not that you establish your coherency, and then you are done for life. You continue living in the world and the world continues to offer challenges to the coherency of your world view and view of self. Despite the fact that most of these challenges are quickly dissolved by the alchemies of deletion, distortion and generalization, it does happen that we *do* change. How?

We change in the same way coherency is established in the first place, through reference experiences. That is, we have an experience or a set of experiences that are compelling enough to both "break" certain connections that we currently hold *and* to establish new connections in their place. Innumerable examples could be given, but will offer a few we consider striking:

> Lee Atwater (the Republican National Committee Chairman in the late 1980's) was aggressively partisan and notorious for his ruthless politicking (the nadir of which was the negative presidential campaign he ran on behalf of George Bush in 1988). In 1991, at the age of 39, Atwater discovered he had a benign brain tumor. "It's going to be hard for me to be as tough on people," he said. "Forget money and power. I had no idea how wonderful people are... What a way to have to find out." (*Tribune News Service, March 1991*)

> Prince Sultan ibn Salman al Saud of Saudi Arabia, the first Arab astronaut, described his experience aboard the space shuttle Discovery, an experience that truly brought home to

him the need for world peace: "On the first and second day of the flight, we were all noticing our countries, saying, 'That's my home.' By the third day, you only see continents. By the fifth day, you see only the Earth—it becomes one place, your home...It's an amazing feeling." (*Los Angeles Times, September 15, 1985*)

Documentary filmmaker, Ken Burns, was eleven years old when his mother died of cancer. He noticed that his father had responded to this loss with little apparent emotion. His father did, however, "...permit me to stay up late and watch movies on TV on a school night or take me out to the movies... And it was watching a movie, 'Odd Man Out,' about the Irish troubles with James Mason by the great director Sir Carol Reed that I watched my father cry for the first time and I instantaneously understood the power of the films to provide a kind of expression for emotion, for human beings of all sorts and a way to perhaps express emotions when the stuff of life makes it harder to do or the facades we erect to protect ourselves do...And I vowed then to become a filmmaker." (*The Diane Rehm Show, WAMU, September 11, 2014*)

A stroll through your personal history will provide you with your own examples of experiences that changed your world. These experiences may have been pleasant or unpleasant, and may have lasted only a moment, or spread out over days, weeks, or months. But in each case the effect was the same: the experience was sufficiently compelling to break some old threads and to weave new ones into the fabric of your world. The experience pushed—or carried—you across the "threshold."

Threshold

When we speak of "threshold," we are talking about that point which a person must reach in order to create new connections in experience. This is completely unquantifiable, unspecifiable, unpredictable and all of the other un-ables you might think of. Had Lee Atwater been beside Prince Sultan ibn Salman al Saud aboard Discovery, there is no knowing if Atwater would have come to see the world as one home. Similarly, the brain tumor diagnosis that so affected Atwater might not at all compel someone else to change their ideas about the importance of people. And (going in the other "direction" of threshold) another person could come to Atwater's realization about how wonderful people are simply from being shown some small kindness by a stranger.

While we cannot control or predict threshold, it is still an important concept because it reminds us that there *is* a threshold. As we all know, the fact that an idea is true or useful or in our best interests or desperately wanted does not mean that we will take it on and make it a part of our coherency. Making a new connection—that is, change—requires that some personal threshold of connection must be crossed. A reference experience is an experience that is capable of taking you across that personal threshold.

There are many factors that can affect how compelling an experience is and, so, how likely it is to become a reference experience. Some of these are that the experience:

- Appeals to your self-concept
- Addresses core criteria ("values")
- Comes from a credible/authoritative source (person, book, etc.)
- Resolves a felt need or vexing question
- Is surprising
- Generates intense feelings (pleasant or unpleasant)
- Makes sense

Keep in mind that all of these qualities of a compelling experience are, in a sense, given *to* the experience by the person having it. There is nothing inherent in any particular experience that necessarily makes it a reference experience. For instance, many, and perhaps all, identical twins have had an experience like that we cited above of the woman in our seminar, but not all of those twins came away from it changed in the way she was. The effect of a particular experience depends upon the person who is having that experience. For instance, suppose one evening you decide to take a walk through your neighborhood instead of watching television. You have a pleasant walk, chat with a neighbor or two along the way, notice a lovely garden just a block away, and so on. You might return from this walk refreshed and delighted, but unchanged. It remains just one of countless experiences you have had. Another possibility, however, might be that you were surprised at the relief you feel having gotten away from the television, and notice that you feel more a part of where you live, which is something you have often wanted for yourself. As a consequence, you start going out more often, seeking interactions with your neighbors, and so on. In this second scenario, you return from your walk changed; without your intending it, the walk became a reference experience for you.[58]

Magnitude and Repetition

We have been talking about reference experiences as though you need to find only one, or *the* one, in order to establish new connections in your map. That can be true, provided that the one experience is itself of sufficient "magnitude" to take you over your personal threshold. An example of this is the experience of the participant in our seminar who was mistaken for her twin sister by her grandmother. For her, that one experience was compelling enough to forge new beliefs regarding her identity. As we previously noted, however, what constitutes "enough" depends completely on the individual. A different twin having the same experience might be equally hurt, surprised, or disappointed, but not be pushed over the threshold of belief formation. This twin might instead think, "Oh, grandma is just tired," or "Everyone makes mistakes" (avoiding a challenge to the coherency of her world). Perhaps, for this

---

[58] For those interested in exploring the relationship between reference experiences and the evolution of personality and behavior, there is no better resource than the therapeutic casework of Milton H. Erickson. In particular, Jay Haley's book on Erickson's work, *Uncommon Therapy*, is a gold mine of examples.

twin, a belief changing experience of sufficient magnitude would need to be something on the order of her mother making such a mistake.[59]

The threshold of change does not necessarily need to be crossed in a single leap, as it does with experiences of sufficient "magnitude." The threshold can also be crossed by taking little steps, that is, through the "repetition" of experiences. The repetition of an experience can eventually create a connection strong enough that it becomes an integrated feature of your subjective world. We had an example of this in Temple Grandin's description of the effect of her squeeze machine: "As my nervous system learned to tolerate the soothing pressure from my squeeze machine, I discovered that the comforting feeling made me a kinder and gentler person."

Repetition and magnitude can also function together. It may be that each repetition of an experience is *not* wearing the "path" of connection a little deeper. Instead, the repeated experiences are "stacking" themselves, one atop the other, until their cumulative "weight" (magnitude) eventually topples you over the threshold. Regardless of how it occurs—through magnitude, repetition, or repetition leading to magnitude—what is important is that you manage to get over that threshold of connection that makes the elements of a model real and alive to you.[60]

---

[59] An aside: While "old dogs" certainly can learn new tricks, it is easier to acquire new ideas about "the way things are" in childhood. This is at least partly because there is less competition from other beliefs. Coherency is operating from the earliest ages, but relatively little is "set" in those early maps. While growing up, we are frequently entering new contexts of experience for which we do not already have beliefs, responses, and behaviors. As time goes on, however, the extent of self-validating connections grows wider and deeper, creating more and more filters and layers of filters on subsequent experiences.

[60] Another aside, more formal and very brief: Meaning at every level – from physiological responses, to instrumental behaviors, to abstract concepts – is created through system references to existing causal and equivalence relationships. Changes in existing causal and equivalence relationships are brought about through reference experiences of sufficient magnitude or repetition. Though not necessarily immediately obvious, a case can be made that this pattern describes what is going on at the most fundamental level when *any* therapeutic modality is effective in bringing about change. As exploring this would take us far from the topic of modeling, we leave it to the interested reader to find those connections.

Acquisition Protocol: In General

The fundamental process of acquisition is very straightforward. A model is a description of a structure of experience (patterns of distinctions, relationships and actions) that we want to integrate into our own structure. On the page, this structure is just information. You need to lift that structure from the page and have it become a living part of your own experience. Transforming the described information of the model into actual experience requires that you do two things: first, find those experiences in yourself (*Access*), and second, then bring them into operation in the context in which you want to manifest the ability (*Rehearsal*).

ACCESS: Establishing the Model

In the "Stepping-In" model we presented in Essay 6, an essential element was the belief that "experience has structure." We (David and Graham) obviously already believe that "experience has structure." We have reference experiences that convince us that this is so. But for *you* to believe that it is so, you probably need more than our claims and arguments. For it to become real for you, you need your own reference experiences. And so, in that Essay, we asked you to search through your *own* personal history for instances that demonstrate the fundamental relationship between structure and experience. We hope that in doing this you found examples that were sufficiently compelling to serve as your own reference experiences for the idea, "experience has structure." We then followed this same process for establishing the rest of the elements of the "stepping-in" model. And it is the same for all models: the first step in acquisition is to find your own reference experiences for each of the elements of the model.

Oceans of Experience

We have been talking about "finding your own reference experiences" as though they are already there, just waiting to be retrieved. And for the most part, they are. There is an ocean of experiences in each of us ready and waiting to be fished. When we suggested the example above of taking a walk in the neighborhood one evening, one result may have been that you recalled having had a pleasant walk... and at the time, that was that. That pleasant walk experience did not serve as a compelling reference experience; that is, it did not bring about change. But that does not mean the experience then evaporated. Instead it joined the ocean of experiences that you have been acquiring during your lifetime. There it drifts, and may drift forever, of course. But it—along with endless other experiences—is still there, ready to be recalled. Perhaps a week later or a year later, you are sitting in your house, feeling restless and depressed, when you see on television a neighborhood street...and you recall your own walk in the neighborhood. But this time (perhaps because of your restlessness and depression?) it takes on a significance it did not have before, pushing you over your personal threshold and becoming a compelling reference experience for the importance of being out in your community.

In fact, no matter what patterns of believing, thinking, feeling, or behavior are described in a model, they almost certainly already exist somewhere in your experiential ocean. This is so much the case that, when taking on a model, you can assume you already have the experiences you need, and that you have only to "bring them up." The difference now, however, is that they are being raised in relation to your desire to acquire a particular ability. This gives those experiences a *collective* relevance and significance they did not have before. The vast majority of experiences you need are already in your personal history, waiting to be retrieved *and put to use*.

Of course, it can happen that a model asks you to take on an experience that you have not had. If that is the case, you need to somehow give yourself that needed experience as a prerequisite to taking on the full ability. For example, the stepping-in model requires that you be "open to the experience of another." If you do not already have any experiences that can serve as references for this, you could (for instance) actually spend some time on the floor with a child, learning to play in her world, as a way of acquiring the needed experience. Creating reference experiences for yourself or others is a vast topic in its own right, and would take us too far afield from modeling. Hopefully, the example conveys the essential point, which is that if a model asks for an experience that you do not already have in your personal history, you need to put yourself in a situation that naturally offers that experience. (Again, the work of Milton H. Erickson is filled with instructive examples.)

TO RECAP: The first general step in acquisition, then, is to access reference experiences, that is, to access sufficiently compelling examples from your personal history until the needed element of experience becomes real for you. That may happen with one example of sufficient magnitude. If so, great. If not, you need to continue finding (or creating) experiences until the subjective weight of these examples puts you over your threshold.

REHEARSAL: Becoming Competent

A young man was wandering around New York City, obviously lost, so he stopped an old man passing by and asked, "How do I get to Carnegie Hall?" Noticing that the young man was carrying a violin case, the old man answered, "Practice, practice," and walked on. This is an old joke, but one worth remembering. You can have a wonderful instrument and sheets of beautiful music, but they don't play themselves; you have to learn to play them. We are in the same situation regarding model acquisition.

To be "competent" is to have integrated the ability to do something. The one thing we cannot model is competence. We can certainly create models for *becoming* competent at some ability, but it is still the case that the competence itself will come only through *practice*. There will always be more to the structure of an ability than is captured in our models of them. For the exemplar, years (if not a lifetime) of actually *using* that structure has developed innumerable layers of experience, each of which includes webs of minute and unconscious perceptions and behaviors. We cannot model the depth and breadth of connections that have come from the exemplar's personal history of using the structure, but only the structure itself. If we want more than a taste of her ability, if we want to be competent (and eventually proficient, that is, exemplars ourselves of that ability), we need to establish a similar depth and breadth in ourselves. And that comes from *using* the model.

Ultimately, you will be using the ability you have modeled in real world situations. But before stepping out into those often deep waters, it is useful to rehearse the new ability in the safer pool of your imagination. To begin with, each time you use imagination to rehearse manifesting the ability, you are increasing your facility at accessing its structure and, at the same time, strengthening the connection between being in the context and accessing that structure. (In other words, you are establishing the "habit" of manifesting the ability in the situation in which you need it.)

In addition, rehearsing the ability is an opportunity to get out the bugs. Even when trying out the ability in imagination, things can go wrong, or not go well enough. You may discover that an element you thought you had access to is really not yet in your experience. Or that some element of the structure bumps up against something in who you are, and therefore needs to be addressed. Or that you are missing some important piece of information or structure that you need to make it all work for you. It is better to find and deal with as many of these difficulties as you can during rehearsal, rather than in the real world where these stumbling blocks might send you into a downward spiral that leads you to abandon effort to develop the ability.

And finally, as you rehearse the ability in your imagination you will be developing and exercising that depth and breadth of perceptions, associations, and behaviors that support competence.

Monkey Wrenches

Anyone can be proficient when the world "reads its lines," responding just as we want it to. When we rehearse in imagination, we tend to imagine things going smoothly, and this does not fully prepare us for real life, which is rarely so accommodating. However, one quality that makes someone an exemplar is that her ability is robust. That is, she is able to respond effectively regardless of the monkey wrenches that the world might throw into the works.

While the world will always provide surprises, for the most part we have pretty accurate ideas about what can typically go wrong in a particular situation. An important part of rehearsal is throwing as many of those potential monkey wrenches into the works as you can, and then discovering ways to usefully respond to them *while continuing to operate out of the model.* By doing this, you create an opportunity to extend even further the depth and breadth of your ability to manifest the ability. This makes your ability—*you*—more robust and resilient. In the process of throwing in the monkey wrenches, you might also discover a limitation that you don't know how to deal with and, therefore, for which you need to get some help (perhaps from your exemplar). It is better to do that now rather than later, when you are manifesting your newly modeled ability in the real world.

Persevering

A dusty childhood memory of one of the authors: In the 60's, professor Julius Sumner Miller conducted a weekly television show on physics called, "Why Is It So?" As a teacher, Miller was fiery and crusty...and passionate. He always had several high school students sitting beside his lab bench so that he had someone to harangue, while the rest of us eavesdropped from our homes. In one particularly memorable show, he ran an experiment that did not go at all as he said it would. In a flash, he turned on the students and barked, "Okay, what happened?! What happened?!" One of the students sputtered, "The experiment failed." Miller scowled at the student wrathfully and said, "An experiment *never* fails! There is always a result!" And then he smiled and said, "In fact, you will learn more from those experiments that don't turn out the way you expected them to."

Once you have rehearsed the ability you are acquiring, the next step is to manifest it in the real world. It is not likely that you will have rehearsed yourself into mastery; mastery comes with actual use. No amount of rehearsal and monkey wrenching will provide you with experiences as rich as those you get in the real world. In that richness is the opportunity to really exercise the muscles of your model, to integrate it more and more thoroughly with who you are, and to learn the countless subtleties that will make you proficient at the ability. So it is important to persevere through that initial fumbling period when you are making the model your own.

Building experiences/connections is like building a tower to get a good view. When you lay the first bricks you don't get the better view; knowing that eventually you will get that view is what keeps you at your bricklaying. Similarly, you need a compelling motivation for learning the ability in order to carry you through the clumsy period of acquisition. The ability you are acquiring needs to be worth the time and effort you put into it. We will soon deal with how to build in this level of motivation in the section below on the Motivating Cause-Effect.

Even when you are motivated, though, the promise of the future may bump up against the difficulties of the present. When you exercise your nascent ability in the richness of the real world, there will be plenty of opportunities for making mistakes. Few of us enjoys making mistakes: if we make enough of them—or even just one "doozy"—the whole enterprise can quickly become daunting and make giving up seem attractive. As Professor Miller reminds us, however, those mistakes are opportunities to learn, to recalibrate, to extend our grasp to include yet more of the subtleties of the ability. Responding to mistakes and difficulties in this way, that they are opportunities to learn, is absolutely fundamental both to perseverance and to mastery.

TO RECAP: The second general step in acquisition is to rehearse in imagination (in thorough detail) manifesting the ability in the context in which you need it. And of course, rehearsing means doing this again and again until you have worked out the "bugs," and the structure seems to be operating smoothly for you. Even then, you want to intentionally look for real world difficulties and work through those, as well. And finally you need to practice the ability out in the real world, where it gets truly integrated as your own.

1) Identify an actual situation in your future when you will want to manifest the ability.
2) Access reference experiences (from your personal history, or newly created) for each of the various elements of the model.
3) Rehearse the ability in imagination by stepping in and out of your actual future situation with the elements of experience you are acquiring, doing this until they easily "come up" and operate for you in that context.
4) Make your ability robust by imagining scenarios with as many of the possible difficulties ("monkey wrenches") as you can think of.
5) Practice manifesting the ability in the real world, learning from your real world experiences (including mistakes) as you integrate the ability.

Now we can dive into some of the details regarding acquiring the elements of experience.

Acquisition Protocol: Specifics

In the same way that no organ in your body is more important than another, no element of experience is more important than another. An ability does not reside in any one element of experience, but in the collective acting and interacting of them all. Still, if we were building a home, we would put up walls before trying to put on a roof, and we would pour the foundation before erecting the walls. The sequence we are about to describe is one we have found naturally supports the acquisition of an ability, with each step providing the experiential foundation for the next.

The sequence we will describe is the ideal, of course, and, also of course, it is often not possible to follow this ideal sequence. As always, the needs and tendencies of the individual determine what to do, when, and how. The sequence is useful as a guide, however, and we suggest following it when you can, and abandoning it when appropriate.

> REMEMBER: In the following protocol you will often be asked to *step into the context of the ability*. By "context" we mean an actual situation in which you want to manifest the ability you are acquiring. It is that context that you will step into each time as you bring more and more of the elements of the ability into play in your experience.

The Shell

A snail has a shell to provide it with support and protection, and body for locomotion and feeding. We think of an ability as being much like a snail in that it can be thought of as being made up of two, interdependent parts: the "shell," which includes the beliefs and states, and the "action," which includes the strategies and behaviors. Both are necessary. The beliefs and states organize and direct the action taken through strategies and behaviors; and strategies and behaviors give expression to the shell of beliefs and states. No matter how beautiful the shell, it needs the actions of the snail-body to go anywhere; and without the support and attachment afforded by the shell, the snail-body can only flop around.

In acquiring a model, we begin with the shell: the Criterial Equivalence (Criterion and Definition), Evidence, Motivating and Enabling Cause-Effects and Sustaining Emotion. Without these elements in place, actions have no point of focus, relevance or direction.

Criterial Equivalence

Since everything in the Array is happening in relation to the Criterion, that is where to start. You can certainly access other elements of the Array first, but they are likely to seem fuzzy and irrelevant if you have not first established what it is that you want to satisfy or fulfill (the Criterion). Because the Criterion is the exemplar's label for an important class or kind of experience, and because different folks can have different experiences connected to the same Criterion, the whole Criterial Equivalence—the Criterion plus its Definition—needs to be accessed together. That is, you begin by searching through your personal history for reference experiences for the Criterion *as Defined in the model.*

You may already have in your ocean of experience references for the Criterion-Definition connection made by your exemplar. If so, great; you have only to access them. But even if you do not, you will almost certainly have examples of the *kind of experience* your exemplar defines as being her Criterion. That is, you have had the experience, but do not have it identified (labeled) as she does. If that is the case, establish the Criterial Equivalence for yourself by first accessing your own reference experiences for the exemplar's Definition, and then recognize that *those* experiences are what is meant by the exemplar's Criterion.

For instance, suppose you are taking on Bridgit's ability to be patient with children as they are learning (Essay 13). You would begin by accessing her Criterion of "Movement." By this she means, "The child can do something she couldn't do before, or understand something she didn't understand before. Even the tiniest of things is enough." Let's say that you retrieve your own reference experience for "movement," which is of when you are dancing. But for you, "movement" when dancing is about "expressing yourself through your body." Or perhaps you identify times in your life when you made great strides as examples of "movement." Both are instances of wonderful experiential connections that can be made with "movement." But neither of those criterial equivalences is what "movement" is to Bridgit.

To take on Bridgit's ability, you need to find examples in your own experience that fit with how she perceives "movement." You do this by starting with the Definition. Instead of starting with the criterial label (in this case, "movement"), you search for the *kind* of experience that is needed (the experience as it is defined). In the case of Bridgit's model, you look for examples in your personal history of being able to understand or do even the "tiniest bit" more than you had before. And then label *that* "movement." For example, you recall learning to play the violin. You are unpleasantly squeaking and squawking away when your teacher straightens your bowing arm and suddenly the tone becomes pleasant. As you re-access that beginning of a growing mastery of your violin playing, you can now label *that* "movement."

Evidence

It is the Evidence that lets you know that what you are doing to satisfy the Criterion is working and, so, to keep doing it. Or the Evidence lets you know it *has been* satisfied and you can now move on to something else. In Bridgit's case, for instance, she is working to create "movement" in a child, and she *knows* that is happening when she sees that "the child is intent on what she's doing, and looks proud. Sometimes smiling."

Once again, you dip into your ocean of experiences to retrieve your own experiences of seeing, hearing and/or feeling the kinds of things that serve as Evidence to the exemplar. If you were acquiring Bridgit's ability, for instance, you would search for your own examples of seeing children intent on what they are doing, and looking proud as a consequence. Once you have recalled that evidence into the present of your experience, you can glue it in by using it as you rehearse the ability, both in imagination and in the real world.

It may be that you do not already have experiences that can serve as references for your exemplar's Evidence. As with the missing Definition example above (and, in fact, *any* time you do not already have reference experiences in your personal history for any element of a model), you can seek out or create the reference experience you need. If you were missing personal experiences for the Evidence in Bridgit's model, for example, you could visit classrooms, or a daycare, or a children's museum to find examples of intent and proud children that you can then use as reference experiences for Evidence of "movement."

Motivating Cause-Effect

Place a billiard ball on a pool table and it just sits there. Its spherical shape and smooth surface make it utterly capable of rolling across the table. But without an impetus to move, this capability remains potential rather than kinetic. Similarly, when it comes to any of us taking action in a particular direction, the need for motivation of some kind is obvious. The impetus can be as subtle as a draft on the back of the neck or a whiff of perfume, as demanding as a hunger pang, or as ephemeral as the momentary memory of an old friend.

In this jostling crowd of moment-to-moment motivators, the Motivating Cause-Effect clearly has the biggest elbows. After all, it often directly connects to some aspect of your personal identity and, so, is likely to be inherently more compelling. Even so, it may not be immediately obvious why establishing the Motivating Cause-Effect in a model is crucial to having a model that actually works. After all, presumably you are acquiring a model because you want to have the ability. That should be motivation enough to get things rolling once you have the structure of what to do, shouldn't it?

The answer is "yes," but only if what you really want is to simply *test drive* the ability, rather than *acquire* it. The model provides a structure which gives rise to an ability by organizing your experience and behavior along certain lines. However, you are probably going to need to actually use the model, perhaps over a period of time, for the necessary breadth and depth of discriminations, understandings and responses to coalesce into proficiency and, ultimately, mastery. *That* is acquisition. In order to stay with the period of acquisition long enough to actually *have* the ability, you need to causally "hook" manifesting the model to a motivation that is intrinsically important to you.

But what if the model is easily acquired, requiring little or no through-time dedication to effectively implement? In that case, is wanting its benefits sufficient to ensure that it is used? Even then, possibly not. Whatever the model requires of you, it is undoubtedly something unfamiliar and new (otherwise you would already be doing it). Left to our own devices, we tend to respond to a particular context with those patterns that are familiar to us. This automatic "grab the familiar" can provide a sufficiently high bump in the road to hinder the implementation of even the most innocuous, easily grasped model. So even simple abilities may require a Motivating Cause-Effect capable of providing the impetus to engage the new internal processes and external behaviors through time.

The next question is, *whose* motivation to use? Bridgit's motivation for pursuing "movement" in children is that it will lead to "freedom."

; something that is of intrinsic and compelling importance to
t it may not have that same level of significance for you. If the
Motivating Cause-Effect is to be truly motivating, then the Criterion needs
to be connected to something that has a palpable pull on *you*. And so this is
the one element in the Array that we suggest you *not* take from the
experience of your exemplar.[61]

Instead, you need to causally connect the model's Criterion in Focus
to fulfilling something that is inherently motivating for you. We can offer
you two ways to go about doing this:

> Imagine manifesting the ability and consider what being
> successful at that ability makes possible that is *truly*
> important to you. Once you have identified what that
> compelling motivation is, find (or create) reference
> experiences that lay down a connection between the
> Criterion and that *(your)* motivator.

- OR -

> Identify what is inherently motivating to you, almost
> regardless of context (e.g. "independence," "connecting
> with others," "spiritual growth,") and then find (or create)
> reference experiences for how satisfying the Criterion of the
> model contributes to fulfilling *your* motivator.

In both cases, the goal here is to establish in yourself a cause-effect
relationship between the Criterion of the ability and something that is of
deep importance to you. Turning once again to our example of Bridgit,
suppose that (rather than her motivation of "freedom") what is closest to
your heart is "connecting with others." Your acquisition task at this point,
then, is to find sufficient reference experiences for you to forge a link
between "Movement" ("the child can do something she couldn't do before,
or understand something she didn't understand before") and your

---

[61] Of course, if by chance your exemplar's motivation is one that you share, great.
We are not suggesting that yours has to be different, only that it has to be
personally compelling to you.

personally compelling goal of "Connecting with others." For instance, perhaps you tap into a childhood experience of your own when, because you were—*finally!*—able to catch and throw a ball, you were accepted by the neighborhood kids.

Just as in when you take on a new Criterion (or any new belief), once you have made this connection, your new Motivating Cause-Effect will cause you to notice in your ongoing experiences more and more examples that support that connection. So, using our example, you will start to notice how your efforts to bring "movement" to your students also makes it possible for them to "make connections with other people."

> AN EXCEPTION - While most of the Motivating Cause-Effects you elicit from your exemplars will simply be the content of some deeply held value or desire, you may sometimes find that there is a particular structure to that Motivator that is essential to the ability working. We have an example of this in Lenny's ability to maintain a diet to control his diabetes: "So I can have the life I *want* to have, rather than the one I *don't* want to have." As we described in Essay 8, this structure of holding both future-toward and future-away is essential to his ability. So in taking on his ability, we need to take on the structure of his Motivating Cause-Effect, as well. But of course, the content of Lenny's two futures will be *Lenny's* content; the content of those futures is inherently motivating for him, but may not be for you. So in acquiring the Motivating Cause-Effect for his model you need to substitute what is inherently motivating for *you* into his future-toward/future-away structure.

Now you have what is of central importance (Criterion) and why it is important (Motivating Cause-Effect). You want to support these relatively new stars in the heavens of your experience until they, too, become constellations, fixed and reliable. The Sustaining Emotion will help you do that.

Sustaining Emotion

As we described in Essay 10, Sustaining Emotions are a way of "holding" the structural distinctions that are important in a particular context. Another way to put it is that the Sustaining Emotion is holding *in the body* at least some of the essential relationships that are held in the conceptual framework of the beliefs. Which is just what you need to do now as a way of holding the Criterion and Motivating Cause-Effect as you integrate them.

The ocean of experience that is *you* includes emotions, of course. Although each person's feelings tend to stay within a particular family of emotions, it is still the case that you probably have somewhere in your ocean of experience instances of feeling almost everything that human beings can feel. And so this ocean will probably contain the Sustaining Emotion specified in the model you are acquiring.

Depending upon the emotion, you may be able to access it directly. If this is difficult, range through your personal history until you find an instance—even a momentary one—when you felt that emotion. Recapture that experience, making it more and more vivid, until you can strongly feel the emotion of that past experience. Then bring that emotion into the context of the ability, feeling it while holding the Criterion. Repeat stepping in and out of the context of the ability until the context itself automatically accesses in you that (now Sustaining) emotion.[62]

Enabling Cause-Effect

With the Criterion and Motivating Cause-Effect in place you have, in a sense, set your direction: the Enabling Cause-Effect expresses what helps to make it possible to move in that direction. Find instances in your own experience that can serve as references for the exemplar's Cause enabling (or at least supporting) the satisfaction of the Criterion. Then step into the context of the ability with that cause-effect and discover how it affects what you attend to, think about, and actually do.

---

[62] For detailed strategies for accessing emotions, see Cameron-Bandler and Lebeau's, *The Emotional Hostage.*

If you do not already have examples of this causal relationship, imagine being in the context in which you need the ability, pursuing the Criterion, and *discover how* the exemplar's Cause can significantly help you fulfill the Criterion. Generate enough of these examples until the causal connection between the two becomes real for you. Even if this connection seems to be more information than real to you initially, each time you use that Enabling Cause-Effect when manifesting the ability (particularly in the real world), you will generate more and more confirming experiences of the reality of that causal connection.

Supporting Beliefs

Like the other elements of the "shell," you almost certainly already have experiences in your personal history that can serve as references for the Supporting Beliefs of the ability. Retrieve each of these reference experiences into your present experience until you find the one (or find enough of them) that makes the Supporting Belief become something you recognize as true. Then step into using the ability, noticing how that Supporting Belief affects your experience and behavior, and supports you in manifesting the ability.

The Action

Now that you can step into the ability with both its relevant points of focus and a state that sustains that focus, you are ready to act. Now when you engage the strategies and behaviors, they will be in relation to the same Criterion and Cause-Effects that guide your exemplar. To help ensure that they do, as you access and rehearse each of the elements of Strategy and External Behavior, be sure to continue to hold the Criterion in your awareness.

Levels of Competence

Before moving on, we need to make a point essential to acquisition in general, and of particular importance when acquiring strategies. The way to eat an elephant is one bite at a time. A Strategy (indeed, any experience or behavior) can sometimes be a pretty big elephant to swallow. As always, this naturally depends on who is doing the eating; different people can take different sized bites. The goal in acquisition is not to take on the Strategy all at once, but to take it on, *period.*

No matter how big an experience or behavior may seem at first glance, it can always be chunked down to smaller, constituent elements. For instance, someone who has never danced may have no conceptual or body idea about what to do out on the dance floor. For this person it seems to be an overwhelmingly complex task. Nevertheless, it can be broken down into smaller internal processes and external behaviors. He can begin by simply moving his body to the music. And even this can be chunked down if it proves too difficult. For example, we can have him pick out just the bass line in the music and tap one foot to it. What we are doing is finding the level of complexity at which this person *already has competency,* then building upon that. If you go "small enough," you will always find a level of current competency upon which the larger Strategy can be built. Obviously, this may take some time, but if the ability is worth having, the investment is one of going slow now, so that you can go fast later.

Primary Operation and External Behavior

Typically, the Primary Operation is a blend of internal processes and external behaviors. Of course, the behaviors specified in the Strategy do not operate independently of those specified in External Behavior, but in concert with them. It is the combined action of all of these behaviors that make it possible to fulfill the Criterion. So when it comes to acquisition, it is best to include the External Behaviors when you are taking on the Strategy. (Just a reminder: the Array is a conceptual framework for gathering information; no lines separating the elements of experience into little boxes will be found in anyone's brain. The purpose of establishing a separate box for External Behaviors during elicitation is to draw our attention to those behaviors that are essential to the ability *and may not be automatically initiated by the rest of the Array.* For instance, in the Array for "Stepping-in," being on the same level or below that of the exemplar is a behavior that may not automatically result from taking on the rest of the Array, but is important enough that we want to be sure it is marked out and used.)

The fact that Strategies are often complex sequences and sets of process and behaviors can make them seem daunting to acquire at first. Once again, however, the vastness and depth of your ocean of experience is there to help you. It is very likely that there is a context in your life in which you already use the same (or similar) Operations as those described in the Strategy, even though that context is very different from the one of the ability. For example, you might discover that the strategy a stock trader uses to pick good trades is much the same strategy you use in selecting presents for your family. The "shells" for these two contexts are obviously very different, but the form of the internal processes and external behaviors may be very much the same. If so, transfer the Strategy from the context you are already familiar with into the context—and "shell"—of the ability you are acquiring.

If you do not have a similar strategy already operating somewhere in your experience, chunk down the model's Strategy into its smaller, constituent processes and behaviors, and find *those* in your experiential ocean. Remember that any internal process or external behavior can always be chunked down to a level at which you already have competence somewhere in your personal history (our learning to dance example above).

As you have been doing all along, once you have access you will want to step into the context of the ability and rehearse the Primary Operation. But before doing that, make sure that you first reacquaint yourself with the Criterion and its Evidence. These are, after all, what the Strategy and Behavior are intended to satisfy. Of course, you have already accessed the Evidence when you were taking on the Criterion. Now, however, it really becomes relevant and useful, because now you are beginning to run the Strategies that are intended to fulfill that Criterion/Evidence.

ess the Criterion and its Evidence. Then step into the context the ability, imagine running the Primary Operation and, as a resuit, ., hear and feel the Evidence being satisfied.

Secondary Operations

The Evidence tells you how to know when you are "getting it." What do you do if you are not getting it? Engage the Secondary Operations, of course.

As with the Primary Operation, first make sure that you can access the repertoire of internal processes and external behaviors called for in the Secondary Operations. (And, as before, this may require chunking down to the level of your current competence any of those processes or behaviors that you cannot already do, that is, for which you do not already have reference experiences.) Then step into the context of using the ability and run each of the Secondary Operations (i.e. the Evidence is not sufficiently satisfied, not at all satisfied, cannot be satisfied) until you are comfortable with them.

In a Nutshell

1) Identify an actual situation in your future when you will want to manifest the ability.

2) Access reference experiences (from your personal history) for each of the various elements of the model.

  a. Begin with the Criterion and its Definition, and then add the Evidence.

  b. Establish what is inherently motivating *for you,* and then connect its fulfillment to the Criterion.

  c. Add the Sustaining Emotion.

  d. Add the Enabling Cause-Effect

  e. Add any Supporting Beliefs

f. If possible, find a reference experience(s) for the Primary Operation. That is, find an area in your life where you already have a strategy that is essentially the same as the Primary Operation, and bring that into the context of the ability. If not, make sure that you can access each of the steps of the Operation. Anything that is unknown or difficult can be chunked down to a level at which you are already competent.

g. Imagine difficulties in satisfying the Criterion, and add in the Secondary Operations.

3) Practice stepping into an actual future situation with the Array and using it until it easily "comes up" for you in that context.

4) Rehearse the ability in imagination, including as much as possible the various difficulties ("monkey wrenches") you might run into.

5) Practice manifesting the ability in the real world, learning from your mistakes as you integrate the ability.

Of course, it may happen that there is a conflict between an element of experience prescribed in the model and who you are as a person. For instance, suppose you are taking on Lenny's ability to maintain a diet to control diabetes, an essential element of which is the Enabling Cause-Effect, "I have to maintain focus and discipline in order for the diet to be working." But your response to anything requiring discipline is that you are being *told* what to do, and you resent—and invariably rebel against—that. Conflicts such as these—"hindrances" in our parlance—do not mean that the model cannot be taken on, but only that they need to be resolved in order to take it on. Obviously, depending upon the nature of the conflict, resolving these hindrances may be easily done (e.g. "Hey, wait a second...being disciplined is me telling myself what to do, and that's fine with me!") or may require therapeutic work with any one of the many change modalities and approaches available for resolving hindrances to taking on new beliefs, ways of thinking, emotions or behaviors. No matter what the hindrance is, it is just that, a *hindrance*. If the ability you have modeled is worth acquiring, then it is worth pursuing the bit of change work needed to get over that hindering hump, and be on your way.

* * *

"We can't start perfectly and beautifully...
Don't be afraid of being a fool; start as a fool."

Chogyam Trungpa Rinpoche

Appendices

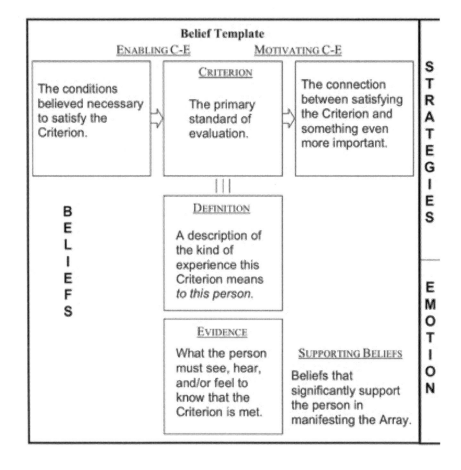

Belief Template

ENABLING C-E   MOTIVATING C-E

CRITERION

The conditions believed necessary to satisfy the Criterion.

The primary standard of evaluation.

The connection between satisfying the Criterion and something even more important.

B E L I E F S

DEFINITION

A description of the kind of experience this Criterion means *to this person.*

EVIDENCE

What the person must see, hear, and/or feel to know that the Criterion is met.

SUPPORTING BELIEFS

Beliefs that significantly support the person in manifesting the Array.

S T R A T E G I E S

E M O T I O N

Appendix I

Array Definitions

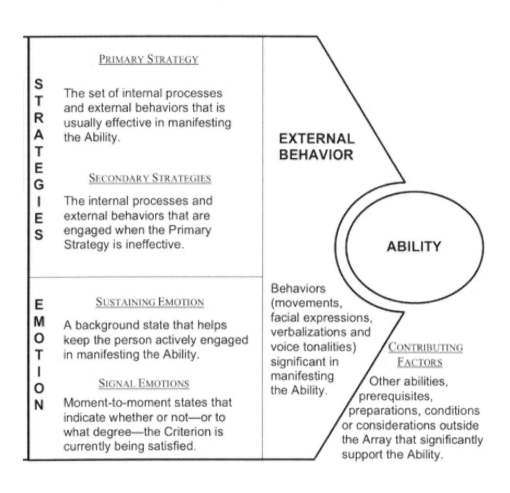

STRATEGIES

PRIMARY STRATEGY

The set of internal processes and external behaviors that is usually effective in manifesting the Ability.

SECONDARY STRATEGIES

The internal processes and external behaviors that are engaged when the Primary Strategy is ineffective.

EMOTION

SUSTAINING EMOTION

A background state that helps keep the person actively engaged in manifesting the Ability.

SIGNAL EMOTIONS

Moment-to-moment states that indicate whether or not—or to what degree—the Criterion is currently being satisfied.

EXTERNAL BEHAVIOR

Behaviors (movements, facial expressions, verbalizations and voice tonalities) significant in manifesting the Ability.

ABILITY

CONTRIBUTING FACTORS

Other abilities, prerequisites, preparations, conditions or considerations outside the Array that significantly support the Ability.

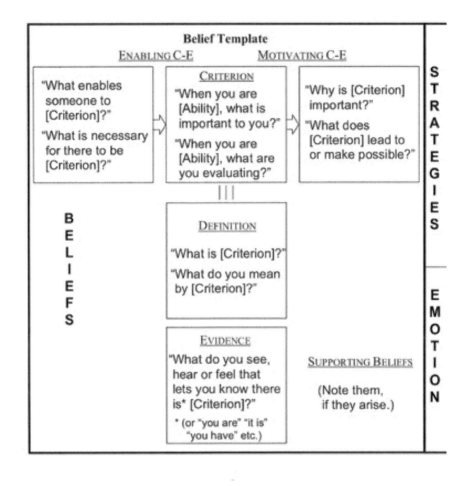

Belief Template

ENABLING C-E   MOTIVATING C-E

"What enables someone to [Criterion]?"

"What is necessary for there to be [Criterion]?"

CRITERION

"When you are [Ability], what is important to you?"

"When you are [Ability], what are you evaluating?"

"Why is [Criterion] important?"

"What does [Criterion] lead to or make possible?"

B E L I E F S

DEFINITION

"What is [Criterion]?"

"What do you mean by [Criterion]?"

EVIDENCE

"What do you see, hear or feel that lets you know there is* [Criterion]?"

* (or "you are" "it is" "you have" etc.)

SUPPORTING BELIEFS

(Note them, if they arise.)

S T R A T E G I E S

E M O T I O N

Appendix II
Array Elicitation Questions

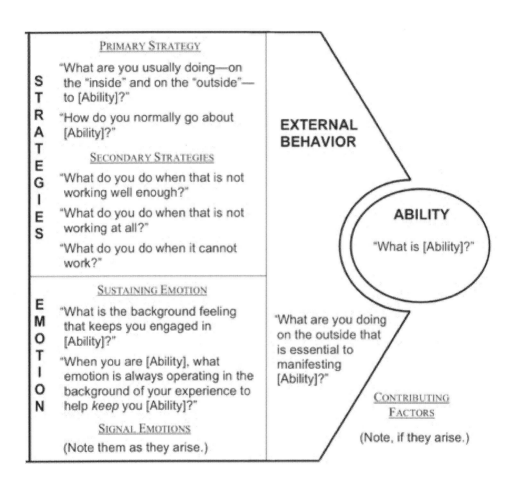

S
T
R
A
T
E
G
I
E
S

PRIMARY STRATEGY

"What are you usually doing—on the "inside" and on the "outside"— to [Ability]?"

"How do you normally go about [Ability]?"

SECONDARY STRATEGIES

"What do you do when that is not working well enough?"

"What do you do when that is not working at all?"

"What do you do when it cannot work?"

E
M
O
T
I
O
N

SUSTAINING EMOTION

"What is the background feeling that keeps you engaged in [Ability]?"

"When you are [Ability], what emotion is always operating in the background of your experience to help *keep* you [Ability]?"

SIGNAL EMOTIONS

(Note them as they arise.)

EXTERNAL BEHAVIOR

ABILITY

"What is [Ability]?"

"What are you doing on the outside that is essential to manifesting [Ability]?"

CONTRIBUTING FACTORS

(Note, if they arise.)

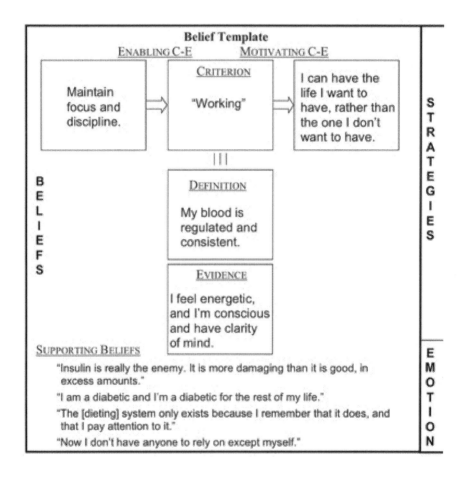

Belief Template

ENABLING C-E   MOTIVATING C-E

CRITERION

Maintain
focus and
discipline.

"Working"

I can have the
life I want to
have, rather than
the one I don't
want to have.

S
T
R
A
T
E
G
I
E
S

B
E
L
I
E
F
S

DEFINITION

My blood is
regulated and
consistent.

EVIDENCE

I feel energetic,
and I'm conscious
and have clarity
of mind.

SUPPORTING BELIEFS

"Insulin is really the enemy. It is more damaging than it is good, in
excess amounts."

"I am a diabetic and I'm a diabetic for the rest of my life."

"The [dieting] system only exists because I remember that it does, and
that I pay attention to it."

"Now I don't have anyone to rely on except myself."

E
M
O
T
I
O
N

Appendix III

Lenny's Array

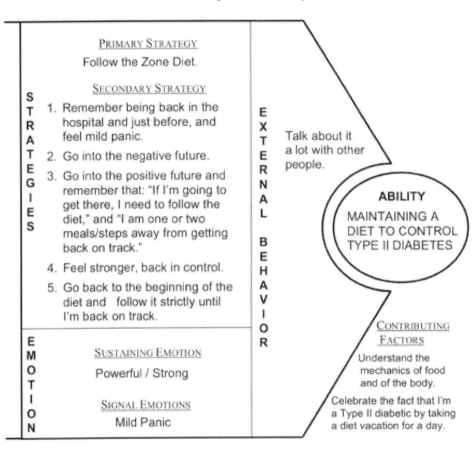

STRATEGIES

PRIMARY STRATEGY

Follow the Zone Diet.

SECONDARY STRATEGY

1. Remember being back in the hospital and just before, and feel mild panic.

2. Go into the negative future.

3. Go into the positive future and remember that: "If I'm going to get there, I need to follow the diet," and "I am one or two meals/steps away from getting back on track."

4. Feel stronger, back in control.

5. Go back to the beginning of the diet and follow it strictly until I'm back on track.

EMOTION

SUSTAINING EMOTION

Powerful / Strong

SIGNAL EMOTIONS

Mild Panic

EXTERNAL BEHAVIOR

Talk about it a lot with other people.

ABILITY

MAINTAINING A DIET TO CONTROL TYPE II DIABETES

CONTRIBUTING FACTORS

Understand the mechanics of food and of the body.

Celebrate the fact that I'm a Type II diabetic by taking a diet vacation for a day.

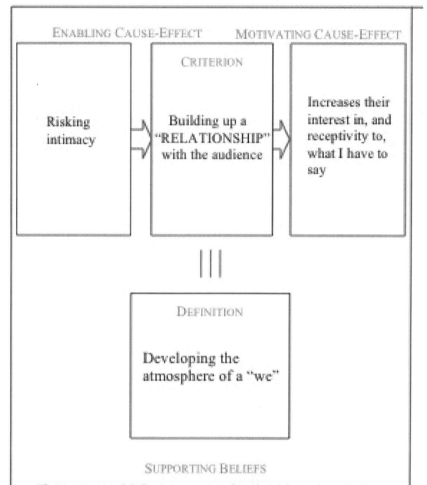

SUPPORTING BELIEFS

"Important to risk I present not only what I have to say, I present me as a person."

"Not being perfect allows other people to involve themselves. Perfection brings you points on the career list but doesn't bring you the audience."

"Most people are primarily interested in what kind of person is it who speaks, more than what does she or her or he say. At least, it goes together."

"The relationship is more important even than what you say."

"I think you can get contact with every audience."

Appendix IV

Ulrike's Array

TEST

"Building up a RELATIONSHIP": I feel comfortable and relaxed. It is much more silent; people don't move that much or talk to each other.

PRIMARY OPERATION

- Be present
- Monitor your own feelings, using them as indicators of what may be happening in the group. Look after the group by letting them know you are aware of questions such as:
    How is the atmosphere?
    How is the state of exhaustion?
    How much are they able to digest?
    How is the pressure on us all [e.g., time]?
- Say some free sentences [not read]
- Include a personal sequence, a sequence with "I"
- Give them breaks [by shifting focus of attention], to relax for a second [brings back more concentration afterwards]
- Express appreciation of them
- Make people laugh
- Look at them
- Dare some movement
- Let the audience participate in the process of your thinking [e.g., meta-commenting on your thinking]

SECONDARY OPERATIONS

Not Sufficient – [continue using the Primary Operation]

Not At All – There can be two reasons for this:
- When I feel the audience expects somebody / something different. I say that.
- I am at my end [exhausted]. I come through only. I do my duty. Don't put myself under pressure.

Can't – You can get contact with any audience, but do I want? Maybe I have to betray myself or something like that; I'm not interested.

SUSTAINING EMOTION

Excitement, with a slight fear

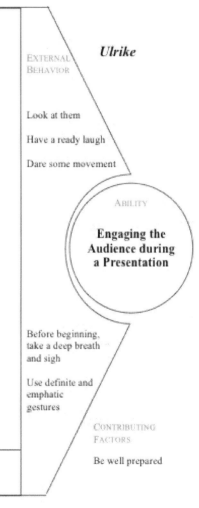

Ulrike

EXTERNAL BEHAVIOR

Look at them

Have a ready laugh

Dare some movement

ABILITY

Engaging the Audience during a Presentation

Before beginning, take a deep breath and sigh

Use definite and emphatic gestures

CONTRIBUTING FACTORS

Be well prepared

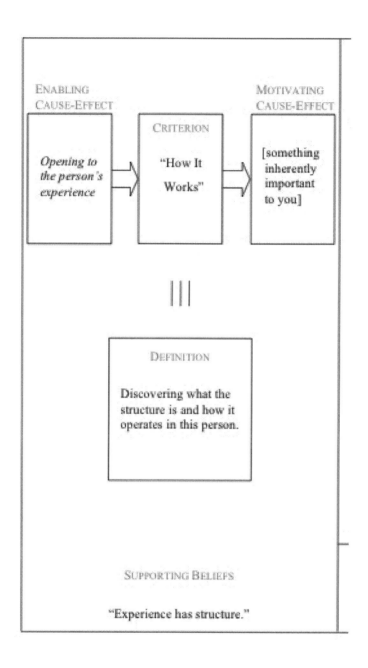

Appendix V

Generic Array

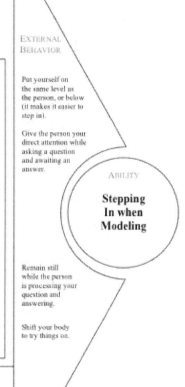

TEST
"How It Works": I can do it; in the exemplar's context, I experience myself feeling and acting like the exemplar.

EXTERNAL BEHAVIOR

PRIMARY OPERATION

1. Get a description of the context they are usually operating in.
2. Become very still and quiet inside, and devote your full attention to the other person. (This may include tunnel vision and a lower, slower and softer voice.)
3. Ask your questions (using plenty of framing):
   * Look for the way that person does it. Look to see if it can be done in more than one way; if so, ask for more detail.
   * Let what they say take over your body.
   * Feel in your body what you see them doing with their body (esp. anything unusual, characteristic or exaggerated).
   * Things they say, say to yourself (internally).
   * Things they say they see or feel, access inside yourself.
4. Check for confirmation of how you are experiencing them through matches between your experience and what they subsequently say or through asking direct questions.
   * As soon as your experience stops making sense, stop the client and say, "Okay, something's not right. I'm missing something." Ask further questions until your experience makes sense again.

Put yourself on the same level as the person, or below (it makes it easier to step in).

Give the person your direct attention while asking a question and awaiting an answer.

ABILITY

**Stepping
In when
Modeling**

SECONDARY OPERATIONS

Not Sufficient – Experiment with the experience by moving things around a bit. If anything is missing, indistinct or potentially misunderstood, ask the person questions about it from a different angle.

Not At All –
   * "I haven't set myself aside enough." Re-set yourself (empty yourself of the former structure) by shifting body posture. Check each element of structure with the person as you "load it on." (You are checking for congruence, disconfirmation, or different quality.)
   * "I've come at this from the wrong direction." Re-set yourself (empty yourself of the former structure) by shifting body posture. Take a different tack.

Can't – Admit you are unable to entirely get the structure. Acknowledge, and express appreciation for what you did get from the exemplar.

Remain still while the person is processing your question and answering.

Shift your body to try things on.

SUSTAINING EMOTION

LOVE
(Appreciating and honoring who this person. is.)

BIBLIOGRAPHY

Ashby, W. Ross (1956) *An Introduction to Cybernetics*. London: Chapman & Hall Ltd.

Anderson, Walter Truett (1990) *Reality Isn't What It Used To Be*. San Francisco: Harper & Row.

Bandler, Richard and John Grinder (1975) *The Structure of Magic, Volume 1*. Palo Alto, CA: Science and Behavior Books, Inc.

Bandler, Richard and John Grinder (1975) *Patterns of the Hypnotic Techniques of Milton H. Erickson, M.D., Vol. 1*. Cupertino, CA: Meta Publications.

Bateson, Gregory (1966) Slippery theories. *International Journal of Psychiatry. 2*/4 pp.415-417.

Bateson, Gregory (1979) *Mind and Nature: A Necessary Unity*. New York: Bantam Books.

Bateson, Gregory (1972) *Steps to an Ecology of Mind*. New York: Ballantine Books.

Bateson, Gregory (1991) *A Sacred Unity: Further Steps to an Ecology of Mind*. New York: Harper Collins.

Bateson, Gregory and Mary Catherine Bateson (1987) *Angels Fear: Towards an Epistemology of the Sacred*. New York: Macmillan Publishing Company.

Bohm, David (1985) *Unfolding Meaning*. London: Ark Paperbacks.

Bohm, David (1989) Meaning and information. *The Search for Meaning: The New Spirit in Science and Philosophy*. Paavo Pylkkänen (ed.). Northamptonshire: Crucible.

Bohm, David (1994) *Thought as a System*. London: Routledge.

Bohm, David (1996) *On Dialogue*. London: Routledge.

Cameron-Bandler, Leslie, David Gordon and Michael Lebeau (1985) *Know How*. San Rafael, CA: FuturePace, Inc.

Cameron-Bandler, Leslie and Michael Lebeau (1986) *The Emotional Hostage*. San Rafael, CA: FuturePace, Inc.

Cameron-Bandler, Leslie, Michael Lebeau and David Gordon (1985) *The Emprint Method*. San Rafael, CA: FuturePace, Inc.

Clavell, James (1981) *The Children's Story*. New York: Dell Publishing.

Damasio, Antonio (1999) *The Feeling of What Happens: Body and Emotion in the Making of Consciousness*. New York: Harcourt Brace & Company.

Darwin, Charles (1872) *The Expression of the Emotions in Man and Animals*. Chicago: University of Chicago Press (1965).

Dawes, Graham (1997) "The Significance of Neuro-Linguistic Programming in the Therapy of Anxiety Disorders". *Clinical Management of Anxiety*. Johan A. den Boer (ed.). New York: Marcel Dekker Inc.

Dawes, Graham (1999) "Faster Than a Speeding Bullet: The Quick Change Speed Trials". *Anchor Point*. Vol. 13, No. 2.

Dawes, Graham and John Killman (2000) "The Excellent Auditor". *Qualityworld*. Institute of Quality Assurance. Vol. 26, Issue 3.

Diamond, Jared (1984) "Race Without Color". *Discover Magazine*. pp.82-89.

Dilts, Robert, John Grinder, Richard Bandler, Leslie Cameron Bandler and Judith DeLozier (1980) *Neuro-Linguistic Programming: Volume 1*. Cupertino, CA: Meta Publications.

Edelman, Gerald (1992) *Bright Air, Brilliant Fire*. New York: BasicBooks.

Edwards, Betty (1999) *The New Drawing on the Right Side of the Brain*. New York: Jeremy P. Tarcher/Putnam.

Elbow, Peter (1986) *Embracing Contraries*. New York: Oxford University Press.

Festinger, Leon, Henry W. Riecken, and Stanley Schachter (1956) *When Prophecy Fails*. Minneapolis: University of Minnesota Press.

Feyerabend Paul (1978) *Against Method*. London: Verso.

Foerster, Heinz von (1979) Cybernetics of cybernetics, *Communication and Control in Society*. Klaus Krippendorff (ed.). New York: Gordon and Breach.

Foerster, Heinz von (1991) Through the eyes of the other. *Research and Reflexivity*. Frederick Steier (ed.). London: Sage Publications.

Frankl, Victor (1984) *Man's Search for Meaning*. New York: Washington Square Press.

Gordon, David (1990) "Reference Experiences: Guardians of Coherence and Instigators of Change". *Brief Therapy: Myths, Methods, and Metaphors*. Zeig and Gilligan (eds.) New York: Brunner/Mazel.

Gordon, David (1988) "The Role of Language in Therapy". *Developing Ericksonian Therapy*. Zeig and Lankton (eds.). New York: Brunner/Mazel.

Gordon, David (1985) "The Role of Presuppositions in Ericksonian Psychotherapy". *Ericksonian Psychotherapy, Volume I: Structures*. Zeig (ed.). New York: Brunner/Mazel.

Gordon, David and Maribeth Meyers-Anderson (1981) *Phoenix: Therapeutic Patterns of Milton H. Erickson*. Cupertino, CA: Meta Publications.

Gould, Stephen Jay (1996) *Full House: The Spread of Excellence from Plato to Darwin*. New York: Three Rivers Press.

Grandin, Temple (1996) *Thinking in Pictures*. New York: Vintage Books.

Haley, Jay (1973) *Uncommon Therapy: The Psychiatric Techniques of Milton H. Erickson, M.D.* New York: W.W. Norton & Company.

Hall, Edward T. (1959) *The Silent Language*. New York: Doubleday & Company.

Hall, Edward T. (1966) *The Hidden Dimension*. Garden City, NY: Anchor Books.

Hall, Edward T. (1976) *Beyond Culture*. Garden City, NY: Anchor Press/Doubleday.

Hall, Edward T. (1983) *The Dance of Life*. Garden City, NY: Anchor Press/Doubleday.

Hofstadter, D. R. and D. Dennett, eds. (1981) *The Mind's I: Fantasies and Reflections on Self and Soul*. New York: Basic Books.

Jaynes, Julian (1976) *The Origin of Consciousness in the Breakdown of the Bicameral Mind*. Boston: Houghton Mifflin Company.

Johnson, Mark (1987) *The Body in the Mind: The Bodily Basis of Meaning, Imagination, and Reason*. Chicago: University of Chicago Press.

Keeney, Bradford P. (1983) *Aesthetics of Change*. New York: The Guilford Press.

Koornhof, Piet (2001) "The Makings of Genius". *The Strad*. Vol. 112, No. 1338.

Korzybski, Alfred (1958) *Science and Sanity*. Lakeville, Connecticut: The International Non-Aristotelian Library Publishing Company.

Korzybski, Alfred (1951) "The Role of Language in the Perceptual Processes". *Perception: An Approach to Personality*. Robert R. Blake and Glenn V. Ramsey (eds.). New York: The Ronald Press Company.

Kuhn, Thomas S. (1970) *The Structure of Scientific Revolutions*. Chicago: University of Chicago Press.

Lakoff, George (1987) *Women, Fire, and Dangerous Things: What Categories Reveal About the Mind*. Chicago: University of Chicago Press.

Lakoff, George (1988) Cognitive semantics. *Meaning and Mental Representations*. Umberto Eco, Marco Santambrogio and Patrizia Violi (eds.). Bloomington: Indiana University Press.

Lakoff, George and Mark Johnson (1980) *Metaphors We Live By*. Chicago: The University of Chicago Press.

Lakoff, George and Mark Johnson (1999) *Philosophy in the Flesh: The Embodied Mind and Its Challenge to Western Thought*. New York: Basic Books.

Lakoff, George and Mark Turner (1989) *More Than Cool Reason: A Field Guide to Poetic Metaphor*. Chicago: University of Chicago Press.

LeDoux, Joseph (1998) *The Emotional Brain*. London: Weidenfeld & Nicolson.

MacDonald, Celia and Steve Nuttall (2000) "Team Magic: An Exploration of Competencies and Abilities in Team Working". The National Training Organization for Oil and Gas Extraction. Internal report.

Maruyama, Magorah (1968) The second cybernetics: Deviation-amplifying mutual causal processes. *Modern Systems Research for the Behavioral Scientist*. W. Buckley (ed.). Chicago: Aldine.

Maturana, Humberto (1987) Everything is said by an observer. *Gaia: A Way of Knowing*. William Irwin Thompson (ed.). Great Barrington, MA: Lindisfarne Press.

Maturana, Humberto (1988) Reality: The search for objectivity or the quest for a compelling argument. *The Irish Journal of Psychology*. 9/1 pp.25-82.

Maturana, Humberto and Francisco Varela (1987) *The Tree of Knowledge*. Boston: New Science Library.

McCloud, Scott (1993) *Understanding Comics: The Invisible Art*. New York: Harper Perennial.

Merleau-Ponty, M. (1962) *The Phenomenology of Perception*. Transl. Colin Smith. London: Routledge and Kegan Paul.

Miller, George A., Eugene Galanter, and Karl H. Pribram (1960) *Plans and the Structure of Behavior*. New York: Holt, Rinehart and Winston, Inc.

O'Hanlon, Bill and James Wilk (1987) *Shifting Contexts: The Generation of Effective Psychotherapy*. New York: The Guilford Press.

Ornstein, Robert and David Sobel (1987) *The Healing Brain*. New York: Simon & Schuster Inc.

Pearce, W. Barnett (1989) *Communication and the Human Condition*. Carbondale: Southern Illinois University Press.

Pearce, W. Barnett and Vernon E. Cronen (1980) *Communication, Action, and Meaning: The Creation of Social Realities*. New York: Praeger.

Penfield, Wilder and Phanor Perot (1963) "The Brain's Record of Auditory and Visual Experience". *Brain*. VOL. 86, PART 4.

Pert, Candace B. (1997) *Molecules of Emotion*. New York: Touchstone.

Petitmengin-Peugeot, Claire (1999) "The Intuitive Experience". *The View from Within: First-Person Approaches to the Study of Consciousness*. Francisco Varela and Jonathan Shear (eds.). Thorverton, UK: Imprint Academic.

Pylkkänen, Paavo (ed.) (1989) *The Search for Meaning: the New Spirit in Science and Philosophy*. Northamptonshire: Crucible.

Rheingold, Howard (1988) *They Have a Word For It: A Lighthearted Lexicon of Untranslatable Words & Phrases*. Los Angeles: Jeremy P. Tarcher, Inc.

Rose, Steven (1973) *The Conscious Brain*. New York: Alfred A. Knopf.

Sachs, Oliver (1995) *An Anthropologist on Mars*. New York: Alfred A. Knopf.

Thompson, William Irwin (1989) *Imaginary Landscapes: Making Worlds of Myth and Science*. New York: St. Martin's Press.

Vaihinger, I. (1924) *The Philosophy of "As If"*. London: Routledge, Kegan and Paul, Ltd.

Varela, Francisco J. (1987) "Laying down a path in walking: A biologist's look at a new biology". *Cybernetic* 2: 6–15. (available at http://cepa.info/2069)

Varela, Francisco J. (1992) The reenchantment of the concrete. *Zone 6: Incorporations.* Jonathan Crary and Sanford Kwinter (eds.). New York: Zone.

Varela, Francisco, Evan Thompson, and Eleanor Rosch (1997) *The Embodied Mind.* Cambridge, MA: The MIT Press.

Watzlawick, Paul (1984) *The Invented Reality.* New York: W.W. Norton.

Watzlawick, Paul, John Weakland, and Richard Fisch (1974) *Change: Principles of Problem Formation and Problem Resolution.* New York: W.W. Norton & Company.

Zeig, Jeffery K. ((1980) *A Teaching Seminar with Milton H. Erickson.* New York: Brunner/Mazel.

Books and CDs by David and Graham

Ordering information for these books can be found at
http://expandyourworld.net/books.php

Expanding Your World
Modeling the Structure of Experience

by David Gordon and Graham Dawes

This book puts in your hands a clear, concise and practical process for accessing these otherwise hidden patterns of thinking and behaving. Every chapter builds upon the concepts and skills of the previous one, so that by the end you will have a detailed and thorough picture of the process. To make the modeling process fully alive for you, Expanding Your World has 2½ hours of modeling Elicitation and Acquisition video demonstrations embedded into the text. This means that you will be able to watch an actual demonstration of what you are reading about at the moment you most need it!

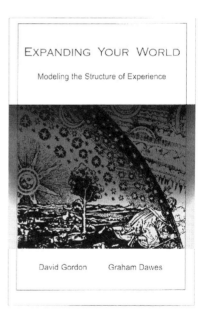

WWW.EXPANDYOURWORLD.NET

The Emprint Method
A Guide to Producing Competence

by Leslie Cameron-Bandler, David Gordon, and Michael Lebeau

This is one of the few books written on the process of modeling. In addition it is one of the very few approaches that also offers a companion book of modeled abilities (see *Know How* below), all of which were modeled using The Emprint Method format.

Know How
Guided Programs for Inventing Your Own Best Futures

by Leslie Cameron-Bandler, David Gordon, and Michael Lebeau

A treasure trove of successful patterns for dieting, loving relationships, effective parenting, and more. Even though these essential abilities were modeled using The Emprint Method (see above), *Know How* is written so that anyone can easily understand and use the practical patterns it describes.

An Introduction to Modelling with NLP (CD)

by David Gordon

This is a recording of David teaching a seminar on the fundamentals of modeling. Here you will find a presentation of the Experiential Array, modeling exercises, and elicitation demonstrations with several people.

Phoenix
The Therapeutic Patterns of Milton H. Erickson, M.D.

by David Gordon and Maribeth Meyers-Anderson

The vast majority of books about the acknowledged master of hypnotherapy, Milton H. Erickson, focus on his use of hypnosis. *Phoenix*, however, reveals the effective patterns of thinking and intervention upon which all of Erickson's therapeutic (including hypnotic) work was based.

Therapeutic Metaphor
Helping Others Through the Looking Glass

by David Gordon

Metaphors provide a depth of association and potential for insight often not available in more direct approaches. Stories create a shared language between a therapist and a client, and can lead to great personal transformation. *Therapeutic Metaphors* provides an explicit and practical format for creating impactful stories for change.

Stories That Change People (CD)

by David Gordon

Here is a complete introductory seminar on the structures and subtleties that go into creating effective therapeutic metaphors. The seminar includes exercises, demonstrations, examples, and delightful explorations into the many aspects of therapeutic metaphor.

The Handbook of Work Based Learning

by Ian Cunningham, Graham Dawes, and Ben Bennett

This is a practical guide to supporting organizational learning in ways that lead to success. The three main parts of the *Handbook* focus on the strategies, tactics and methods that are the foundations to ongoing learning in an organization, and are presented from the perspective of both the learner and the professional consultant.

The Authors

DAVID GORDON

As one of the original developers of Neuro-Linguistic Programming, David has helped create and shape the field for nearly 40 years. though his work has touched virtually every aspect of NLP, David's primary areas of contribution to the field have been in the use of therapeutic metaphors (inspired by his work with Milton H. Erickson) and in the pursuit of modeling. Modeling has consumed most of this professional attention for the past 30 years. In addition to training thousands of people in NLP, hypnosis, therapeutic metaphor, and modeling, David has written many articles on NLP, as well as books on various aspects of therapy, including *Therapeutic Metaphors*, *Phoenix: The Therapeutic Patterns of Milton H. Erickson*, and *The Emprint Method* and *Know how* (both with Leslie Cameron-Bandler and Michael Lebeau). David lives in the Sonoran Desert with his friends the coyotes, rattlesnakes, tarantulas, scorpions, lizards, and other beautiful creatures.

GRAHAM DAWES

A founder of the UK Training Centre for NLP (the first center outside of North America), Graham received his doctorate in management Learning from the University of Lancaster, for an exploration of the nature of reality, meaning, and change. An exponent of the Self-Managed Learning (SML) approach, both for those in organisations and for school-aged students, he has edited and contributed to two books on the subject, and was on the team that designed SML-based programmes for an MBA (University of Sussex) and an MSc in Managing Change (University of Sheffield Hallam). He is also the author or co-author of a workbook on humanizing organisational change (with Roger Harrison, the primary theorist of organisational culture), a training pack to develop coaching capability (for the Chartered Institute of Personnel and Development, and published in the US by the American Management Association), the chapter, "A Bermuda Triangle of the Mind," on the work of provocative therapist, Frank Farrelly (in *Der Zirkel des Talos*), and the recent, *The Handbook of Work Based Learning*.

51352840R10279

Made in the USA
Middletown, DE
02 July 2019